CW01652944

Well, Dearie!

The Letters of Edward Burra

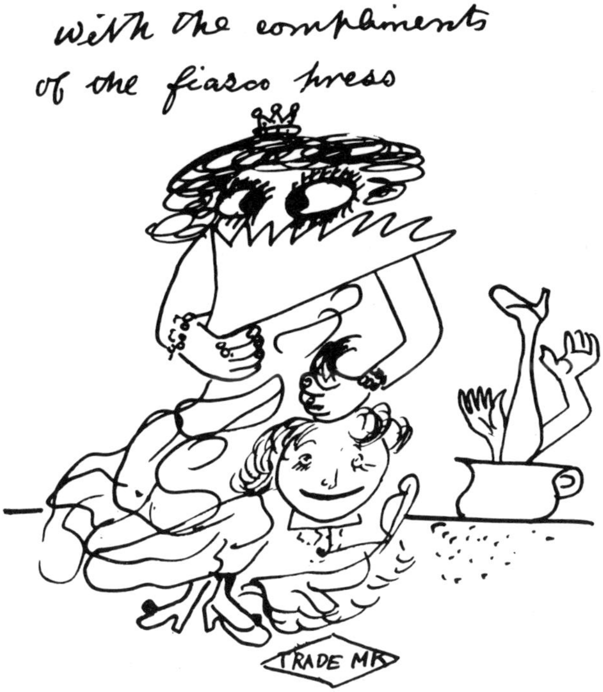

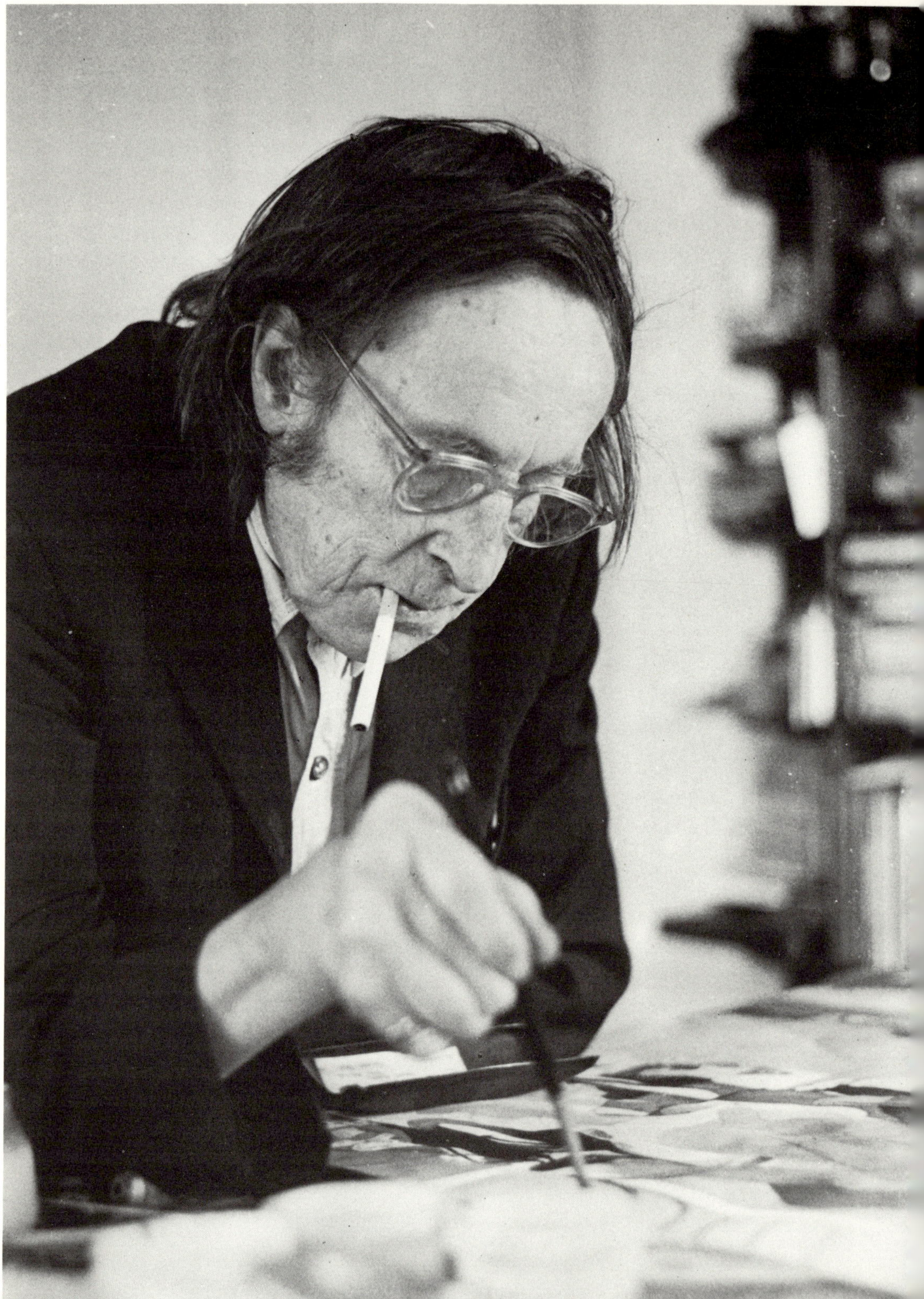

Well, dearie!

THE LETTERS OF EDWARD BURRA

Edited by William Chappell

Gordon Fraser · London

First published 1985 by
The Gordon Fraser Gallery Ltd, London and Bedford
Copyright © William Chappell 1985
Letters copyright © Gordon Fraser Gallery Ltd, 1985

All rights reserved. No part of this book may be reproduced or utilised in any form or by any means, electronic or mechanical, including photocopying, recording or by any information storage and retrieval system, without prior permission in writing from the publisher.

BRITISH LIBRARY CATALOGUING IN PUBLICATION DATA

Burra, Edward
Well, Dearie!: the letters of Edward Burra.
1. Burra, Edward 2. Painters—Great Britain
—Biography
I. Title
759.2 ND1942.B85

ISBN 0 86092 076 3

Typeset in Monophoto Photina by August Filmsetting, Haydock, St Helens
Printed by The Roundwood Press Ltd, Kineton, Warwick
Bound by Hunter and Foulis Ltd, Edinburgh
Designed by Peter Guy

CONTENTS

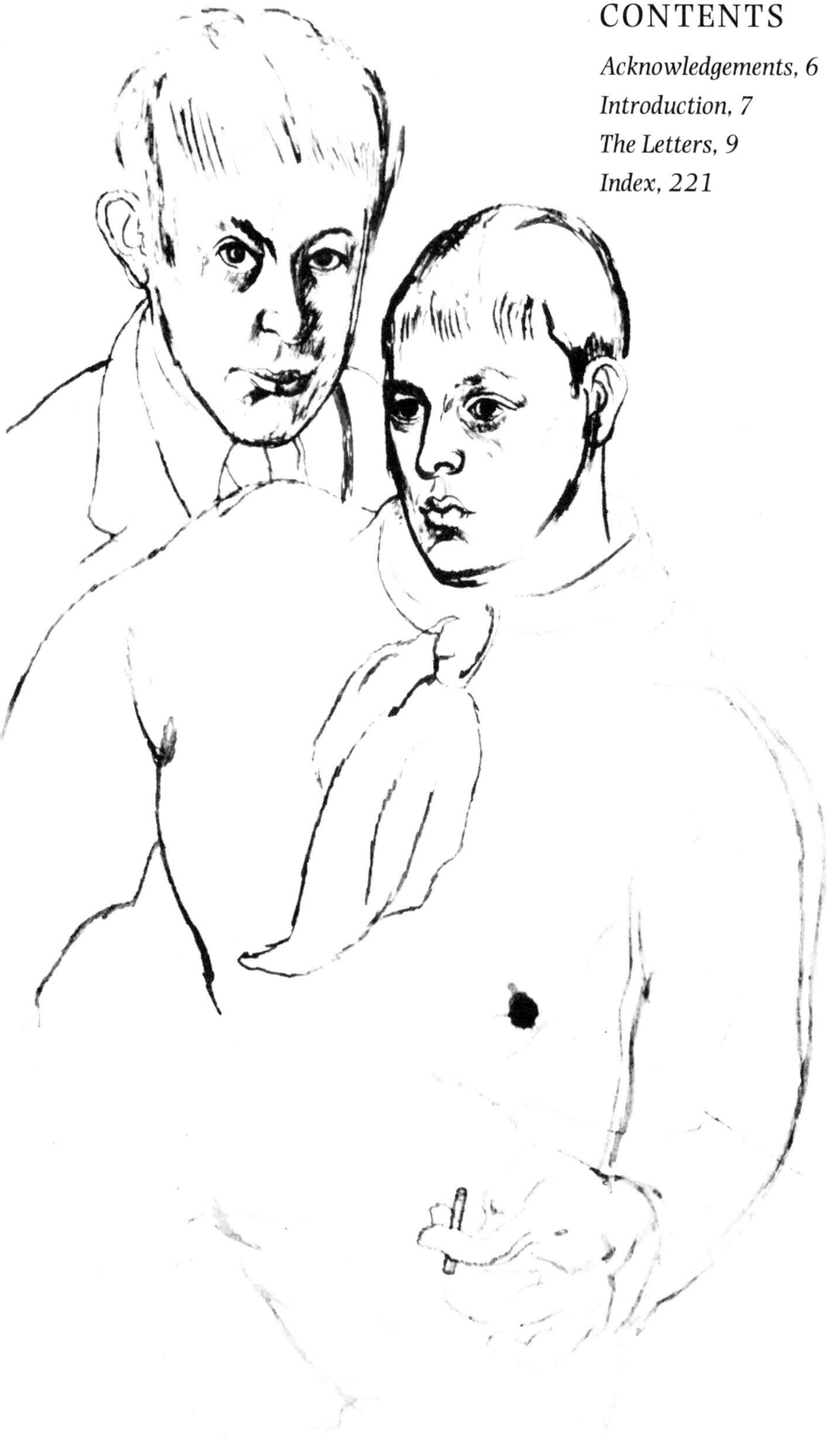

ACKNOWLEDGEMENTS

I would like to acknowledge the help I have received in the making of this book. I must particularly thank Anne Ritchie, Barbara Ker-Seymer, Clover de Pertinez, Beatrice Dawson, Gerald Corcoran, Mary Augusta Aiken and Monica Wodehouse for not only keeping their letters from Edward Burra but for making them available.

My thanks are also due to Simon Kingston and Peter Guy, for the wonderfully tactful and complete co-operation they have shown throughout the preparation and presentation of the book. I owe more than I can say to Gerald and Desmond Corcoran of the Lefevre Gallery for their unfailing support, and great generosity in allowing me the use of their reproductions of the Burra drawings; and I must thank Jacquie Cartwright – also of the Lefevre – for her patience in helping me to make a selection. I am also deeply grateful to my friend John Aiken (without whom there would be no index) and for the kindness of Mr Douglas Byng in permitting me to quote from some of his brilliantly funny lyrics.

Finally I have to thank Amanda Pugh for weeks of typing and retyping; and Van Phillips for introducing me to Andy Beard, to whom I am indebted for his skilful reproduction and enlargement of the photographs.

PUBLISHER'S NOTE

Although Burra's spelling and (lack of) punctuation have been retained, a few small corrections and adjustments have been made for the sake of clarity.

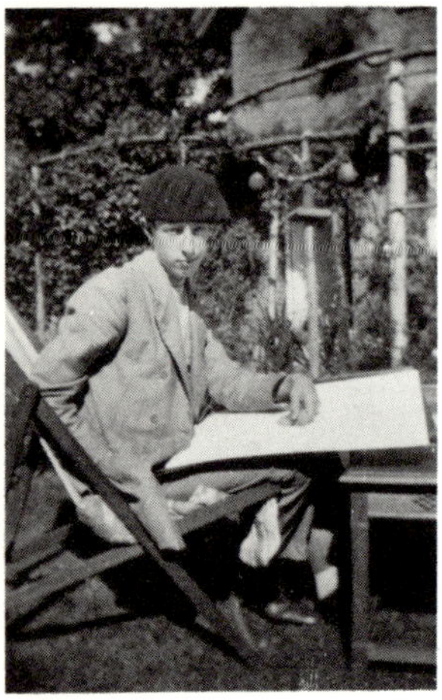

INTRODUCTION

During his adolescence Edward Burra discovered five friends who were to remain close to him all his life. The bulk of these letters are addressed to them.

Ker-Seymer, Pritchard and Chappell were his fellow students at the School of Art in the Chelsea Polytechnic. Beatrice (Bumble) Dawson and her future husband Gerald Corcoran he met a year or so later.

Within Edward's circle – regardless of their own comparatively unlikely and not altogether unsuccessful careers – it was tacitly accepted he was the star turn. He took a passionate and predominantly benign interest in even the smallest activities of his cronies – these were later to include Frederick Ashton and Robert Helpmann, for both of whom he produced magnificent theatre designs[1] *– but he showed little patience with any nonsensical or pompous behaviour of a kind sometimes indulged in by his chums. It can be noted how often in his letters when his friends got out of hand he made great use of a series of highly denigratory nicknames for each one of them. These became a favourite weapon for the deflation of any over-grandiose ideas. It was clearly difficult to stand on one's dignity when reduced to Mrs, Mdme, Nurse or Fishnet Annie (Chappell), the pagan laundrywoman (Ker-Seymer) or Hotsy Trackles (Ashton). In the twenties and thirties it was practically a point of honour to send everyone and everything sky high. These letters should finally put paid to the idea of Edward as a deeply reclusive eccentric. He was in fact naturally gregarious if – and let that 'if' be noted – he could choose his company. He liked strangers and was much given to long rambling conversations with drunken old wrecks grumbling in a run-down pub. Throughout his life he continued to accumulate new friends. His actual need to lead a life of activity was only curbed by his delicate constitution and his always-ailing body, yet he managed to get around the world as much if not more than many of his contemporaries. The letters are a testament to his inventive wit and his brilliantly lively mind. We are sometimes made aware of the dark melancholy in his being but it is only fitfully revealed; more suggested than emphasised; for it was his unquenchable interest in life and people which made him see at once and with crystal clarity the terrible jokes always embedded in the very worst of events.*

W.E.C.

[1] *For Ashton,* Rio Grande *and* Don Juan; *for Helpmann,* Miracle in the Gorbals.

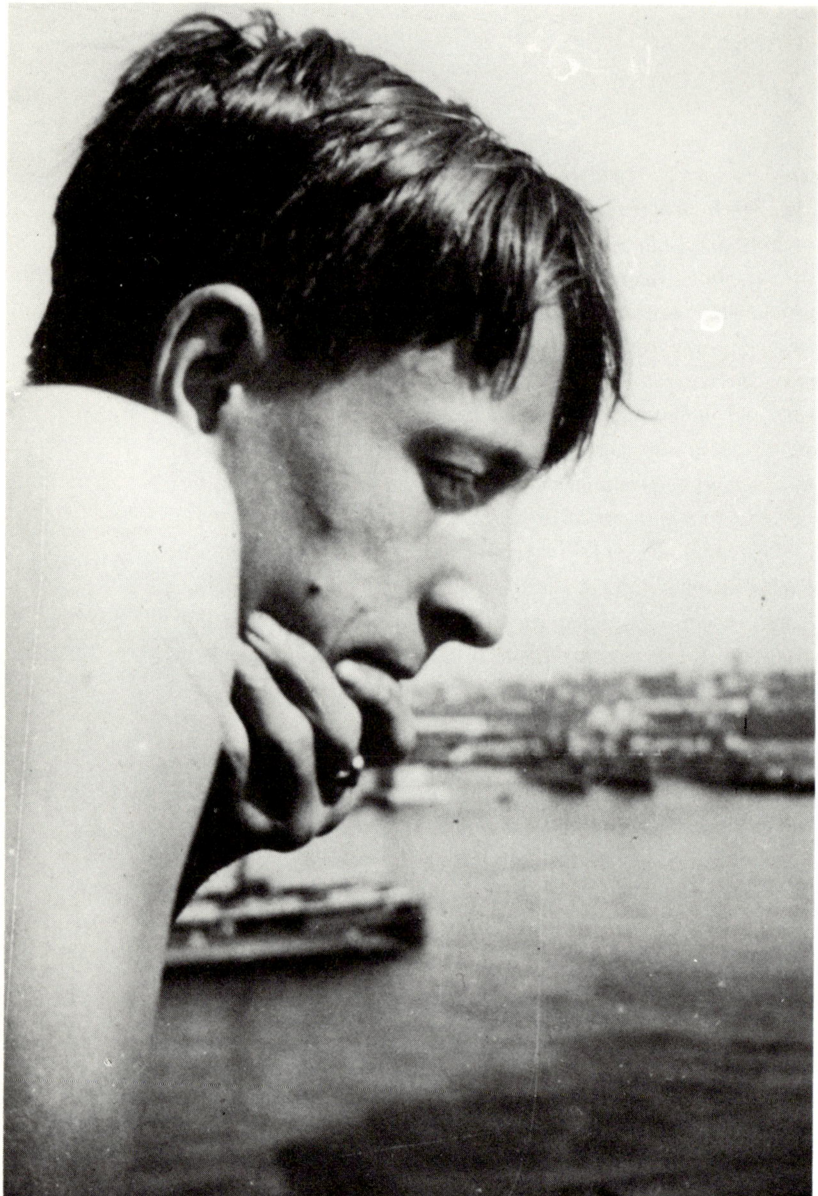

Edward John Burra was born on 28 March 1905 at 31 Elvaston Place, his maternal grandmother's home: a tall, handsome house in one of the many solid and dignified early Victorian terraces which to this day represent the dominant architectural style of South Kensington.

It had been his good fortune to be born into a well-to-do family, as it was his bad fortune to be born so frail a child, cursed as he was at birth (as though by some vindictive Carabosse) with a deep-seated arthritis. This horrid ailment, worsening as he grew older, was accompanied by pernicious anaemia, and later in life by an hereditary affliction, an enlarged spleen. The doctors were, understandably, pessimistic: 'He will not', they said, 'make old bones'.

Doomed, it seemed, to a short and pain-filled life, he not only achieved those three score years and ten Nature so grudgingly concedes to the average man: he also added a further year and a half. Such extra time can be seen as a typically defiant bonus given to himself by himself: a gift made possible through his possession of an unusually strong will-power. This alone sustained him throughout his life.

Between the ages of six and seven he wrote (from his birthplace) to his mother.

31 Elvaston Place. S.W.

Dear Ma is Cotkland nice we had a fog yesteray a very bad wone. I am stil in London I am righring this letter this mornen I am and a very nice letter too the best wone I have riten for a long time.
Miss Forbs came to meat me here on Saterday I dont know if Billy is any Better I roat him a letter yestern
I am going home
tomoro I am OH yes.
Love from
Edward Burra.

He continued to spell Saturday as Saterday for the rest of his life; and he never gave up his addiction to a good deal of purely phonetic spelling. It brings an early English, almost Chaucerian, look to the words in this childish letter: yesteray, wone, righring and mornen; riten, roat, yestern and tomoro. From about the age of four up to ten or eleven years children are, in their own way, mysterious as creatures from another planet. They are born wicked, and grow into a kind of innocence. Very early they let us know they are observant, cunning and inventive; they are also cruel, ruthless, unpredictable, deadly secretive; and they seem, one and all, able to paint and draw with fluency and wit. These gifts are a normal part of those secret magic worlds in which young children live. Alas, when they move into their teens the greater proportion move away from (and completely forget) the enchanted groves full of signs and symbols and strange creatures where once they had their being. It is only the exceptional ones, the truly gifted, who continue to walk the earth for the duration of their lives still wrapped in an invisible carapace, crowded by disturbing and enigmatic images.

When he was nine, Edward Burra was sent to preparatory school at Northaw

Place, Potters Bar in Hertfordshire. He was well aware his work was to be directed towards passing the entrance examination for Eton. Reading his letters from school, apparently so utterly typical of a schoolboy's mind, it is hard to believe they were not written tongue-in-cheek.

18 October 1914

Dear Ma
Will you send me my tortch with a new battery in I want it as quick as you can send it. I wich you wood hurry up and come and see me. You seem to be never comeing. I think I am gitting on quite well with my lessons . . . I hate that little boy more and more that I never speak to him now . . . Please when you send the tortch send a cake with it.

With lots of love to all
from E. J. Burra.

1915

Dear Ma
. . . Two of my teeth came out a few days ago. I am keeping them for you . . . There is a magnet crase now it was ships last Christmas Term. I finished my book now and would like In white Rayment. I have survived chicken pox so far quite successfully . . .

To his mother, 13 October 1915

. . . I wonder what the Hastings pantomime will be this year we must go to the gallery this time because of the war and eat oringes and drop the juice on the pit. . .

17 October 1915

Dear Daddie
We heard the Zepps on Wednesday night and the windows shook. How exiting for Tunbridge Wells Ma says they dropped some bombs there. I dont know where I am in Form this week whitch is horrid. Love from Edward.
P.S. I am third and please tell Nana to send me my tortch.

20 February 1916

Dear Daddy
Rainbow cups are the craze now like the one Uncle Dick gave me. There was a match today but we got beaten . . .

5 March 1916

Dear Mummie
. . . there was a match yesterday not hear we got beaten by 13 goals we only got 0 goals . . .

To his mother, 21 June 1916

. . . I was third in the Latin paper last week and 4th in the Half Term order. I am doing better than I did last term . . .

29 November 1916

Dear Pa
. . . I had an awful shock when I heard the bomb had fallen just behind Harrods I thought of doing some Xmas shopping there . . . theres only 3 weeks more not counting the 20th on which we brake up . . .

10 December 1916

Dear Ma
. . . We will have our last Catechism lesson tomorrow and I am very glad. I've got just a little more than half of Westwood Ho to finish now I hope I shall finish before the end of term only a week and 2 days more though. We will have standard bread though so it doesn't matter to me much . . .

20 May 1917

Dearest Mummie
I'm top of the form this week. P.C.U. has been perfectly violent lately and has been down on everyone. He delights in smacking people and jawing them. I know its his favourite pastime as he told us so!!! . . . Thank you very much for the Zig-Zag music I can play it slowly[1] . . .

The next two letters are undated

Dearest Daddie
I hope you have got my letter by this time. I shall have been up here 2 weeks tomorrow & at this rate of going I shall be up here for the rest of this term. I'me sure I could get better far quicker at home. According to Old Moore there is going to be an accident in May next year I wonder which railway it will be. I hope it wont be the S.E. & C.R.! . . . I have got through 2. W. de Queux's, one called The band of Black and the other called The Temptress they were both very exciting indeed . . . I shall die if I have to stay in this room another day . . .

Dearest Mummie
I have been up here 2 weeks on Saterday & at this rate of going I shall be up all the term I am getting awfully tired of this room Sister says she wishes that I would be sent home as she is getting sick tired of me. I am longing to see Betsie again she must be getting quite big . . . I am in bed with a horrible little boy called Levy . . . I shall commit suicide if I stay in this room much longer.

The truth about the letters sent from school has nothing to do with tongue-in-cheek. They were an instinctive use of material from which might be manufactured

1 *He had begun piano lessons.*

the mask of a 'good conformer', the mask behind which many a child can lead its own absorbed and private life. There are no complaints in those letters. The requests for goodies and books; the recounting of favourable reports and good places in class; the apparently sincere interest in the fortunes of the school's lamentable football team; the marking away of the days till the end of term; each and every one of these routine reactions has a ring of truth, for the good reason that Edward, both in his youth and for a great part of his mature life, was always completely able to adapt. The strongest part of his will-power rose from a stoicism inherent in his character. He proved incredibly 'British' in this respect for it was never made easily discernible, and antipathetic as it might be to his true character, the boring and restrictive routine of school life held few real terrors for him. So it is not until we read the two undated letters to his parents recording one of many sojourns in the school sick bay that we hear the faintest cry for help. 'I'm getting awfully tired of this room', he writes to his mother. And to his father, 'I'm sure I could get better quicker at home'.

The letters conclude with more acute cries. 'I shall commit suicide if I stay in this room much longer', and 'I shall die if I have to stay in this room another day'.

Whether this particular state of collapse (brought on by his acute anaemia) was the one to terminate his school days we cannot tell. We do know his recurring attacks culminated in a bout severe enough to make it imperative that he should return home at once. Subsequently it was arranged he should complete his education at an art school.

Now no particular mask was worn. He could relax back into home life, and into a private world invented by himself and shared with his cousin, Lawrence Rich, who sent to him in the summer holidays an interesting and unusual letter. Unusual to us; not to the writer or the recipient. The envelope which carries 'Please Forward' in the top left hand corner is addressed to:

Miss Phylis Dilly
c/o E.J. Burra Esq.
Flat 9
Liberty Buildings
Lower Tartan Street
GEV. N.W.2

The address is scored though, and Springfield, Playden, Sussex has been written beside it. There is a note enclosed with the letter.

Dear Edward
I am coming over on the sixth when Mummie is playing in the tournament at Rye so dont go out. Gladys & Phylis can meet.
Lots of Love
Lawrence

Gladys and Phyllis Dilly! The notorious, the infamous Dilly Sisters! Louche, low-class, liberated women; mafia mobsters who ruled and dominated a city organised and planned by the brooding presence of Edward himself in association with his henchman, cousin Lawrence.

Flat 8 Soho Block, Tivoli Alley, San Sebastian

Darlin Sis
Thank u so much for your letter to the paper. I henclose a photer of self signed which u can ang up in the flat – Will yer send me one of you. Sara tore yer photer up in a fit of rage because I didnt payer. She rarely is most tiresome she broke me last butter dish last night. I ad the most awfull row with perewinkle the other day she took all otel writing paper disgraceful woman no manners and she as got into Tangles at the Soviet All, awfull hupstart she dont know ow to act. These Goonies are awfull they ave taken all the rooms in the otel and dont pay. An orficier kicked Sara up the stairs because she was late *pore dear*.

Well I opes Mother is better now and you are all right

LUV
and tons of kisses
Gladys
x x x x x x x x o o o o o x x x x x

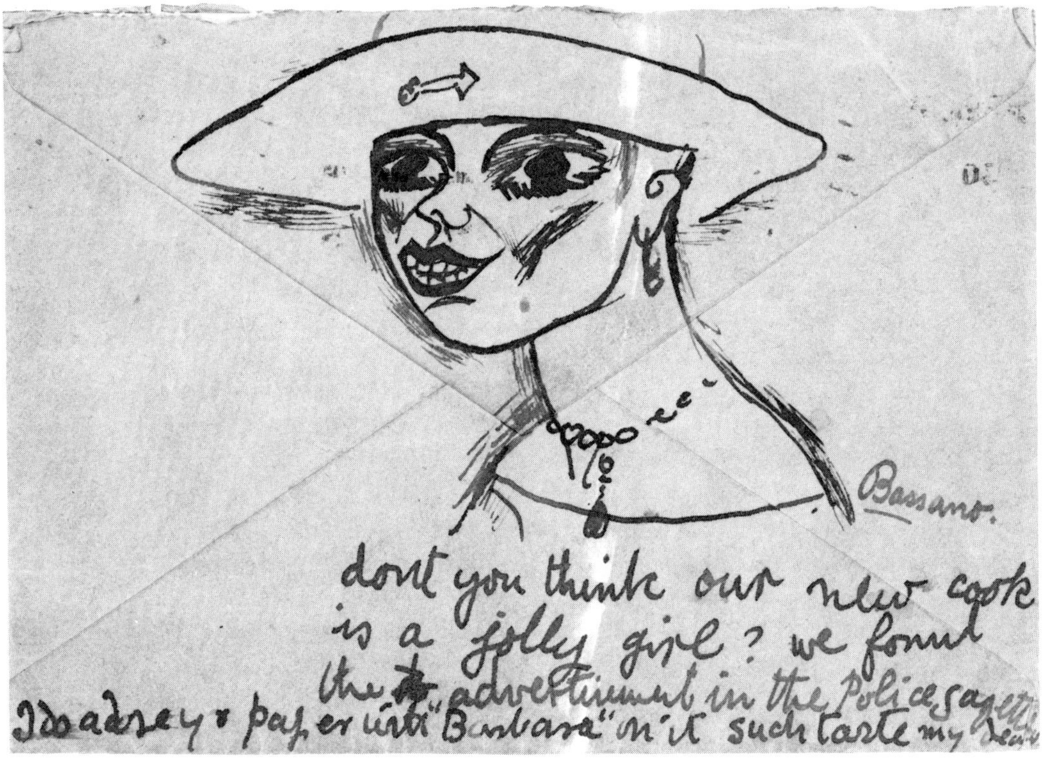

*This conglomeration had been born from the marriage of two media, the cinema (children's matinees at the local movie house) and the weekly comic papers (*Chips and Comic Cuts*). These were a potent and direct influence on Edward's earliest work. The towns he built and destroyed with his cousin; their Soho Blocks, Tivoli Alleys, and Lower Tartan Streets, their cinemas and theatres (both the Dilly sisters had theatrical pretensions), were certainly progenitors of the bars, the*

music halls, the markets, dance halls and cafes which were to become the backgrounds of the mythic world of Edward's work at art school.

In these toy towns, crowded with monstrously unequal and immobile toy people of every type, shape and size, the intricate imagination of a child breathed a frantic life into the wood, stone, china, plaster and metal that made up the inhabitants. When much later in his travels Edward discovered all those Southern ports crammed with tarts, pimps, layabouts, gigolos, street vendors and working people, he found every building and every character instantly familiar and recognisable, because he had already invented them.

Burra was still two months short of his sixteenth birthday when at the beginning of 1921 he entrolled as a student at the Chelsea School of Art, a department of the Polytechnic in Manresa Road. Despite the hideous destruction and conflagration of the First World War, it appeared after the fighting had burnt itself out that nothing in England had changed. Nothing at all. Neither modes nor manners, morals nor ways of thinking. The modes were still shapeless and dowdy. The manners still stiff and formal, the morals discreetly lax – and thought, in general, remained unadventurous and predictable. A way of life predominant in those years preceding the war persisted, appearing to the young simply as a series of reflections caught in a dusty mirror; something preserved, Pompeii-like, in the ashes of its own destruction. Preserved; and as dead as the dodo.

Seen in retrospect, the potent era so inaptly dubbed the 'Roaring' twenties (screaming would possibly have been more suitable) leapt into being – as Minerva from the brow of Jupiter – fully armed and kitted out with knee-length skirt, cropped head, futurist colours and spike heels. She appeared clutching a foot-long cigarette holder of enamel and jade in one hand as with the other she tucked a small pack of cocaine down her plunging decolletage. Her sudden and subversive appearance was heralded by a blaze of black jazz, her whole person aglow with an aura of spectacularly appalling behaviour.

The change – in fact *– happened very gradually indeed; and the final transformation needed three or four years to prepare and present its perfected image.*

The young and frivolous, like Chappell (Burra's first friend at Art School) and Burra himself, longed for the metamorphosis they scented in the atmosphere to be actually seen taking place; if not in their own behaviour, at least in their own ideas. For a teenager Burra was unusually sure of himself, a characteristic induced by his complete and utter indifference to what others thought of him. From early childhood he had been quite a 'show-off'; and a deep-rooted antipathy to any signs of conventionality, primness or conformism, combining with a natural mental exuberance, gave him a manner of expressing himself which was rich with youthful exaggeration and affectations. Chappell, obedient and delighted, splashed along in his wake; he was at the time only thirteen and a half (his mother had lied about his age to get him into art school).

In the autumn of 1921 these two juvenile loonies decided they might admit into their confidence another student, Barbara Ker-Seymer, with whom Chappell had begun a tentative acquaintance. In 1922 the trio became a quartet with the arrival at the art school of Clover Pritchard. With no doubts, no considerations, no questions (these arose decades later, as invariably they must, between close and lifelong friends) they happily discovered exactly kindred tastes and fell immediately into unusual communion.

Had they been told in 1922 they were to remain close to one another for well over fifty years they would have been incapable of contemplating, let alone accepting, so vast a panorama. Each buttressing the others' egos, the quartet was quite formidably self sufficient and almost unsupportable: noisy, over-pleased with themselves, determined, above all, to shock. Their antics were regarded by most of the female students with amused tolerance. Not so by the men (predominantly a cloddish lot) who were overtly suspicious and hostile; an attitude returned a hundredfold by its recipients. Burra revealed his contempt and dislike in a surprisingly virulent postscript to a letter written to Chappell in 1923:

God rot the tea club.
& may L and his foul sluttish friends
fall and break their necks.
    Bugger them.
and T and his friend
are stupid oafs
    not worth bothering
    over by sensible
members of the human
race – annoy everyone as
much as possible dear & my
blessings gang with you.
Messages, Messages.
    xx Ed xx

The arcane rituals of the 'Tea Club' took place during the mid-morning and afternoon breaks when a privileged élite of a dozen to fifteen senior students and pupil teachers endured maximum discomfort by squeezing themselves into a completely windowless, airless cupboard in one of the school's corridors. Biscuits and canteen buns were handed round, and tea was brewed on a gas ring from which fumes added flavour to the claustrophobic and exclusive atmosphere. Chappell and Burra were introduced (producing a dead silence) into this hallowed precinct by a small, soft-voiced, bosomy person, Florence 'Birdie' Rushbury, whose sharp tongue and married status (her husband being an R.A.) gave her an undisputed authority to do as she wished. She had taken a great fancy to the dreaded pair, and was delighted to give them this unparalleled opportunity to 'annoy everyone as much as possible'.

The letter itself, written from Springfield in the summer of 1923, bears no date.

Thank you dear, for your nice letter which was so very discreet. Everyones bin ill. The house stinks of rhubarb & sickness one is much better now and comes downstairs & plays the piano very well my dear 'La cathedrale Engloutie' von Debussy & Soirée dans Granada also Debussy & everything very nice that you would have liked so much I wished you had been wafted here on a zephyr. So La Tottie[1] has deigned to say she would come I am quite looking forward to seeing La Tot again I feel sure she has grown into a fine woman Madame Zara says avoid a cadgey we Tottie with a face like Ernest Torrence & above everythink avoid WOOLWORTHS OXFORD BOULEVARD.

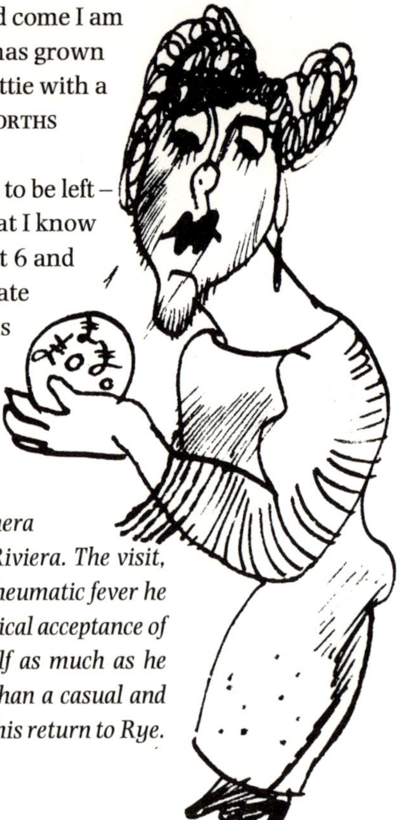

So you are going to have a nice time avec Tottie and I am to be left – alone – sob – Ime comeing back to College never fear not that I know when it begins yet Granma is coming back to London on Oct 6 and college begins some time last week in Sept so wont be very late I am sorry you could'n.t come dear what a pity maybe it was for the best who knows. Lazy bones Ime not *at all* sure painting is his milieu he photographs well its a bad sign[2] but still who knows Give my love to Tottie not that you will dear but still Edward.

In the spring of 1925 Burra was taken by his mother to Bordighera (a faintly seedy resort as he immediately notes) on the Italian Riviera. The visit, intended to be curative, proved disastrous. Stricken by a severe rheumatic fever he was hurried home in a very poor state of health. His unfailing stoical acceptance of physical weakness, combined with his capacity to mock himself as much as he mocked the world, made it impossible that he could give more than a casual and passing reference to his illness in the letter he wrote shortly after his return to Rye.

To William Chappell from Springfield, 1925

Dear Billy we came back from Bawdi in the Blue train which is *sposed* to be ever so mondaine but all I saw was ancient invalids and a couple with a baby that looked as if it came off Margate Sands there were a few mondaines tho to lighten the gloom I caught a glimpse out of the corner of my eye of one or 2 *demoiselles de haute monde*? or as good as *haute monde* you cant tell the difference unless you look close Bawdi is *not* mondaine and is just a wee bit enclined to be scabby but the native population are too beautiful and wear such exotic garments speshly the men I saw some most exotic shirts with Kubismus decorations all over them I would have got some if I'd had any money its just like an enormous Berwick St[3] only more soo Reely you do seem to be quite the rage of the nobility and gentry where will it end? this orgy of pleasure never rivalled since the days of Nero can end in nothing but ruin and disgrace. The well known Doris, Lady

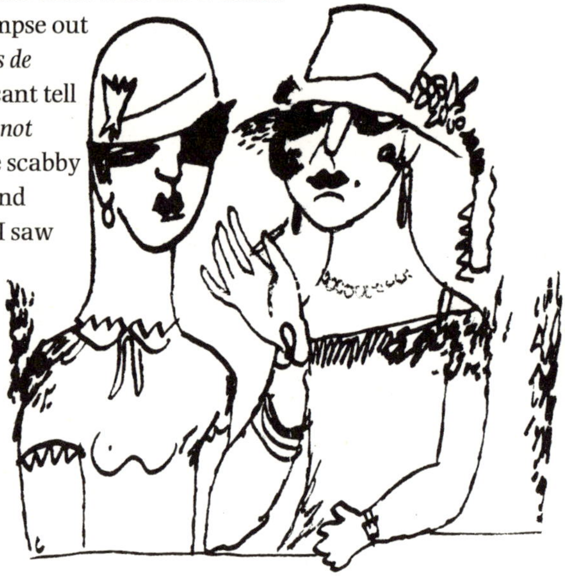

1 *One of many nicknames for Barbara Ker-Seymer.*

2 *A comment made about Chappell by Florence Rushbury.*

3 *Berwick Street in Soho (London) is full of market stalls and cheap shops.*

The castle Springfield

Sweetlist Queen of Adorableness
Thankyou so much for your dainty wee-letter as soon as I recognised your writing I had such a scrumshus ~~Shiver~~ shiver. I have been to that passionate outpouring "Men" and reely I never saw anything quite so kinki in all my life the exquisite art of the Negri reduced all classes to Hysteria can she rule men with a twinkle of her bust boddice? not!

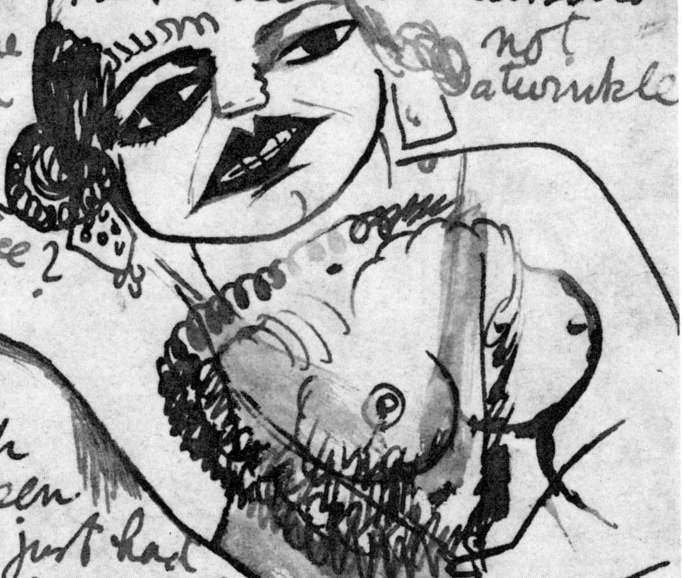

I cannot do justice to such volupté my pen falters I have just had a long letter from Billy who

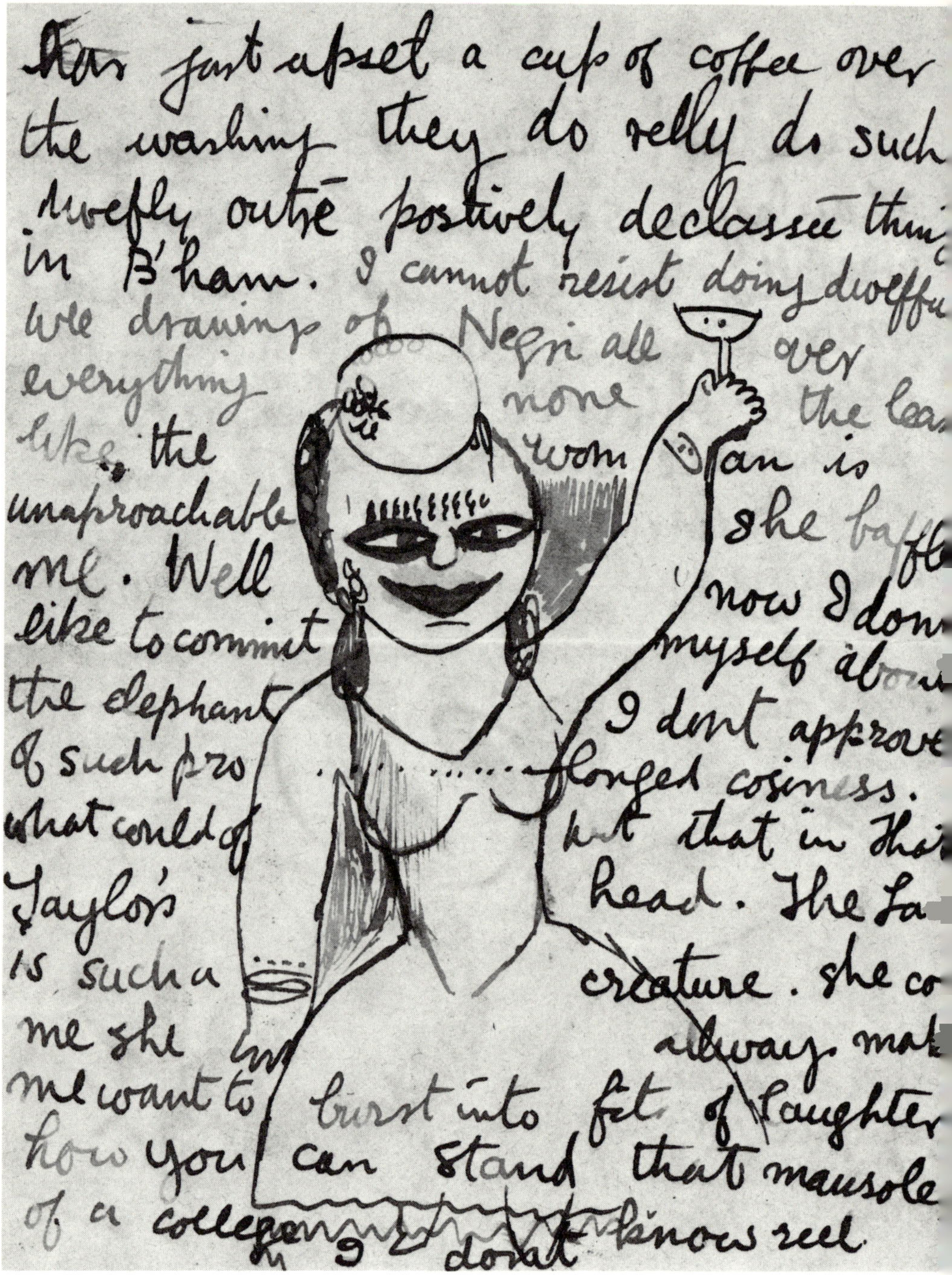
Have just upset a cup of coffee over
the washing they do relly do such
dreefly outré postively declassée thin
in B'ham. I cannot resist doing dreffu
wee drawings of Negri all over
everything none the lea
like, the woman is
unaproachable she baffl
me. Well now I don
like to commit myself abou
the elephant I dont approve
of such pro longed cosiness.
what could of put that in Thai
Taylor's head. The La
is such a creature. she co
me she always mak
me want to burst into fits of laughter
how you can stand that mausole
of a college I know reel.
m I dont

courageous I calls it ah you can
see the girl comes of the good old
sticking English stock My sister
is having such a rollicking time
in Florence what with fascisti
officers and only the other day a
perfect brute pinched her on
the → ....

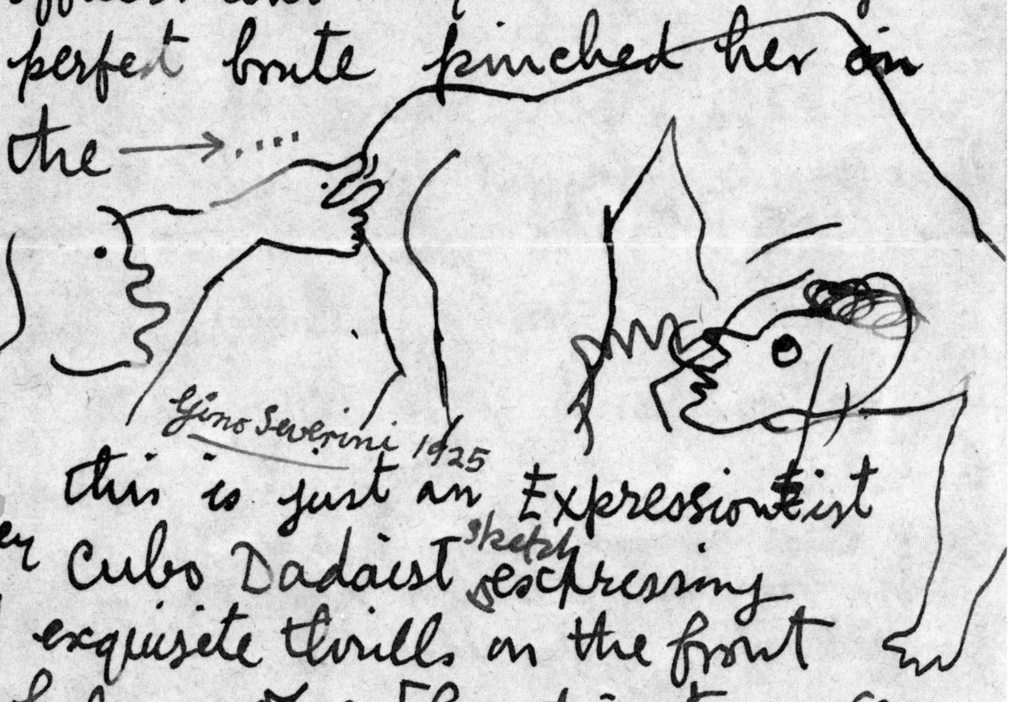

this is just an Expressionist
Cubo Dadaist sketch escpressing
exquisete thrills on the front
balcony of a Florentine tram car
and her that ticklish in that part
and whats more dearist she kept
skipping up and down cos she's

so <u>dweffly</u> tidish just there and
couldnt for the world think what
was the matter me being a
innocent well brought up girl of
the wickedness of the big city I'me dreading
what she'll write and tell us next
daughter of a family before you can say
Knife. I have been Reading Therese Raquin
par Emile Zola dr such a passionate
morbidity!! "The young woman tasted
all the bitter joys of adultery": chap 2
"he ~~ea~~ rose and took her roughly to
him after a short struggle she crushed
her lips against his, the bitter smell
of his body irritated her strangely, she
sank down upon the tiled floor —— the act
was brutal!" etc etc etc translated by E Barra
copyright applied for in all countries. Well dear
I am doing an oil painting a perfect madness
nobody knows what its supposed to be
nor do I. Miss letter seems rather hectic yr Eddie

Langley[1] gave a charming little first night *affaire* au Coliseum *all* the intelligentsia were present and a few besides witty conversation flowed like water – Did you see the House Party with decor by Marie Lawrencin I'd give anything to see it and I never shall get a chance Ime sure for I still hobble and cant do this and that and I want to see Delysia[2] and what's his name who was the Dauphin in Saint Joan I cant remember his name [Ernest Thesiger] and he is so good. all Ime going to see is the 10 commandments at the local pictoreum and flea course with luck monster and pig to go to 6 theatres I have again heard from the Rushbury who wrote such a sweet demure dainty little 15 century letter I was quite overcome but I am sorry to say us Parisiennes du quartier Latin are not at all mondaine in fact *all* our Paris friends are quite beyond the pale! She said she would ask me for a sejour when they had got a studio and if there was a room which would be ever so nice but I shall still probably be tottering and impotent. Also Cupid[3] has been given the boot and rushed forth with murder in his heart and persperation on his shirt Ime sure there will be a passionate suicide or something dredful Exair hero found hanging from weeping willow in Wellington Square is there a woman in the case? The woman Rushbury then came into the box (played by Isobel Elsom[4]). Ime reading a book by D.H. Lawrence which is so full of guts and maleness and femaleness it gives me the fidgets.

A style of writing favoured by Burra in his adolescence was a direct (if somewhat overblown) lampooning of a gossip columnist, as in the Tatler's *'Jennifer's Diary' or* Vogue's *wonderfully snobbish 'How one lives from day to day'. One of these letters has an added eccentricity in being inscribed on a sample double sheet of writing paper bearing the printed legend 'Truslove and Hanson Booksellers and Court Stationers Sloane St', and the specifications and prices. The front page carries an embossed address: 120 Grosvenor Square, W.1: and a diamond shape enclosing the name 'Marguerite'.[5] Burra has added a phone number Gerard 090909090[6] and the month, July 1925.*

My dearest Billy, realy what with the polo and my divorce case I haven't had a moment to write I have done right in divorcing the duke I know, the creature is quite *unbearable* in hot weather and perspires dreadully no English gentleman perspires, its not done. I am just going down for a long week end to the 'wee dustbin' my country cottage we realy cant afford to keep up the Towers any more still I do regret my marble and chalcedony bathroom you know my dear a hip bath is *not* the same thing be it ever so

---

1 *Doris Langley Levy (later Moore).*

2 *The French star of C.B. Cochran's revue* On with the Dance *by Noël Coward at the London Pavilion.*

3 *An admirer of Florence Rushbury. It was possibly the son of R.A. Bevan the painter.*

4 *A British silent movie star.*

5 *Marguerite was a natural, faintly better-class descendant of the bossy and obnoxious Dilly sisters of his childhood games. She paved the way for the arrival of the dreadful Doryse Ex Bureaux, who was to become a regular intruder.*

6 *An echo of a song,* Naughty Naughty One Gerard, *sung by musical star Teddie Gerard.*

quaint and dinkie also all the rooms opened into one another at the Towers which was so convenient! (?) You must come and have dinner with me before I go at Lyons Corner House the new poor cannot choose of course in my palmy days it would have been the cafe de Paris. Realy I must tell them not to put advertisements all over my best writing paper Truslove is getting positively dreafly careless. Poor Mama has got typhoid fever[1] but is much better she got it from dirty milk isn.t it dreadful.
Well my dear I must say goodbye as my rose coloured hispano Suiza purrs at the door.
Love to all
Your ever loving
Marguerite xx
As you may have noticed the heat has affected my head. M.

To William Chappell from Higham House, Robertsbridge, Sussex, 1925

Dear Billy Theres no peace for me for as soon as I returned chez moi about midnight on Fri they said you are going to Higham[2] tomorrow are.n.t you *dear.* Oh no I ses its quite impossible only 4 days ago I slept there with 15 guardsmen I couldn.t go there without being payed and little Tatsy does nothing but make little pools on the stairs out of spite spose someone reely important should see & granma is positively too mad and locks up all her illegitimate children in the coal cellar of course I dont mind Pongo and Wuffles seeing it all my dear but if someone reely reely important should see whatever should I do. I.m Manon, Manon Ker-Seymer[3] you know? There is nothing at all nice chez Woolnorth but wee narrow belts in vermilion with gold bindings comme ça and plain gold and gold and black check and vermilion and black reely dear they are quite twee I got one for Anne I had Heinz baked beans and a tasse de Cafe at the squalid Lyons opposite Charing X of course as soon as I arrived at Charing X it poured the drabness was bitter and I went to Tottenham[4] in the tube. Pa shows no sign of wishing to call on Queen Mossbottom[5] I think it was nothing but a passing whimsy and seems very pleased I should go to Paris *Anna* departs for Italia[6] on the 25th or something like that for years it seems she wont be seen again before next summer. its vewy sad that families should be so separated I think pwaps we may go to Florence some time if so I shall do shoppings and get some more lovely jerseys I think dear papa might stump up a little money for you I heard him muttering to himself I shall intrigue when we return on Monday Oh the good form ici it quite freezes me

Dear Papa did indeed stump up, making it possible for Burra to take Chappell (the pair of them closely chaperoned by Henry and Florence Rushbury) to Paris, where

---

1 True.
2 His grandfather's house.
3 Barbara Ker-Seymer's elder sister.
4 Tottenham Court Road.
5 Florence Rushbury.
6 To finishing school.

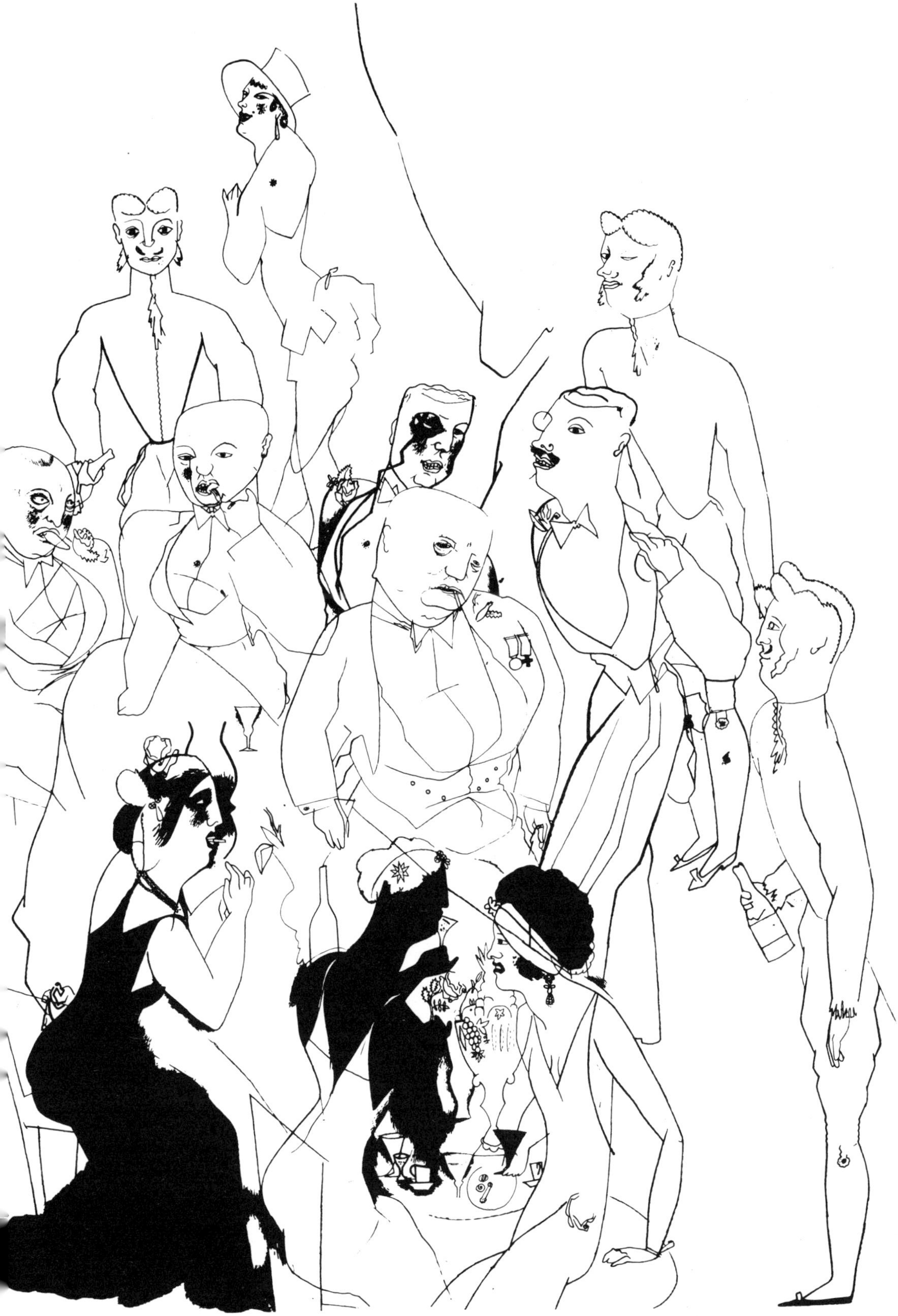

they saw Josephine Baker make her first violent impact on the music hall theatre, her beautiful body naked except for a fringe of diamanté bananas, in the ravishing Revue Negre *at the Champs Elysées.*

To William Chappell from Springfield, 1925

Dear Billy did you get my cultured wee cardie sent off in a moment of dementia I have heard from the Rush who has asked me to the cott[1], but doesn.t know when till she has consulted Rush. I hear you had a tête-a-tête diner avec Barbarina dear was it actually in the sacred Gledstanes![2] and the family was away paddling and reely how risqué but Aunty Alice was beneath the kitchen sink. I think I might come and do life at the P. next term in the evening for I couldn.t manage the day you know dear I am such a creature of the night I could not go back to the College again that is finished for ever. I am very dissatisfied with everything at present and yet not at the same time so temperamental it is realy because if I draw too much my eyes get sore and I should like to draw all day without stopping but it cant be done. Today has been the fine hot day just as I like I hope there'l be no thunderstorms to upset it. Anne does nothing but play in tennis tournaments such sporting bright young people and dances at week ends in the country club never mind the heat in 2 minuts we shall be in the pool kind of thing you never knew never speak to me again of tennis. I cannot go on I am quite beyond myself   yrs Ed.

Toward the end of 1925 Edward's letters to his cronies began to proliferate. Until then the quartet had been inseparable. Each day (all day, if possible) in one another's pockets; meandering through London afloat on a shimmering buzz of high-pitched childish conversation. Let loose into the world separately, they became intent (and none more so than Edward) on keeping track of each others' lives, habits and behaviour. Being natural and inveterate gossips they had long since discovered deep pleasure in the close discussion of one another, and woe betide any in the tetranity who dared to show the tiniest sign of taking themselves seriously. With zest and vigour they performed a private version of the School for Scandal. *Edward was Crabtree; Barbara, Lady Sneerwell; Billy, Backbite; and Clover, Mrs Candour.*

During his year's sojourn at the Royal College of Art, Edward acquired four new friends, each an interesting subject for elaborate vivisection. The pas-de-quatre became a pas-de-huit. It included a girl of great looks, Irene Rose Hodgkins, newly arrived from the Art School in Eastbourne, on a scholarship to the RCA. Her life was to prove as unlikely as her name. Being a romantically inclined person, she fell almost instantly in love with a fellow student, Basil Taylor,[3] a tall languid young man whose sad bloodhound eyes belied his oblique sense of humour. Hodgkins had already made friends with another student, Lucy Norton, a generous and infinitely

---

1 *At Burton Common near Petworth, Sussex.*

2 *Barbara Ker-Seymer's home in West Kensington.*

3 *Bi-sexual and fundamentally melancholic, he was to commit suicide and she to die, tragically, from cancer at the height of her beauty in her early thirties.*

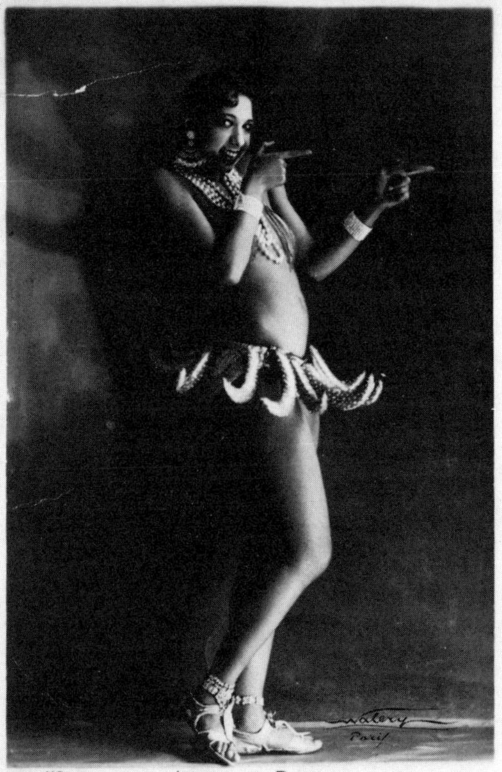

116 JOSÉPHINE BAKER

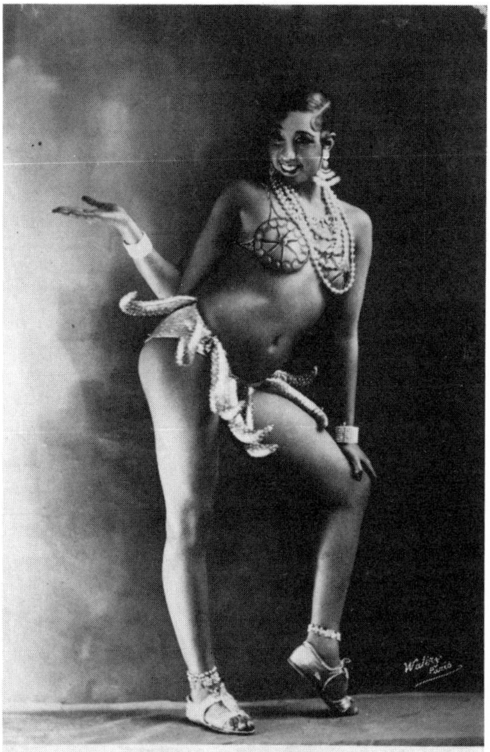

JOSÉPHINE BAKER
– Folies-Bergère –

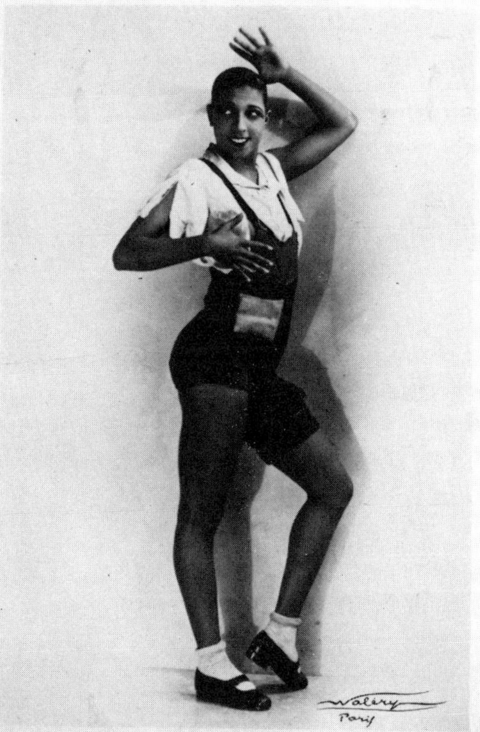

114 JOSÉPHINE BAKER

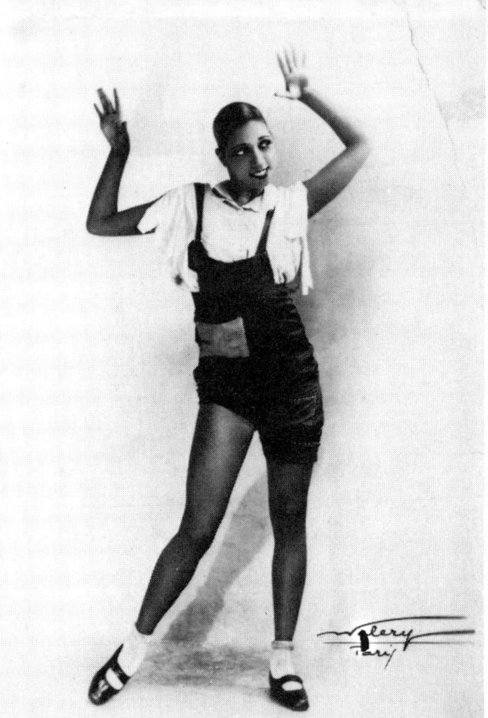

115

JOSÉPHINE BAKER

good-natured girl, well acquainted through her brother Harry in literary and artistic circles. Much later she enjoyed success through her elegant translations of the journals kept by Saint-Simon. The unexpected figure in this new foursome was a scholar and a blue-stocking, Doris Langley Levy. A close friend of Basil Taylor, who produced and presented her to the appraising (and faintly hostile) eyes of Edward's self-absorbed coterie, she was awaiting the imminent publication of her version of the Odes of Anacreon.[1]

This impressive group could have been a little daunting to three of the original quartet. Edward, it hardly needs to be said, remained undaunted. His great gifts were obvious. Still in his teens he drew like an angel with a strength and purity of line more than exceptional. The years at Art School nourished and developed his obsessive interests. His absorption with the fantastic, the grotesque and the absurd, and always with visual truth; his passion for the cinema which had been wonderfully catered for by the continual showing of the most excellent silent movies at the two Kings Road cinemas; the Kings Picture Playhouse[2] *and one sweetly subtitled Chelsea's House of Enchantment. Add to these the bonus of a first rate Variety Theatre, the Chelsea Palace, on the corner of Sydney Street;*[3] *and yet another of Edward's joys was accessible. The cinema is given much attention in the post Art School letters. He revelled in its every aspect. The purple prose of the subtitles; the extravagant costumes; the exotic personalities and faces of the stars (the men as heavily painted as the women): all this crystallised for him into something as hallucinatory as the effects of opium. Life itself had begun to show a similar quality of dreamlike unreality.*

To Barbara Ker-Seymer from Springfield, 1925

Dear B
We've not settled when we're going to Paris I.me so looking forward to it and we shall return so vewy continental positively like Ivor Novello in the rat n'c'est pas? I am going to Manhandled tomorrow at the local cinema pathé gazette comedy and Episode 709000 of the Pink faced horror Black Duggan lures Lulu Platinum who has a clew to the treasure of the Idols Eye concealed in her false teeth to the disused cellars beneath the old corset factory. Lulus fiancé Jack Mushbottom daredevil boy journalist finds a blood stained fragment of Lulu's mouchoir outside a ventilator of the old corset Factory meanwhile Lulu and Duggan fight hand to hand for the possession of Lulu's teeth Lulu escapes to the top of the great chimney 20,000 feet high and the pink faced horror (Lulu's maternal grandfather thought to be dead) sets fire to his hidden powder magazine in the nethermost disused cellar of O[ld]C[orset]F[actory] Duggan flies to the airodrome and charters an airoplane which flies rapidly towards the 200000 ft chimney of the O.C.F. on which Lulu guards her false teeth. Jack finding a cannon in

1 As Doris Langley Moore (after her marriage) she became well known as a novelist and the author of several enthralling books on Lord Byron. In addition she is an expert in period clothes and the founder of the Museum of Costume in Bath.

2 Now a Classic with four cinemas and several shops crushed into the shell of the original building.

3 Now a very nasty building with a Reject Shop in it.

the back yard ties himself to a shell and hires Rasmus (an old retainer) to fire him off at the 20000C[himney] of the O.C.F.

Duggans airoplane
&
Jacks shell
meet exactly
above
the
old
factory etc etc etc.

How I run on when the creative spirit is on me theres no holding me I declare also Forbidden Paradise is coming which I.ve been itching to see.

This is Auntie Maisie's[1] latest photo as you see my dear shes got over the twiplets

like anything even the landlady is quite reconciled now the twiplets are the tweeest tweetles of pets positively a necklace of twees and they dont wear nothing but bathing dwesses cos its so economical.

Vewy muchest
of love & kisses
dearest lots of
love from
Ed.

Edward and his friends were scrambling out of adolescence into a world of high, and excessively perverse, sophistication. How tempting and dangerous, beautiful and wicked, gloriously anarchic and strange, Life appeared. Sexual ambiguity was the rule. Sexual promiscuity and sexual aberration the mode. Had Edward known quite ordinary strength and health there is little doubt he would have become extremely wild. Wilder than any of them. The foursome made valiant (comical-tragical) attempts. The outrageous talk, the sexual precocity of their mental attitudes, and their immense theoretical *knowledge could not hide the fact they were in* practice, *virginally innocent. Set beside today's teenagers (a generation of boys potently fucking, and girls often pregnant at thirteen) they could only appear touchingly retarded. Possibly it was an attempt to improve so depressive a condition which prompted Edward to talk and write of his friends as a collection of hardened hustlers, prostitutes and alcoholics. He produced a score or so of scurrilous nicknames, accepted with delight by the nominees.*

To William Chappell from Springfield, 1925

Dear B.
I am delighted to come up whenever you like for it seems to me I haven't been near London for years Today one swoons with the heat crocodiles langurously move their speckled bodies through the odorously intertwined

1 *Another monstrous fable. The 'photo' is lost.*

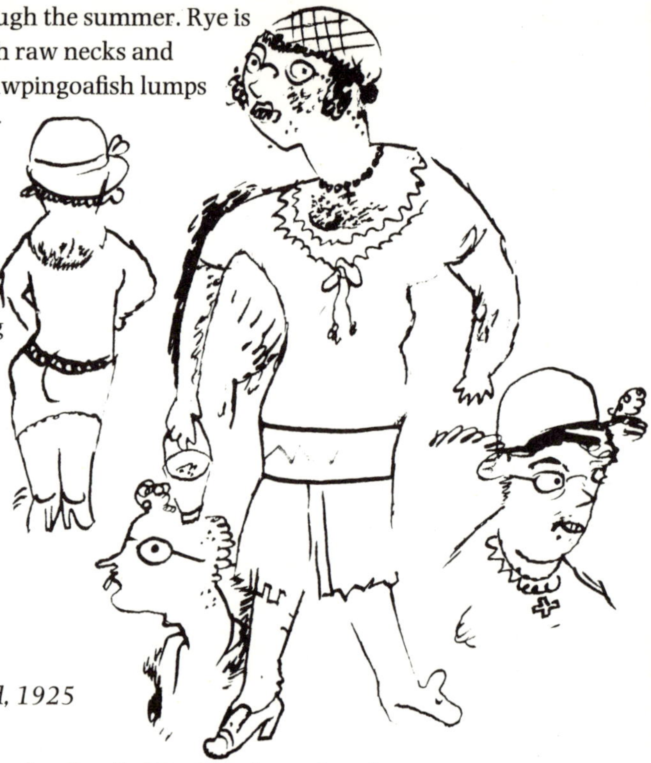

oleanders I hope it will go on all through the summer. Rye is hateful now full of abominations with raw necks and sports nets you cant imagine such gawpingoafish lumps of raw beefy FLESH flesh and butchers meat how I hate people I feel all the culture that goes on in Ilkley Yorks is due to darling Doris, the amoureuse of Byron. myhair continues to fall[1] But not quite so profusely I may yet be saved from looking like Pablo Casals yes we do seem to be answering our voluminnous. correspondence very prompt I thought you couldn't have vewy much to do to be so quick and bright Oh Lor I cant go on anymore now hoping to see you again in the future
yrs truly E
This space to be filled in by sender.[2]

To Barbara Ker-Seymer from Springfield, 1925

Well mi old pouf.
I have a new playmate in the neighbourhood called Paul Nash my dear I went to see P last week in great trepidation & was met with the greatest charm he showed me all his wood engravings and some lovely stuffs he's had printed. he said he thought Lu's flat wanted knocking about a bit and Lu[3] had a charming invention but she is realy so social I dont know if she'l do anything realy. Also Warren and L have been having another tiff over Dottie making so much use of L 'Of course' ses; Paul 'Lucys *so* good natured and will do *anything* for *anybody*' reely I ses anything for some people I suppose anyway darling Peter has been sticking up for our little Princess and saying Dottie mustnt treat her so badly isn't it twee. I went to the worlds sweetheart in the film you allways hoped she would make yesterday afternoon, I adored it that young mans smile I thought would crack, talk of spitting in a novices mouth it wouldn.t be difficult to land something with no malicious intent in his, his teeth are a lighthouse in my dreams I adored Carmelita Geraghty she was so low especially in her peignoir trimmed with swansdown I have been trying to get Santal from Mudies select library but they comes back at once with East Side West Side & the Wild Body with to the lighthouse put in for luck I should love to read Valmouth such a coarse book as the grand duchess Po Po of Pisuerga was heard to remark whilst roaming in the ruins of Sodorlahoma. I am dieing to see 'rain' or alias Sadee Swanson at the Capitol. Did you see an example

1 *He had been ill again.*
2 *This p.s. heads the empty half of the sheet.*
3 *Lucy Norton.*

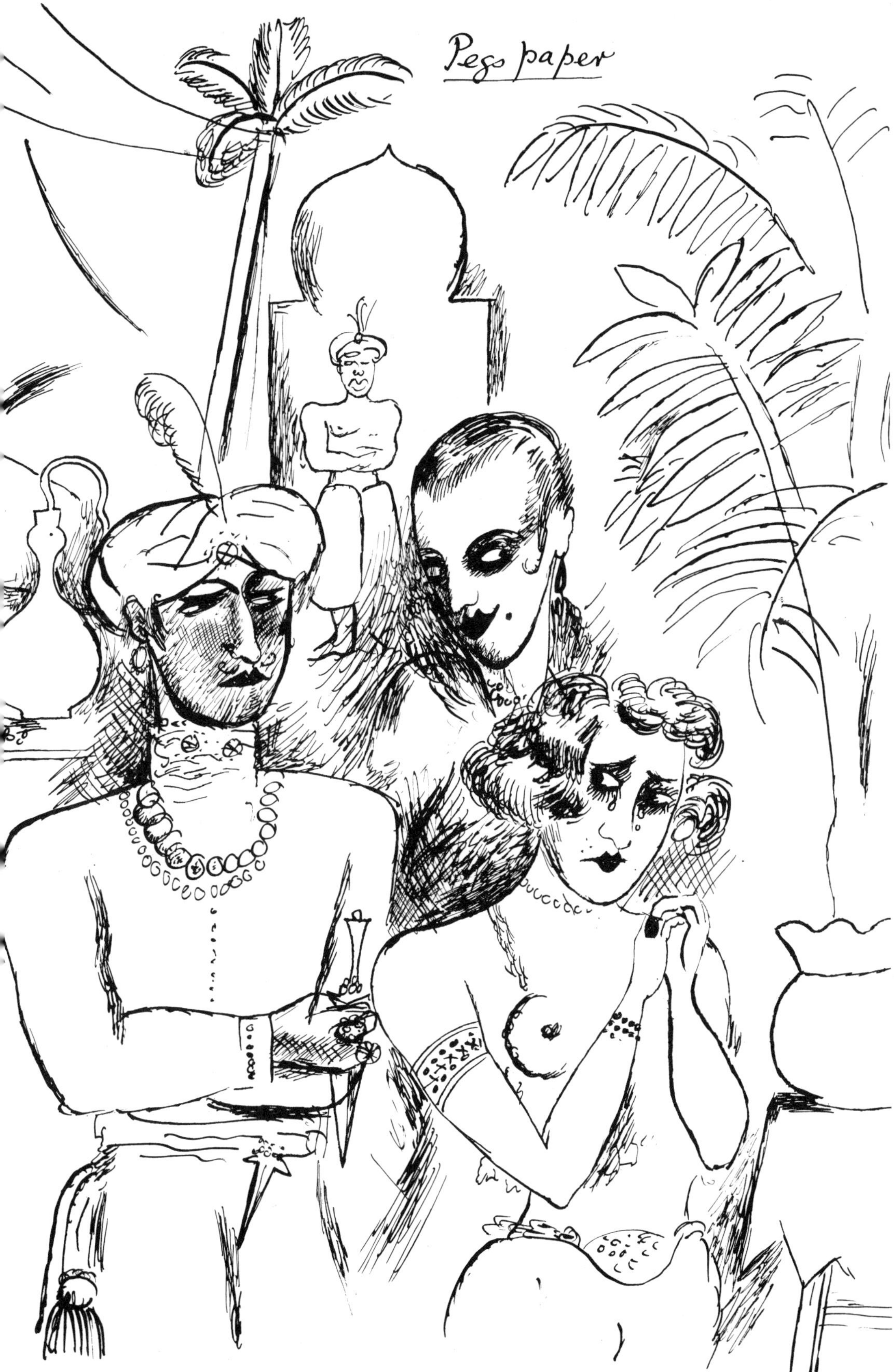
Pegs paper

of one of the subtitles of Sadie Swanson in the Evening S? 'Pogo Pogo where the men dont need any blankets as the rain comes down in sheets' theres wit for you director Raoul Walsh put that one in when no one was noticing, him and Dolourous Del Rio put their heads together whilst filming the legs of Carmen & thought of it then. My dear I see in the local paper such reviews at the grand theatre Brighton but never a matinee always the soiree at 6.30 and 9 so they always begin too late for the train. Married Bliss in 15 peeps also the Show boat produced by Lew Lake a musical nautigal review to say nothing of the Irish Follies which have been on the streets for the last 10 years or my eyes are incorrect when 'Splinters' with Reg Stone & a male chorus of 90 in undies appears I.m going over for the night. I enclose the most beautiful still of the month posed by Lionel & Gloria Entitled 'Dont sit goggling at me I tell you a scorpions run up me & wont come down' I think its very beautiful. Well dear I remain your loving pros

To William Chappell from Pensione Simi, 12 Piazza Donatello, Florence, Spring 1926

Dear Billy
Mama has come having been somewhat diverted by the strike[1] in fact she seems to have roamed all over France when she got to Boulogne no train to Paris of course so she went to Calais having stayed at Boulogne the night in a taxi taking the hall porter with her as a chaperon my dear she then stayed another night at Calais and then she finaly arrived in Paris having lost the Rome express she remained there the night & went to Her Sister from Paris featuring Connie T[2] and to the Louvre and to the Luxembourg and the Luxembourg gardens she tried to find the Rue de la Grande Chaumiere[3] but couldnt my dear all I hope is that the 1£ stirling will keep up and not fall for if it does we shall have to clear out rapid, I'me so glad you liked my lovely cards I have plenty more up my sleeve my dear the movies here are too mad for words they have William Duncan Olive Thomas Larry Semon Ben Turpin Tom Mix and all sorts of demented Italian films. If I hear Valencia again I shall destroy myself every one shrieks it theres no escape at all you see an innocent infant toddling along and just as it comes level with you out comes VALencia drin drin-drinnn all the children here have such fine powerful singing voices. I read all about the strike in Le Petit Parisien today it was Triste 'weekend' à Londres it certainly seems Triste and no mistake I see the Fulham & Stepney Electric lightworks are closing up my dear Lucy will grope with the aid of a rushlight and fall with a crash down the stairs into the salle de bain it seems to me perfectly terrible also I saw there were grave fears about comestibles that would be the last nightmare but allways remember the sound common sense of the british working man will win in the end and the back-

1 The General Strike in Britain.
2 Constance Talmadge.
3 Where Edward and Chappell had stayed when visiting Paris with the Rushburys.

bone of England is the middle classes what my granma must be like I cannot *think* for at the best of times she fears a revolution & Lives in mortal terror what she must be like what must she be like, Walham Green and its stretchers are'n't so far from Elvaston Pl. We went to the Arizona Express this evening its too twee at each critical moment the express arrived and everyone lept on to it

yrs E

P.S. Tell me dear when you are finally starving and I will send a quarter of an lb of chocs. Do not tell me you are yet deprived of cinemas?

To Barbara Ker-Seymer from Springfield, Summer 1926

Dear Baba Thank you for the baiser which I call stop pressing so hard George do or you-ll have my false teeth up your nose. My dear I cannot do justice to Lya de Putti on a p.c.

Oh her hubbie was such a jealosy box and when they had been to a gorgeous play in which a gentleman(?) strangled a blonde out of '*jealosy*' just like that my dear Putti said you would not ever be so jealous of me as that would you darling? I dont know so much said I from the 1/2s[1] & sure enough in the last reel she nearly got strangled but for a friend arriving and finding her puffing on the floor like a fish out of water it was such an emotional film Lucy went to a farewell party to Gypsy and had 3£ removed out of her handbag also they sang such bawdy wee songs all about mothers womb falling in and heaven knows what else. Billy seems having quite a tiring time at Ostende[2] I heard from Mrs Rushbury who is sharing a room with Bonzo[3] & the leading lady[4] who is realy too lovely according to her every one is in love with her & they live in an atmosphere of hot house roses crêpe de chine & chinchilla she also says the chorus are very beautiful and some are even vertuous. I allways was quite a one for vertue. Mind you do not get entangled in a new French Revolution which seems to be iminent anyway you can fly to San Sebastian in a roadster. We went also to the Ballet Tamar Jack in the box, the good humoured ladys & Zephyr & Flore and there was such an Ammerican sailor in the dress cercle he was so delightful I didn.t know what to do I enjoyed him as much as the ballet. How did you like my card of the Naldi[5] which I bought in Firense it was such a photo so typical I think they must be very fond of Negri[6] in France for she has always been on everytime Ive been there, last time she was in La Femme du Monde & the time before it was Mon Homme avec C. de Rochefort which is what you saw I am very fond of Rochefort you dont seem to see him very much. Everyone has gone away so I am quite alone

1 One shilling and twopence was the price of a seat.

2 Where he was dancing in cabaret with a partner.

3 Chappell's partner – real name Mildred Challenger.

4 A dazzingly pretty girl called Joan Langton.

5 Nita Naldi, a silent movie star.

6 Pola Negri, a German movie star.

for the time I recline in my bower emptying slops on the heads of the passers by when it is an Ammerican sailor that passes by of course I drop a cupids kiss sundea out of respect you know dearie. I have also visited the show of the Rye local artists. Oh dear you should see it No. 1 is old Mill at Twinkleton no 2 is moonlight and old tinned Salmon & no 3 is 'Church of Santa Maria del Tomato Assisi'. I have sent a dreadful little thing I did at the Chelsea P my dear very sweet so as not to enfuriate Mr Revel[1] Everyone is positively overcome with piety and kneeling about in corners also a very real life wee sketch which someone has bought for 3£.3.0 so good as come from Evil. Well dear mind you write again & have your photo taken in your Barkers hat & Selfridge 2/11¾ 2 piece bathing suitette with papier maché belt to tone I am all expectation

love from Edward

The young have many bad habits. One of the most maddening is the elaborate secrecy they tend to practise toward their elders. Edward and Anne were equally dedicated to this cult, using it mostly as a harmless irritant with which to goad their tolerant and benevolent parents. Secrecy reached a pathological pitch should either of them be asked, however tentatively, for information as to past, present or future movements. Anne was able to turn a routine visit to the tennis club into a secret mission for MI5.

'Where have you been?' her mother might enquire, mildly. 'Did you see anyone? What did you do?' In return Anne offered the solid negatives 'Nowhere', 'Nobody' and 'Nothing'.

Edward carried the process a good deal further. No one was given a chance to question him. Any morning he might meander down the garden. He could have been merely walking to Rye to buy cigarettes, going to Hastings for the day, or to London for the weekend. On the other hand, it was just as likely he was on his way to America for an indefinite period. He vanished as though the earth had opened and devoured him. He left as always, apparently *empty-handed, for if his usual morsel of luggage (much the same for a weekend or a six-month visit) were needed, it would have been hidden beforehand in a convenient pick-up spot, and taking the backway through the fields to the station he walked, as it were, into limbo, leaving behind him dead silence.*

This could well presage illness, accident, even death. It was hardly surprising that after some weeks Dah Burra began to make discreet enquiries amongst Edward's friends, all of whom had been immediately notified of every inch and every event of his journeyings from the moment he reached his destination. On one occasion Dah had at last tracked him down to Paris where he was staying with Lucy Norton, and wrote him a gentle enquiry as to his well-being and the possibility of an eventual return home. This was treated by Edward as a gross invasion of his privacy.

'Do not fuss', he wrote. 'I am still here and mean to remain till L[ucy] returns then I might come back for a week after which I might go to Marseilles for a little I

1 The headmaster of the Art School at Chelsea.

don't suppose it's very expensive. I am reading the "Rouge et le Noir" which is not unlike the Chartreuse de Parme and then I shall get L'Abesse de Castro. Love Ed.'

The roles were reversed. Edward had become the firm parent reproving the foolish chattering child. It is a marvel he had not added a PS: 'and be good enough to not bother me with any more unnecessary questions.'

To Barbara Ker-Seymer from the Hotel Paris et New York, 148 Rue Vaugirard, Paris, 20 January 1927

Cara Barbarina
We have just been to the last days of Pompei dear which I adored my dear the orgy in the temple of Isis excited us so we shivered all over the high priest & his protege reclined in a bower of roses and in every direction there were Doctor Blotto's living statuary and at the back there was a mummy case in which their appeared a creature all wrapped up in bandages who tottered swaying forward & dear the bandages began to unrole disclosing the serpent of old nile in no clothes but a small size Kotex sanitary pad with 1 tasty dimond placed in front in a commanding position she then did a dreadful dance and hurled herself on to the high priest & then covered up her bust all too modest with rosebuds it was quite a treat dear I can tell you We[1] have such an acquaintance among the haute monde here you.d never guess only the other day we went to tea with some ladies in a hotel bedroom everything in our eden of a hotel has been or is out of order the lift the lavabo (my dear we didn.t know what to do when that went wrong) so the infuriated mob burst into the private suites with W C privé and salle de bain downstairs & thus in the end nature had her way as she allways does my little dears also the central heating & water supply have been afflicted with the rickets Did my daintie card arrive with all the dear little babys under the toad stools Aunty Maisie tells me she finds hers there in fact more than is good for her. We have been to the circus which was heaven oh the acrobates & the Fratelinis were so twee well dear do write to your doting Edykins.

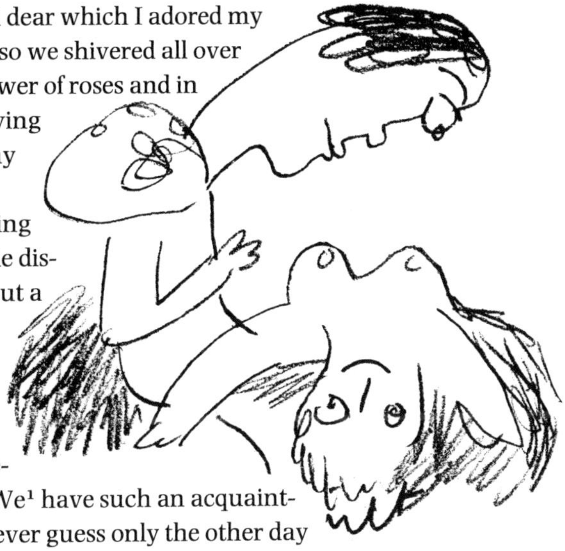

To Barbara Ker-Seymer from 148 Rue Vaugirard, Paris, January 1927

Dear Babykins. Thank you for yours to hand on Sunday afternoon we went to Palace aux femmes. at the palace music hall with Dranem (a cross between Ernie Mayne & Will Evans) also Harry Pilcer who is old enough to be Ellen Terrys father from what I could see of his pretty face such a ruin has never been seen he danced the black bottom in the middle of a fearful transformation scene in which 90 Fisher girls and the 50 Ballerines de Bigiarelli the 80 Palace beauties and the Chicago naiades whatever

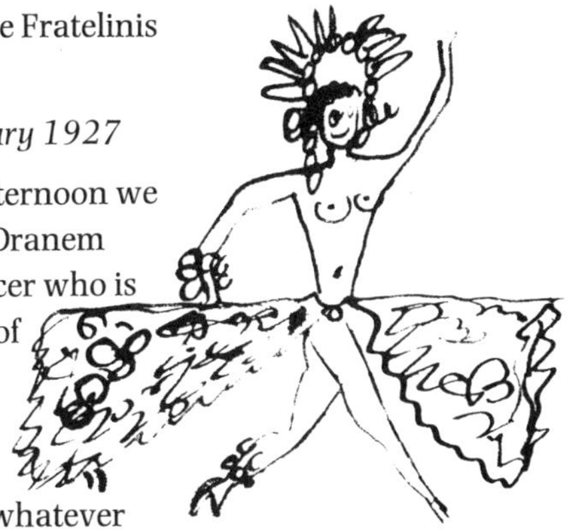

1 He was travelling with Lucy Norton.

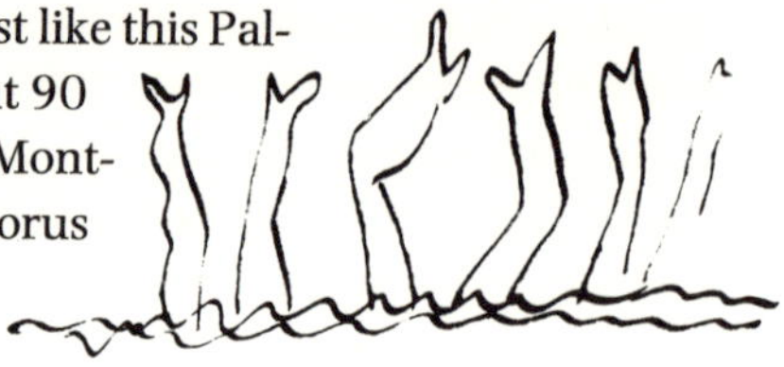

that my be walked about with the most awful costumes just like this Palladium pleasures holds no thrill for me now they had about 90 grand tranformation scenes entitled 'Broderie Anglaises' 'Montmartre Negro' & 'blossoms in the orchard' in which the chorus lay on their backs and swayed their legs about to the voluptuous strains of Bye Bye Blackbird or Barcelono (indigo yes indigo) more like asparagus than anything else it looked like Jenny Golder was supposed to be in it but we saw another creature instead called Aileen Hamilton an American she looked like the offspring of Edith Evans and Alice Terry[1] she was so snappy she leapt on a piano and sang Sweet child y'our driving me wild accompanyed by Spadaro who was the only realy good person in the piece he was a dream he did an opera as everyone in it would sing it which made us roar Norty[2] did not think Palace aux femmes at all good but for Spadaro it was so awful I enjoyed it I never can resist such scenes in the last grand outburst 3 creatures appeared with nothing on in a sort of fountain that voluptuous my dear chains where passed round to keep everyone in their places especially when they had a jolly mauve lime put on them. I hope the water was warm otherwise it will be Palace aux pneumonia for someone shortly I'll look around for a likely looking gingham if I dont see a gingham I.ll get some other stuff in tartan everything seems to be tartan here as far as I can see. Well dear 'Judas sister Judas sister' as Sybil Thorndike said in that interesting play 'the lie'[3] I think it was what is this about *alienating* Manons fellows affections whilst she is in Malta beware you do not know to what lengths a Jealous woman will go. I'de give him seduction a good kick in the right spot would soon put him right my dear thered be no more seductions then.

I think we should collect all our letters and publish them in serial form in the Pink un. You know dearest I think we might earn quite an honest penny by it & How is my monster my notorious Taylor mind you watch out and see Billy doesn't go out too much with Emile or someone will be carrying within them the burden of their fault. Well love and hugs from Edykins.

To Barbara Ker-Seymer from Paris, January 1927

Well my duckykins
our letters must have crossed this does not do justice to my Paul[4] my dear I never thought anyone had ever known him I allways thought he was quite a sort of mystery well dear I know you will like the cards when they come Please expect a rain of little Swanns Aunty Maisie remembers him as such a nice manly little fellow You havent had Hardboiled Virgins yet I suppose but realy I dont think you should read such books as Hot Sat his

1 *Who starred opposite Rudolph Valentino in* The Four Horsemen of the Apocalypse.
2 *Lucy Norton.*
3 *By Henry Arthur Jones.*
4 *A fairly outrageous French juvenile.*

hands were like hot dogs upon the flake white of her spikey nipples. I wonder where your mother could have got the Photo of Josephine[1] I've been looking all over the place for her but all I can find is Swanny Dorothy Dalton & the Fratellinis also Jack Dempsey now and then. This afternoon I saw 2 of the most dissipated men I ever saw in the Café they gave me the shivers they had 2 Jolly girlies with them but my dear I dont feel they will be jolly long one mans face looked like a cross between a crossword puzzle and Clapham Junction. Carmen is on next week and Ime all agog the photos look as if it was a dream of a film such dirty looks are exchanged Raquel M.[2] looks lovely I hear its very dull says Horty Norty having bought the Sunday Pictorial and read film flicks by Filbert Fan however go she must dull or no. We went to a terrible film called Lovey Mary featuring Bessie Love oh dear it was so cute we left in a maze of happy faces hollyhocks cottage gardens first love lambkins and Mrs Wiggs of the cabbage Patch. Norty is on the gad to night I said I was so tired and didnt go Ive no doubt I shall be in a position to tell the scandals off all the courts of Europe tomorrow princesses are as common as black eyes in our cercle lots of kisses and love from Edykins.

To Barbara Ker-Seymer from Springfield, 1927 (Monday Eve)

Dear old Pros
Thank you for your last.
I did have a fine time last Saturday. The Lady Norton and her aide de camp the Marquis Chappell came to lunch in their 6 cylinder limousine after walking round the grounds in a tearing gale you could hardly keep up in we went & had a squint at Paul Nash we found the great artist at work in the garden at one with the nature he so tenderly portrays. he was robed in a seamans jersey and kerchief bought at the village shoppie. Mrs. N was not at the cot to eye us through her lorgnette. I like Paul he is quite a petty. The Marquis C read all the letters from you he found lying about to see if there was anything about him self in them unfortunately there was nothing. Next time I am in London my dear Let & Cedric[3] want Billy to bring me to tea to show them my work I went to such a strange film today featuring jolly Marion Davies she was a mass of dutch boudoir caps realy it was such a frenzy I wasnt quite myself on coming out of the cinema & eat a whole packet of stuffed dates straight off. Well dear old Tot I remain your fairy Princess. E.

In the September of 1927 Chappell accompanied Edward on a visit to Marseilles and Cassis. They travelled third class by the longest and cheapest route. On 24 September 1927 (wearing his gossip columnist's hat) he wrote to Barbara from the Hotel Cendrillon, Cassis.

---

1 *Josephine Baker.*

2 *Raquel Mellor, marvellous Spanish diseuse and actress.*

3 *Lett Haines and the painter Cedric Morris, whom Edward and Chappell had met at a louche party in Paris in 1925.*

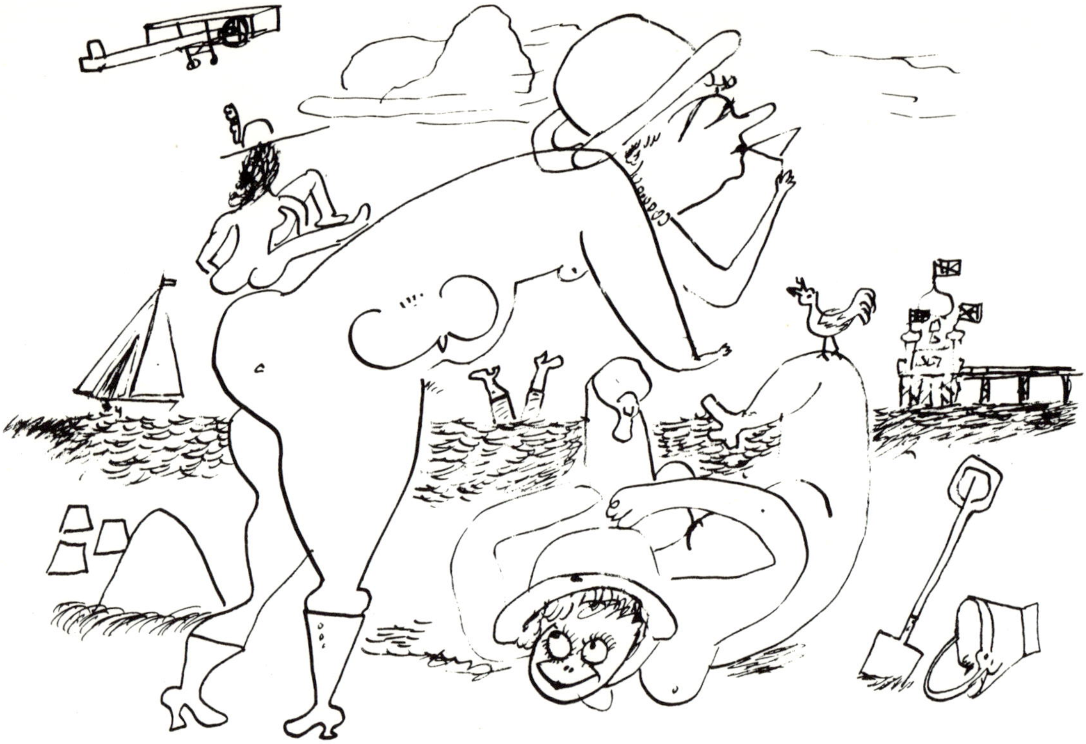

RIVIERA CHATTER *by Prausette*

Well my whoreingest.

If you could see the jolly men bathing at the bathing beach everyone skilfully undresses on the plage in full view of everyone prizes are given to those who manage to undress and not show the organs only this morning it was won by the celebrated poet of the advance guard William Chappell, Mdlle Ida Rubinstein gracefully gave away the prize which consisted of [a] charmingly fashioned whirling spray which when opened by a secret spring disguised in the spout discloses a tangee lip stick with powderette & a bottle of Piver's Pompeia. Well my dear what do you think Josephine B. is making a debut in the movies in a film called the Siren of the Tropics *Ciné Miroir* is full of it I enclude a jolly photo of our *vedette* also the story is by Maurice Dekobra[1] I.m sure it will never come to England. Our hotel is a dream of delight there is a couple that intreeges us no wedding ring my dear the man is very tall and thin & the woman is very small & thin, they have such a twee doggie that violates every puss it lays hands on the chic wear here is ripping red print hankys round the neck & head white linen trews and bathing shoes in blue, white striped or rose pink everyone walks about with drawing books and canvasses the canvasses look a bit futurist you know you cant tell if its the old manse at twilight or death at the festival. We are going to Marseilles on B's birthday you know us men must be satisfied and there aint no facilities here is.n.t it twee all about the Grand

1 *Author of a famous novel,* La Madonne des Sleepings.

Rue where we get our jolly marin ware and linen trousers the guide book says is a veritable ghetto of houses of ilfame my dear I stares into every window hoping for a thrill but all I see is little Georgette having her nappy changed by loving mothers hands. Billy has come out in a lovely toilette of linen trowsers bathing shoes a pullover & red kerchief and a jolly beret boutht at Elli's hatshop Marseilles, Oh you know old men have young ideas when they see Bill, Marie Prevosts only rival well write to your old moke by return yes Prowsette.

To Barbara Ker-Seymer from the Hotel Cendrillon, Cassis, 4 October 1927

Dear old catin
Yesterday evening I saw Billy into the Paris train at Marseilles. such a panic was never seen every one rushed in at the doors and got jammed in the corridor community sensations. thinks I jumping up and down and up and down with about 3 chinese 10 senegelese a few turks 3 french 4 widows with crepe vills and Billys suitcase outside the compartment we were all trying to break into. If you feel a little relaxed and down go to Marseilles its like Berwick street gone mad with six lines of trams a sprinkling

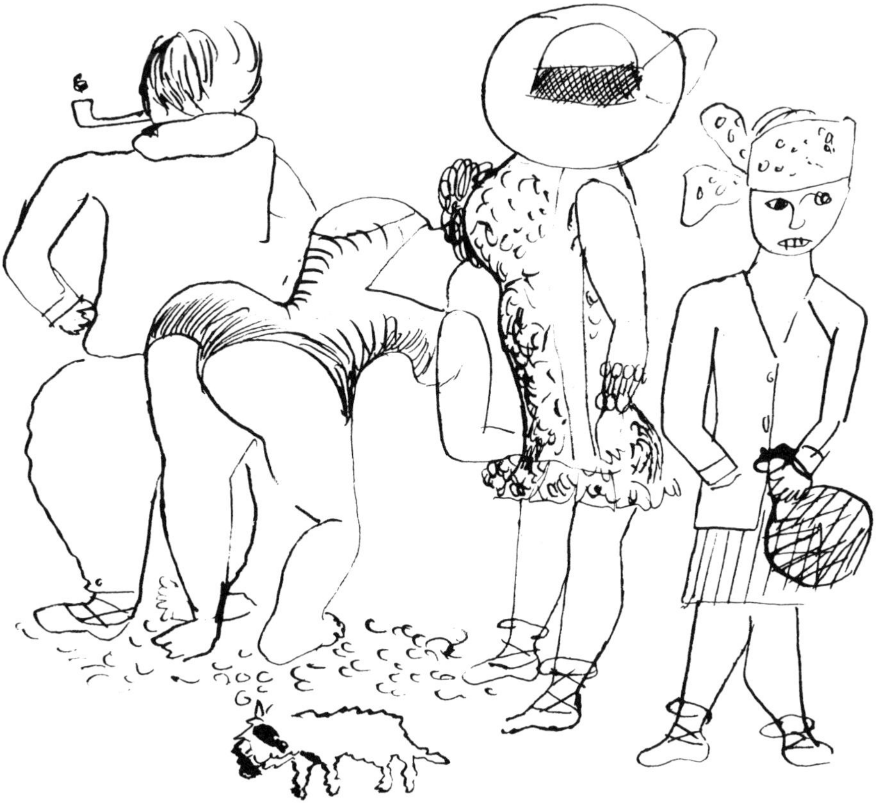

of nigs in blue boiler suits and a bevy of cafe bars all over the pavement I.ve never heard such a din we are getting more and more artistic here quite the royal college my dear only a bit more chic there is one glory who is perfectly immense and is the mistress or wife or concubine of a Japanese. She has an enormous body & weeny arms & legs and quite a thin face heavily farded such a treat you never saw I adore her especially when she lies on the beach with a handkerchief over her face to keep the sun off she looks

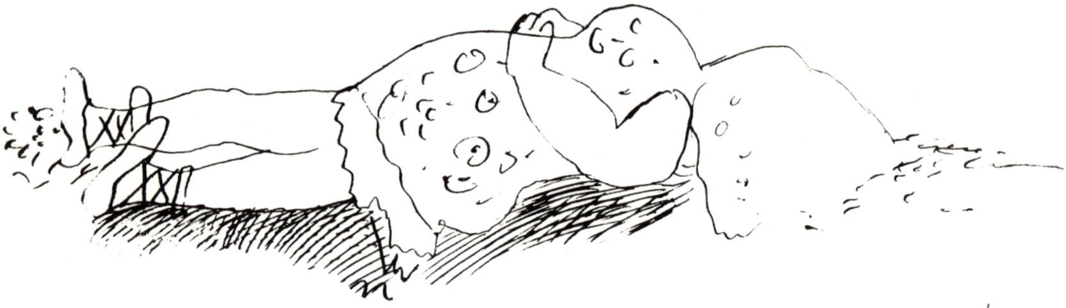

like a relief map of the lake district in play wax by the pupils of Bermondsey Board school what the jolly artists colony thought of Billy and me remains to be seen the looks we received from time to time however I comes back with something as acrid well dear old catin I suppose Billy will be hanging on the end of the phone long before you get this to tell you all the news I have bought such a pair of shoes in Marseilles for 17/6D in two shades of brown or I may say tan a much favoured mode about here is cream coloured sort of glacé kid with a tan toe cap and a sprinkling of tan lines here and there also sham crocodile uppers are a perfect rage tho of course you know dear I like everything to be real you know realy good. Has Clover Pritchard returned from Vichy yet, I hope the waters have made fathers nose a somewhat lighter shade of red mind you give her my love. My dear you can get the most glorious rings in M. large signets with enormous green and ruby stones I think of getting one just to give a good impression mind you write dear to me love Edykins.

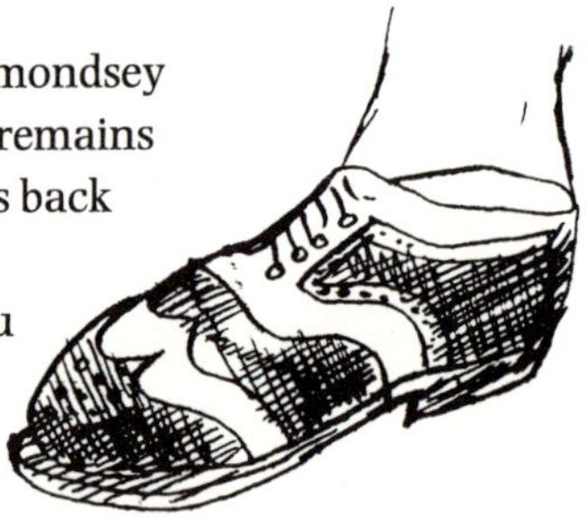

To Barbara Ker-Seymer from Springfield, 14 October 1927

Dear Baba
Well dear I'me sorry I'me not as good as the Tatler but London Life & the Worlds Pictorial News flavoured with the police gazette is more my line old tart as we know. I'me sorry it didn.t give J a sophisticated thrill like reading Aldous Huxley to read my letters. Well dear I am sorry to leave Cassis or at least Marseilles I missed Billy when he left there was no more picking over the neighbors after Prince Gossip had left, I heard from B this morning and he said he had been to see Miss H and Basil was there, who 'had been trying rather late in the day to raise his social value 'and was also' very much 'his own master' what does that mean please? also Barbara was there and had been trying to get her own back on me by saying I was in love with John Aldridge and Lucy believed it. I have been reading such a lovely book called The devil in the body by Raymond Radiguet there is a piece in it where the heroine becomes enceinte and the hero says 'when I kissed Marthe upon the stomach it was not her I kissed . . . but my child!'

now we know of a new place to caress. I went to Don Juan on Wednesday, my dear what next if you please? I couldn.t resist the peice where Jolly Barrymore Fairbanks leaps up upon the Borgias balcony to attack the hand maid & says 'A maid in the hand is worth 2 on the balcony' also Phylis Haver as 'Imperia, a famous frailty' was quite a treat arriving at the prince of lovers house in a sedan chair drawn by 2 negros I thought it was a meat safe when I saw it first I.me sure Warner Bros must have hired Mack Senett to write the scenario. I liked the bit where Don J. offers Estelle Borgia née Dempsey[1] the poison cup and Borgia says 'we Borgias never share with another', & Don J pours it on a rose which at once curls up in smoke like a chipped potato and Don J says 'The rose is richer for an experience' H A H A I thought I should be ordered out of the movie and I had to leave before the end however the end I must see if I have to go to the Boltons in 1929. The Rye Electric Palace is my only hope. I may be coming up on Monday to stay at Granmas Joint 31 Elvaston Place S.W.7. Gran is in a nursing home in Portland Place I thought Ide wandered by mistake into the Berkley when I arrived & was confronted by a hall porter in medals and a uniform the home kept by Lady Carnarvon who sweeps among the sick in pure white with a nurses cap upon her head such an angel of mercy, what she knows of illnesses I cant think anyway Ma and my sister Anne are staying at 31 in Grans absence so I have wrote a P.C. and asked to come to if I do I daresay I shall see you au resevoir as they say well dear old Pros no more now from yr. faithfull Prowsette

NEWS OF THE WORLD
STRICTLY COPYRIGHT

To Barbara Ker-Seymer from Springfield, 1 December 1927

Dear Ba Ba
How are you getting on dear old thing? I am not getting on so well. We went to Granmas funeral on Monday carrying a wreath of chrysanthemums maiden hair fern and moss oh it was lovely such a beautiful wreath my dear never do I go to another funeral I thought I should collapse at any moment I never thought they dug graves so deep they let the coffin in with ropes and realy I thought when is it going to arrive? all I can say is dearie you may be afraid of lifts but youl be much more afraid of graves when your time comes going down such a long way. we fled as soon as it was over and the cold I didnt dare get my handkerchief out of my inside pochette as my suit was a rich brown and everyone else was dressed in deepest black well to get to more merry things we get nothing but jolly advertisements for Derry and Toms gift section cheap gifts consisting of novelty manicure set and pen wiper in the shape of an amusing Dismal Desmond mascot 10/6 post free Woolworths pocket handkerchiefs in Debenham and Freebody boxes is all I can afford at present. My uncle has just bought an upright H.M.V. gramophone costing 25£ if you please and

1 Estelle Taylor, who played Lucrezia Borgia, was married to Jack Dempsey.

what do you think we were treated to when we went to hear it? Ruddigore & the Vulgar boatmen (featuring William Boyd and Elinor Fayre says I at once on hearing it begin) also a jolly organsolo. Whats this I ses when the organ begins, The pipe organ at the Majestic Clapham I suppose broadcast recording 1/3^{D} at Marks and Spencer and then we has a lovely record of the choir at somewhere or other, such trebles my dear. I do adore a Eun . . . I mean boys voices says I but pulls up in time knowing Eunuchs are to some what red rags are to bulls. Bumble[1] and me had such a time leaving our pictures at the New English[2] we roamed about in a thick fog and finaly arrived at what looked like a charming new block of residential flats in course of erection a creature flew out and shouted out 'pictures' in a furious voice so we said yes and he grabbed our pictures and stuck them against some scaffolding so by now they are built into the wall securely I should say never to be discovered till 1999 I havent heard a word about mine so I fear the worst. Well old tart I can keep up no longer I'me so busy doing a cover design for The Buggers own Bumper Joybook mind you write yrs with love Ed.

To Barbara Ker-Seymer from Springfield, 9 December 1927

Dear old prosser

Thank you for yours. The private view[3] must have been a treat Mother and Father went & Mother said 'yours killed all the other water colours so they hung it in the roof and all you could see was feet' HA HA. I was in London for the day on Wed (cheap day) buying jolly yuletide gifts or trying to it was so awful I.ve never seen so much rubbish displayed so I finaly staggered into Selfridges Book Dept nothing so crazy has ever been seen Tiger Tims Annual and England reclamed rub elbows with Our little dots and The scented garden. I tryed to get the flower beneath the foot[4] but I might as well have tried to get Ulysses at the Roman catholic book store however I discovered in a catalogue which an assistant produced a piece by Ronald Firbank entitled 'the misadventure of Cardinal Pirelli' or something like that[5] so of course they didnt dream of having it in stock & said they would send it what on earth will it be like? finaly I went to Lil Dagover in Matrimony at the Astoria Lil is too divine & Gosta Eckman is in it as the vilain. Have you heard anything of Tearsheet Hodgekins lately I want to know her address so as to send her a congratulatory card on getting into new premises just to hope trade will be good you know. Have you seen the December vogue? its Cecil Beaton Baba Beaton Annie Beaton Mrs Beaton Father Beaton Lizzie Beaton Beaton Beaton and even one of those amusing drawings by Cecil Beaton of Cecil Beaton impersonating a fragrant old staffordshire peice representing Apollo well cheero Old Pross from Prou Prou.

1 *Beatrice Dawson, a new friend of Barbara Ker-Seymer. She later married Gerald Corcoran, who became Edward's dealer.*

2 *The New English Art Club Exhibitions featured work by young painters.*

3 *At the New English Art Club.*

4 *By Ronald Firbank.*

5 *Actually* The Eccentricities of Cardinal Pirelli.

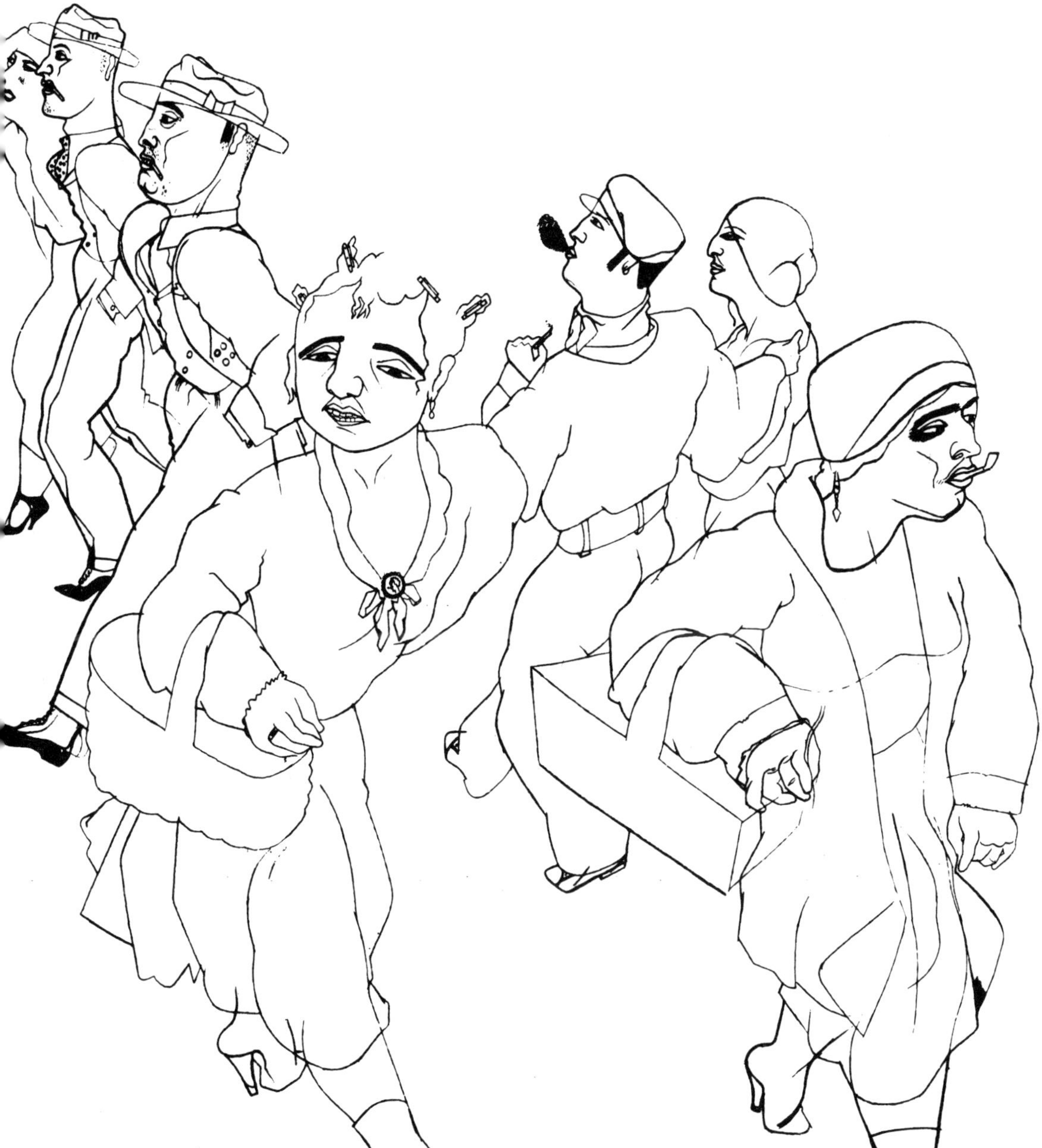

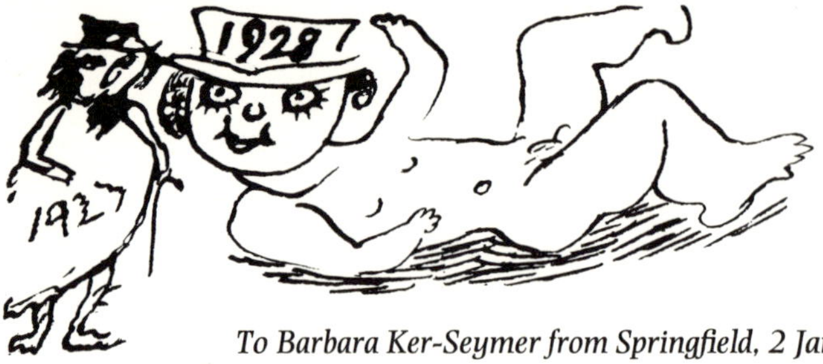

To Barbara Ker-Seymer from Springfield, 2 January 1928

Lack a day we are so gay with our jolly New Year hops at the local tennis club you know. I heard the bells ringing oer the silent fields and meads on New years night so I made a good resolution never to go and see Chrissie White and Henry Edwards in 1928. On Sat I went down to the beach to

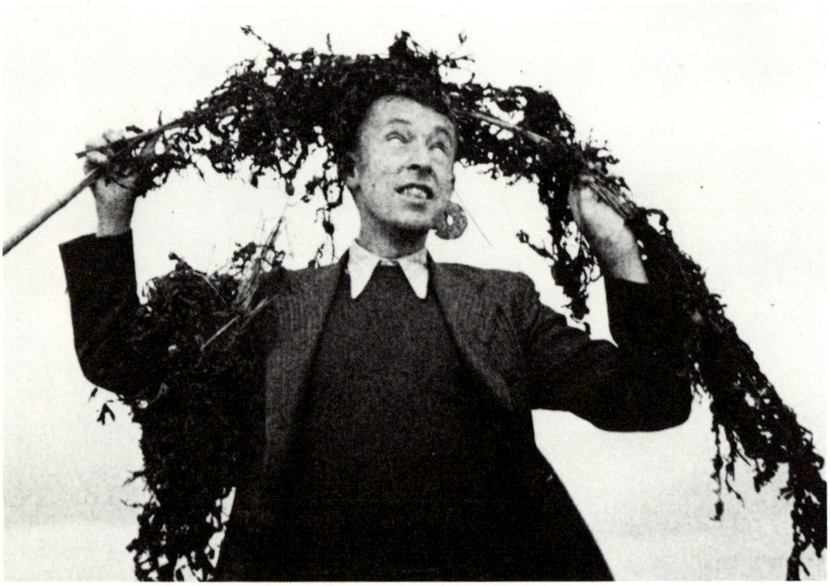

look for seaweed and shells. I got some lovely tufts of sea weed. I.ve sent it all to Billy so mind you ask him for a share there were some lovely old bloaters and drowned kittens on the strand but enough is as good as a feast so they say the seaweed will look lovely bunched on the shoulder quite like a flower from the Gallery Lafayette only weaved by natures loving fingers in Neptunes marine cavities we went to the Panto in Hastings last week it was a perfect dream the principal boy *would* act through thick and thin even singing 'When I saw Sally coming down our Alley' didn't stop her and as for the ball at the Palace such 18th century has never been seen outside the Lyric Hammersmith. It seems that the princess Pearl is strangely like—ah—little Cinderella—Ah what it is to be a prince, nobody loves you for yourself alone, ah, strange princess you remind me of—ah—Cinderella—ah. Oh sir are you reely a prince my prince? ding dong dong ding ting and then cinderella flew away and left a very large silver slipper (by Sorosis Ltd) which was produced by Dandini from the wings it was so twee the principal B was like this in a silk imitation grey leopard tunic with a bead valence a grey bow gracefully drapé upon the bottom in which was stuck 4 large ostrich feathers black with ruby coloured edges and a smart white cloche hat from Lisette de Berwick Street sprinkled with diamenté and 4 enormous black and ruby feathers stuck on the back but that was not all she also had a hunting kit and a deep mauve diamente

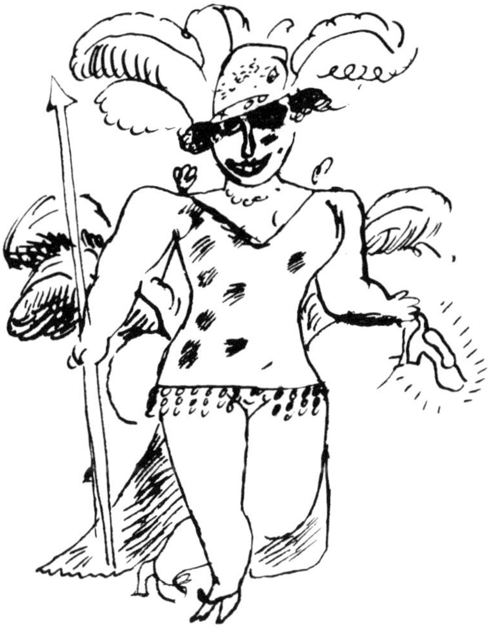

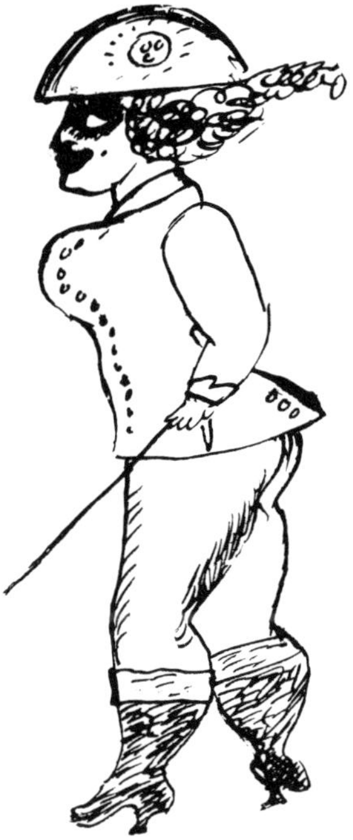

tunic with a train to tone the sisters were a rare treat and made the most terrible jokes such as Cinderella go and take the milk to the local anarchist to be paralysed Oh we did split our sides I can tell you also 'you've got camels feet . . . what d'yer mean camels feet? they have'n.t seen water for a month also Oh I ave got such a beautiful dress for the ball with gussets on the bust, gussets, gussets I may have had a slap on the bust but never a gusset Oh it was a treat. I want to see the Palladium panto with merry old Clarice Mayne and Nervo and Knox as the brokers. Realy what was Granma doing with such a strange postcard as that in her possesion Danses Folles I see it calls itself a portuguese count I suppose he calls himself but I calls him a discount (ha ha) Well you know I hope you will have a nice time at the ball and had no arrestations for indecency this time tho' if you go as drowned sailors with open work net tops I.ve no doubt you will be ordered off the floor[1] anyway I have sent B some nice cockle shells coverd with barnacles so they will keep the boys at bay if they importune too far. It is simply pouring with rain everything is melting and immense floods are appearing its a good thing it was still freezing when I went down to pick up shells as I was able to cross the ice like Eliza in Uncle Toms Cabin with a bagful of shells instead of a baby What is the coloured prologue to

1 *At The Chelsea Arts Ball: Edward christened Chappell 'Fishnet Annie'.*

Uncle Toms Cabin like at the pavilion? very spiritual I feel and no chinee opla opla or Johnny Hudgins[1] nothing but playing golden harps all over gods heaven I am afraid Well old pross I daresay we shall meet again soon if a typhoon doesnt bury me in a frozen snowdrift before the 7th. I hope Queen H[2] will ask us to tea I'me dieing to see the inside of the *cocotterie*[3] I'll have to give her a gilt Buddha to put in the all.

To Barbara Ker-Seymer from Springfield, May 1928

Well dearie
There has been a slip somewhere for I came up on Thursday instead of Wed, I.me sure I put Thursday on the p.c. I sent. I sent one to Mistress Chappell and one to Clova as it is spelt in 'Manjanztsk prvdntsk' or whatever the paper is we went to 'The Street' & 'Blackmail' which was glorious Ive never seen such a programme my dear we waited till ten past 2 for you and Clover showed us her engagement[4] in Hungarian papers & then we went in. You must go old Ellen Richter surpasses herself she first appears as 2 dainty legs in + 4's sticking out from under her car so of course our ruin of a Jack T. gives them a pinch and out comes Ellen in a Austin Reed pull over & leather airmans helmet very fat and walking with her feet turned straight out she was so good tho especialy in the drammatic parts where she went to get her sisters letters ('Evi Eva' with an immense mop she wore the most lovely clothes very tawdry with a striped red bodice & shoulder straps as for shoes my dear sort of Peter Yapp[5] mixed strangely with pinet and walked well down Ellen was not to be outdone and appeared in a chic coat trimmed with flounces of black and white wool exactly like the druids beards in the imortal hour old Ellen had been at them with the shears when they were asleep I'me sure she also had a chic evening gown made of tramlines of diamonté flounces of net & draped velvet. This dress caused quite a furore in the Shaftesbury[6] I hear. Reitlingers party was rather on the dull side Billy said everybody you can think of seems to have been there as far as I can see even Mr. Jowett dressed as a Victorian Beau Mr & Mrs Ethelbert White went as topsy & Eva Mrs White was Topsy and Mr W was eva he needed scarcely any make up.

Throughout the autumn of 1928 the weather in Toulon was particularly delicious. At the end of the last week in September Edward, Chappell and Irene Hodgkins were half way through a holiday, installed in the 'Hôtel du Port et des Negociants' and existing in a state of blissful contentment. Stunned almost speechless by the benevolent sun, they had fallen into immediate lotus-eating. Chappell

1 *A black comedian and dancer who appeared with Florence Mills in 'Blackbirds'.*
2 *Irene Hodgkins.*
3 *The house in which Hodgkins' lover had installed her in Godfrey Street, Chelsea.*
4 *To a very handsome very wicked Hungarian, Adam de Nagy.*
5 *A smart shoe shop in Sloane Street much patronised by the Sloane Rangers of the period. It no longer exists.*
6 *Shaftesbury Pavilion – a cinema near Cambridge Circus, long gone.*

and Hodgkins were natural lotus-eaters; completely idle, staring without seeing; luxuriant and immobile, save for those mornings when they could summon enough energy to cross in the steamer to the beach at Les Sablettes, *and once there, collapse again becoming supine sacrificial objects, devoured by the sun. Occasionally they encountered Anthony Powell the writer. Often the beach was quite empty. For Edward, lotus-eating meant working, always his deepest pleasure and here made doubly pleasing by the soothing warmth. He sat back in the shaded end of the bedroom painting or drawing on a large sheet of paper overhanging a tiny table. Too lazy even to leave the hotel Chappell often lay naked on the floor by the window in a blazing oblong of sunlight, hoping to match up his pale bum to the rosy brown of his back and shoulders. At some point in the day they would all meet – again occasionally with Anthony Powell – either in the Café de la Rade on the Quai or back in the town at Raymond's Bar in the Place Puget where a crumbling fountain smothered in rampant greenery cooled the drowsy air. (This fountain appeared several years later on the backcloth of the set Edward designed for the ballet* Rio Grande.*) Hodgkins was awaiting the arrival of her lover Dennis Cohen the publisher,*[1] *a rich, intelligent and charming man. On her return with him to England she was to embrace the Jewish faith prior to their marriage. However, as pointed out in a favourite silent film subtitle Edward never tired of quoting, 'Fate the Ringmaster of Lifes Circus, cracked his whip' (HA! HA!,) and a suntanned blond god, quite clearly the offspring of Apollo and Venus – disembarked one early evening from a yacht on to the Quai Cronstadt. He turned out to be the painter Tristram Hillier. That then was that. Hodgkins abruptly and quite surprisingly calmly, left Edward and Chappell to their own devices. It was merely a matter of a day or so before the mythic figure had gathered her up and transported her to a ruined castle in deepest Provence, where a year later she gave effortless birth to twin boys.*

Edward's delight in such outrageous behaviour makes it strange that no letter of his records the whole episode. When Dennis Cohen arrived it was left to Anthony Powell to disclose to the wretched man that his mistress had vanished with a new lover whom she hardly knew.[2] *Edward and Chappell lingered a further week and then made their way to Paris, hoping to meet up with Frederick Ashton. As it turned out this meeting was also obviously planned by Fate the Ringmaster of Lifes Circus (HA! HA!) and this time round, he cracked his whip over the idle, empty and sundrugged head of Chappell.*

To Barbara Ker-Seymer from the Hotel du Calvados, Rue du Depart, Paris 14ᵐᵉ, 9 October 1928

Well dear
We arrived quite safely and found every hotel full but this, which is exactly like the hotel in the Loves of Jeanne Ney if only it had a tin fan full of postcards of boxers and *artistes* it would be perfect. We went to a glorious film today featuring Lilly Damita George Alexander & Alphonse Freiland

1 *Of the Cresset Press, who were to publish Edward's* ABC of the Theatre.
2 *He tells of this in* Messengers of Day, *the second volume of his autobiography.*

such luxury has never been seen I didnt think Lilli D could possibly be so chic La Grande Adventuriere it was called you must look out for it if it comes to London Lilli D looks just like a continuous succession of Vogue drawings, covers of Harpers Bazar Vanity fare and drawing by André Lepape Realy you should conquer your claustrophobia and come here for the people are so glorious so chic 500 miles of lip stick 60 gallons of fleshing 40 tons of eye black & 17 miles of false lashes are used in Monparnasse alone each day I.m certain and they all wear white overcoats Les trench-coats as they call them. We have done nothing but rush from end to end of the town searching for Fred after penetrating about 40 miles into Old Montmartre (the heart of the apache quarter you know) to the Rue de Ruisseau[1] we were told by an extraordinary old creature with a riddled face that he had removed a day or two ago to the Hotel St. George Rue Bonaparte which is not far from us so of course we rushed back and visited the Hotel St Georges and they said F was in and after walking into about 5 lavabos by mistake and causing a panic by going into other peoples bedrooms there being no lights in the passages we arrived at Freds chamber which was at the top and having banged about ½ an hour we gave up and swept off in disgust I never went up so many stairs in my life and we are the 6th floor as well and have a lovely view in to an old French courtyard decorated by dainty fragments of old newspapers dead flowers in pots and broken bottles. I have just bought a lovely novelette film Edition of La Tragedie de la Rue[2] tastefully illustrated by stills from the film its going on here somewhere but so far off we'll never penetrate it looks glorious the story is nothing but about painted lips lurking in the shadow of the tortuous Rue lovely I calls it there are a whole lot lovely new Josephine B. post cards come out one by D'Ora in the nude wrestling with a bit of gold lamé, symbolic I suppose well old dear we leave the hotel on Saterday for another which we hope to find Ill send you a few more p.c's
from your old Tottie E.

To Barbara Ker-Seymer from the Hotel Saint Brieuc, Paris 14me,
Friday 19 October 1928

Dear Old Totty
We thank you for your nice letter which was pushed under the door this morning when I saw it coming through I thought it was Belphegor. We went to the Rue de Lappe on Sunday me & Billy danced a beautiful tango my dear you should have seen it and as for Freddie he was surrounded by doubtful Spaniards who terrified him into paying for all there drinks they also took all Sophies cigarettes when she was doing a can can with Billy. Everyone pretended to think she was a man dressed up & kept saying ah monsieur monsieur as for the matelots such buttocks ma chere and the lesbiennes so long drawn out. realy my dear these dainty heads are no

1 *Where Fred Ashton had been lent Lennox Berkeley's apartment.*
2 *Starring Asta Nielsen.*

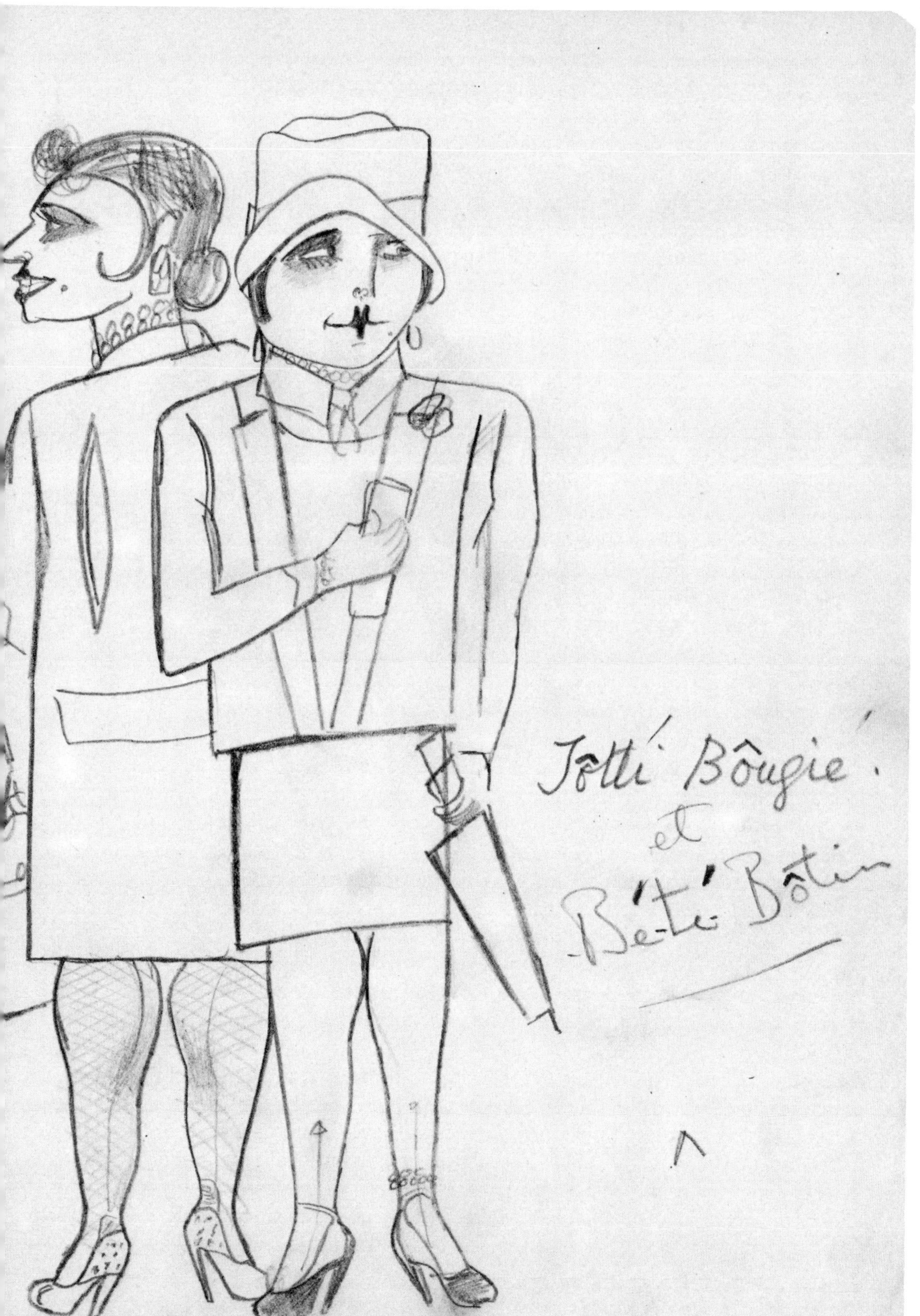
Tôtti Bôugie
et
Bé-té Bôtin

exageration one wreck had a different ring on each finger I have done a drawing of the scene on the strength of it. the orchestra is glorious and consists of a concertina a rattle and a drum & such modern tunes my dear such as Shanghai with a flavour of Hellelujah thrown in. We went to a glorious film (did I tell you) called 'Les Coupables' featuring Vernon & Fritsh & Jenny Hasselquist who fell on bad days and became mistress of the brutal Alexander von Shlettaw. However all ends in a gala by Bernard G killing Shlettow in the charming mirror salon upstairs which consisted of pillars and cushions and mirrors which reflected everything crooked (such UFA photo[1]) & Susi & Willi sailed away to honeymoon castle leaving Jenny H in a nursing home supported by Bernard having been acquitted. Well old dear au revoir & write again to your faithful Tottie E.

To Barbara Ker-Seymer from the Hotel Saint Brieuc, Friday 19 October 1928

Well my dear
And what do you think of the latest Parisian theatrical news? Mistress de la Chapelle will be away from London for many a weary month doing galas in Monte Carlo Switzerland Milan Vienna maybe Berlin and *perhaps* ending up in a great flourish at the London Coliseum where Madame Ida Rubinstein & Chaffers midgets will compete for the top of the bill[2] My dear such a company as it is too 'We are all *vairy* nice, we only ave nice peoples', says La Nijinskas husband to Billy. We met Rupert Doone the other day my dear the look he gave me would have mopped up Niagara falls The fights I have with Rupert, says Fred, only yesterday we shouted so loud coming back in the bus I really thought we should be turned out. So. I see ma chere that there will be some little tiffs before the end of the road is reached[3] We went to Bed and Sofa the other evening with Freddie its the most glorious film you've ever seen Moscow looks lovely a mass of clanging trams & terrible high lamp posts. I am thinking of going to 'The fugitives' to night featuring Hans Brauswetter Kate von Nagy and Vivian Gibson it sounds lovely having been left till Sunday entirely alone & neglected, Billy comes back on Sunday night Fred & me are going to meet him I think I shall probably come back on next Monday week if all goes well. There is the sweetest little Ammerican creature in the company so Ammerican from Boston Mass he wears a large Diamond ring and produces boxes of aniseed & black currant gums and says, 'aave a caandeee' he is a little protegée of Ruperts I believe the vagabond hats he wears are so Ammerican you realy think you are let loose in a Mack Sennett and he has a lovely Raglan overcoat very voluminous with huge mother of pearl buttons realy If I was Billy I should cultivate such a treasure We went to La Beauté de Paris at the Palace the other day my dear talk of the Palladium it was like the palmy days of the whirl of the world back again there were the most glorious sets and nobody

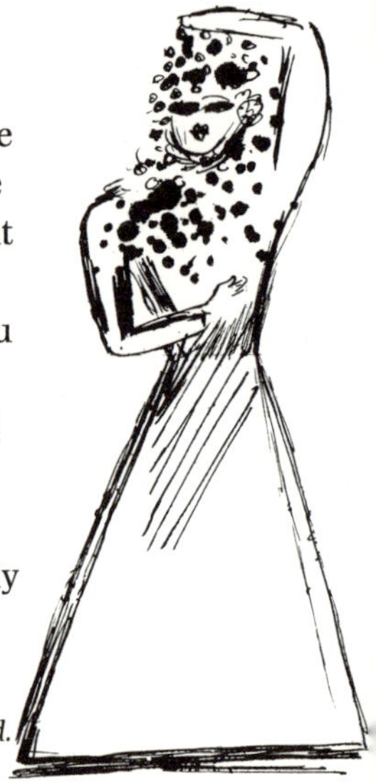

1 *UFA was a famous German film company much given to soft-focus photography.*

2 *'Fate, Ringmaster of Lifes Circus' etc. Fred had forced Chappell to audition for La Nijinska as he needed a compatriot in a mainly Slav company. To Chappell's great consternation he was accepted.*

3 *This remark was quite prophetic.*

in the cast could do a thing except a Spanish dancer called Tina Mellor she had a beautiful dress entirely black and a chenil Mantilla wrapped tightly round her face then she had a lovely white dress like Raquel Mellors[1] in Carmen there was also a argentine orchestra aided by a female singer who sang Spanish tangos. The last scene which represented Metals was a triumph with a set designed by the famous architect Mallet Stevens and as for the costumes my dear they were realy *magnificent* and I'me not joking they were all supposed to be corrugated iron, wire netting, drain pipes etc and realy they looked quite like a very super german film revue, after coming in dressed as falling leaves, spanish signoras, Mexican paesants & Marys flower garden it must be such a change for the chorus to come in dressed as wire netting the costumes were like this only really lovely I am so pleased to hear you are becoming so popular and still popular at the Chelsea P. as soon as I come back my dear I am coming for a little taste of Checko Slovakian hash Japanese stew & Viennese mince No I shant dare go near the common room for fear of having the womans pictorial and Good housekeeping thrown at me Well dear I must end now or Ill never get to Vivian Gibson write again I remain your faithful Tot

E.

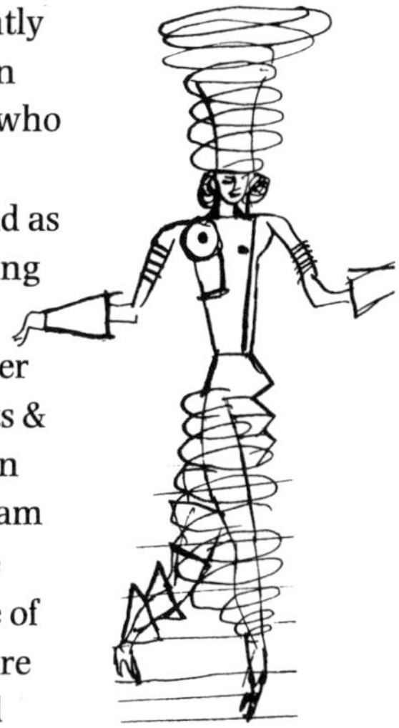

To Barbara Ker-Seymer, from the Hotel Saint Brieuc, 1928

Well my dear old Top

How are you getting on we are all in the pink rehearsing till 12 midnight daily so you may imagine our tempers are a little off instead of Faith hope & charity its vinegar vitriol & acrimony. As for bonny old Ida! Oh Fi Madame will have to have a special arrangement of invisible ropes to keep her for more than 3 seconds on her battered points. Billie says she's just like Beatrice Lillie in her famous skit on Les Sylphides Also ma chere about 6 goods Trains will be required to travel the scenery as it is all real staircases & real columns and real marble and real gilt & everything real put poor old Ida. I went to a dreadful film to night called 'The Dangerous Age' (it was only dreadful because Bernard Goetzke was in it) Asta Neilson my new beau ideale plays Bernards wife she at once falls passionately in love with Walter Rilla and goes to the opera and sits all the time holding Walters hand in the buffet but Walter has a girl friend who looks like Laura La Plante and youth will out thinks Asta as she stares at her ruined face in the mirror so away she goes to her country home accompanyd by the faithful cook who has also been having a few stormy periods in which she gave all her savings to the chauffeur who promptly ran away with the under housemaid so she came with Asta and glued pictures of muscular men in jock straps all over the refrigerator, interspersed with a negro boxer or 2. Asta however is too much of a lady to do such a thing she doesnt even sleep with the police gazette disguised as woman and home under her pil-

1 *Tina Mellor was in fact Raquel's younger sister. She later appeared in London in one of C.B. Cochran's revues at the London Pavilion.*

low but she keeps leaping up in a terror in the night having had a hallucination Walter had come to her neatly dressed in a nice trench coat with a homburg with a bow at the back she keeps writing in her dairy the days go slowly peacefully by Sometimes I think I shall forget but the *nights*!!!!

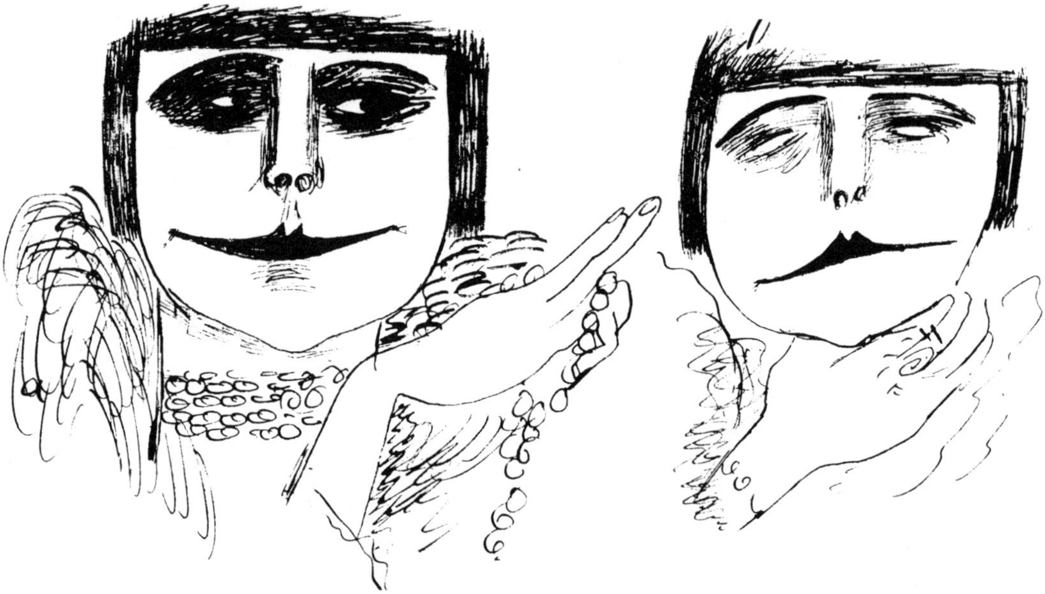

However Walter still loves and comes to her but she says it would be folly I am . . . an old woman so out flies Walter into a tornado made by the studio aeroplane the next day. Asta says she must go to Walter those dreadful nights did it so off she goes and arrives at Walters lodgings only to find him in the arms of Laura La Plante so back she goes to face old age and just as she's facing old age back comes Bernard G. who says you allways will be young to me let us grow old together & so 2 hearts that beat as one strayed together down honeymoon lane realy my dear if ever Asta Neilson is permitted to appear by mistake on Sunday the Kings picture playhouse you must go she's glorious such a wreck you never saw We went to Raquel Mellor yesterday the Empire music hall was about 5 times too large & Ime sure she didnt go down well with the audience as in the cheap seats the only thing that could penetrate to them is Toots Pounds & Miss Daisys performing hippopatamusses playing saxophones her first peice was lovely she swept on in a heavenly Spanish costume with a 6 foot train & shawl she has a perfect mop of hair and a completely white face then she proceeded to be a religieuse. by Lanvin trimmed with a sprig of ivy & with 4 inch heels which of course I find so convenient for vespers matins and visiting the sick. What she ought to do is appear in a night club she would be so glorious there'd be no holding it then we had René 1sts [First's] performing Doggies by way of a change, did I say performing my dear they *performed* in more ways than one

We saw Sheila Hennessey in the Dôme at breakfast the other day so refined when Billy said he was in Ida R's co by way of being impressing she said but do you *like* it? my dear she couldn.t have said it in a more awful voice if he'd said I.m one of the 18 diamond boylies in the Folies B revue When the Princesse Hennessey was at Juan les Pins last summer she was an intimate friend of dear Lady Peel alias [Beatrice] Lillie and she said Lillie was permanently like she was on the stage so I suppose when she sweeps into dinner at the Palace hotel Juan les Pins she says Did you ring mam? she also said she was often drunk but never when working, when working never a drop and one day when she came to go with B[eatrice] to Molyneux in Monte Carlo she found B in bed looking rather queer so B said Ime so tight I cant get out of bed I dont know how I got here someone must have put me. well me old dear I hope you liked the card of the Dodge Twins.[1]

To Barbara Ker-Seymer from Springfield, 4 December 1928

Well dear
As you see I have come back of course the real truth is the place was getting too hot for me by far & who do you suppose we saw on Sunday night as we were taking a drop in the Dôme café but Miss Lucy Norton and Jerry Reitlinger Oh he did look such a fresh pretty thing to be sure Lucy was so charming & said Someone asked me for a list of the best English illustrators so I gave your name in, I know you havent done any illustrations but you can send some of your drawings & pretend they belong to books. As soon as I arrived here who should ring up but Dennis Freeman who said he wished to see me & my pictures so I said I havent any here Barbara Ker-Seymer has all my work in London so my dear when you receive a mysterious phone call you will know who its from as he wants to show them to Eddie Marsh and wants one himself Oh of course I me *so* poor says Dennis I couldnt *possibly* buy one after theyve been to the Leicester Galleries its awful the poverty that strikes everyone when they see my work it appears Scott Goddard is in Paris writing criticisms of the Rubinstein ballets for the Observer so keep a weather eye on the Observer & you may see some dirt. Dennis F. hates Gerry at least he said so 'Ide heard so much about Jerry from Lucy' says D. 'how no one understands Jerry and Jerrys such a dear and then when I met him at lunch I found Ide had a fight with him years before and not known who it was HA HA.'

Well well I suppose the Ballet all troupes off to Brussels on Thurs. I expect Billy and Arthur[2] will share a room there wont be any room for Mistress Chappell my dear as Arthur likes no less than 3 girls a night if possible so C will have to put up a little pied a terre in one of the drawers of the chest of drawers however alls fair in love and war as the saying is. Have you seen Brigitte Helm in A daughter of Destiny yet, also I wouldnt mind

1 *A well-known cabaret act of the twenties.*
2 *Arthur Mahoney, the 'sweetest little Ammerican' Edward mentions in an earlier letter, was a very good dancer.*

seeing Emil Jannings in all for a woman All for the faces is what we go for, Well my dear I may stay for the night at 35 Dornton Road[1] if I go up on Monday & Ill let you know Love from your affec Tot

To Barbara Ker-Seymer from Springfield, Winter 1929

Well dear old sportie!
& where do you suppose I have been staying? nowhere but chez la princesse Lucy Norton on Monday night my dear having been driven up in fine style on Monday morning. Mistress N had been staying the week-end at the Nashes & a merry time was had by all. I read her your letter Oh er how *did* she get to know Olivia[2] says Lucy. they seem *very* friendly Oh yes ses I bosoms my dear I suppose she must of got to know her through Bumble[3] (Olivia's secretary you know) I wish you could have come to tea today at the flat but there was'nt any invitation forthcoming I'me coming up on Wed 20th for the day however so we can go to Anny Ondra in 'The adventures of a chorus girl' which I see is on in Tottenham Crt Rd the beginning of next week. We went to the Wedding march on Monday night my dear such lovely photography they must have dribbled on the lenze and then hung up Erich Von Stroheims pants to dry in front of that it was all such love in a mist what with the apple blossom & fay wrays bun it all looked more like a free fight in a swansdown factory than anything else to say nothing of every button sword eyeglass & bit of old tin glinting & flashing to such a degree it almost blinded you and of course the chief highlight of the piece is Zazu Pitts as the poor crippled princess. Patricia von Wilde Liebe Fuckinspunk she staggers about in a fog with a crutch in long white robes with a sort of black nuns whimple effect round her neck and a dainty fair wig surrounded by false apple blossom & doves she looks more like poor old Auntie Fan whose brains just beginning to go than anything else. Maud George however is just so gloriously lovely as the hard brittle flashy mother of prince Nicki alias Stroheim she keeps appearing in long negligays trimmed with black ostrich feathers and a lovely head of hair à la pompadour smoking cigars in a holder and saying 'Nicki you must marry money' (in other words limping 'Auntie Fan' who is to inherit a fortune from corn plasters) I could look at Maud George for ever then we proceeded to have a bit of dinner at the Gargoyle[4] such a dainty Tudor atmosphere Lucy kept hissing look over there its Lady Dean Paul[5] David Tennant was also there & had a dainty meal of sausages and mushrooms also who should appear but exquise Marcel Boulestin[6] followed by fragrant little

---

1 Chappell's home in London.
2 Olivia Wyndham.
3 Beatrice Dawson.
4 A popular night club of the period owned by David Tennant.
5 A Polish concert pianist, party-goer and junkie mother of Brenda and Napper.
6 Owner of Boulestin's, one of the best and most popular restaurants; also a great writer on cookery, and the cookery expert on Vogue.

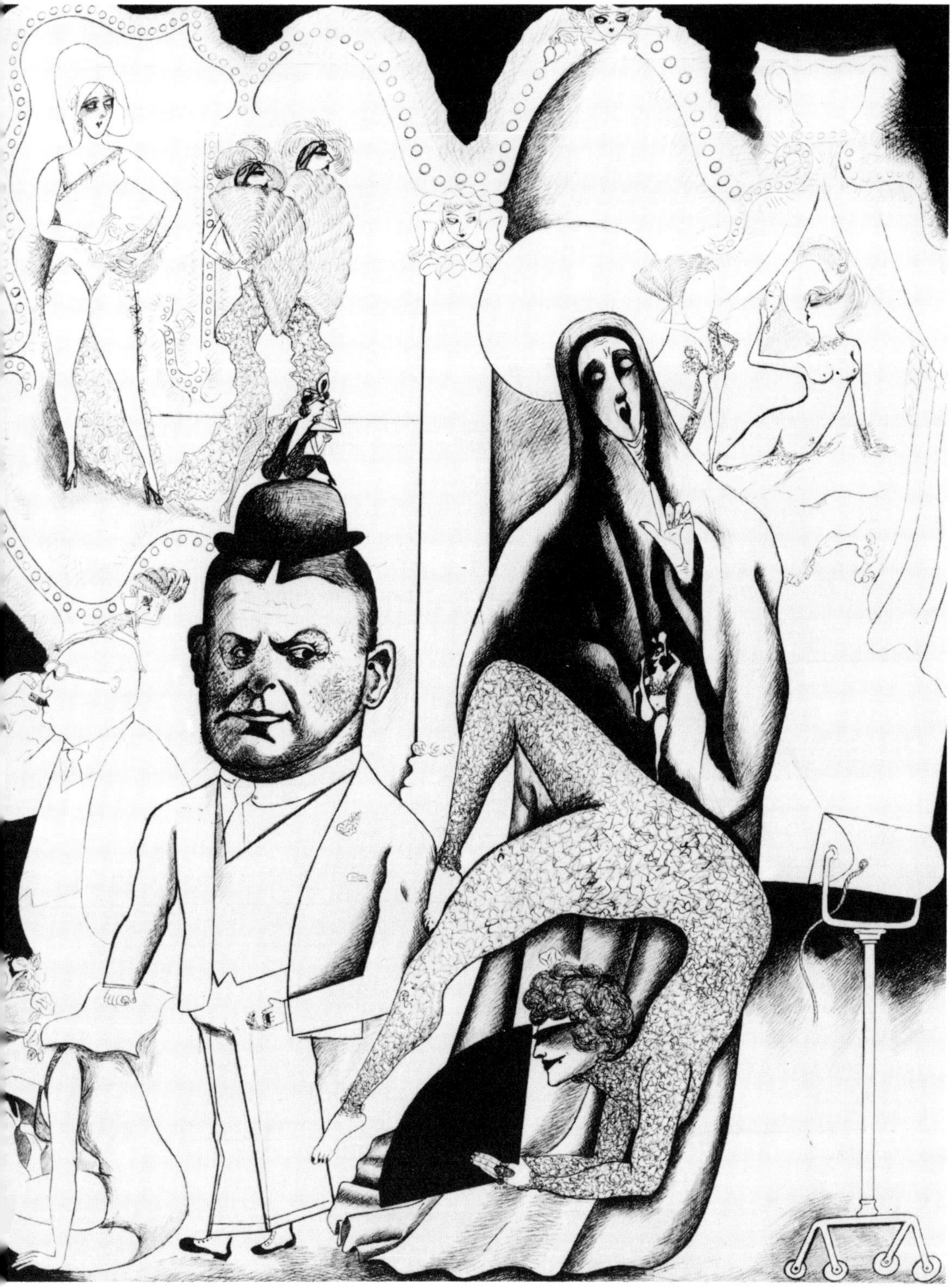

Robin Adair.[1] I find the gargoyle comes a bit more expensive than our dear old Maison [Lyons] but still when you are surrounded by lovely new Matisses whose price runs into 4 figgers and get a squint at Vogue without paying its not so expensive we had to stay there till about the middle of the night as the maid had gone out for a romp at the crickelwood rink with her fancy & dear old L had forgotten her key anyway we had a nice talk. I must say I've never been so cold in my life as I was on the sofa last night tho I did pull up the carpet & wrap myself in it. Yes my dear dame rumour is correct for once I am having a show with 'Ethelbert W.[2] a modern landscape painter' as Mr B[3] put it in a letter so theres a treat Paul asked B. about it and B said well we couldn.t put him with Henry Lamb as the people coming to see Henry L would all be carried off rigid and doubled up with a stricture at the sight of my frivolities on April the 6th or thereabouts I believe the date is if theres a Harry Peel on that afternoon I.me going to it. What did Somerset Maugham think of my dainty sketches! how killing its a wonder Godfrey Winn didnt drop down in a colic at such strong meat as you might say. I heard from Mistress Chappell the other day who has been stricken with flu however everyone was so kind and Lapitzky[4] arrived with a bottle of turpentine and gave B a sharp massage with it they are by way off going to Vienna on the 16th February if Ida doesnt get the staggers in this weather she wont be able to bend those dear old legs so easily I got such a lovely Sophie T its not quite a new one but realy youve never heard anything so twee 'I shant waste no time on talking. Ill just start on sight & if hes never forgotten his bible you bet he will tonight'.

Say for his love Im so hungry that his cheeks Ill start to bite and if hes never. had his moments (HO HO) I guess he will to night on the other side is 'Aint wimmin wonderful aint wimmin grand aint they the rulers of this happy happy land' which is killing well old dear write again from yr affec. Tottie

During the first two months of 1929 Chappell was still traipsing rather unhappily round Europe, making sorties on Paris and the Hôtel St. Brieuc between the visits to various great continental opera houses. The letter Edward wrote to him on 5 March 1929 bears no address, though it must have been from Springfield. Always allowing for a leaning towards dramatic exaggeration (a weakness of all four friends and reaching a high frenzy with the descriptive passages in the letters of Barbara Ker-Seymer and Edward) this particular epistle is a graphic and hilarious blow-by-blow *(see the action) account of 'normal' party behaviour within a group which was to become part of the much over-publicised collection of characters dubbed the Bright Young (and, it must be said, not so young) People: the joy of every newspaper gossip columnist in London.*

1 *Boulestin's lover.*
2 *Ethelbert White, a painter.*
3 *Mr Browne of 'Browne and Phillips', who owned the Leicester Galleries.*
4 *Eugene Lapitzky, one of Rubinstein's company who had also been in the Diaghilev Ballet.*

To William Chappell from Springfield, 5 March 1929

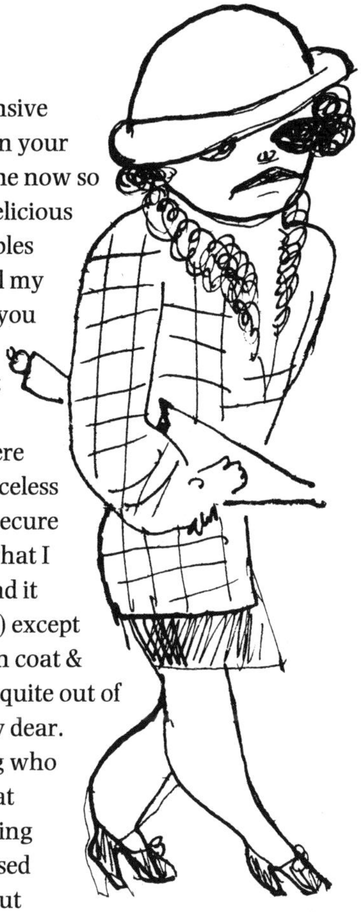

Well dear
I was beginning to wonder if you had been installed in an expensive Viennese apartment by wicked prince schnitzel[1] & had forgotten your old friends you have been travelling to be sure mother is in Rome now so if you & Mama are in Rome at the same time you might have delicious macaroni & heinz Tomato sauce somewhere. I saw dainty Bubbles Ker-Seymer last week her last remaining bonnet is over the mill my dear she's fully launched in the *demi-monde* she says she wrote you two letters and you never answered but one she wrote to Vienna before you went so I dont feel that will ever see the light of day. Well old sport Miss Wyndham gave a cocktail party last Friday and everybody was there the Kings Road & Sloane sq were lined with plainclothes detectives to guard Lady Dean Pauls priceless diamond ankle watch & the princess Haines pearls were the sinecure of all eyes till the eyes saw double which was very soon. from what I hear in my radio grammes they all went down like ninepins (and it was suspected that aphrodisiac had been added to the cocktails) except Lucie Norton who retained her dignity & her lovely bone martin coat & chatted to Jerry[2] and Miss H[3] who is now *so* gay the butterfly is quite out of its cocoon no party is complete without the beautiful H now my dear. Jerry is much struck & she went out with him without knowing who it was to say nothing of Jerry having fallen for who pray but that terrible Dawson[4] girl. Oh ses Jerry over the phone I had something I must say to you but I cant – not now – your going to be proposed to says I to Bum could not your womans wit have helped him out Miss W. Bubbles & Miss H went to the Eiffel tower everybody was there (as usual) & they were joined by Paddy Brody & Drieberg[5] & Dennis Pelley a rather twee young man and they played the gramophone with lovely records Drieberg bought in Whitechapel one was an oriental piece called Sweet Mumtaz with a voice that kept sayin at intervals whip it boys whip it (so suitable to Dreiberg) and come on lets snag 'em snag it the other is immigration blues and the creeper what does snag it mean an it please you no good I'me sure. There was a bit of a brawl at last Tuesdays party & Miss Olivia Wyndham got knocked down in an off moment by George Goodenough a self made man as started as a newsboy then liftboy and lifts was not all he lifted and then butler[6] & then came *discovery* 10 diamond & saphire eternity rings assorted other rings and jools £2–500 per annum and a large car but blood will out dear as Michel Sevier shut the bedroom door by mistake in his face which being *Ivre* put him in such a fury he said

1 *No such luck.*
2 *Gerald Reitlinger.*
3 *Irene Hodgkins.*
4 *Beatrice (Bumble) Dawson.*
5 *Tom Driberg, journalist and later Member of Parliament.*
6 *He was also a very handsome chorus-boy-about-town at one time.*

to M–S come out & fight which M wouldnt so O came up and tweeked his ear & he said WOMAN (thanks for the comp says O) woman the worst of you is your not normal so O flied in a rage and landed him one on the *bouche* & *bon* on the bouche too for blood flowed in floods but not to be outdone Goodenough let out such a biff that O was layed out everyone rushed & held the combattants back and the language *ma chére fidone* nothing has been heard like it since the general strike.

Ill damage your reputation you XX!!OO! says Goodie too late old chap says O having recovered then dainty Marjorie Craigie placed a tea cup on Goodies head which was the last straw so he just swept everything off the dresser Heigh day but we were all friends by the end of the evening & so we go on I am thinking of being London correspondent to the police gazette I just sit by my fireside like Corisande & how the dirt does flow in. We went to tea with O the wed before last and I had a look at all the photos which are lovely one of a bride with a train is beautiful oh that train c'est intoxicating as Mr. Reville ejaculated one day having dropped in and the Queen of Spain oh so *grande dame* er would you mind drawing out those shades under the busts my courtiers are so particular you know ses queenie[1] and as for Lady D. Paul after hanging 2 yards of Lindsay woolsey before the lens a cross between Elsie Janis[2] & Fanny Ward[3] has been arranged theres what you call a clever photograph says O. I went to Man woman & sin the other day its lovely go if you see it about. And then women dawned. on the boy says a subtitle as John Gilbert is seen reading about Love cottage crime with photos of none other than our old Fay Webb as mysterious as a yegg attached then he goes at once to a brothel but rescues a friend who is drunk & then is told off to take Jeanne Eagels[4] who is lovely such a wreck youve never seen to the embassy ball & has to hire a dress suit so while dancing he berrys his nose in Eagels peroxide & says what is that beautiful perfume? moth balls says Jeanne her nose buried in Johns hired dress suit. Also I went to the Edge of the world & waited patiently for Batty Brigitte[5] to burst out as a siren from behind a flour barrel but oh no not at all it was so artistic I thought I should die well write again old tot   yours E love to all.

To Chappell at the Hotel Rosa, Milan (the Rubenstein company were at the Scala), a postcard, dated 11 March, 1929, of film star Nils Asther a current favourite and several times leading man to Garbo in silent movies. The card is a glossy one in the style known as 'hand tinted'; meaning a yellowish tinge to the skin, a brownish tinge to the hair and a rosy tinge to the lips, which made Edward write on the back:

Hot lips like pips[6] I think this card is lovely & the new submarine unnatural colouring. Ime $\frac{1}{2}$ alive and hes driving me mad he's only human if

1 *This was actually quite true.*
2 *American revue star.*
3 *Fanny Ward was billed as the 'Eternal Flapper'!*
4 *Jeanne Eagels, a distinguished stage star in the USA, played in London in Coward's* Easy Virtue.
5 *Brigitte Helm, star of Fritz Lang's famous silent film* Metropolis.
6 *A line from a favourite number 'Louisville Lou': 'Hot lips like pips And no more conscience than a snake has hips'.*

he's to be had I must have[1] Nils Asther. Well dont you hope you find Mither McCree in Roma as my dear *last night* a phone message arrived to say *Betsy* must be operated on for appendix that night so my dear as soon as Mumsie gets wind She'l probably return in a raging fury the address is Pensione Santa Caterina Via Po 'Po' my dear we live on the Po hey dey! I envy you the continent dear hear there is nothing but Vitaphone Variety & Matheson Lang in Jolly Dick Turpin   from yrs E.

To Barbara Ker-Seymer from Springfield, late Spring 1929

Well dear
I actually did write to you on Sunday but lost the letter and couldnt tell where to find it. Thank you for the 2 daintie p.c's they will be so useful for my new pictures we never bother to paint in this part now we just stick on things instead. I have such a twee one started of 2 ladys walking along with pieces of motor engine for heads & a table at the side made of anita paiges[2] legs with a drawn in top and a dishful of heads reposing on it its fascinating. I came up yesterday & saw Billy Freddy & I had lunch at the corner house with our old B what about my new cigarette lighter & cig case in black enamel inlaid with crocodile & ivory?[3] you have done some lovely photo's of B I hear at least 5 times life size Im dieing to see them & I hear milady Wyndham is becoming New Yorks own girl doll maker & about to make a fortune out of Lord Todwaddly[4] J. Carstairs is very pleased I'me Sure How is Baldwin Billy asked me to stay & I couldnt move I just collapsed like everything else since the last gale when the old greek temple[5] was missed by 4 inches by a giant cedar which tore up a weeping willow crushed an apple tree ploughed up the bamboo & crushed everything within radius ½ the garden wall collapsed a fir tree collapsed & the dog was run over & died of an internal injury so gay.

I had such a jolly new year at the Nashs I arrived to find them cowering in the upstairs boudoir the sitting room roof having fallen in now Twit[6] is staying having had a mastoid she's got a large bandage round her head & not content with a bandage she has a crêpe-de-chine veil draped round she looks like Toots Pounds in mothers of the world[7] at the least shock she bursts into tears as everyone went away & left her last week end I went to tea and she told me all about the days when she was Edgar Wallaces secre-

1 *Another favourite, 'I must have that man'.*

2 *Anita Page starred with Bessie Love in* Broadway Melody, *MGM's first big talking-all-singing-all-dancing musical.*

3 *In fact silver and eggshell – very twenties.*

4 *Lord Todwaddley was a doll in naval uniform, mascot of 'Joe' Carstairs, a great lesbian figure of the twenties.*

5 *A folly in the garden at Springfield.*

6 *A relative of Margaret Nash.*

7 *Toots Pounds and her sister Laura, an Australian duo, were the stars of many spectacular revues at the London Palladium. In the incredible production number 'Mothers of the World' Toots (centre-piece of a series of stained glass windows) was the mother of the world – the Virgin Mary; as heavily made up as a tart. The whole concept – Eskimo mother, Indian mother, Dutch mother etc – was much to Edward's taste and to his delight in the more appalling excesses of the music halls.*

tary & he ran a shady racing paper those were the days twit the office boy Edgar Wallace with mistress & mistresses children all used to troupe to Ostende for the week-end Twit & the office B had to stay home and look after the kids when Edgar & his mistress used to go to the casino but when Edgars back was turned T used to creep away & leave the children following Edgar in the 3rd class section of the Tram. I hear you have caused a scandal by appearing with a *black woman* at Olympia I dont know what John Bull would say My dear True blue Lou[1] I snapped up as soon as it appeared isnt it lovely what others have you? I shall hear them next time I come up I shall come & visit you Oh says Freddie in the middle of the Samovar I had *such* a wet dream I was surrounded by Spanish Whores outside the Picaddily Hotel all the audience who had dropped in for a cup after the matinee poured their tea into each others laps. Haleluyah[2] is my favourite film. Ive never seen anything so lovely especially the cabaret which had the most glorious band. the wedding I liked too that terrible barn dance they did it fascinated me no dear Ive not seen Sweetie we dont have them new fangled talking pictures here we have Jack Mulhall & Somebody or other in Actress or Angel & Ted Wells in a Ripsnortin Romeo and such silent Art films here I had a letter from Eve Disher who said youd given her my address early in Jan as she was arranging a show at the Mansard Annexe so I turned her on to Mr. Brown & I think he gave her a pic for the Annex Well well I hope to see you when I come up on my day off next week love from your affec old Tot

E.

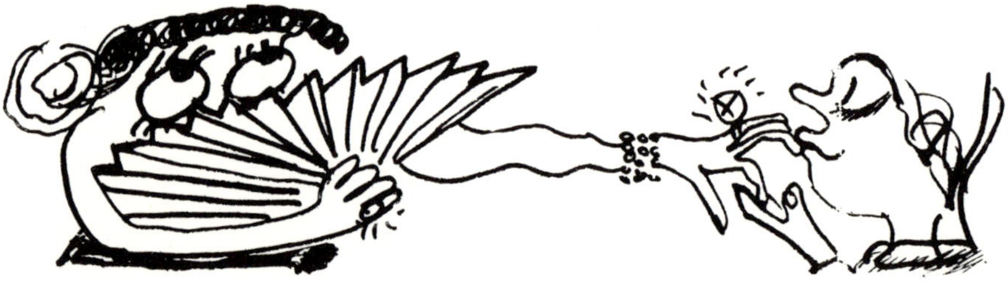

To Barbara Ker-Seymer, 1929

Dear Old Tarty

I have just been staying away for a day or two at a most extraordinary house The proprietress used to shoot big game so of course you couldnt walk an inch without falling over a stuffed zebra all the ink po's were crocodiles feet & the coal scuttles elephants feet and when ever a bit of beam stuck out there were goats heads attached as for the leopard skin mats my dear Louise Glaum[3] would have felt like a home from home as for me I felt like delerium tremens and I was taken to Nurse Sybil Thorndike in Dawn[4] I've never seen anything so tragic heart rendering my dear it is I

1 *A new record.*

2 *A musical with an all-black cast.*

3 *A famous silent film 'vamp'.*

4 *Sybil Thorndike played Nurse Edith Cavell.*

cried and when the lights went up all the audience looked as if they's been having a rough channel crossing. Nurse Sybil walks about with a perfectly fixed expression like death at the festival & all the cast conceal themselves in the cellar disapear in wardrobes and hide in barrels & Nurse Sybil presses electric bells in the carpet disguised as rosebuds when the German army arrives to warn the escaped prisoners cowering in the cellar I'me sure Sybil would be a furore in German films she & our old Bernard Goetzke should do lovely as co-starring partners in rivalry to Ronald & Vilma.[1] It was so funny my visit as of course I was asked to bring *my work* and before the big game woman & her companion saw it they kept rushing into the most awful artists material picture shops & saying 'Oh you *must* come in too, this is *such* an interesting shop dont you *adore* that pointing to a small water colour of the Virgin M nursing an allenburys progressive baby[2] with a gas ring going off round its head seated on a toadstool in bluebell wood. I kept wondering what ever would happen when my pictures were displayed & I couldnt get out of showing them, so they said on seeing my pictures Oh futurist I suppose, of course I dont understand them at all but I am very old fashioned but you paint so neatly & such lovely detail I think it such a pity you dont paint *artistic* things like flowers & landscapes[3] Oh ses I *I* think them beautiful then the big game woman said It doesnt seem right that you should be painting *such things* at your age by that time I got the giggles I didnt know where to look the half of the time joyless street is coming to the Shaftesbury P[avilion] early in June. You must go Greta Garbo is the heroine & Asta Nielsen is driven into a brothel from starvation & poor old Garbo gets in too, the brothel keeper is a glorious woman exactly like Hodgekins & keeps saying to poor old Garbo now dear do take that £200,000 sable cloak (she kept a clothes shop as a blind) pay by instalments and I would *so* like to introduce you to a lovely gentleman of my acquaintance . . .

To William Chappell from Springfield, late Spring 1929

Ai hope you are well and happy I have a frightful cold caught last weekend[4] from Norton As no one was at Thornsdale but J & 'Daintie' the last resort was had in. Ai am writing to ask if I can come and stay with you a day or two on next Saterday that is if you can have me & have no one staying with you dont hesitate to say no. Also I hear from Ker-S. Battleship Potemkin is at the Film Society Ide much sooner it was On with the Show the all screaming yelling revusical mirthquake all in unnatural colours which I want to see to say nothing of Big Time & Street Girl featuring Jack Oakie & our famous old street girl Compson. Well what about the party Miss Norton seems to have frozen all comers with a look but Mr. Gossip in

1 *Ronald Colman and Vilma Banky.*

2 *A phrase taken from a baby food advertising campaign.*

3 *The terrible person was right by chance. Much much later Edward was to produce wonderful flower and landscape paintings.*

4 *At Gerald Reitlinger's home, Thornsdale, in Kent.*

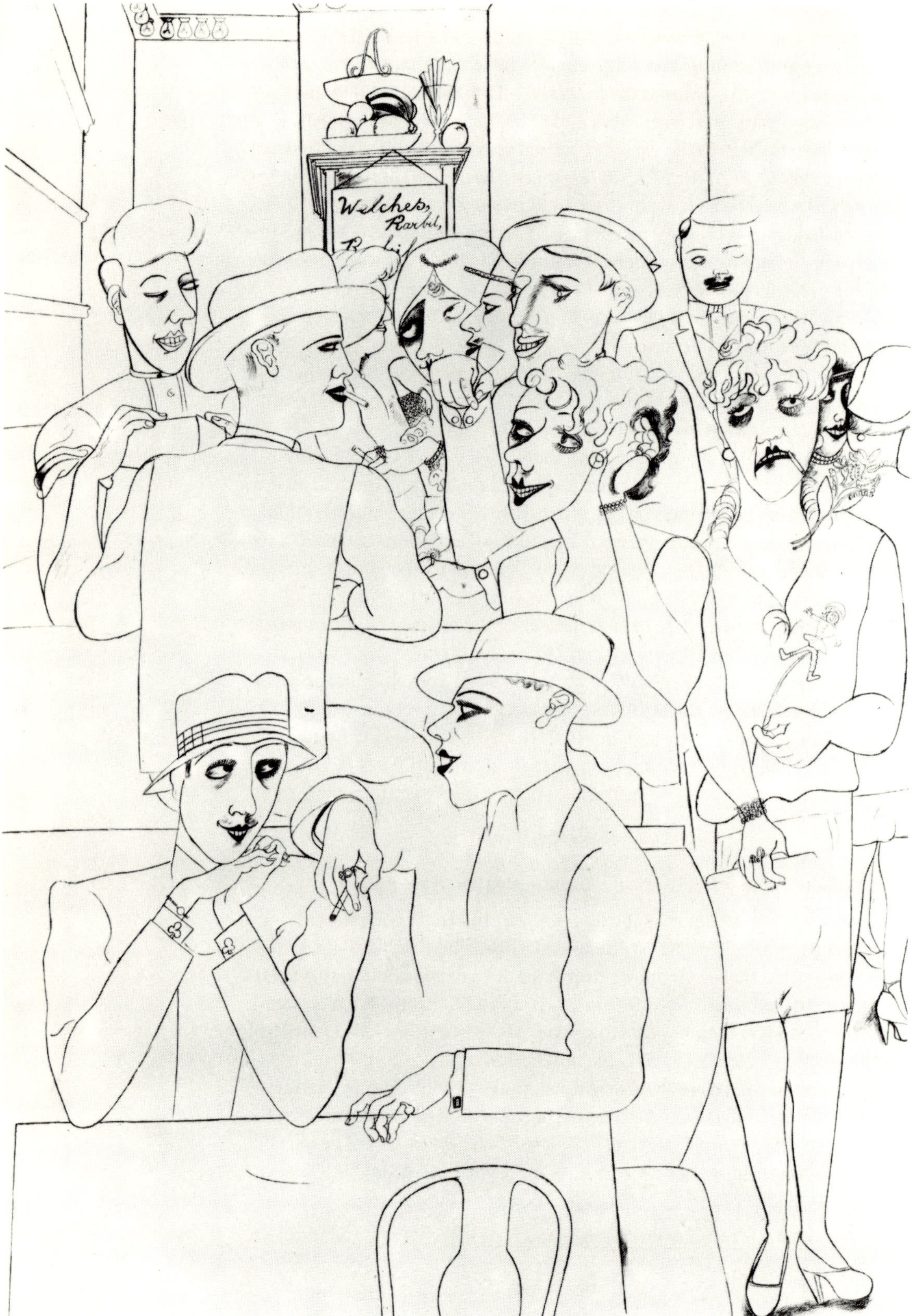
Welches,
Rarbil,

the Daily Mirror couldnt get it off his mind for days. Have you seen the ad for Pandora's work basket[1] or whatever Doris's book is called such a daintie drawing of Doris seated on a pillow with a large tumbler beside her flanked by 2 old world caracters pretty little drawings I think Ime sure they are Hodgekins's. What do you think someone offered me 12 gns for Grog[2] as I told you over the Tassies at the Samovar & I wrote back and said 15 gns was the lowest I could consider well they wrote back & said (through Miss Brinton sec) I am afraid I cannot spend more than 12 gins at present but hope Mr. Burra will make it possible for me to possess one of his works I saw his work at the Leicester Galleries it appeals to me strongly. I am willing to stand aside till the end of the exhib & if it isnt sold for more I should like it so I just wrote back to Brinton to say yes after all 12 gins is better than nothing about £9–10s that is deducting frame & percentage. Mr. Brown would have a fit if he knew but Ill do anything for money. Ive been reduced to the Black Mask magazine (20 cents in U.S 25 in Canada) 3d at Woolworths realy what beautiful English McSlumps windy eyes flikkered wickedly, drop that gat he tensed And your mothers another spat Gertie her fingers worked nervously in her boudoir cap & the corners of her red lips heavily painted with carmine twickered flabbily – 2 shots crashed out – McSlump slumped forward you trollop he managed to lash & crunched a twisted heap on the carpet Ime sure I could write beautifully for Black Mask if I had the plots Well ai still hope you are well from your affec Crazie, princess Mess.

In May 1929 he wrote to Chappell from Paris

Thank you dear for your letter & what do you think pray? the bonnie Companie Benoit has just quietly *collapsed* leaving ½ the poor miserable people without a penny as for Benoit[3] he eats you may know in the Brasserie opposite the theatre not caring a button for the other poor wretches who may get payed in a day or two (or not) I never 'ave been in such a company says Vera Savina[4] reely I never knew anything like it so I said (all *innocently*) surely isn't Massine forming a Co? I divorced 'im y'know Ow we didnt suit at all anyway *Ive* never done anything to 'urt 'im but he never does anything for me the way of the world I suppose she is my favourite woman with shoes like this. as for Molly Lake & Borowski not one 1d have they got Bartholin & me asked them to dinner yesterday & today B gave them 15 francs poor B my dear I insist on him leaving Paris *as soon* as he receives his 50,000 francs[5] as he needs the money I know & all these ravening wolves will fall on him 50 cents will remain & Harold if you please claims 10 per cent as he sold B the ticket such Boloney you never

1 Pandora's Letter Box *was the title of Doris Langley Moore's book.*

2 *A painting by Edward on show at the Leicester Galleries.*

3 *The spelling is right: he is not referring to Benois, the ballet designer.*

4 *Vera Sarina had been a member of the Diaghilev company.*

5 *Birger Bartholin had been a member of the Rubinstein company. He was a neat, elegant dancer from Copenhagen, with a nature of pure gold. Edward was nearly as fond of him as he was of 'the sweetest little Ammerican'. Bartholin had just won 50,000 francs in the Irish Sweepstake.*

heard so dear Rupert Doone told B to write to Ireland & say before sending cheque please deduct 10 per cent & send it to the seller of my ticket (if this is so) which of course its nothing but a perfect gyp on H's part.

Just been to *Paris qui remue* Josephine B's piece tonight I stood dearie so my feet are much in evidence glorious my dear B is now a *grande vedette* & appears out of a golden casket in a very long sea green silk evening gown trimmed with diamonté she looks at least 6 feet high & sings King for a day which is perfectly divine such a drama she makes of it there is also a marvelous adagio team of 3 men & a woman who do the most terrifying tricks. Miss Florence is lovely with back bends & front overs & the jackson boys & girls who Ime beginning to know by sight in the street now we frequent Rues Fontaine & Pigalle yes dear I would love to come & stay with you but would go home for 1 or 2 days first B wants to come to London in September & join with the Maisie Ramparts.[1] Just a mad project Since I have been here I have seen nothing but dancers from morning till night it seems. I shall give a recital at the *Salle Gaveau.* Yes dear talking of Lady Bureauxs eldest sister reminds me of a few anecdotes – Ah wild blood there was in the old colt (out of Mrs Merrick by the prince regent y'know) she was the girl that made Byron lymp & who can ever forget the Tay Bridge disaster & of course she ruined Gladstone & at the hight of her fame & beauty she walked straight up to the Jersey Lilly & upset a bottle of ketchup down her dress King Edward laughed so I well remember but of corse Alexandra never forgave *or* forgot give her an inch and shell take an ell as she used to say whilst knitting Alexandra roses for the boys at the front No more no more
love from Tottie.

From Paris Edward accompanied the Nashes, Paul and Margaret (and the ubiquitous Twit) to the South. In June 1929 he wrote to Chappell from Toulon.

Hey dey here we are in Toulon If you could have seen the fuss with which we left Paris having loaded about 7 suitcases 3 hat boxs and a napsack onto a taxi with string the tyre went flat halfway so we all trouped onto the pavement whilst the driver tried to jack up the tyre to no avail however as the Jack broke Ah Quel fatalité quelle vie says the driver from under the car so we had to pile onto another taxi & got the train allright having bought bars of chocolate sandwiches Evian wine & biscuits I sat gapeing realy we might have been going to Vancouver & there was a wagon rest on the train the next morning Paul never slept a wink & moaned from time to time the floor was so hot you could hardly put your feet on it Twit & Margaret tied-up there heads in handkerchiefs & put on bedroom slippers I fell in a torpor We had a nice time in Paris I had a lovely swedish jewish lunch in Lova's studio.[2] those 2 strange exotic women who are they especially one who is the most yiddish Jewish thing Ive ever seen & with the most terrible *jambes* but very nice Lova reclined in an armchair perfectly

1 Marie Rambert.
2 Elovius Mangor was a Swede working in Paris.

Burra in Toulon w
'The Spirit of Navigati

green with his flies untied saying Oh my stomach. Realy that Bar I lent on it nonchalant & it just gave way as for the photo of Berger de Fucker pinned up at the back 'melting eyes as blue as skies who does she roll them for' You are to be framed in *silver*. I think you are the doyenne of the gallerie A. Mahoney I hear is giving lessons in Boston the sud ammerican *tournée* sounded fierce they tried to do them down on the salerys & Paul & me visited Zadkine he has such a nice studio & with house & a wild back

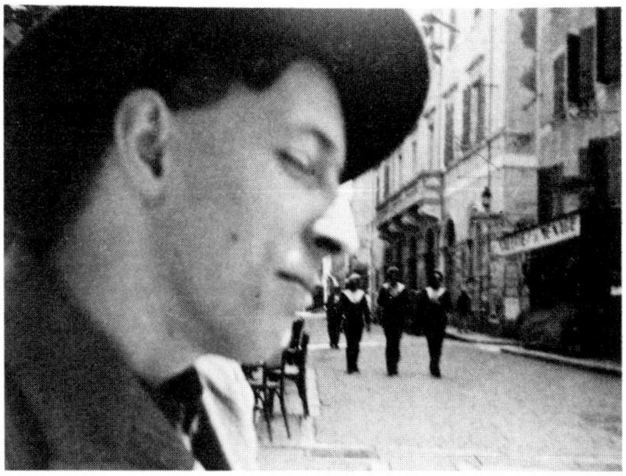

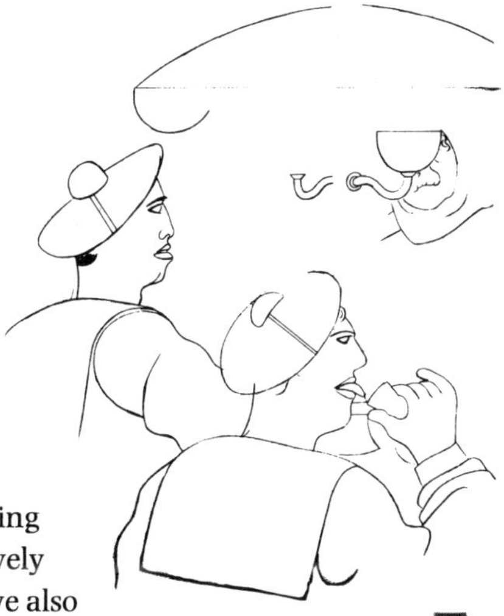

garden full of aviarys & broken up statuary he was charming & showd us all his sculp which is glorious also he has a lovely collection of *antiente peintures* done by unknown people. we also went to gallerie Leonce Rosenberg such a show my dear of Metzinger Chirico Gino Severini Herbin Ozenfant & others (Max Ernst) all very abstract Ive never seen such a beautiful show for years. Leonce R was very charming theres a lovely *surrealiste peintre* called Viollier all red plush birds nests in trees with the Venus de Milos head & shoulders coming thru the top I believe some of them may get shown at the Leicester. Now we know where John Armstrong has been says Margaret glancing round. I went to Anna Sten & J. Kowal Samborski in the Yellow Ticket in Paris the brothel scene is a dream it opens with 1 very thin ruinous pros & a very small pros doing a dainty cotillon round the room then every one joind in and did the lancers dressed in ruinous old wrappers with holes in the edges where they's caught their feet then Spring came & there was a sudden flash of rippling rivers bursting buds & falling wombs & then a flash back to the brothel where the eternal lancers went on & on then a flash of cornfields and back to the brothel where on went the lancers tho the flesh cracked neath the painted grin you must go if it comes to the film Society if only for the brothel. We went to Volpone in Paris such a brilliant bit of acting I enjoyed it very much & very well set but high brows dont have *jambes*. so far as I can see such things are not allowed in the little Atelier Theatre nevertheless I enjoyd it despite extreem discomfort & what of the

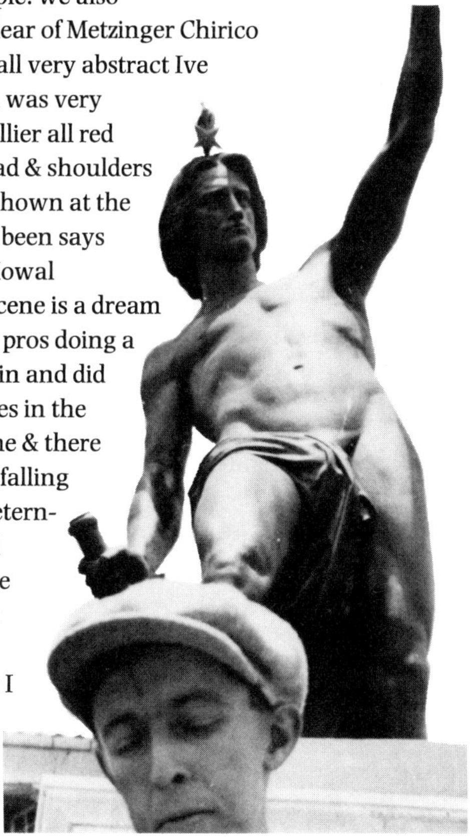

Roccy twins[1] issueing out of lotusus followed by the midget golden haired ballerina & in the wind blown scene Leslies dress was by Lanvin Some of Mistinguetts clothes were too glorious I thought. Isnt she a dream in the sketches her speaking voice is lovely she'd better go to Ammerica & appear in a talkie as Irene Bordoni's great grandmother. Isnt it sad about Mabel Normands[2] demise all my favourite artistes are either off the screen or dead. Tell me about the party. Love to your ma & I hope Gran hasnt fallen flat on her face again   from yrs Tottie

A coloured postcard of a pensive matelot smoking a cigarette came from Edward at the Pension des Lys et les Roses, Tamaris.

Just got your letter
Chérie! We are all gone in a 1d steamer to pension Lys et les ruins. the *quiet* country deary such a deafening din you never heard shrieking cocks & screaming doggies. I wish we had not left Toulon but of course so refreshing to have *quiet* country after noisy town 'Nostalgie' this picture is called dont you think its lovely Would you like a white sweater with a rolled neck Ive got one there very nice here till next Weds.   yrs Tot

Compare Edwards description, in his letter to Chappell (p. 64), of the luggage carried by Paul and Margaret Nash on the journey from Paris to the South, with a repetition of the same story in a letter sent at the same time to Barbara Ker-Seymer. It is as though any form of contact with Barbara's ever present need to dramatise peoples' habits and behaviour acted on Edward as an intoxicant. He wrote on the Café paper provided by his favourite bar, 'Raymonds' in the Place Puget in Toulon.

How are you dear? We are just off to day to Nice (Hotel Funel Avenue Durante Nice) we have been at the Lilys & Roses Boarding house & when not bursting into tears we are O.K. I had a letter from S. Fedorovitch yesterday she said she had a lovely time in London & you looked '*très odalisque*' I allways new you had such an oriental type of beauty Did you meet old Berger Bartholin whilst he was in London? I adore him whatever you say he was hysterics & shows miles of gum. Well dear I hear from my Bureau of Information that the party was a great success the crowning tableau was Mistress Hamnett[3] being sick on a boxer which Carstairs thought disgusting & told Lady de Chappell to biff him one on the jaw of course I took it as a joke says Billy. I have put everything I possess on my back & my leather coat on top so Ime ready to die Oh its chronic. Yew should see the luggage we travel 50 rucksacks a kettle & 90 suitcases. It turns me grey Paul has just picked up an acquantance on the Quai named Cole Such a mist of grey hair you never saw & deaf as a post so the shouting can be heard at Marseilles. Fred is going to write an article in the dancing times I

1 *Scandinavian twin boy dancers at the Casino de Paris.*
2 *A charming comedienne and silent film star.*
3 *Nina Hamnett, the painter.*

hear a special Gala number double the price & copiously illustrated with la Grande Vedette I hope As for Chappell on the road with the new revuesical medley Bright Spots I can see looming in the future (featuring Scott & Whaley) You really ought to come to our Lilys & Roses Boarding house the landlady walks about in a dressing gown bedroom slippers and a piece of black tulle tied round her head. She's about 6 ft broad & 10 inches high shes such a good cook dear If I hadnt left I should have died of congestion a bit drainy on the stairs & no hot water but what you fetch in a jug in the passage but as the Landlady widow Kohrer said in her own words were no palace here its the simple country life such a din of Cocks Alsatians & pianos you never heard. P & M's room was next the lavabo so my dear such rushing water it might have been in the room with you quite a cure for shyness says M. Well Ime off to the Gare yrs

Tottie.

Marie Rambert (dubbed by Edward with his passion for denigratory nicknames 'Maisie Rampart') had for some time been making valiant attempts to forward the careers of her dancers. Her husband, Ashley Dukes, had already provided the West End theatre with a great success in his play The Man with the Load of Mischief. *Now he had finished another work: an adaptation of* Jew Süss, *the best-selling novel by Leon Feuchtwanger, author of an equally popular period piece* The Ugly Duchess. *In Jew Süss (who knows whether by chance or intent?), Ashley Dukes suggested that dancers should appear in one scene. Frederick Ashton was to be the choreographer, with Constant Lambert in charge of the music. It was Ashton's third work for Rambert and was called* Mars & Venus[1], *a pretty trifle featuring the ravishing Pearl Argyle and the handsome and accomplished Harold Turner. The cast included two girls (Andrée Howard and Anna Brunton) and Chappell, who made one entrance in the ballet scene, walked on elsewhere in the play and understudied Turner. The play made an extended tour of the provinces before opening in London.*

To William Chappell, 19 July 1929

Dear
I am just writing a line to hope you have ever such a gai time at Blackpool wrangling with Freddy under the wibble wobble it ought to be lovely if the weather keeps on what has become of Boodle Doodle now you have gone has he insisted on going to Blackpool too. I had tea with Paul & Margaret at ye olde Simone the piemone all over antiente beams we have quite a horrible tea Miss Jill[2] Forbes Robertson was also there having just *finished* at the Royal Academy of Dramatic Art such a naive charming young actress I adore comedy says J, of course Father wants me to join the Old Vic Co but I dont want to. you cant concieve what an equisite well bred young comedy legitimate actress she'l be what she needs is a strong mix up of

1 *He had already choreographed* Leda and the Swan *and* Capriole Suite *for the Rambert Dancers.*
2 *In fact Jean (not Jill), daughter of the distinguished actor Sir Johnstone Forbes Robertson. She was a great Hedda Gabler.*

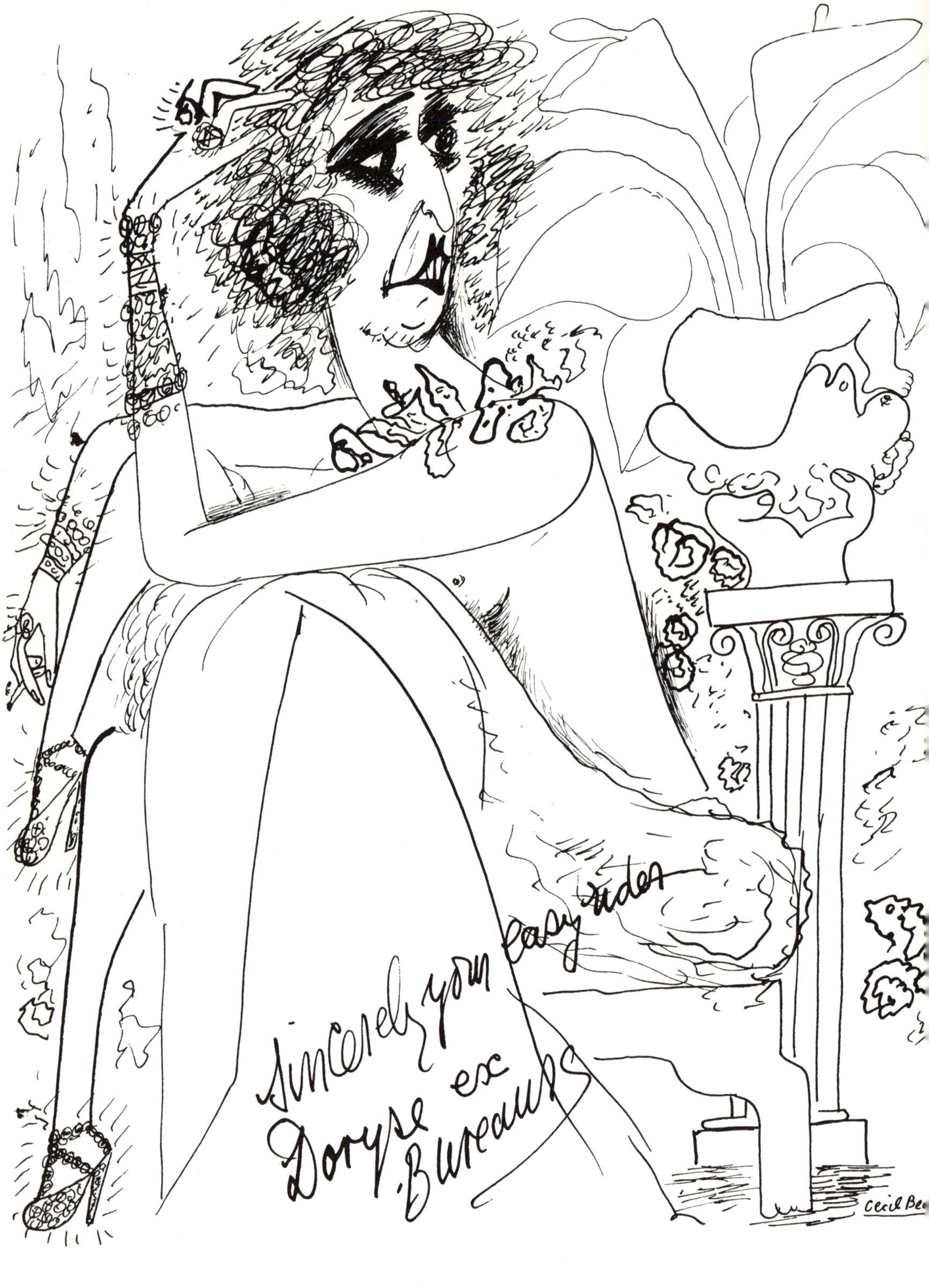
Sincerely your easy rider
Doryse ex Bureaux
Cecil Be

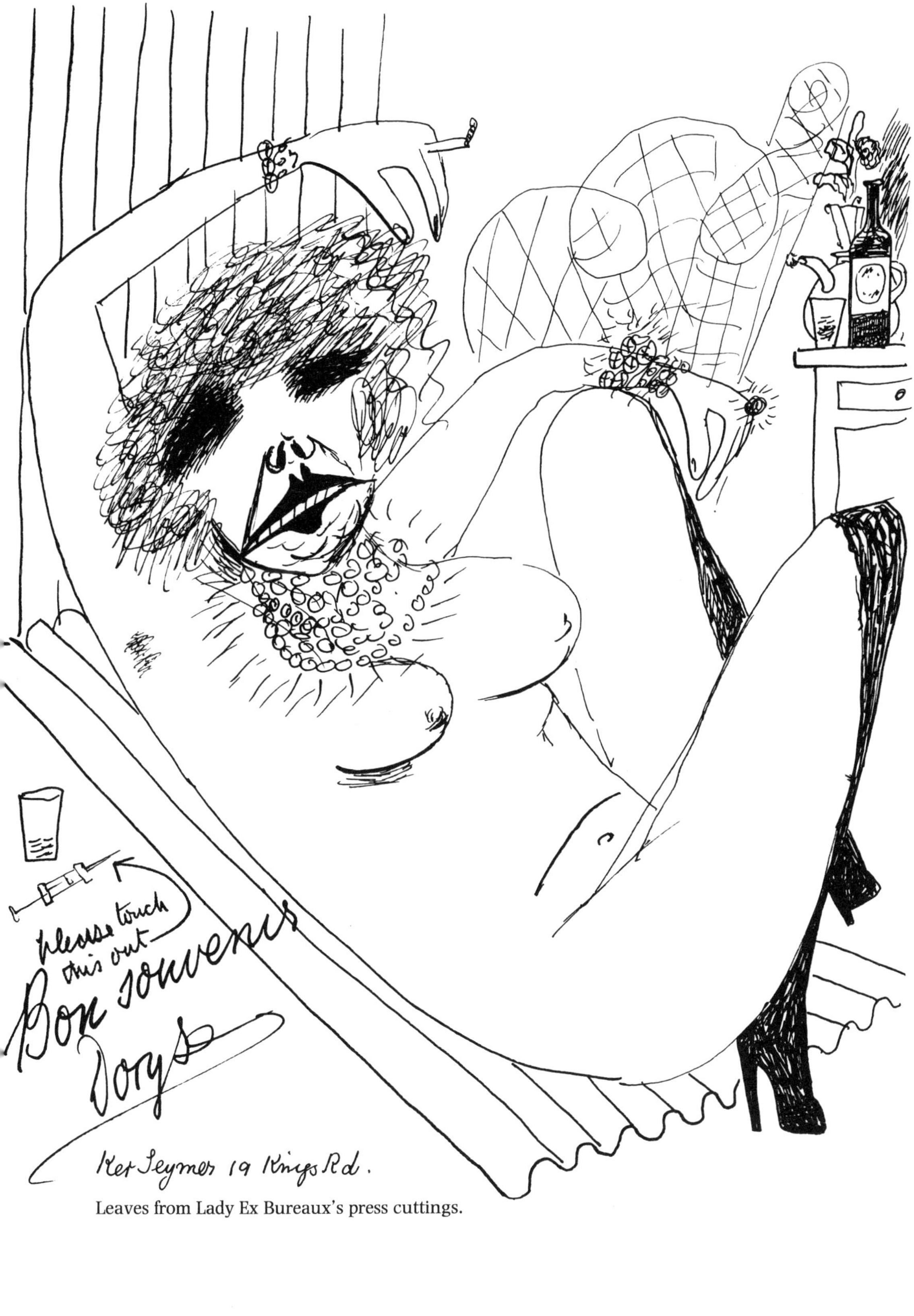

Leaves from Lady Ex Bureaux's press cuttings.

Mistinguette Earl Leslie Harry Pilcer Miss Florence & the late Claude France & perhaps a little Falconetti to put her in order.[1] Did you see in last Sundays Sunday Times in doings of the week how at the opening of those dreadful French pictures we saw at the Leicester, 'M Sasha Guitry was *so* taken with Miss Lucy Nortons amusing long tailed dachshund' Oh she *will* be pleased to see that in the paper says Margaret, she trailed the dog all over the Galleries & everyone fell over the lead Mr. Brown was furious.

at the sight of that terrible imitation Van Dongen in the first *salle* its a wonder the poor wee doggie didnt caca & pipi & everything else over Yvonne Printemps did you & Fred succeed in getting to the Tropic party Ive scoured the daily mirror but havent found a word the *little* hostess was going in shorts Ime told that must have been lovely I believe its champagne & fireworks at Uckfield to night tomorrow morning dawn will break on a string of motors all in various stages of wreck & ruin on the route from Uckfield to London everyone being dead drunk[2]

Well if you want to see a lovely film go & see the Racket featuring Marie Prevost Louis Wolheim & old Tom Meighan Marie is a perfect dream and so is Wolheim its so well acted & breathlessly exciting what with shooting & bootlegging theres not a moments rest even Tom is good so dont miss it if it is on in Blackpool my next favorite film is 'The Fleets in' featuring Clara Bow deodo James Hall & Jack Oakie realy my dear Claras costume is a dream and the dancing at the Roseland dance Hall is so glorious you dont know the subtitles are heavenly too by George Marion Junr. the wise crack[s] crackle so loud you can hardly hear yourself speak James Hall is forced to dance with another dreadful creature in the Roseland & he says to this creature about Clara 'shes sure got me trimmed' 'Yes' comes back this creature *and* trims her own hats *and* walks home alone dont get me wrong' its just the most heavenly awful humour the only humour that reaches down to a low thing like me. Well old sportie send us a line from Black P. I enclose a lovely Art plate of Matheson Lang[3] in his 'Scarlet pimpernel make up' as Lady Blakeney I presume   love to all from Tottie.

Edward's character was thick with contradiction. The letter he wrote to Chappell (Mid August 1929) containing the horrifying news of the imminent death from meningitis of his adored (and adoring) younger sister Betsy discloses the deep division between his upbringing and his natural inclinations more clearly than any analysis. His upbringing – based firmly on the Victorian principles of his father (who was a very good *man) told him to be truthful. Respect the law. Never raise your voice.* And never *embarrass others with an over lavish display of real feeling. His inclinations sent him veering away toward everything the most anarchic and outrageous. There existed a continual tug-of-war between public Edward and private Edward. Where, in the letter, his very real grief breaks through it is quickly pushed away and down in case such a display of sorrow might upset or embarrass.*

1 *She was also a wonderful Peter Pan. Perhaps Edward's 'mix up' was already there.*
2 *Prophetic: this is exactly what happened.*
3 *Matheson Lang was playing the title role in* Jew Süss.

Away and down it goes into his gut where it lives by the laws formed from the stoicism implanted in his character not only through his upbringing but also through his continual uncomplaining fight with ill health. Down there he can keep his strong feelings (rarely, if ever, admitted) for his family and his friends, in a hidden place in company with his overriding passionate love for his work. The sorrow breaks in again in very short paragraphs to be sent almost immediately packing by his usual flow of dotty anecdotes and enthusiasms. The odd interpolated cry shows how a real expression of anguish is often said in very banal words.

To William Chappell (in Glasgow) from Springfield, mid-August 1929

Well dear

So nice to hear from ye as we say in Glesgie if Marsuple[1] knew you were in Glesgie Im sure she would introduce you to some realy nice friends. We are having *an awful time* as Betsy developed a headache last Sunday and on last Sunday week a specialist was sent for & it appears she has meningitis & apparently can only live a fortnight I can hardly write it mother is in a dreadful state and has fits of sobbing Such merry times have been going on at Thornsdale what with dashing nude into the river and Brenda Dean Paul walking about in Lido trowsers the whole village is an uproar (if you can believe the Nashs) when bonny Brenda tripped down to the river for a splash she discovered a young man sitting by the stream, so she said Oh-er-do you mind me bathing without a bathing dress so the young man said no & in went B meanwhile the young man who had been having a lovely time peeping thru the osiers rushed out & said he'd summons her then Jerry swept down just as Farmer Jones wife & daughter were rowing over the ferry & out rushed farmer J & threatened to fight Jerry they have such house parties my dear consisting of Vyvian Holland & Sir Michael Bruce goodness knows whats happened to Lucy. Also the man & wife that do the cooking are top hole Mr rolls home at closing time and is heard to say this place is nothing but a br- but a br- but a bloody brothel Ime sure the village will tar & feather J or something did you get a Variety I sent you to Bpool I'me sure the door keeper now knows all about how much Coconuts grossed at Seatle, what about Diagileffs demise it came as a shock to me will Boris Kochno ever keep those wayward puppets together I see they are still coming to London in the Autumn but realy its a terrible blow to the profession Just got back from a jolly day in town where I bought Artistes materials anything anything to get away from the atmosphere of this house everywhere I look I see a reminder some little book or something and its too awful I got a record at Foyles Victor (9d) of Downhearted Blues introducing 'Chirpin the blues' by Alberta Hunter & Lovie Austin played by the tennessee ten & Gulf coast blues & Sugar Blues (Clarence Williams) also the tennessee 10 & I darent play the phono for fear of making a noise & as Foyles havent a phono downstairs I havent heard it yet but I have no doubts about it Ive got a Boyd Senter of Downhearted so I know thats good

1 The Burra Family's Scottish Nanny.

Well dear write to me again soon. Theres a reproduction of Marriage in the Sept 'Pall Mall' & an article on buy modern painters & make money(?) by Wilenski as soon as I appear in a magazine it fails at once so theyd better take care yrs Tottie.

To William Chappell, August 1929

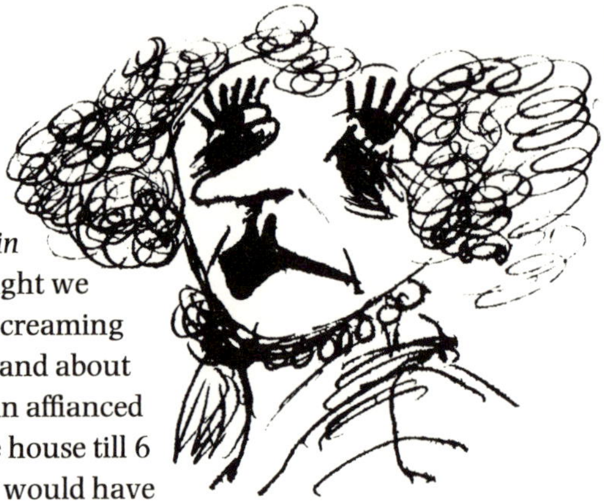

Well old sportie
Thank you for the pc recived yesterday as I have been staying with Madame Ker Seymer at 19 Kings Rd since Sunday Olivia having succombed to flu Baba came here for the day on Sunday *by train* so you may imagine she was on her beam ends alright we returned to London in the evening with about 18 screaming babies dribbling Hastings Rock we talked so much and about such *intime* things no one else spoke a word esept an affianced couple in the corner. Wretched B couldnt leave the house till 6 each day and as even Mrs. Brown leaves at 1 there would have been nobody but about 1 phone message saying can I speak to Miss Wyndham? Oh Miss Wyndham is away no I wont leave a message Mistress Norton put in an appearance on Monday to fetch her photos shes quite a beauty in the phots & so charming she was we went to the Mystic Mirror featuring Fritz Rasp and the Docks of New York my favourite film Betty Compson has a wild peroxide towzle and a railway system under each eye Baclanova is a rare old gem of the streets too in a blouse & skirt a protruding tum (and bum) we were even permitted to come back to supper of Lyons Fish cakes at Adam Street. We went to the water Rat on Tues (after working hours such a press my dear 2 phone calls & what with that & reading Variety we were quite worn out) Babs went out with the Girlies after supper so I leant out of the window & played the gramophone till about 1.30 when I staggered to Bed about ½ an hour afterwards a loud crashing was heard which was Ruth Baldwin & Babs dropping in Ruth was quite drunk after a bit more crashing & screams they went off I dropped off Ruth Baldwin is my beau ideal I think I like them fat I cant resist anyone that goes about with an airoplane in dimonds where there ought to be a tie. On Wed we went to the Innocents of Paris with the Baldwin my dear Maurice [Chevalier] is glorious but its *the* most dreadful production youve ever seen then we saw Raymond Hatton in the talkie mirthquake Dear Vivian if thats a mirthquake then Ime the unknown soldier it was awful. I went to supper with Paul & Margaret Saterday last & jolly Lance Seiveking was there so picturesque the tall muscular form was in brown tweed trow[s]ers a biscuit shirt & a tie to match the tie arranged so romanesque & just after the sea beast[1] has had a reissue too so what will happen

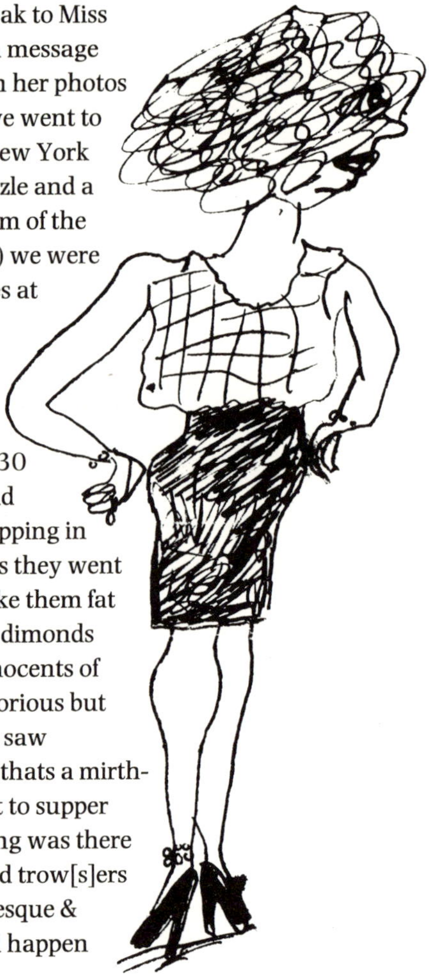

1 *A film starring John Barrymore.*

when Don Juan gets reissued I dread to think. Did I tell you of Sophie & me picking corn to compose a suitable bouquet for Sockalova[1] in Sacre[2] last Monday week? Sophie insisted on having corn so having climbed over a high hedge full of brambles we picked an imense sheaf of corn & staggered back with it looking like a bit of old Russia as Gerry said such a useful bouquet as with a little grinding & kneading you could make ever such an economical pudding with it. looks more like Sacre de L'Automne to me says mother. If you want to get a glorious record get Doing the new Lowdown & Digga Digga Doo by Duke Ellingtons wonder orch; on the Parlophone Ive never heard anything so lovely both have vocal chorusus I play nothing else Well there dont seem much else in the way of news theres a strange composite photo of captain 'Dick' Wyndhams amusing old fashioned fireworks party in the sketch I think all composed of bits of photos that have come out its a good thing it didnt all come out from what I hear Heydo Ime afraid the season is over & were all gone to the moors & Blackpool Well boy dear you treat me worse than any dog.[3] How is Fred and *dont* forget Mrs. Ashley Dukes 7/6 for it would be so awful if she had to live on her hub.

Au reverie old Tot

send us a line to say how the show is going

From your affec

Tottie

A unique stream of consciousness (or should it be unconsciousness?) in the letter which follows is explained by a nice phrase in the letter: 'As you see my dearie cheery more than a grumbler of gin I took' The address is:

Sprin fidil kidle kadle and
his Dublin Dowdili ow dow

Are you ankshus to hear of me mo moo? I haf made up a new numberr called 'Chop Suey girl of old Sing Sing' The set is Maxims chinese rest and all the show girls parade as different chop sueys whilst the tiller troupe does a chopstick dance the finale is the 24 lancashire laddies and their 24 sugar dada dada dddddda das raiding the place and we all said grace and instead of truncheons they have little fickle nickle saxophones groins in the groans never make old bones stweet dont you think? yes? And my dearest dearest do. You *must* have 'Film photo wie noch nie (5/9 net)!!!! from Tommix in Fred Salm whilst under the Lilian Hall Davis Lee parried John Gilbert licking lian liane Haide ay Lili Damit Dagover and complete with Harry Piel and never do I enjoy Jack Trevor & Werner Fueterrer fouettant Willi Nilli Fritsch so Bitsch my Jenny Jugo jugged hairs marcelled little Lilian Harvey full of sauce the saucily Susi Andra Vernon as usual & Saxo-

1 *Lydia Sokolova (née Hilda Munnings), one of Diaghilev's leading dancers.*

2 Le Sacré de Printemps, *the ballet by Stravinsky choreographed by Massine. This must have been the last season given by the Diaghilev Company with Boris Kochno in charge in London.*

3 *An esoteric quote from a conversation in Paris the previous winter, having no bearing on Edward at all.*

phun with Henny Porten not so small porten Astor Neilsonals Hamlet! ! ! also Panoramique du Cinema & Films von Soviet Russia from mama and 'Inclinations' from Anne. Let me give you Film photo for Xtase Xmas 1929 How you would enjoy! As you see mon beau mon wee ta pipi t'aime toujours & those cock sucking cunters every day at Gunters spitting skunking spunking raised it up from the dust and away into the Buggers Lantern Jaws How goes the bright young persons Gertie de Gonhorea Hardie Chancre and Softie Chancre & the darling Barbie? so darling & Wo Wodent B jalous of a bo like you and mes fillettes each with an Andoillettes Antoint ainoint. *How* it aches my dearest derring dont do it again tonight I forbid you puss dont lick jew Süss again tonight! ! and so say all of us.
(As you see my dearie cheery more than a grumbler of gin I took)

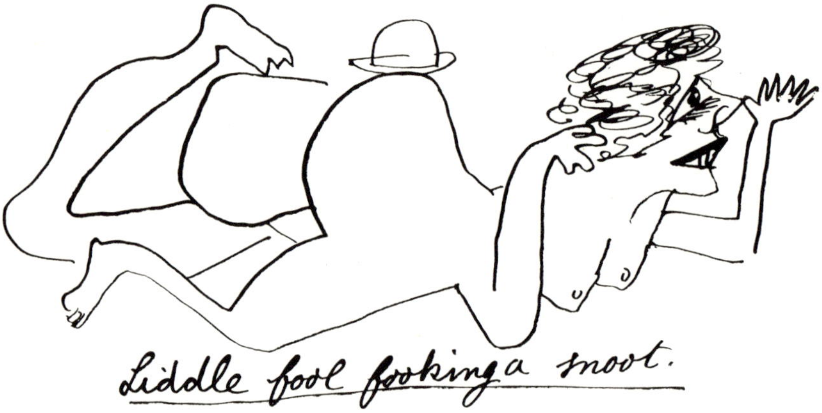

Meilleurs souvenirs a mon Freddie et mon Renée (51 Godfrey) & the Arts Theatre. Write to me wave to me waive & aint Miss behaving from you Gin soddy sodomie.

In 1929 Barbara Ker-Seymer had shown signs of possible maturity by leaving home. She had, in Edward's words, 'flung her last remaining bonnet over the mill' and was 'fully launched in the demi-monde*', a jokily dramatic statement (as always) on Edward's part. In this instance perfectly true. She was on the brink of becoming assistant to Olivia Wyndham, an agreeable and handsome woman who had set up in business as a 'society' photographer at 19 Kings Road Chelsea, a maisonette over the Post Office. It was not long before Barbara became a resident. Clover had already broken away from her family, having (on 8 November 1828) married her dark angel, Adam de Nagy, on a freezing morning at a Catholic church in Budapest. She then appeared to vanish. It was a long time before her friends discovered she had been throughout her marriage (it lasted three years) virtually a prisoner, incarcerated in the lonely house at Jakfalva, her husband's estate outside Budapest, whilst he, consistently unfaithful, was carousing in the night spots and the brothels of the City. It was so like a novel by Ouida (currently one of Edward's favourites); she had become identical with the heroine of* Moths*: icily beautiful, desperately unhappy. Driving, wrapped in sables, in a sleigh through a winter-*

struck landscape. It has to be pointed out here that both these great bids for freedom of choice were made by women already in their mid-twenties. By today's ideas they were almost middle-aged and very tardy in escaping parental control. Today's youth would find this not only comical but puzzling. The boys would have puzzled them more. Chappell, twenty-one, and Edward at twenty-four (grown men both) showed not a sniff or sign of rebellion, nor the smallest need for real independence. Despite the continued fanciful sophistication of their talk, their tastes and their ideas, and the real maturity of Edward's gifts as a painter they remained emotionally and sexually childish. Financial considerations would have prevented Chappell from fleeing his matriarchal suburban background of grandmother, mother, sisters and aunts – unless he had been lucky enough to be set up in an 'expensive Viennese apartment by wicked prince Schnitzel!' as Edward had suggested. Chappell never showed a need for more independence than was already afforded him by his doting mother. Edward, had he asked, would without doubt have been allowed to live among his chums in London. He remained in the family home (his only protest being to remark, periodically 'Dont FUSS') until his parents died. Well into his sixties he abruptly found himself in complete charge of his own house; and discovered rather late that such a situation suited him to perfection. 1930 found 'Maisie Rampart' slowly but surely pushing Frederick Ashton into becoming a choreographer, and Chappell into a possible career as a dancer and a designer. He showed both aspects by designing the costumes for, as well as appearing in, a new work, Capriol Suite, *given by Ashton at a matinee in the Lyric Theatre Hammersmith on Tuesday 27 February 1930. Just to make certain that Chappell should not get too carried away with pretensions to being 'artistical' (a venial sin), Edward sent him a mock fan letter. No address. No date. It was written on a sheet of Schiaparelli pink writing paper.*

Dear Mr. Chappell
Nite after nite I have admired yr legs they certinly r yr trump card. When you come on as a nun I can hardly stay still and in 'Vitriol Suit' by that wonderful Frederick Ashton you are a *dream* especially wen yr shoes fly off[1] showing a beautiful foot. PTO

May I hope for a photo?? most other stars (Gertie Gitana, Scot & Waley etc) have sent me ones. believe me you do not guess at what you bring to my life. Thanking you in anticipation from

your 'shadow Fan'

P.S.
I am an othor & send one of my little booklets for even dancers have kiddies.

Back in 1928 Edward had written to Barbara Ker-Seymer: 'I hope you will have a nice time at the ball and have no arrestations for indecency this time [there never had been any] though if you go as drowned sailors with openwork net tops Ive no doubt you will be asked to leave the floor I have sent B[illy] some nice Cockle shells covered with barnacles so they will keep the boys at bay if

1 This did actually happen.

they importune too far.' *The ball in question was of course the famous Chelsea Arts Ball given each New Year's Eve at the Albert Hall; and Barbara Ker-Seymer and Chappell were regular guests, dressed always identically. In the letter Edward wrote to Ker-Seymer early in 1930 we find that she and Chappell had been at the Ball as usual. Unfortunately Edward does not tell us what they wore.*

Dear.
I hope you enjoyed the bohemian chelsea Arts ball We went to puss in boots the other day in Hastings. it was heaven such a ruin I never saw Dame Dorking got so worked up having had a few nips in the wings she sang put your bubbies through the mangle instead of put your worries etc then she appeared in the grand finale in a beaded model with a long cigarette holder and kept making jokes about women in + 4's so we are trying to make Radclyffe and Una go you should see Radclyffe in hers this little sketch is very lifelike[1] admiring the Nash's Christmas tree the antiente town is getting a regular Montparnasse I am thinking of opening a branch of the fétiche[2] with old world beams and lanterns Im sure it would pay hand over fist I am just going to hire Sheila Kay-Smith[3] as hostess at my fétiche branch she is so popular here. Have you been to the Lyric Hammersmith[4] its a great success I believe tho hearts (*and* faces) are breaking out under the make up[5] I saw Anna Christie a day or 2 ago Garbo's voice Chaliapine is but a coloratura soprano to it. When next I come up I will give you a ring I havent been since you saw me in Shaftsbury avenue what with rain fog & ruin I saw Lucy the other day she had so many saddles & bridles hanging about her you could scarcly see the wood for the trees

Well dearie love to all
from Tottie

Edward wrote what amounted to a eulogy on a gramophone recording of two songs written and performed by the immensely popular cabaret star and inimitable dame of innumerable pantomimes, Douglas Byng. Edward admired him a great deal. The letter is not dated, and it bears no indication as to the name of the addressee. It is without doubt written to Chappell, the clue being a reference to a paperback novel Monsieur Venus, *by an extraordinary writer named Rachilde. The outrageous plot (much enjoyed by Edward and Chappell) concerned the necrophiliac habits of its immensely wealthy heroine, who kept the embalmed corpse of her lover – the Monsieur Venus of the title – in a tomb set in the gardens of her house. Here at dead of night she would visit and make love to the exquisitely beautiful cadaver.*
The letter plunges in:

Dont you like my new paper Comtesse Bond it calls itself Lattice grain I bought it cheap for 4d. I've just bought "Sex Appeal Sarah" by Douglas B

1 *Radclyffe Hall, author of famous lesbian novel,* The Well of Loneliness, *and Una, Lady Troubridge, her friend. The sketch is lost.*
2 *Lesbian night club in Paris.*
3 *A Sussex novelist.*
4 *Where The Marie Rambert Dancers were appearing.*
5 *Chappell had caught impetigo at a grubby barber's shop.*

on the Zono youve never heard anything so lovely its so Spanish and sung in such a voice why the Zonophone co didnt blow up I dont know also on the other side is She may be all thats wonderful (but she dont appeal to me) Byng & Wade[1] such words

On the bridge of sighs she used to roam till she got such a size that she had to go home, oh she may etc . . . but shes no damned use to me, ting-ting Oh she may be all thats wonderful but she dont appeal to me, she may be all thats wonderful but she's not having meals with me, She drove round Paris on New Years day & got a nasty bump in the Rue de la Paix Oh she etc . . . by electric light she's not bad to see but she looks like death with the morning tea, oh she etc. also I got Ethel Waters theme songs which are lovely Ime sure the audience will all get up & walk out as soon as Birmingham Bertha begins Nobodys fooling Birmingham Bertha she's had schooling this particular Bertha eye for an eye jaw for a jaw's my plan As for Am I blue it suddenly turns into 'hes a good man to have around' however compared to Margaret Johnstone & Bessie Smith Ethel is very refined. The Lady Lucy Norton was seen last week twice. (I'm Sex appeal Sara my body gets barer each time I appear on the screen, I know the Lupinos I go to their beano's they start off with cocktails and end up with Eno's, shes the courage of her own convictions when she starts to spoon . . . I think she'll get convicted for her courage very soon heigh ho the meryho. When she bows her head to say her grace you thank god for the moment when she hides her face she may be all thats wonderful but shes no damned good to me. Hey dey)

We are all one big county family now theres riding yachting (?) croquet, darts, shove halfpenny & shooting soon therl be murder. My next favorite tune is if possibly you possibly could possibly why possibly couldnt you possibly maree me posibly posibly dream & think about you I cant help thinking possibly Hodge didnt have it.

I am just putting on Douglas Byngs version of the famous novel M. Vénus (at the Arlequin Nottingill) Venus playd by Barbette & Raoul de Vénérande played by Bert Errol & sister played by Hermione Baddeley & the financey played by John Barrymore. dance ensembles by Mdme. Ashlie Dukes who will dance the waste paper basket polka during the intervals to a mecanicle piano I must stop now I feel quite ill mind ye gae tae thi London Group Exhibition Ive got an oil painting in it however it got in I cant think the private V is on Saterday Love to Fred when you see him next. from yrs affec Ive got those absentminded blues Tottie.

The years from 1929 to 1935 were – in certain raffish circles – noticeable for almost non-stop party giving. Many were in fancy dress: and the 'Bright Young (and not so young) People' chose the themes. Go, they said, as babies (some alarming results). Go Tropical. Go Greek. Go Sailor (with Tallulah Bankhead who sat on a glass-topped display table which collapsed and cut her behind). Go suitably

1 *Hugh Wade, who played the piano at the Blue Lantern, a cheap and lively night club in Ham Yard frequented by Chappell, Ashton and Ker-Seymer.*

dressed to 'celebrate' the End of the World (Ashton wore black silk pyjamas, gardenias and a black straw boater with a widow's veil). Should you have no invitation a bottle would gain you admission. Gatecrashers, a period phenomenon, arrived in dozens, offering anything from Guinness to a magnum of Bollinger. Edward's sharp eye took in every absurdity and parodied them perfectly in an invitation he sent to Chappell in 1931.

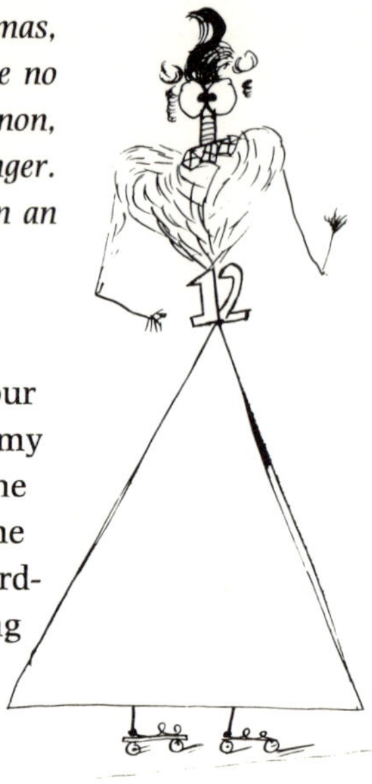

To Barbara Ker-Seymer, 1932

Heres a beautiful thing turn to rotogravure pages & see something to your advantage Mata Hari!! My dear never have I seen anything so lovely in my life my favorite picture a man & woman behind me kept saying why – she looks like a deths ed (5 mins later) why she looks like a *man* now Madame Mata Hari Blair[1] – Dietrich is so busy being Garbo & Dietrich she can hardly speak she sweeps about with her hair tied up with bits of string looking inscrutable

Goodbye for present

To Barbara Ker-Seymer from Springfield, 1932

Thank you very much for your letter dear, I am driving everyone mad as I havent yet found out the date of my show Ime *far* too busy to bother about little things like that so I shall be sitting here working at one of my beauty panels & will wake & find it all over perhaps Ime coming up on Monday or Wednesday next as I have some more peices to deliver so will drop in on the old tea things. Longing to see your new Ammericans they sound lovely talking of Ammericans I met one only the other day John Gould Fletcher[2] he looked as if he had been pulled thru 18 thorn hedges 14 baths of cocaine & then painted green he was very ill and could hardly speak all he said to me was are you portugese? then he produced a small notebook full of Zodiacal signs & said you were born on March the 28th!! 29th I says so he says Ah yes double sexed Are you going to take photos of the ballets can I have some prints of Rio if you take any Dont speak to me of Banting how did he get away if only some one could spirit me away!!! Oh hot digetty Do I reely must go for a holiday after the show as I am becoming a little crazie How is B & F[3] I havent heard of B for years I suppose hes doing all the sewing[4] for everyone free of charge I see a print of (Negative) of Nancy Cunard in the Architectural review How grand dearie I must see women who do things why not women who do nothing it would be so much more original I think I see in the Daily Mirror all the debutantes are working their fingers to the bone all thru the season at the Slade school well dearie Ill be seeing you

Hettie Bureaux My favorite film is Finn & Hattie also Mae Murray in High Stakes Ime curazy over Mae Murray the same as ever.

---

1 *Madame Mata Hari Blair was Chappell's younger sister Honor, at this time a well-known London chorus girl.*

2 *A writer, and friend of Conrad Aiken.*

3 *Chappell and Ashton.*

4 *At the Mercury Theatre.*

To Barbara Ker-Seymer on hotel notepaper with printed heading: Palace Hotel Place Jules Ferry, Lyon; actually from London, 1932

I do hope you like my new fangled pictures Ime just crazy over bird folk now & in Lyon right this moment am studying bird folk from my window in the palace. we spent 8 hours sitting in the cafe Royal & Lyons corner house last night I also visited the 2 cinderellas of Shepherds market no sooner had little prince Bartholin[1] & myself got in the house when in came Sophie Bunny Rogers & boy & we all started to talk of the cinema Sophie curled up & went off to sleep nestling in a packing case covered by 3 sheets of talc 8 ½made cellophane hats a few sheets of the N.Y. evening graphic and 2 or 3 licquorice all sorts & gramaphone records as a pillow the sash of Bums window broke so her bedroom is impossible & of course you are coming to my little exhibition the 24 or 25 May of bird life at the Leicester Galls you soitinly must not miss this Oh why cant I be in Paris! ! Bumble made us all jealous Dear Paris in the Spring with chestnuts boisting in the Bois – But it is autumn now   sincerely Madame Mata Hari

To William Chappell from Springfield, 1933

How are you getting on with your bitten neck and all?[2] I have been busy doing a few ideas for an opium ballet for Wylie Tates Aladdin[3] to be presented at the Empire Leeds. Paul saw it by mistake and was *horrified* so crude I see Dave Apollon is back again at the New Victoria. I was wondering if you could have me next week. Bum is supposed to be coming for this week end so I thought I might come back with her if she comes that is I havent heard anything Foyer de dance[4] seems such an exquisite thing according to the Times Mrs Ashton is such a gallic maitre de Ballet I want to see it. I saw Vilma & Dickie Dixon last Friday Vilma was so feminine in primrose mousseline Dickie looked like an insane child games mistress in a pince nez and baby shoes a daintie "colony" is forming to go to Spain in January as we have found a pension about 3/- per day the "colony" will be down each others throats in 2 ticks I may add Have you seen "Madame Hydrangea"[5] the new *pensionnaire* at ye olde Belte and gew gaw Shoppie which is only an alias more belting than belts belting the clients & they love it. If you want a lovely record get parlophone R 1297 Original Memphis 5 playing Anything also our old pal Apollons orch in a tango no te enjones carazon with a vocal chorus by one of the boys Pedro Gonzales? I want [to] see Tiger Shark its full of horrors so they say Edward Robi[n]son is a mad portuguese sea captain it sounds lovely Richard Arlen Zita Johann support. sharks no like dark meat

Well dear hoping
to see you sometime soon
Ed

---

1 *Birger Bartholin, dancer, who was in the Rubinstein company with Ashton and Chappell.*
2 *Bitten by a wild lady fan at a birthday party.*
3 *Fred Ashton and Edward were planning an opium dream ballet, but it did not materialise.*
4 *A ballet by Ashton for the Rambert company.*
5 *Birger Bartholin.*

When in 1931 Irene Hodgkins paid a visit to Cassis to catch up with her old set who were on holiday in Toulon, Edward, for some reason, did not see her. Back in France two years later, in the early autumn of 1933, he moved as always irresistibly South to his favourite port, Marseilles. Discovering that Hodgkins was in Martigues, and it was not far away, he decided to visit her.
He wrote to Chappell from

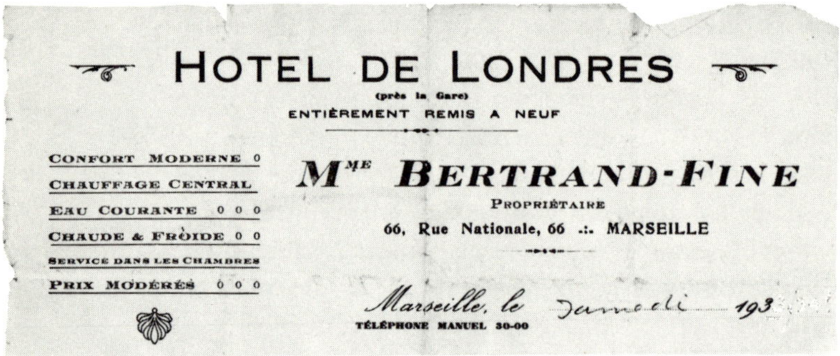

HOTEL DE LONDRES
(près la Gare)
ENTIÈREMENT REMIS A NEUF

CONFORT MODERNE
CHAUFFAGE CENTRAL
EAU COURANTE
CHAUDE & FROIDE
SERVICE DANS LES CHAMBRES
PRIX MODÉRÉS

Mme BERTRAND-FINE
PROPRIÉTAIRE
66, Rue Nationale, 66 .:. MARSEILLE

Marseille, le Samedi 193
TÉLÉPHONE MANUEL 30-00

How are you getting on with the new show at the Troc.[1] I went to Martigues the other day as Barbara told me Hodge lived pres de Martigues when I got there I found the house was three kilometres away so I sat down 2 lunch. in the restaurant were 2 men who looked so artistic they must be English who I took no more notice of. ½ an hour later I turned round & there was Hodgekins so of course Ide been staring at Birdie Hillier without knowing who it was she hasnt changed *at all* swathed in backless cotton dresses & eating ice cream cones just the same only thinner & better looking Mr. & Mrs. Dennis Cohen[2] then arrived on the scene on their way to Spain I had dinner with them in Martigues an enormous dinner of lobster & chicken it nearly killed me after we met some people in a bar a poet called Roy Campbell roaring drunk apparently theyre allways getting drunk there was another man staying with them whos name I forget you need never go home to see your friends says Hodge they all trickle here sooner or later. The twins are a dream & live in a pen tended by a french maid. I feel tempted to go over to Toulon in the bus for old times sake just to see how many monsters I can recognise. from what I can gather B & M[3] are returning some time next week they said they might stop over in Marseilles. I felt very ill yesterday & sure enough after waking up from my noonday siesta (at 4 o'clock) storm clouds had gathered by 6 it was pitch dark all the lights in the Vieux Port failed all the trams stopped & there was a flood at the bottom of the Cannebiere in which lay stranded motor cars. I realy shall have to leave soon as I am getting in such a state of decay yrs with love Ed

How do you like Marie Dubas new star at Casino de Paris?

---

1 *Chappell and Ashton had been performing in C.B. Cochran's* Magic Nights, *a midnight revue at the Trocadero in Shaftesbury Avenue, for the past nine months. Chappell was now designing costumes for the next show.*

2 *Dennis Cohen had found a substitute Hodgkins in an American girl, Kathryn Hamill, who was much the same physical type.*

3 *Barbara Ker-Seymer and Marty Mann.*

The letter shows the pleasure Edward took in the company of children. He had been a wonderful elder brother; first to Anne then, even more devotedly, to Betsy, a late addition to the Burra family. Apart from his interest in seeing the twins, he knew Hodge was well worth seeking out for herself. Her life had resembled (and continued to do so) nothing so much as an old-fashioned, over-romantic novel.

To William Chappell from 1890 7th Avenue Apt 2A NYC, 18 October 1933

Really dearie if only if you all were here New Y is marvelous. Am comfortably ensconced in Harlem 1890 7 Av (apartment 2A) in a pitch dark bedroom of a pitch dark apartment the property of Edna & Lloyd Thomas[1] who are both Charming Olivia [Wyndham] is such a figure in Harlem society you cant concieve she seems to know all the neighbourhood. we went to a little party the other night to a hermeticaly sealed "oriental" flat lit by old moorish incence burners with red electric bulbs you couldnt see a thing theres so much talent at the partys here that its more like non stop Variety we went to an outrageous place called the theatrical grill a cellar done up to look like Napoleons tomb and lit in such a way that all the white people look like corpses. Ive never seen such faces the best gangster pictures are far outdone by the old original thing. The chief attracles of the cabaret was "Gloria Swanson" a mountainous coal black nigger in a crepe de chine dress trimmed sequins who rushed about screaming Clappy weather, just cant keep my old arse together keeps runnin all the time etc and rush up to the table dragging his sequins up and disclosing a filthy dirty pair of pink silk panties how he managed I dont know no balls or anything else so far as I could see I discovered an Arthur Mahoney in the phone book & rang him up of course it was the wrong one so how to get hold of our old ex Mahoney God knows at the oriental party who should I see but our old pal John Godwin as silly as ever and I never knew he asked mother Ker Seymer to marry him if only Fred could come here he would adore it Ime certain if he doesnt come hes crazy despite the broad Atlantic. Dame Ruthie Baldwin got a nasty shock when she found me round but has recovered somewhat Sophie is in her element hanging round hot dog stands Mae Wests new pic is packing the paramount from 12 noon to 4 in the morning I am dieing to see it and prepared to beard a howling mob for Mae & pay 55 cents into the bargain we are staying at Mineda Farm this week-end the country is *lovely* & my dear the autumn tints the interior of the Regal cinema is nothing to it dame nature has weaved her spells with lavish brush How are you two boys getting on do write to me love to you all Ime thinking of becoming a naturalized Jewish citizen (Hitler is mud in New York)
yrs Ed.

1 *Edna Lloyd Thomas was a distinguished black actress and a close friend of Olivia Wyndham.*

pictures are far outdone
by the old original thing
the chief attraction of
the cabaret was "Gloria
Swanson" a mountainous
coal black nigger in
a crepe de chine dress
trimmed sequins who
rushd about screaming

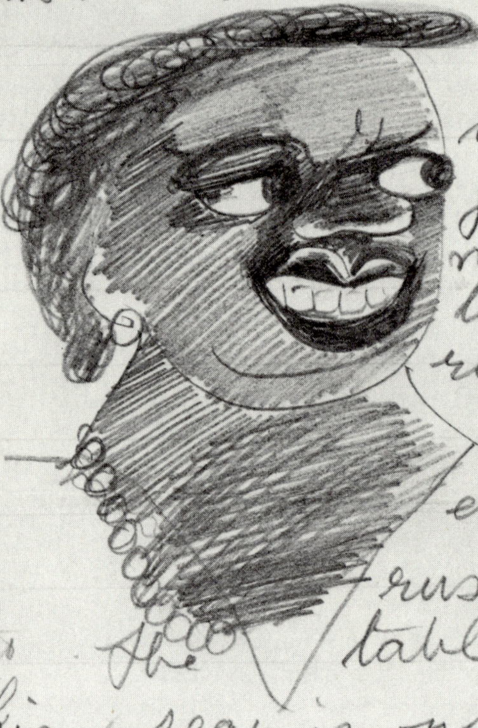

Clappy
weather,
just cant keep
my old arse
together, keeps
runnin all
the time
etc and
rushd up
to the table dragging
his sequins up and
disclosing a filthy dirty

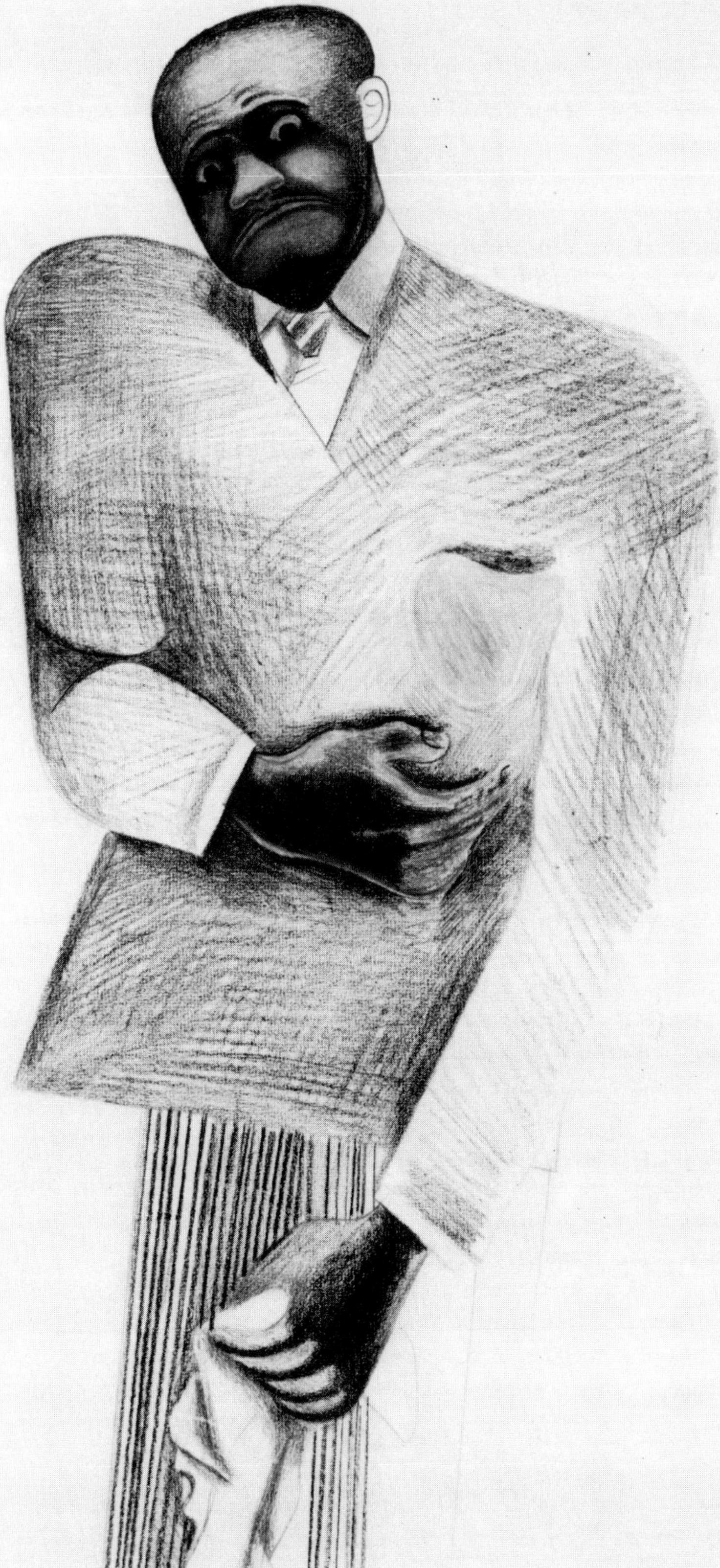

To William Chappell from 1890 7th Avenue NYC, October 1933

Yes sir were having a heat waaaave a tro-opical heat weeyave as Madame sings every night at her famous "Club Madame" corner of 42nd and Mad, and Mads the word. Well well I have written you a letter and a post card but I suppose something must have ganged agley Dear Arthur[1] has been found again as a Dresden China statuette at the Roxy we took him to the Askews[2] yesterday where he was a great success especially with Virgil Thomson every time I go to Constance & Kirks I get roaring tipsy as for Kirk and Soph Soph by the end of the evening they were teaching each other Jiu Jitsu. Have been to 2 gallerys[3] – Levys – I was too "literary" in subject dearie Constance said if only youd come from across the channel it would have been quite a different story however Levy gave me an intro to John Becker (Beckers Gallery) and he likes them very much and said I should redecorate the new Bar at the Yale Club I feel everyone will get up and say it ought to be an ammerican artist to do a job like that.

If you want a nice record dearie buy "Harlem on my mind" from as thousands cheer sung by Ethel Waters other side is Heat Wave Harlem on my mind is lovely – The count Mahoney has not changed a tittle I may say and has the same trunk and even the same overcoat I cannot tell you how glad I was to see him I thought hed gone for ever Arthur still looks back on those happy Rubinstein days in the Select as his most golden happy period hey dey will write and send a few papers I wonder why you didnt get the cards I sent best wishes Mrs. De Pyster Bureaux née Polly Tangletale. I just did you up a packet of papers and left them on the EL[4]

You should have seen the tabloids on Tilly Lo[s]chs Taxi accident Poor Bankhead seems desperately ill we heard her life is dispared of its too awful.

Edward proved, in the paintings that resulted from his first visit to the USA in 1933–4, how closely and affectionately he observed every physical characteristic of the black people. He had grown up with the rhythms of jazz and the blues during the twenties and thirties when a positive Niagara of black talent crashed and splashed its way into the nightlife of London.

C.B. Cochran (probably the most enlightened impresario of his time) was much given to importing rare and specialised entertainments into the West End theatres. His was the first management to bring to London a complete company of black performers (to provide the second half of a revue, Dover Street to Dixie, *at the London Pavilion). It featured three notable talents: Florence Mills was huge-eyed, and thin as a bird, with the pure high voice of a nightingale; Edith Wilson was a singer in the true traditions of the Blues who delivered with relish what was without doubt the most undermining statement ever written into a popular song: 'He may be your man but he comes to see me, sometimes; and when he's with you*

1 Arthur Mahoney.

2 Kirk and Constance Askew had a permanent 'Salon' in their apartment where all the young and talented people gathered.

3 Edward was hoping to fix an exhibition in New York.

4 Elevated railway.

I'm always on his mind.' The third remarkable performer was Johnny Hudgins, a comedian who managed to be simultaneously frenetic and lugubrious, and had a voice like a creaking door.

Edward found himself (in October 1933) not only in the USA but also in New York city; not only in NYC but actually living in the mythic world of Harlem. The acute delight he felt springs live from the pages of his letters.

To Barbara Ker-Seymer from 1890 7th Avenue NYC, October 1933

Well old dear
New York would drive you into a fit. Harlem is like Walham green gone crazy we do a little shopping on 116th St every morning there are about 10 Woolworths of all sorts also 40 cinemas & Apollo burlesk featuring Paris in Harlem which I am plotting to go to It must be seen to be believed. Sophie and I go out and have breakfast at different quick lunches we hope to try the Arabian nights luncheonette tomorrow the food is delish 40000000 tons of hot dogs & hamburgers must be consumed in N.Y. daily as for the pies & sodas 2 minutes after arrival we were being treated to sodas in ye patio soda shoppie done up in the Mexican fashion. There was a cocktail party the other day Taylor Gordon[1] was there who is delightful also Douglas Parmentier and Esther Strachey whos face I couldn't take my

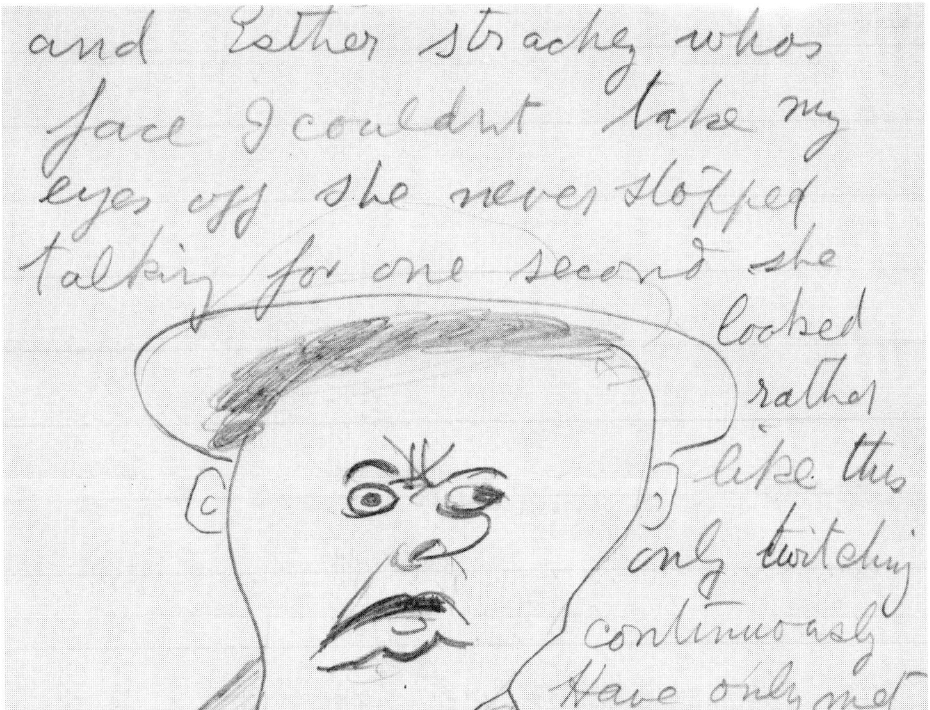

eyes off she never stopped talking for one second she looked rather like this only twitching continuously we went to the Savoy dance Hall the other night you would go mad Ive never in my life seen such a display an

1 A black singer.

enormous floor half dark surrounded by chairs & tables and promenade on one side and the band on the other with a trailing cloud effect behind Ive never seen such wonderful dancing they also had an initiation ceremony in which all the men had to crawl under a row of mens legs and be beaten with a stick going through and the women had to be twirled round ten times its most extraordinary they also had amateur specialities one couple were marvellous a thin marmoset of a creature with cropped crinckled hair and baby shoes and a woollen jumper its an experience not to be missed at any price. The East side is lovely too a tangle of firescapes washing and fruit like a Berwick street thats burst all bounds everything here is more so we went to Harlem Opera House to see moonlight and pretzels and arrived in the gallery to find one solid mass of dusky faces there were about four white as far as I could see a marvellous stage show also to a revival meeting no one did anything dramatic except an old negress who shouted Lawd aint that so with a shrill scream at intervals & everyone shook hands last night soph soph and me went and [to] Pilar Arcos at the Cubo Spanish theatre down the road our old Pilar is heavan 1 inch high she has such a presence and carries on so she sweeps all befor her I feel we are going to have Baldwin trouble Soph Soph cant bear the sight of her Ah we all have our little crosses to bear

Well dear au revoir write to 1890 7th Ave

Yrs Ed

January 1934 found Ed still in New York. He had left Harlem and moved to the East side. Ashton had finally dared the 'broad Atlantic', having accepted an offer to do the choreography for an opera by Virgil Thompson, Four Saints in three Acts, *with a libretto by Gertrude Stein and an all-black cast.*

To Chappell from 125 East 15th Street NYC, 3 January 1934

Well dearie and how are you I just sent you a bundle of comics and among them a few ties inserted which have all been *sent back* on the spot how they found out the comics were stuffed with ties god knows. Fred is in the midst of rehersals for Lily Lucy and Saint Theresa half in and half out of the door (lyric by Gertrude Alice B. Toklas Stein) none of the cast ever dream of arriving at the right time no negro ever does it seems Madame A[shton] disappears up to Harlem at 9.30 each morning & returns a grey white shadow screaming for steak at about 6 each evening. We went out for a jolly evening last night Ashtonette "Sophie the Pole" myself the Duchesse de Clermont Tonerre and her lady in waiting Madame Guy and Tom Howard if you can believe such a combination Madame la duchesse is perfectly crazy and speaks fluent Yiddish and English we visited a few hot spots one in the village which was camp lovely my dear a monster rose up in an old red wig with a bit of spinach hanging off the back and sang "they call me red head brick top carrot tops and strawberry garden but *I* dont care (scream)" my favorite number then we went to the Savoy and then to Hot Cha (Mrs. Cooks gone mad) where a shame making man sat down at

as fat as a pig she

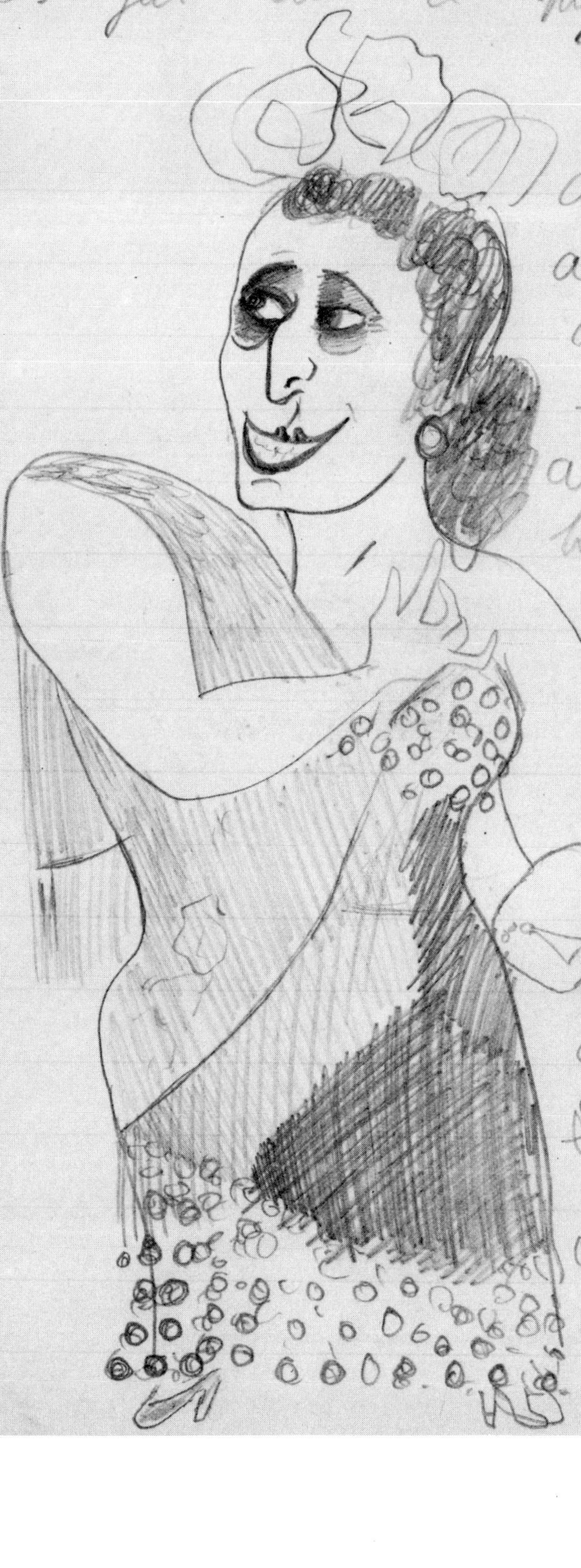

has such
a presence
and carries
on so
she sweeps
all befor
her we
saw the
Askews
yesterday
I feel
we are
going to
have
Baldwin
trouble
soph soph
cant

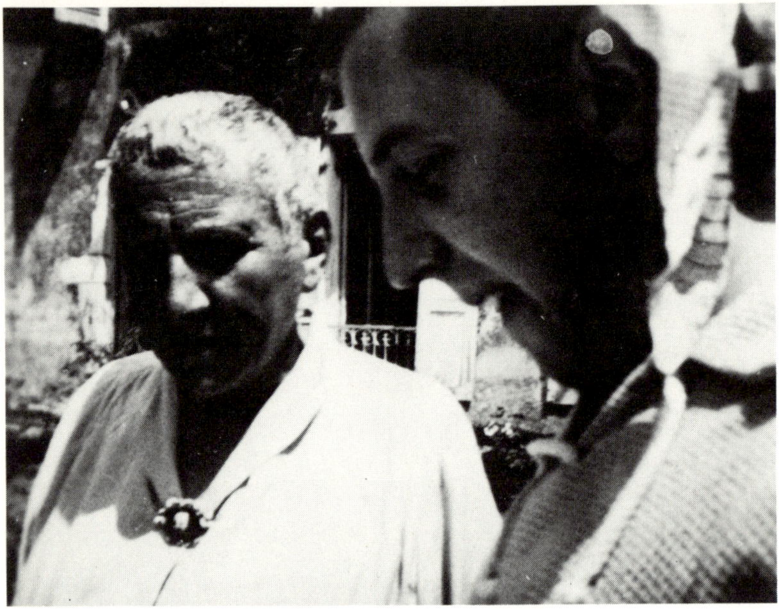

Gertrude Stein with F. Ashton.

the table and burst into La Paloma Clermont Tonerre at once asked for une veille Kentucky darkie song which flung the whole place in an uproar then we went to a underground grave yard called the log cabin my favorite resort in which a terrifying negro midget with a mouthfull of gold teeth sang a repertoire of dirty songs Madame was delighted. Fred is going crazy what with one thing and another. good talk about art and the Askews gin as for Arthur he arrives roaring drunk at 3.30 sharp every morning I am in the same house he shares a ground floor hovel with a piano and gilt mirrors with a strange person a Barman at the Club Richman who never comes home A has been fined 10 $ for missing his appearance as a wise man in the Xmas nativity tableau at the Roxy A is burning Murray Anderson has just been rehashing the follies by putting in 50000 $ of new scenery and Jacques Cartier. Our old Palls Cuffski and Hymanski[1] are here together with the manski who writes the books on the ballet and I forget the name[2] Best wishes love from Dorothée Trala (Madame that was)

To Barbara Ker-Seymer from 125 E. 15th St. NYC, 8 January 1934

How are you dear I am in my usual daze we went to cocktails at Constance (Twitch) Askews yesterday Iris Tree has arrived much to Soph Sophs joy. Hotsy Ashton is becoming frantic as the caste learn everything perfectly befor lunch and forget it after he works from morning to night in an old Harlem ballet club that used to be a church so its quite dear old Notting hill all over again we had a nice little round of the Clubs the other night the Duchesse de Clermont Ferrande[3] who aged 70 appeared with a small pan cake on her head and a piece of carpet wrapped round her neck and her

1 *Betty Cuff and Prudence Hyman, ex-members of Maisie Rampart's troupe.*
2 *I believe it was Arnold Haskell, author of* Balletomania.
3 *Edward has re-titled the Duchesse.*

companion Madame Guy who had such poise 50 gins hardly undermined
it The next day I went out with Madame Guy to buy "disques".
Il me faut des blues says G at once buying Empty bed blues by Bessie
Smith then we had lunch with Duchesse *Esther Strachey* & Eugene
McGowan both of whom were stricken dumb at seeing East
side Annie in Madames pocket it was very funny I saw Bessie Smith at
the Harlem opera the other day die Ruth Baldwin yellow and blow for
24 hours with a bicycle pump and pour into a long wine coloured
dress with paillette short sleeves and you have Smith. There is a
lovely Ethel Waters record out of "Just cant take it baby (lovin you the
way I do) 'Trackle' Hotsy Ashtons favorite numero I heard from Clover
again she said she might be over in London about Christmas
she seems to be spending her time playing hide and seek in the shadier
quarters of Paris from Madame Romains and, enjoying it every moment
We find out that Krishy Wisham was quite unknown in New York
and nobody knew anything about him so it needed exportation to
bring out the glammer.[1] Well dearie au revoir and please write.

Love to all Ed.

From the day of her marriage to Adam de Nagy in Budapest on 8 November 1928 there had been no word from Clover. By 1931 the marriage was breaking up. Her husband's wild behaviour and endless infidelities became insupportable and Clover ran away. Not very far: only to her parents who were staying at the Hotel Gellert in Buda. A decision had to be made as to whether or no she would rid herself of her dark Lucifer. This took over a year and it was not until June 1932 that she at last returned to London where she was received back into the collective bosom of Burra, Chappell and Ker-Seymer. A mere six months later her irresistible penchant for European gents had carried her off to Paris on an invitation from a highly respected French writer, Jules Romains, whom she had met at the French Institute in London. Since M. Romains was a married man it was no time at all before Clover had turned into a typical Jean Rhys heroine hanging about in small hotels on the left bank 'playing' (as Edward points out) 'hide and seek in the shadier quarters of Paris from Madame Romains and' (quite unlike *a Jean Rhys character) 'enjoying it every moment'.*

Edward was very partial to Victorian novelists; a particular favourite being an authoress who called herself Ouida. She was a remarkable writer with an extremely personal style. At the height of her success, she was considered so beyond the pale, so scandalous, any young lady known to have read her works could well have risked social ostracism. Chappell's mother had told him how, as a girl, she had been driven to locking herself in the lavatory with Moths *(one of the most popular of Ouida's novels), breathlessly devouring a short section at a time, and keeping the 'depraved' work from the sight of her father, who had forbidden his daughters to read it. Ouida exerted on both Edward and Chappell the same fascination as Monk*

1 *Walter Crisham arrived in London as a dancer with a troupe of lady harpists, for an act at the London Palladium. He became a popular and skilled revue performer and partnered Hermione Gingold and Hermione Baddeley in many shows.*

Lewis, Mrs Radcliffe, Harrison Ainsworth and Sheridan Le Fanu. Two of Edward's letters from 1934 involve the work of Ouida. One is a scene (invented by the letter writer and catching perfectly the spirit of the original) featuring the notorious Lady Dolly Vanderdecken, mother of the icily beautiful, doomed heroine of Moths. *The second has an actual passage quoted in full; a perfect example of Ouida's prose in a typical descriptive piece from* Chandos.

The first letter is to William Chappell from Springfield.

Oh! If you say Ime "flabby' said Lady Dolly flushing as much as Piver[1] would permit. Lady Dolly blanched beneath her enamel. H'm thought Lady Stoat of Stychely if Dolly gets any sillier nobody will receive her and she will have to be content with horrible second class salons and 3rd rate watering places and 5th rate counts and 7th rate countesses and "the World" will laugh and forget over the latest new *Saleté* –

Les Corcorans are supposed to be arriving to day from Bournemouth!! what they were doing so far outside our "world" in such a 2nd rate watering place I cant imagine. I wish Ide summond up enough force to come but Ime so comfortable here with my thick boots and my bible and geraniums and district visiting I see Blackbirds of 1934 are coming to the Coliseum it was a flop in N.Y. except for me who was forced to go alone against all oposishion there is the most wonderful chorus and Aileen Stanley who looks exactly the same I will send Color of the East but am deap in it the stories are absolutely fascinating there so colorful its quite blinding love to you all *Ed.* If you want to be just a kiddie once again by memories of Love Piano solo by Eddy Lowry *Decca* consisting of Roses of Picardy – Rose in the bud Little Grey home in the west etc and you will be transported to the local cinema the 2nd feature before the orchestra comes on its wonderfull.

To William Chappell from Springfield, 1934

How is youse boys? I here Fred[2] is the worse and has turned blue & had to be lanced realy it is too awful he never seems well. I heard from Ker-S today he was ill. shes been in bed too with itch black spots in front of the eyes claustro nausea shivering fits & the pain. Last Monday I weekly said I would drive up to London for the day with A[3] who couldnt get any one else Ma Cherie! driving down on Monday night at 6 in the worst fog that has flung its tawny mantel oer the black smoken pile since the old curiousity shop nobody could satisfy their curiousity as when we finally stopped we were in Greenwich high st!! *Dieu sait comment*, swathed in a mass of fog we finaly groped our way back to the Marquis of Granby New Cross and proceed on our way at 15 MP.H accompanyd by little boys with electric torches such fun for Princess Marina's wedding day if its the same pay 5 guineas

1 Piver was the nineteenth-century equivalent of Lancôme or Elizabeth Arden.

2 Ashton.

3 Anne, Edward's sister.

and see some pea soup that you canmake yourself for 2^{D} love to Tony I see Dante en folie[1] the new non stop show at the Shaftesbury is coming on nicely   Love from E.

To Barbara Ker-Seymer from Springfield, 1935

Thank you for your letter I think of having Lecuona's Cuban boys chasing a fox into "the home covert" tattooed down the back next time I visit the

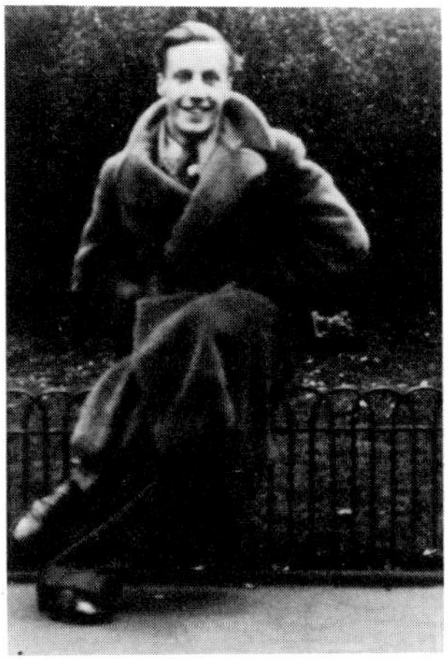

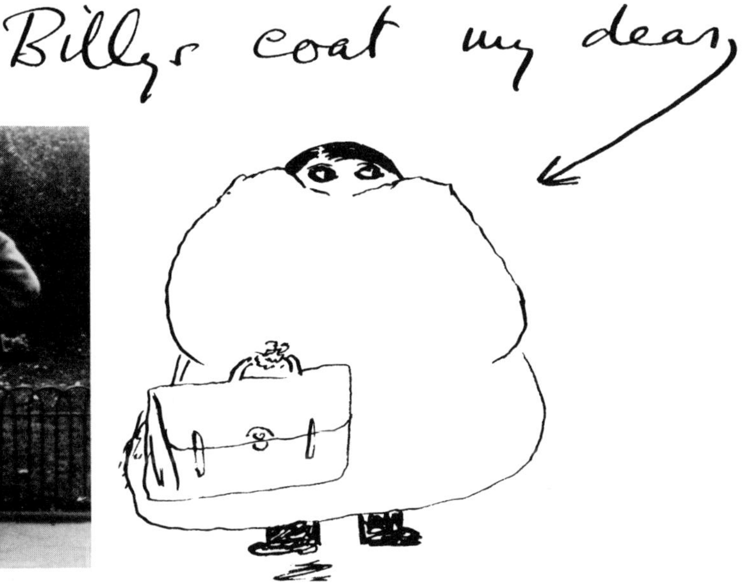

Waterloo Road[2] Billys coat my dear like this but cosier and much thicker Ime sorry to say that despite all adverse criticism of meanies Mae West remains my favourite since seeing Belle of the 90's which I enjoyed more than anything Ive seen for a long time my favorite scene is when she stands draped in diamonte covered reinforced concrete with a variety of parrots feathers ammerican beauty roses & bats wings at the back[3] and ends up waving an electric ice pudding in a cup as the statue of Liberty some of the sets I thought were the best Ive seen. I heard from Madame de N[4] she had had a few rare editions addressed to Mr. de Nagy and shrouded in grease paper from Jules I would like to go to Paris for a bit I must say and hang about shady bistros keeping out of the *wifes way* I will come up soon I promised to go & stay in the mews[5] if such a good for nothing influence is allowed there am looking forward to an afternoon in the Fitzroy – a Panto at the ballet club with Mim as Idle Jack Ashley as the dame Susie Salaman as Dandini & who? as fairy queen? Best wishes yrs Ed

1 *In fact a serious play about Dante starring Eric Portman and Margaretta Scott. Anthony Hankey, Chappell's flatmate, was in it. It was a Flop.*

2 *Where an expert tattooist, much patronised by the Services, could be found. He had already decorated Edward's shoulder with a Chinese head and a dagger.*

3 *The very costume and pose Edward painted of the immortal Mae West.*

4 *Clover.*

5 *Number 44 Queens Gate Mews, where Chappell was now living.*

To William Chappell from Springfield, 1935

Dear B.

I see there is a panto at the Mercury Rene and Ashley Dukes as the Ugly sisters I suppose.

Phylis Neilson Terry sang a few whispering choruses from what I hear of the Nottingham lace scene Ime dieing to go Have you seen Mdlle Ker-Seymers new "*cocottes bonbonieres*"[1] where tout Bloomsbury are going to loll on Louis quinsy settees stuffing their mouths with *bouchées* in the heart of the demi monde? it realy is lovely opposite Kettners so convenient to Rosins Jewish Bakery. I got a wonderful Ouida Yellow Back "Chandos" at our old shoppe in Hastings for 2^D Chandos is ruined and sinks to the depths–: "men who had the Trackers of turf law or of social law on their trail, & hiding for very life knew no nest surer than this foul one – all these were here in the tawdry glitter of the flaring gas jets – & there were women too – some young – some fearfully young – loveless & rogued with *hacking bitter coughs or laughing ghastly laughs* playing, playing, playing insatiate, with the thirsty eager devilish glare, aching in their painted eyes – Among them stood Chandos" – Its lovely love to you & Tony from Ed.

To Barbara Ker-Seymer from Pension Carmona, Alhambra, Granada, 1935

How are you getting on dear we have a romantic gypsy moon lighting up the old Alhambras fairy traceries I wouldnt have thought it possible that there could be so many flies as there are here the only place of escape is the cinema. This week "Luces de Buenos Aires" featuring Carlos Gardel & his old south Ammerican guitar Carlo is really Wyndham Lloyd The heroine was glorious with a mouth like a trap and a Jewish nose she made a fortune singing in the Buenos Aires follies till she got lasso'd from the stage box by 2 of Carlos Wyndham Gardels gaucho pals. I hear you have Madame de N[agy] in your midst again having finaly been driven into the lower depths of Montmartre Kensington Palace M[ansion]s is the only refuge now all the papers here are all over pics of Jules Romains who is one of the delegates at the League of Nations cultural meeting[2] in Madrid also Aunty Dolin[3] & his girls et boys are appearing in Madrid but no photos of them I went to a bull fight last sunday my dear its gorgeous all the bulls gore everybody and do the bulls bleed yes sir and do the audience roar with laughter the costumes are lovely my favorite costume was vermilion trimmed with black lace

a monster has just arrived

Best love
& wishes
from Ed.

I dont want to leave
Spain not till
I must

1 *At 4 Church Street (now Romilly Street), Soho.*

2 *A detailed account of Clover's meeting with her ex-lover is given in* Edward Burra: a painter remembered by his friends.

3 *Anton Dolin, the dancer.*

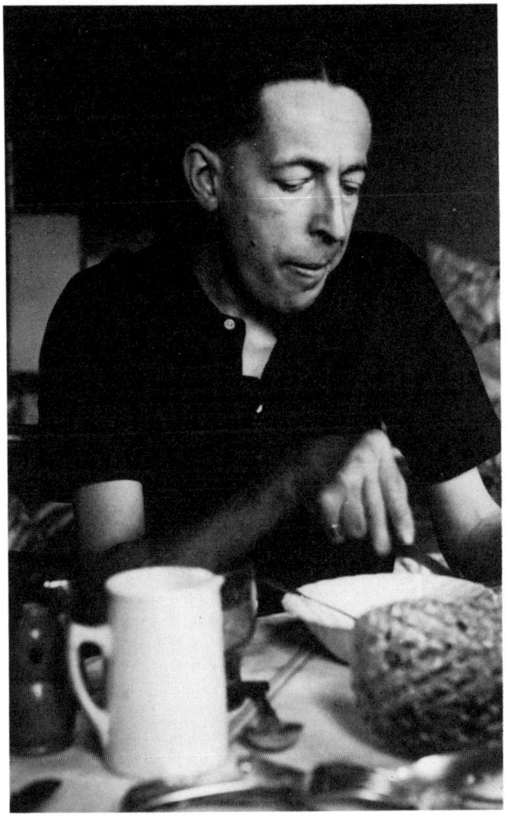
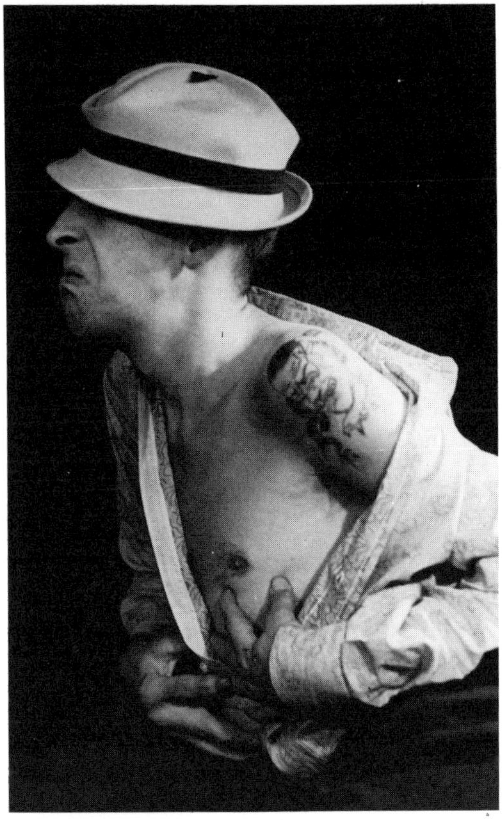
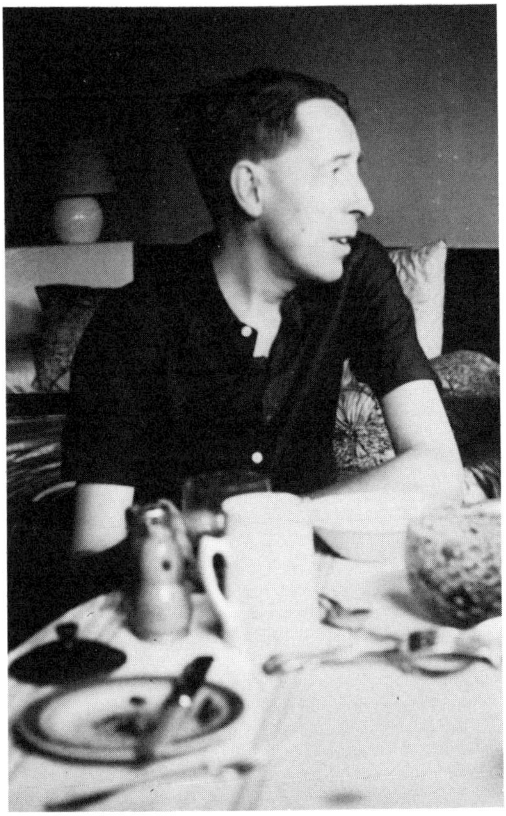
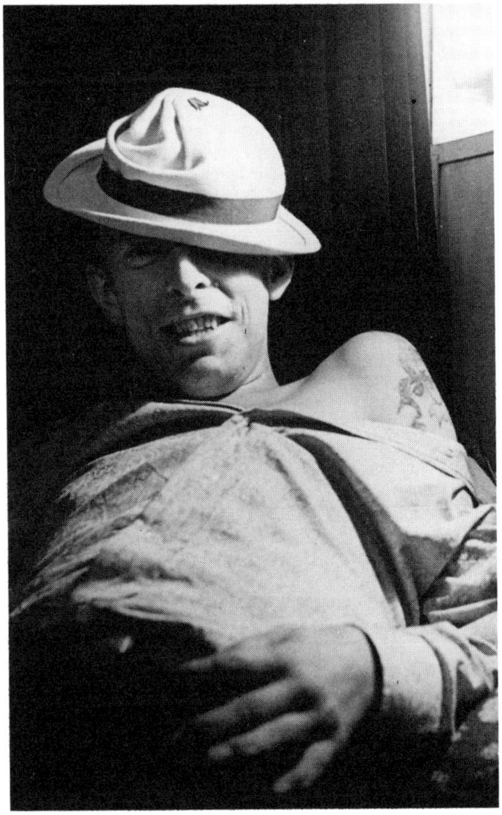

To William Chappell from the Hotel Aragon, Madrid, 1935

How are you dearie & how did Barabau[1] et ses boys go off we are suffering from a little trouble here today every shop & cafe is shut & all the trams & taxis have stopped I suppose it will be O.K. There is a vast crowd police, ambulances & firemen Miss Ker S said there was to be an influx of Bloomsbury but no sir I havent seen any as yet no rough tweed & kindly faces peering through specs. Mdms man[2] is charming & very respectable exactly like one of her own drawings only greener with bags under each eye very funny he kills me Ive been feeling like death as before I left I had 2 teeth out & have had neuralgia ever since De Nagy of course is in her element I have been doing a little work on a minute table that sways rhythmically belonging to the Mdme

well dearie I will end now

yrs E

Spain possessed every element most pleasing to Edward's senses; satisfying his eyes, his ears, his nose, his emotions, and his taste buds. The fabric of Spanish life might have been specially designed for his pleasure. In Barcelona, encountering for the first time the unsafe chaotic night world of the Barrio Chino he felt at once the pleasing tingle of a faint disquiet he instantly recognised and to which he gave immediate response. Like an insect or a small nocturnal creature, he possessed – or could assume – protective colouring, and settle unremarked into any kind of background.

He could not have enough of the grand old entertainers in the music halls, patrolling the width of the stage, up and down, up and down, belting out the paso dobles. Strong sounds, strong characters, strong colours. Above all the flamenco: the hoarse despairing voices of the singers, the machine gun rattle of the heel beats in the zapateado, the noble swirling arms of the women flicking their flounced trains, and the divine melancholy of the chords falling like golden rain from beneath the fingers of the guitarists. 'A sound', Edward said, 'to bring tears to your eyes, it's so beautiful.'

'I don't want to leave Spain', he had written to Chappell. 'Not till I must.' There was real feeling in those words. Sadly, 'must' became inevitable. The civil war erupted, followed by the poison out of Germany which spread across Europe.

With Toulon and Marseilles and Paris in the twenties, Harlem in 1934 and Mexico in 1937, Spain in the thirties became another strongly atmospheric and formative influence on his work. He was to pay a last visit in 1953, with Barbara Ker-Seymer.

To William Chappell from the Hotel Aragon, Madrid, 1935

Thank you for your letter dearie arrived today Monday I sent Varley & Prentis a drawing from Paris but Ime certain it never arrived & now of

---

1 *A ballet which Edward had designed for De Valois at Sadler's Wells Theatre for the Vic–Wells Ballet company (now the illustrious Royal Ballet).*

2 *Clover's future husband, Antonio de Pertinez.*

course its too late somebody must have opened it in the post mistaking it for filthy French pictures we are all getting along nicely here Mdms man is a perfect gentleman bright green green hat & face & looks like a deaths head he has a mania for *south sea island* pictures so has rushed off to Mutiny on the Bounty "Mandalay" is my favorite now with Kay Francis as Spot White a hostess in Nicks place in Rangoon Raffaiela Ottiano that was stabbed by Mae W[est] in the Mae W film & was Garbos maid in Grand hotel is the deposed hostess known as *the countess* shes wonderful with such a face of vinegar Ive never seen and always appears in full evening dress, tossing off glasses of scotch in the middle of the day its the best film Ive seen for years Ive been 4 times on Mae dae were all to be queen of the Mae with bomb garlands & called ever so early with mothers head flying through the window I have just been to a flamenco singing competition at a place called the lirico Price realy Ive never seen anything like it I went in at 6.30 & came out half dead at 10.30 & it was still going on I left just after a wonderful old cook had shouted for an hour she must have been at least 60 with grey hair there was also a marvellous little boy aged about 10 in a red jersey accompanied by my new favorite Niño de Sambucar a guitar player to bring tears to your eyes its so beautiful. his *feet* I've never seen anything like in my life such elegance tiny and the most wonderful shoes have been feeling half crazy since I had the 2 teeth out but thanks to a mysterious German product called Veramon its been kept at bay I'm sending you 4 tabs and I hope they dont get taken in the post. *They are wonderful* & will *stop anything within 15 mins* or less theres nothing so good in England I wish you could come here would you come if you had the cash you now get 40 to the 1£ note (*not* travellers cheques or bank cheques but *notes* dearie, *notes*). Well write again when youve pulled yourself together
love from Ed
Ime sure Barabau was a pretty sight.[1]

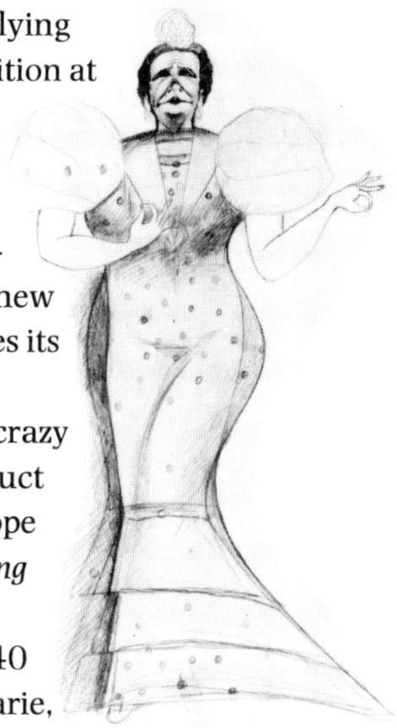

A postcard in the hand-tinted style so popular with Edward and his clique was sent to William Chappell from Barcelona. It is undated and the post mark is unreadable. The hand colouring is particularly good and lurid. The photograph is of an Amazonian female with a smile of quite deadly charm. She is so enwrapped in a deeply fringed flower-embroidered shawl she must have inevitably fallen flat on her face had she attempted to move one inch. Her huge mantilla is obviously made from a Nottingham lace curtain and she holds (in a daintily wristwatched hand) a flag, a tricolour in scarlet, lemon yellow and a virulent purple. Above her head the following verses are printed.

> *Quando estoy en tierra extrana*
> *y contempla tus colores*
> *al recordar tus hazañas*
> *yo recuerdo mis amores*

1 *It was indeed. He had done wonderful designs for the setting and the costumes.*

mira si yo te guerre
banderita di mi alma.[1]

Edward's message brings a new slant. 'Turn again Whittington Lord Mayor of Barcelona Espana is proud of you. Huguette ex de Nagy is suffering from boils she went to the Dr and was immediately taken for a Jackson girl[2] *in trouble until she produced 25 pesetas then she was a lady again.'*

Edward returned to USA in 1937 staying with Conrad Aiken at 17 Ellwood Street Charlestown, Nr Boston, Mass. He arrived on 11 February and wrote later to Chappell a contented, lively letter. No one could foresee the dire finish to his five month sojourn in the USA and Mexico.

Well dear
& How are you battling with lifes storms?
I am very happy here in an Irish ammerican midden of decayed grandeur parts are reminiscent of Bloomsbury I went to see the new piece by Maxwell Anderson "the Winterset" man & realy *Jamais jamais de ma vie ai je vu de telles choses* – Mayerling the plot is The Emperor played by Dudley Digges[3] so I at once mistook him for an inebriated old retainer Henry Hull[4] as Rodolph went on like a head waiter in a tantrum & Margo who should have been Vetsera – but it was played by a small under house maid – was having "*la grippe*" and if you ask Mame I say she doesnt fancy the part & probably is going on having *la grippe* The only bright spot was Pauline Frederick[5] who appeared in a dark crimson bustle & black net & *looked volumes* not that she was allowd to say much but in the last act during the shooting in walk Dudley & Fredrick & Dudley says "we – have – lost – a son" Pauline rushes at the 60$ scenery & beats on the door saying merciful heaven let me in – in her best fashion the whole wall of Schloss Mayerling tottering beneath the drama – realy I must say for all the furs & theatre guild it was frightful a mass of pretension Nobody dare say a word against Maxwell Anderson who is bringing "grandeur" to the ammerican theatre Winterset was very good I thought all vast close ups of Margo but the beautiful language was a bit balled up if you ask me however I was so busy looking at the production I didnt hear much. I thoroughly enjoyed Tallulah B's Reflected glory or rather Reflected Bankhead never off the stage a moment thats where a star should be I say having paid 2$75 a seat. Have heard from A Mahoney who is in New York as usual & would like to come to London as usual but will never get there I feel he says first a

1 *When I'm away in foreign parts*
and I see your colours
and remember your great deeds
I also remember my loves
Look how much I love you
little flag of my heart.
The translation is by Clover de Pertinez, who explains the flag's colouring: 'When Spain became a republic in 1931 a bright purple piece was added to the famous red and gold of the Spanish Flag. Then Franco of course tore it off and now there's a monarchy it hasn't been sewn on again.'

2 *The Jackson girls were a troupe of English dancers almost as well known and admired as the Tiller girls.*

3 *An Irish-American actor of distinction.*

4 *A leading man of the period.*

5 *A great star of the theatre and cinema.*

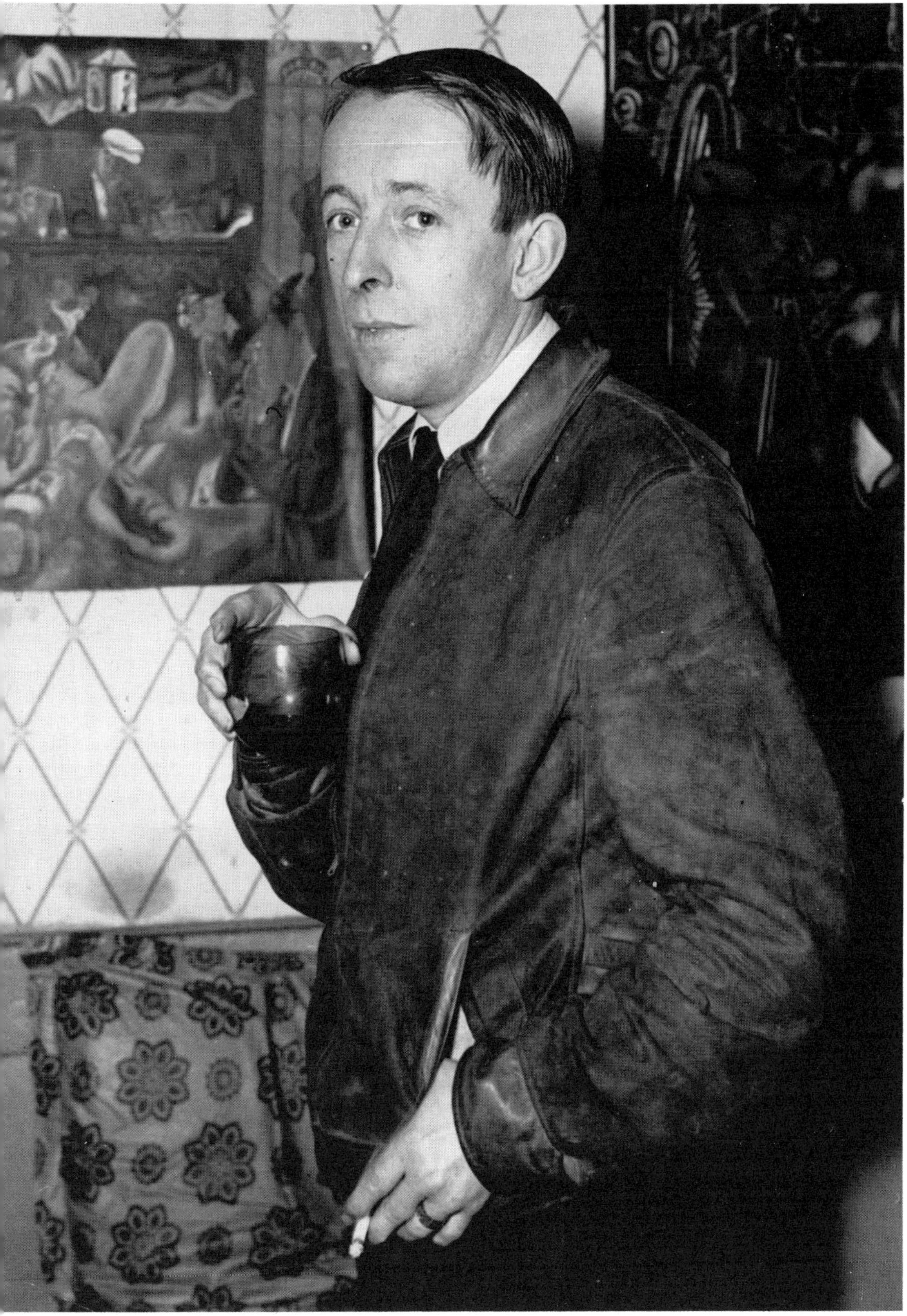

bottle & then a job prevents him There are many quaint corners of Boston I find quite unapreciated but the hats are what overcome me there was a hat show at the Copley Plaza reported in the Boston Ammerican surrealistic influences combined with tip & tilt which means I dont know what one daffy pill box model made of a bone [&] a bit of something was voted too extreme for Boston by Betty Tosspot Boorsqueeg of Beacon Hill who

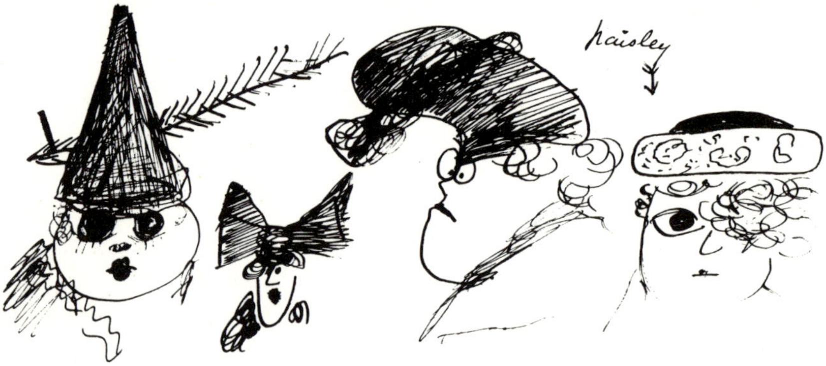

said such models could only be worn in New York but what is worn in Boston my dear tip & tilt is more surrealistic than anything Ive ever seen Ime hoping to see Aunt Fontanne & Uncle Lunt in "Idiots delight" shortly coming here also Plough & Stars by the director of the Informer with Una O'Connor as a screaming Irish char throughout the rebelion & I see Mother Swanson is about to make a come back under the auspices of Metro Goldwyn Mayer Ime so glad – did you see about Marie Prevost I was so sorry & I saw in Variety her body was not discovered till after some days by the howling of her pet dog – & the janitor came up to see & found her dead realy I think it disgraceful that such an artist should be neglected however fat & alcoholic she was always funny. Have heard from Clover who says a coach & horses is driving round her stomach at 5 every evening I suppose she is "expecting" pretty soon[1] my love to Fred & Bobbie write to me if *you can* yrs Ed also our old pal *June Caprice* is dead very young too awful.

Edward's visit to Mexico precipitated a physical crisis producing lasting ill effects on his always precarious health. His behaviour – easily misinterpreted as purely self destructive – sprang in fact from a deep rooted need to find out how far he could push his body before it gave in. He had spent much of his life challenging his delicate stomach, just as he challenged his arthritic hands and tormented feet and knees. It irritated and depressed him to find his efforts to lead a normal life continually thwarted by his frail physique. Preceding the expedition to Mexico he spent quite some time in Charlestown, near Boston, where Conrad Aiken was living with Mary Augusta Hoover, who was to become the poet's third wife. Boston and its environs suited Edward well, despite Aiken's lethal dry Martinis. These were at least made from drinkable spirit, so were far less destructive than the

4 *Edwardde Pertinez was born in a nursing home in Maida Vale on 1 March 1937.*

rotgut firewater of the Tequila, the Mescal, and even the appalling pulque, all of which Edward imbibed regularly. In Mexico it could well be he denied himself two or three extra years of life through his reckless acceptance of the native drinks and the native cuisine; and seeing it had never agreed with him his fondness for overspiced food was foolhardy to say the least. The native dishes of Mexico were wildly spiced and blazing with Chili, making it impossible to ascertain either the condition or the provenance of the meats which went to their making. Bad fiery food and cheap fiery liquor: the combination could only be disastrous. Staying in the house of the writer Malcolm Lowry in Cuernavacca he suffered a total collapse. His journey back to Charlestown must have been a nightmare. There, he lay prostrate, living on a diet of fresh oysters brought to him daily by the kind hands of Gordon Bassett, a close friend of Aiken. Finally he found enough strength to make the journey back to England. It was a dehydrated, emaciated, almost corpse-like figure who crept into Springfield. He had written one of his illustrated letters to Clover Pritchard (who was now Clover de Pertinez) on the voyage.

To Clover de Pertinez

Cunard White Star
"Scythia"

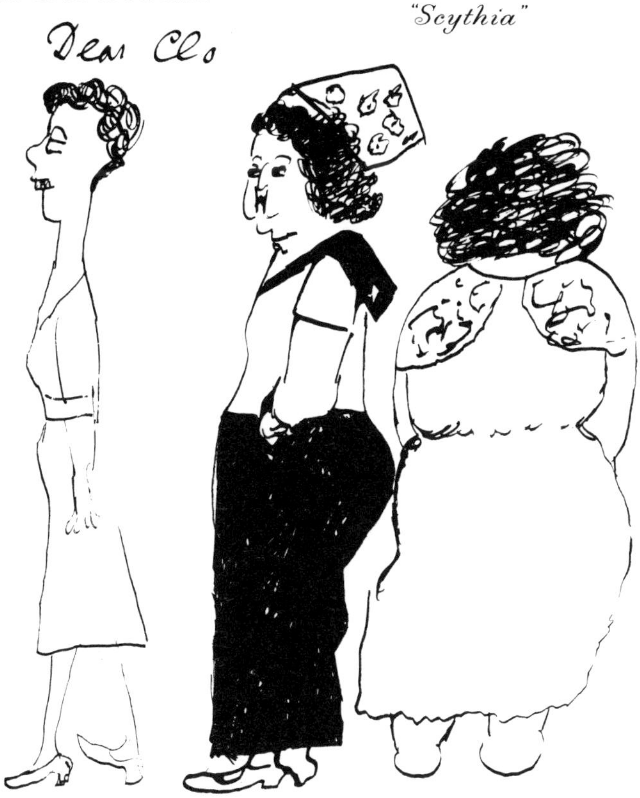

Never in my life have I seen such a collection of "*Sorciere Hysterie (avec sa bouche flétrie) succubes salamandres et scarboucles* letting out hysterical shrieks of demoniac laughter all 2 feet high purple in the face & square as boxes the boat is quite awful vintage 1910 My funeral nitch is two flights of stairs & 20 miles of rabbit warren from les waters & with my feet my dear its quite a calvary when nature calls the food however is good when not turned to gall by a "Get together dinner" when all the *salamandres* get red hot in paper caps somewhat damp with sweat & cry shilly or burst in to *carcajadas* Dantes inferno I say they had a fancy dress dance last night I wish Ide had the strength to go to see what pinnacles of horror had been reached. Thank heaven Im alone in my cabin there would be no room to turn if there was anyone else. 3 or 4 people are supposed to be squeezed in & what that calvary must be like dieu sait! I was very sorry to leave Charlestown & had just discovered a very nice young doctor who specialized in rheumatic complaints & I believe is very good & said what a pity you are going we could do so much for you here unfortunately at 10$ a time so its cheaper to remain stiff at the price I dont think US doctors have quite that interesting mania for *surgery* the English have. My favorite character on the boat is a *jeune fillette de 45 ans* avec *Madame mere* (pic on front page) she has about 10 *toilettes* & appears in a different *robe de style* each evening yesterday was roses & cream Mother a raddled balloon wears a chintz cap with a visor also 900 boy scouts going to a Dutch jamboree such big boys too & should be in long pants There are 2 or 3 elderly "boys" Aged between 40 & 50 *siempre fresco* decked in pocket knives and garters with tassells & felt medals pinned about I cant take my eyes off there must be something wrong its not natural Thank god it has been quite flat so far if it gets rough Ime bed bound as I dont entend to risk my neck up & down 90 stairs with my feet & hands & entend to get home as quickly as poss I cant face 'Towne" Any way you might venture over for a week end if I could arrange it Ime sure it would be a nice rest for you all Have been passing the time reading theatre by S. Maugham quite amusing for ship board a sort of mythical Gladys Cooper Oh says Lady somebody to "Gladys" your father was a doctor wasnt he he often used to come up to the house. Yes says Glad a Vet he used to come up & deliver the bitches there were thousands of them – No Percy W[yndham Lewis]'s in the ships library however bad for the passengers not that they have strength to read theyre quite worn with screaming. Well dearie *mil recuerdos* & *misericordia* which you must lend me. yrs Ed

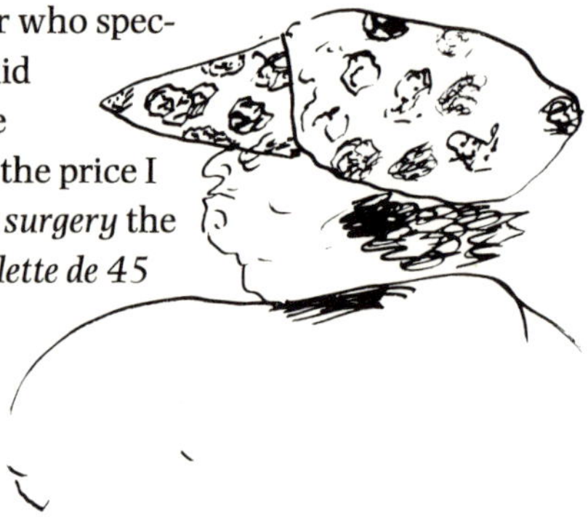

To William Chappell from Springfield, 1937

Well my dear Thank you for yours.
Old Mexico was the cause of my downfall I should never have left Boston Mass which suited me down to the ground not that Mexico isnt lovely if you can stand it. Did you all wear shorts and Dirndls at the Schloss Kempinski?[1] The Duke & Duchess of Kent I saw dressed firmly as human beings nothing will drag off the Duchesses turban when will you be in Edinburgh[2]

1 *I'm afraid we all did. The Schloss Kempinski was in fact the Schloss Kammer, on Attersee in Austria, one of the many homes of Alice Von Hoffmanstal, a beautiful and elegant highly-educated American who was born an Astor. Helpmann and Chappell, who had been on holiday in Dubrovnik, had joined Ashton and Alice Von H in Venice. Ashton was at the time her lover.*

2 *On tour with the Sadler's Wells Ballet Company.*

as we had thought of going there its such a bracing place & I need bracing & Ime sure a nice front room in the LMS Hotel overlooking the Tram stop would be wonderful I think its much more bracing than Glasgow which seems given over to a tepid damp Aunt Bumble came down for a weekend it was very suitable as neither of us could hardly move she had a blister & tottered about with a modish bit of lint sticking out of her beach sandal Have you seen the new thing in the B.B.C *Chay*kovski who I mistook for a new Soviet Russian composer (not yet disgraced) till I turned on Chay & suddenly heard a familiar peice Valse des fleurs so of course Chay was realy Tchai can you tell me *way*? Ay would so much like to see Saratoga not that I will Ive not been to a cinema since landing in England theres such an epidemic of British pics I cant go either that or Bobby Breen who looks like a dwarf Heather Pilkington with a dark wig Miss Ker S & H. Pease[1] arrived yesterday Miss pouring at the nose in a paroxysm of sneezing & holding bottles of hay fever cure so we *at once* went to Hastings Baths which I must say are wonderful looking just like one of those drawings full of tiny figures by Ensor I saw *quelque jolis choses* but considering all things the Varicose vein harvest is very poor *cette année* & today we go to the Daily Mail Beauty contest prize a cardboard suitcase lined pale blue sateen full of unusable nail files & a celuloid hair brush we had a dainty tea of Cadburys cup (coco) chocolate to you & butter fingers in a cloud of wasps I was sorry you couldnt come down my dear as I would like to have seen you but perhaps after your tour we hope to visit La Pertinez the wonderful old retired Manchester Andalucian bailarina in her flamenquisimo corner of High S[2] tomorrow as I am dying to see baby[3] who is getting a very pretty boy now I was driven over to Brighton the other day it being such a nice run no sea air can reach the town owing to a solid string of fried fish shops all along underneath the front so a solid screan of smelling fat rises up screaning the metropole from any nasty fresh air send me a PC on tour I sent you a dainty one from Mexico
yrs E.

To William Chappell from Springfield, 21 December 1937

Dear B.
How are you getting on The cigs are for you & Book token for mother I cant enter a shop without having an attack of Tic douleureuse so cant buy any presents I hope to come up after Christmas to stay at 4 Church [Street] I hope to pay a visit to Wigmore[4] too but shall go to church 1st for if I first went to Wig my dear There would probably be a frightful scene and I should be driven to Portsmouth or the Isle of White I went there on a visit and found Clover established in an ex sea captains pied a terre where he lives with his "Ward"(?) I must say I liked it Ive never seen anywhere so

---

1 *Humphrey Pease was a well-liked drunken 'man about town' whom Barbara married. It was not a success.*
2 *High Salvington in Sussex.*
3 *Edward; Clover's son by Antonio de Pertinez.*
4 *Bumble and Gerald Corcoran's flat in Wigmore Street.*

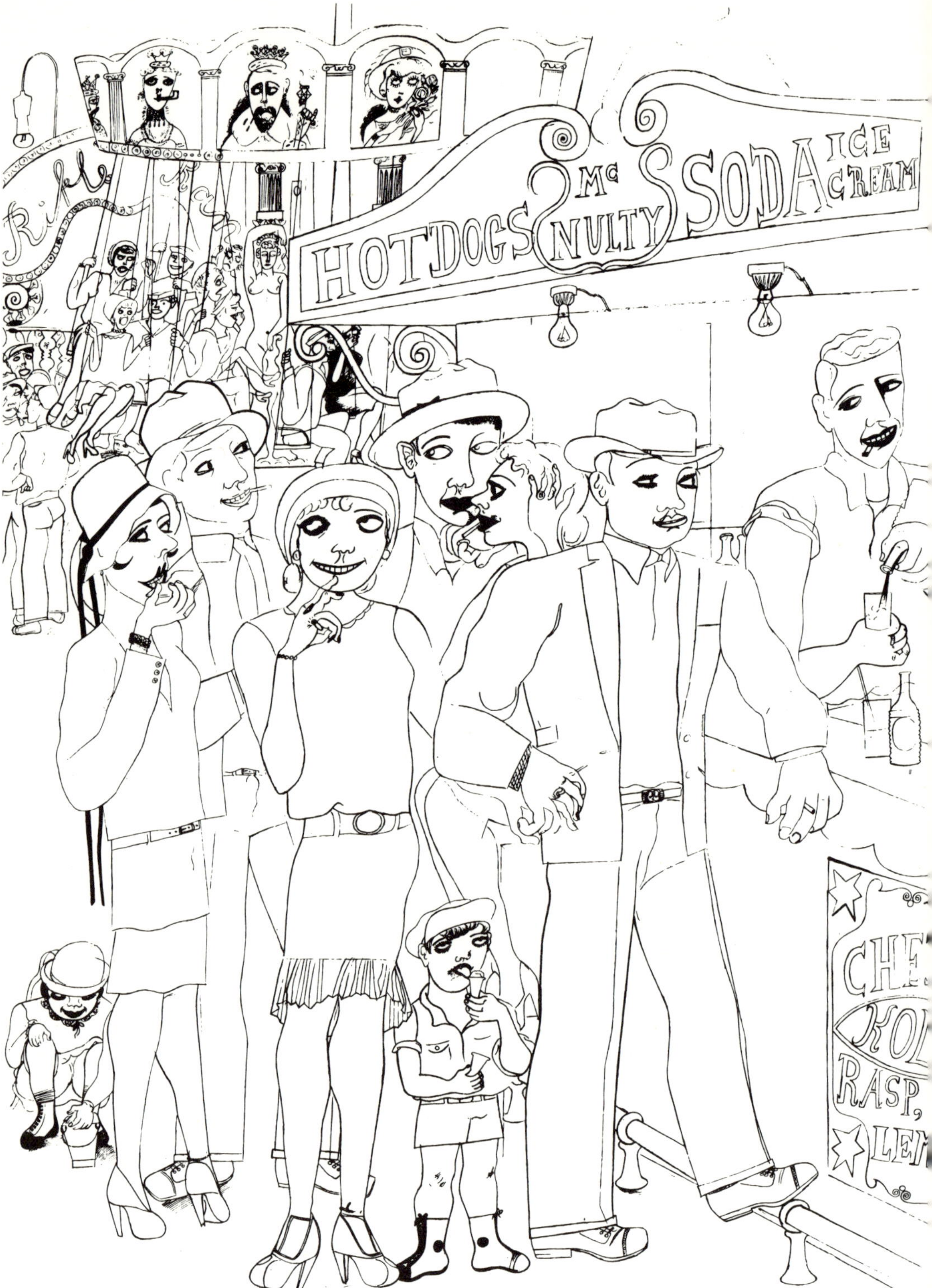
HOT DOGS
Mc NULTY
SODA
ICE CREAM

empty I was horrified about Lilian Baylis[1] I really dont know what will happen without her to keep order Miss Ker-S seems very busy photographing Miss Modern washing her panties in Trex etc what I should like to photograph is daintie ladies in combinations I went to see Carnet de Bal[2] which I thought was a triumph especialy a frightful scene in an abortionists parlor in Marseilles Ive never seen anything so squalid and a frightful virago exactly like Mae Busch[3] Dolin is going to revive *Rhapsody in Blue* next season he and Valaida[4] should make a hit together in a revived version of the Black Bottom in top hats made of ammerican cloth (on points) Ime told Heartsease Helpman is *not* going to fly after all at the Vic[5] Ime bitterly disapointed Well I hope to see you in the New Year Old Moore[6] is very ominous about 1938 so happy new year dearie love and wishes to Dony[7] & your mother

yrs E.

To William Chappell from Springfield, December 1938

Dear B.
Thank you so much for tome which unfortunately I have read so could you change it for "Anabasis" by Saint J. Perse (translated into English by T.S. Eliot) 5/- Faber & Faber and "The Georgiad" by Roy Campbell also 5/- & I believe published by Faber & Faber too if you would change it dearie it seems cruel to waste 10/- – I have been prevented from carrying out my good deeds this merry season by the weather *un vrai temps de Macbeth* here with thick snow frozen into one vast slide. I wanted to go to Hastings but all the trains are 1½ hours late so I dont fancy waiting at the *gare* as for the new fangled buses they have long since given up. I hope I shall see you in the new yr I wish to see *notre grand vedette*[8] in his great role[9] at the Old V[ic] that and G.S. Melvin[10] I consider are the seasons theatrical high lights There was a wonderful photo on the cover of the Radio Times of Nelson Keys in a mob cap and mittens looking exactly like Bumbles old French maid I thought for a moment she had been captured for "In towne to nayte"[11] as what an old French maid *realy* thinks – she thought a good deal when I was last in Wigmore strasse *and* out loud both in Anglitsh *and* French. Well merry seasons wishes from yrs E

from yrs E

1 *Lillian Baylis had just died after setting up the Old Vic and the Sadlers Wells Theatre. She actually started off the roots of the National Theatre, the Royal Ballet and the English National Opera.*

2 *A brilliant French film directed by Duvivier, starring Marie Bell.*

3 *Star in Erich Von Stroheim's* Foolish Wives.

4 *A rather awful singer-dancer of the period.*

5 *As Oberon in* A Midsummer Night's Dream.

6 Old Moore's Almanack, *which Edward read religiously every year. O.M. was right to be Ominous.*

7 *Chappell's sister Honor.*

8 *Robert Helpman.*

9 *Oberon in* A Midsummer Night's Dream *with Vivien Leigh as Titania.*

10 *A wonderful pantomime dame and comedian.*

11 *A popular radio programme introducing 'interesting' people who happened to be 'In town tonight'.*

To William Chappell from Springfield, 1 February 1939

Dear B.

Thank you for Anabasis arrived yesterday Ime sorry about Campbell I wonder if you could get "very foreign affairs" by John Scanlon. I wish you could come down one day and visit the Hastings emporiums I must say they have the most extraordinary collection of objects and furniture I've ever seen thanks to the inhabitants of Hastings being continualy on their last legs I presume they continualy sell off theyre few poor sticks. Mdme Pertinez has been looking at rooms and flats in the purlieus – Hastings fascinates me. We went to look at a Bungalow near Guestling on the way to Hastings my dear! *Jamais jamais* have I seen such squalor the proprietress was a school mistress *défroquée* we think. Every room had about 3 sordid iron Bedsteads in it with outside lavabo and mysterious outhouses and tin cans no garden Ive never seen anything so sinister rather like a bedroom in "real Detective" all it wanted was a touzeld corpse in a blood bath and a few policemen. then we visited an oblong green box on pillars on the side of a hill not a very fortunate day for house hunting. the proprietress of that was a lady gnome doing a bit of gardening with her feet tied up in brown paper dressed in about 10 coats and a Japanese fishermans hat on quite a lady of course no one else would have dared – well I hope to see you soon and visit Bumble at Maddox St. Best wishes from yrs E.

I had some cards from Soph she seems to have enjoyed herself in the states.

The outbreak of the Second World War fully revealed (and accentuated) every one of the contradictions buried in Edward's character. His general reaction to the ghastly situation was epitomised in a letter to Chappell. "Everythings a proper cunt and no mistake." By turns horrified, disgusted or bitterly amused, he let loose a series of broadsides, ranging from a surprisingly Blimpish mixture of nationalistic and patriotic sentiments to attacks on all the events, decisions and people he considered guilty of starting the war. In spite of these outbursts of spleen his innate practicality and his sense of self preservation never really deserted him. Nor did his sense of humour. Throughout his life Edward's inclination to anarchy fought the conformist elements induced by his upbringing. The anarchy he encouraged. To the conformist side of his character he had no wish to give the time of day. None the less it continually made its only semi-dormant presence felt.

Edward wrote to William Chappell from Springfield in August 1939. He had inscribed below the address:

1st *Triumphal* week
Shit

Well my sweet

How are you getting on in these stirring times? Nobody seems to have dared sing Keep the Home Fires burning – except me – Ime singing all the dear old hits – they dont seem to go down very well now Sister Susie sewing shirts for soldiers was a terrible flop the other night also we dont want to lose you BUT WE THINK YOU *OUGHT* TO *GO* Mdm Ker-S couldnt keep away from her *infame reduit* Ive just heard from her she flashes her torch in the Blackout and surprises the strangest things going on. We've got some kiddies here 'Arry, Fred, Sheelah, Vera and Lily. Vera wets the bed we 'ad to buy some draws at Marx & Spencers (before they went up in price) Mother says shes got a weakness. I saw in the Times you were to be accompanied by Constant[1] and Maud Hoare[2] or some name like that on 2 pianos! White pianos I hope one on each side of the stage with 2 standard lamps and some lilac in a golden basket I hope otherwise I shouldnt feel a bit at home Ime waiting for scarlet fever & diptheria to break out among the Refugees. The mothers are getting a bit restive for the dear old Elephant and Castle and feed the Kids on osborne biscuits & potted crab one was offered some *Fresh* vegetables the other day it nearly killed her poor woman she had to be brought round with a Japanese crab meat sandwich and some smiths crisps. Work parties are a cinch such fun making swabs to fill the cracks in the Maginot line & every 2nd person is an air warden. Thank God the theatres are shut for if Drury Lane was open I dread to think what sweet Ivor of old Novello would be thinking up with Mary Ellis as the spirit of Democracy including a real line Maginot real destruction of Warsaw the Derby Day 1914 and the Battle of Bunkers Hill Miss K-S says you are getting 3£ per week why pray as they probably will do enormous business write me a line you will find me here at my post yours Ed

In a letter dated '16th day of the great SHIT' he wrote again to William Chappell from Springfield

Thank you for yours dearie I wrote you Saterday to Cardiff Prince of Wales[3] seeing in the Times among the "French Victories" between the Maginot & Siegfried that the Ballet was starting bravely off accompanied by Constant[4] with a bottle of whiskey hidden under the keyboard. Well dearie "they" are all busy "stopping" Hitler as hard as they can in my opinion they might have allowed him to romp over Poland & little Rumania who are a bunch of gold digging crooks anyway whilst we paid attention to the Empire and built up a huge defence force "He" has got Poland anyway "divvyed" with Uncle Joe Stalin and Brave little turkey after having received 600000000000 £ from the British Treasury as a bribe is now going to pay a visit to Comride Molotoff between you and me & the gate post I wonder how our pinks are feeling Manys the time I used to stay in the best houses in Romilly Ex Church St the trim little soubrette[5] used to bring up the times and the Daily worker for the big boss upstairs I

---

1 *Constant Lambert.*

2 *In fact Hilda Gaunt, almost as striking a name. She was the stalwart rehearsal pianist for the Sadler's Wells Ballet for many years, and saw them into Covent Garden when they became 'Royal'.*

3 *The Prince of Wales Theatre. The Vic–Wells Ballet were on tour without Chappell, who was awaiting call-up.*

4 *Constant Lambert.*

5 *Barbara Ker-Seymer.*

received a mysterious missive from the Ministry of Labour Nat Service dept. They are compiling a register working through expert committees considering the position of artists they sent a form to fill & I filled it saying I suffered from rheumatism and an enlarged SPLEEN *spleen* sweatheart bigger than ever these days and distilling *venom* also I said I was particularly good at water colours! ! ! I have brought up all the Aspirin I could lay hands on "*l'opium des pauvres*" it was referred to in a book I've been reading. Write again yours E.

In the small hours of the night after the official declaration of war the whole of Great Britain had been woken by an obscene howling of sirens: a fanfare surely, heralding the apocalyptic end of a beleagured island, quite obviously unprepared for any attack from an implacable enemy. The beastly sound was not only a false alarm, it was also one of the great anticlimaxes in British history and was closely followed by another. This one was to be much longer, more uneasy and infinitely more lowering to the spirit: the months of the 'phoney' war. Finding himself confined for the duration (apart from occasional sorties on battered and shabby London) to Rye and its environs Edward at once set about making certain that whatever they *– as he always designated the authorities – might be concocting in the way of disruptive* plans *he was not, in any circumstances, prepared to lose touch with his friends; nor be made to leave his home Springfield, sitting firm and foursquare in its lush pastoral surroundings. Situated only a matter of minutes from the invasion coast it offered a continual subject for wonder, as to why the house, and its productive kitchen gardens and orchard were never commandeered. Edward became, at this point, like an agent in charge of an elaborate network of communications. He poured out a stream of letters in all directions. He sent off bags, baskets and tins, full of fresh fruits and vegetables; dispatched books, papers and magazines: and kept each individual in his immediate circle as cognizant as possible of the health, the whereabouts and the states of mind of the others. The complete cycle of the war letters would fill a volume. Even the selection given here presents a detailed and graphic account of how life looked, sounded and felt in the south-eastern corner of a grimly defiant island during a long hard war. At his most enraged and cynical the unfailing liveliness of his irrepressible sense of humour continually surfaces. It is interesting to discover (though he might have disagreed with such an idea) how essentially English he was in his own oblique and original fashion.*

To Pilot Officer Gerald Corcoran from Springfield, 1940

Dear Gerald I was wondering about yr new address. I just mailed a paper off this morning to Harrogate Yorks. Fred has been down somewhere in Sussex he flies to and fro in a bomber. Now Ashton old boy they say[1] lets fly upside down! I dont know what Harrogates like but terrible I imagine full of escapees so its far too full The garden is wonderful now with strawberries & *asperges*. I sent some strawberries to Bumble but Im expecting to

1 *'They' was in fact Peter Townsend.*

hear a mass of creeping *pourriture* has arrived. Bum & I went to see "The Spoilers" Dietrich she really was a sight well worth the price. I sold 2 pictures at Brown & Polsons corn flower Galleries Leicester Sq and have been sent 30£ on account so welcome

yrs Ed

To William Chappell from Springfield, 1 February 1940

Well dearie Im glad you can be seen writing to the notorious Bella Donna who has been trailing about in a sea of frozen slush with a suppurating bunion. A thick *grey mist* as well. You can have no conception of what the "Hay road" is layke. Nowadays when I go to Hastings to do a little shopping I always get to the station at 2 and travel on the 1.30 we have no burst pipes thanks to the central heating but all over the town. whenever I pass the cemetery I find a flood of mutes waiting outside the door or a trail of taxis & blowsy wreathes winding through a grey substance 2 feet deep in places like a melting water ice. Anne has turned into "An Army Wife" (by the author of Ponjola[1]) and has been sharing a house with other wives of officers in Wilts no one knows from day to day what any one else is going to do they are supposed to be going to France nobody knows when nobody knows how many people are sleeping in the house or what time the meals are. Before they are done if you ask me they will find themselves sailing away to protect the Royal Dutch Standard Shell Mex Benzine at Mosul. I feel the war may take place where its least expected. Ime fully expecting the Hastings rep co in "The *Last* of Mrs. Cheyney" to suddenly be blown up with a mine coming in contact with the pier. I should be very nervous. What has become of Gay Mrs. Corcoran of Maddox St. She frightened me last time I saw her she seemed to be tormented in some way and kept saying she never went to bed befor 6 in the morning I never hear from her do you ever see her? "gaiety" does no good to me. I *never* forget. I heard from the little flower of Romilly St[2] who said that everything burst & I should think shes gone away. I would like to see Freds new piece[3] it sounds very good any thing to do with the powers of evil dearie. Ime a great believer in them. I dont think the war is very "popular" do you? I dont care for the future at all. All I can see is crowds rather blueish & very under nourished running about breaking windows and being shot at by a few rather half hearted special constables. The city they say is buying "land" The vicious spiral of inflation sweetheart we shall soon be having Woolworths 100£ & £200 stores instead of 3^D & 6^D Well I hope your musical comedy comes off a success has it a cast yet? This weather must have been death to show business.

Write again yrs E.

---

1 Ponola *was by Cynthia Stockley, a popular and prolific novelist whose books were mostly set in South Africa.*

2 *Barbara Ker-Seymer.*

3 Dante Sonata *at the New Theatre, St Martins Lane.*

To Gunner Chappell W.E. 979498 from Springfield, 1940

Dear B
How are you bearing your cross? and where if I may be so bold as to enquire? We are still here. Camber & down there have been evacuated – all the week enders fled from their caravan block houses with earth closet – but there were some old inhabitants – out they went loseing everything in the way of potatoes & hens all going for no price at all the chickens and arriving in Rye with nowhere to go all poor & no money – so enormous rents were then asked – so I was told – you may imagine it was like asking for sarsaparilla from "Arthurs Seat" They would all prefer to be quietly bombed away among the potatoes & their own poor eggs (at the price they are) but oh dear no. If they go on like this they will have a revolution. Some natty officers came round here & were met by Madame Anne Huntley who said *she* had no intention of going. So they said did she know what "terrible things" would happen to her? if we stayed. However here we are still thank god. I cant cope with anything any more realy. I heard from Gerald at Loughborough camp – Leics – wherever that may be we are realy very quiet a paroxysysm takes place over Dover & we dont hear a word – I never hear the siren anyway – A bomb fell in Hastings I hear – our temporary cooks mother was in Hastings Hospital when a casualty in the last stages of fragmentary wreckage was brought in and gave her such a turn she is mad to come home even with her stitches in.

"Everyone" is at their war work like mad creatures Ime sure they all enjoy it. I believe I sold a picture from Matheison to the Tate and that double pic that was at Zwemmers Ayve not seen the colour of their money yet dear but you know we artistes live by beauty alone The career of Beauty Darling[1] Stefan Lorant, Noel Coward & Madame Tabouis have all gone to the U.SA I see in the Times. do write & let me know if you want anything love E.
Ime awaiting the *End*.! Clover is O.K. baby is learning to ride!!

To Gunner Chappell W.E. 979498 from Springfield, 1940

Well dearie how are you dreeing your weird? In pouring rain & a high S westerly gale. The only thing that ever stops airial activity is a 90 mph gale I find. Corcoran has had 7 days leave and was going to meet Bumble at Bunny Rogers for the weekend. Then I've heard no more but I hope to. Farewell Leicester Square dear I notice in the papers a photo of a large *vacant* lot – The Peroquet and La Leicester Sq cinema looked to me to be a sort of empty shell & very much the worse however. Pride & Prejudice[2] goes gaily on in a whiff of lavender & old fug (from the Leicester Sq tube station when the doors are opened in the morning[3] Where burning Sapho loved & sung burning up Ime waiting to hear Winston Churchill has landed from a

1 *A wonderful turn-of-the-century novel by Dolf Wyllarde, a great favourite of Edward and Chappell.*
2 *A current stage production.*
3 *Used as an air raid shelter as were all the London underground stations (those* deep down).

milk white tank with a casket of Lord Byrons curls from Newstead Abbey & whats next on the menu I wonder. Frederic[1] you remember has been back on leave in a fit of giggles his friend in Rye had all his clothes incinerated by an incendiary and they went to Hastings to buy some more every shop they went into they had dozens of extrordinary things pushed at them to buy before the Purchase Tax. My arse. As for *that* dearie. Ime already in rags & mean to continue in them it scarcely seems to me to matter A woman of no importance featuring Fae Comp & Milton Raspberry[2] (stoll Films) I see darling little Mischief Bergner[3] having disapeared last July to the frozen N with a 200000 £ film unit to make a Briddish brobaganda film has suddenly rushed to Hollywood & wont return to finish the pic. I wonder *why* she wont return? isnt it odd & shes a British subject now too so unless they can arrange to finish the pic in Hollywood they stand to loose quite a lot of dough re mi – youd have thought anyone so patriotic as Bergie would be rushing "home". The Dly Express was a bit sniffy on the subject.[4] Ive taken to combing the papers with a toothcomb I find some very tastey little animals too one very odd little "trouvaille' in the Times was that Mr. Noel Coward had arrived in Yokohama! ! ! old Judah Bergman (Berg[5] to you, got a nice little round sum for being called a tottering old thing of 31 from McAdam of the Dly Exp I see. I must say it was rather insulting Ive since seen a photo in Air Force Blue looking tremendous. And what of our Ballerines! I hope they dont whirl onto a land mine & end up in a double transformation on a windswept East Coast Fenn somewhere in Lincolnshire.[6] Come on get back into my Lincoln I know exactly what your thinkoln as Vaughan de Leath sang in happier days when all the trees on Clapham Common were green lad. I suppose nothing will move Dame Blair & mother from Gt Ormond St But the whole house falling in the Street. How are you getting on comparing Rags of Rodier under the shadow of the Druidic altars or over tea & doughnuts in Ensa canteen? It must be very difficult to keep one thought together I see a squawk over no coal – they say theres plenty at the pits & everyone is mad for it & they are putting off thousands of miners but they cant get transport & suggest army trucks should be used. You should see the army trucks here my dear. Not *one step* do they ever walk – no wonder theres no transport! Its a miracle to me where all the petrol comes from I should think they wash in it. Its a pity you cant come & be a gunner somewhere down here there are enough in all conscience. Well dearie drop us a line yrs. E.

1 *Frederick had become part of the domestic staff at Springfield as a teenager. He remained with them returning after the war, and nursed both Dah and Ma Burra through to their deaths.*

2 *Fay Compton and Milton Rosmer (an actor of unusual heaviness).*

3 *Elisabeth Bergner, a whimsical wistful Viennese–German–Jewish movie star and actress, probably the most unsuitable Rosalind in* As You Like It *ever seen. She was the wife of the film director Paul Czinner and had a vast success in England.*

4 *How beastly of them!*

5 *'Kid' Berg, a champion boxer, was a friend of Chappell and Ashton, who met up with him when he was courting Bumty Pain, one of the Cochran Young Ladies in the cabaret revue at the Trocadero in which Chappell and Ashton appeared.*

6 *They very nearly ended up getting caught by the German invasion of Holland.*

To Gunner Chappell W.E. 979498 from Springfield, 5 September 1940

Well dearie Nous avons *la grande scéne de Phedre* followed by excerpts from "The dumb torturer of Barnstaple" at 8.30 onwards non stop till 8.30 the next day. about 2–3 weeks ago bombs fell right on ye antiente towne flattening that nice pavilion with a bow window next to Bensons[1] house which was cracked Ye myrmayde recieved *quelque chose* on the roof that sent off all the tiles etc also 2 small houses vanished into dust to dust down on the road to Hastings. Mrs. Huntley was down picking about in the ruins soon after befor that there had been a special *degringolade* on the pylons on the marsh you remember and now every day & all day mumsie is getting a shade nervous. I told her she should be "grim & gay" thats what old Churchill said on the radio. Me, dearie *Ayme* very grim & gay. The night befor last there was a terrific thump about 11.30 that stirred them up dearie – such a rushing up and down stairs I asked Mama "I wondered why the French *gave in?*" She was rather cross. Only my "gaiety" of course it sometimes goes a bit too far. Such weather! I realy feel quite dry and warm for a change and the beautiful nights *so* full of starlight and searchlight mercifully there are no aunty aircraft guns round here all we have are air battles overhead with machine gunning swooping roaring & carrying on. You must write to me when you get back to Brighton & tell me when your off and on & I might yet come over for a weekend. London sounds deadly. I *particularly* dislike sitting in shelters they drive me crazy the boredom is so awful and interminable I remain firmly *au lit* impossible to go to Astings my dear the last time I went off the sireens went Madame & I spent three quarters of an hour in a grocers cellar missing my bus & no bombs

yrs Ed.

To Gunner Chappell W.E. 979498 from Springfield, 1940

Well dearie – I got your little note on Sat evening about 7.30 – quite by mistake as we have no second post now unless someone fetches the letters – no one ever does of course – so in the natural course of circumstances it wouldnt have got here till Monday morning. I am still plucking up courage to come as I see myself sitting for hours in the train with the line blocked as it often is and being forced to spend a night in Brighton & missing you I should become *Mad* if that happened. Do you ever get any leave? if so you might come & spend it here but I expect you go and visit Mama who I hope is alright as for Honor shortly Dame Honor O.B.E. doyenne of chorus girls & mother grand cross of equity! twice I've bought the Daily Mail and every time I see columns about Blair (who supports her widowed mother). Do give me Ashtonovas address – underneath Drakes Drum Mavavargavissey *South* Cornouailles as possible Ime sure we have been very quiet the last day or two but for a vast hord pouring over yesterday morning & afternoon the nights are very restful but for an occasional rumbling droaner over-

1 *The author E.F. Benson.*

head. In the direction of the outskirts of 'Taowne" I've noticed some of the most picturesque activities such as twinkles in the sky and mysterious flashs etc the usual of course. There was a very dainty picture in yesterdays Dly Chronicle of people queuing up for some ghastly underground den in East London. They all looked like *death* dearie and Tiggety Boo to Bebe Daniels – The cold seems to me intense the last 2 or 3 days I hope you wont freeze too much if you ever get to Egypt perhaps it will save you frost bite on the Brighton Metropole Blockhaus Beach that in a swathed gas proof hat sounds deadly I rather like being up at night in fact if I didnt paint I should prefer to be up all night & sleep all day. the effects at night especially at moonrise & set are so wonderful. Why isnt Ernest Hemingway here typewriting a leftist play in Claridges called The Last Days of Madrid I mean London. London is much "hotter" than Madrid I feel they didnt do too much damage there. I hear they had to evacuate Claridges (from Sheila Hennessey)[1] owing to unexplodids you can imagine just 2 or 3 days ago I saw in the Times the Queen of Holland had returned there "after a few days absence"! Hennessey was entertained by friends at the Dorchester & says she *never* saw such sights. dossing down for a lovely night in the lounge at 10 guineas an armchair H[ennessey] is rather sour as she escaped from Bordeaux *en bateau* the family are very much the worse for wear it seems to me. Its a miracle Fleet St hasnt been hit such a pity I think but I suppose the devil protects his own. What about little lunch time Ballet bravely struggling on. Can you imagine how alarming Mim must be. One of Londons most popular little theatres has been gutted so I saw I wonder which. I fully expected there would be a loud report and when the smoke cleared Helpman (black from head to foot) would be found in the middle of an imitation of Mrs. Patrick Campbell in "The Molly Bawn" without George Alexander but even he couldnt stand it Ime not surprised I must say. I dont dare go away I feel there will be an invasion whilst Ime away and I shall never find anybody again! or the house will be reduced to Ashes yrs E & write again & tell me Ashtonovas address if you know that is.

To Gunner Chappell W.E. 979498 from Springfield, October 1940

Dear B.

How are you getting on I dont know how long it is since I wrote but there have been two murders and various machine gunnings from the air since I dont know if I told you we live in an ambiance de crime the last one pas/s/ionel/le as the garage proprietors wife stabbed him in a fit of jealousy. the other was Christmas night. the children gathered round the tree got *so-o* rough one was kicked to death & howid police (military) shut all the childrens parties up tight. I have been doleing out change and $2\frac{1}{2}^{D}$ Tiffin at a canteen of unexampled squalor cups washed up in a thick *velouté* sauce I often think of taking a cupful home for braiseing Clara Carrot. Ime glad Madame Celiméne Helpman has tossed up a fine part[2] for herself with

---

1 *Sheila Hennessy and her sister were daughters of the Cognac family and close friends of the Burras.*

2 *In Webster's* The White Devil.

a few resounding speeches she does as only her inimitable self can do did you get a book with a play by Middleton was it I sent you called the Changeling (I believe) with a villain in it called De Flores it would be lovely for Celiméne.

Winston has come back to a bad egg *et comment* – if you ask me no wonder he stayed away so long I foresee a terrible row "suppressed' as much as possible, over Malaya. freezing hard here, I've entirely ceased to care or bother about anything now. so restful I find. if I think Ive got enough cigarettes & sausages 35 per cent meat 999 per cent Elizabeth Ardens under arm paste for 3 days ahead Ime fine. I do hope I shant meet any more machine guns. Teddy Till[1] has just had nice time to arrive safely in Singapore!

From your old pal.

E.

You should see the regiment we have here Rochdale & Tinned Salmon have done their worst poor thing[s]

To Gunner Chappell W.E. 979498 from Springfield, 15 October 1940

Well dearie what a whirl of Messershmidt this evening they love it a little cloudy. about a week ago 2 houses in the council housing estate were reduced to ruins & the backs of Prospect Terrace a regular prospect I was at the top of the hill and was reduced to crouching in the hedge – the lorry drivers fled like autumn leaves (falling early *this* year) & were all in hedges & ditches letting out a stream of fuck sod etc etc Its a sort of British Ave Maria each sod a pearl each fuck a prayer to twist a bugger by absence wrung Where will it all end may I be so bold as to enquire? All the theatrical world is at Blackpool I read in Charles Graves column so-o gai dearie Hanging their fucking washing on the Blackpool front and a do hope a whacking whistling double distilled Vitriol 1000 ton Molotov bread basket hits them fair & square Thats how I feel charitable & full of mothers milk turned to Eiffel tower lemonade & citric acid burns to the bone acts like a charm I hope this reaches you by Christmas tayde Post early for the near east they say. Shucks!!

yrs Ed.

Heard from Ashtonova this morning going a 4 weeks ENSA tour to brutalize the troops.

To Gunner Chappell W.E. 979498 from Springfield, 23 October 1940

Well dearie I presume you are dragging your cross up and down Calvary Lark Hill. I was wondering what had happened to you so I wrote to Brighton in the hopes theyd forward. I cant imagine what Lark H must be like at least having crossed the plain in a blinding rain storm on one occasion I can well imagine. Perhaps you will have Ashtonova Crummles et ses

1 *Teddy Till was a friend of Bumble and Bertie Dawson, and so a friend of Edward. He was taken prisoner.*

Barnstormers down upon you[1] The *Spectre* and Job I should suggest & my new production "Nervous Indigestion" music by Herman Finck arranged Respighi. what about the purchase tax? 3^{D} extra on a stick of Shevallo my barber says with a sniff.

The little sweet chewing gum cashew and Dly Chronicle fruit shop has received an oil incendiary in her back parlour doing some damage the front shop looks lovely of course also a toy shop next door got ditto on the back I saw figures in tin hats passing in & out bringing heaps of blackish rubble and sodden copies of Tiger Tim Mrs. Hippo & Our little Dots annual etc "The High" was machine gunned too they say everyone creeping along on all fours as for Lydd that whats known as bombing troup concentrations close to Dungeness. the Spire of the church looks just as usual from a distance but a closer view tells a different tale. Today there has been such thick cloud and fog there has been scarcely any activity not that Ime not rather nervous of thick clouds as things suddenly appear "Out of the Fog" (not Nazimova[2]). I sympathise with your mother as it is terrible to have to leave all your things however decayed books etc. as for *money* dearie there wont be any very soon. Mrs. Cohen will be appearing in a priceless necklace of potatoes having changed her emeralds for a bunch of pigeons eye radishes & a *lavaliere* of swedes. Let them eat cake. Bumble has been swept away like an autumn leaf and finally has shared a basement in St. James Sqr or St. James place with some woman from Paquin. Sooner death than Aberystwyth.[3] Little Miss K[er] S[eymer] is of course as snug as any thing always on the right side that girl isnt it wonderful. The 35's are to register I see Fancy that If they take me they can give me Free Medical treatment HA HA Father flew in a fuss and got a certificate from the doctor & what it *says* my dear! *C'est une vrai peste! un cholera promenant* and locomotor a taxi and call a taxi with an *arrier gout* of syphilis and leproserie. Where shall we end dear? We know the street do we not? Ime so sick of it. Mrs. Huntley has been very busy of late very dutiful she is until death so to speak allways at the work House all night ARP and the canteen where she listens to tall stories from the Irish Fusiliers and dispenses dough nuts bars of aero milk when they can get them and cups of tea *À toute heure*. Everybody got so sour over Gracie Fields getting out with her dough. Why? A scape goat I say make a squawk over Gracie whilst some bonny little tractations are in progress in her *shade*. If anybody earned her money by the sweat of her stomach ulcers it was surely her she's entitled to all she can get away with I say. What mysterious errands do they send dear Noel off on? Well dearie you can always come to deaths head corner if you want some where to lay your head and the house is still standing or we havent been driven away. Not if *I* can help it my dear tooth and nail to the soil I am now look at the price of vegetables and fruit Oh everythings a proper

1 *The Ballet specially asked that the tour should include the Larkhill Garrison Theatre so they could see Chappell.*

2 *Famous silent movie actress;* Out of the Fog *was a silent film in which Nazimova starred.*

3 *Where Gerald Corcoran was now posted.*

cunt and no mistake Well I will say *au revoir* tho I suppose I shouldnt "Chatter French" or we shall soon be in the Isle of Man from your old pal E.

To Gerald Corcoran from Springfield, 1940

Dear Gerald Did you mention choc if so here is a little travelling cutex set so that I can spread my nails with chocolate & prevent biteing. The weather is beyond anything thick snow & ghastly I went to see Billy a week ago I got a lift we had a nice little double Hooch-gin they said – & a dainty lunch at the Cafe Blue very good Old Compton St curri de Horse. We are very quiet here now only Trench mouth to worry over cups are now washed in disinfectant & old tea wash & leaves. if you could *see* the "washing up"! ! La La! but I suppose every coffee stall & cafe is the same & worse. Billy was scarlet in the face & swollen from the weather on the plain and with feet like burned corn beef hash full of fissures & cracks I recommended Glycerine substitute from Boots it is wonderful. I had a cousin went down on the Barham his poor wife knew all about it for months & wasnt allowed to say so everyone had been wondering why she was so quiet. I suppose theyl all go every one of my male relations, near ones, are in the navy Was Rosa Lewis hotel blitzed as I seem to remember a *debacle* in Jermyn Street. The RAF have been warned against Hooch I see in the Dly Mail do be careful it brings on a pricking at the extremities they said blindness paralysis and I dont know what all quite like the Bloody 30th Ward in the Roaring 20's Capone and all   Much love Ed

To Gunner Chappell W.E. 979498 from Springfield, 1942

How are you freezing dear? I enjoyed our little lunch at the Café Blew it was lovely to see you & Ive been meaning to write for weeks. It seems rather difficult to get spirits in taowne. Rum and tonic I find very good a double Rum & ½ a Baby tonic – nothing here we are very quiet I had lunch at the Café Blew on Monday it was horrible but good enough for me – pure grey mare and tough. What about the terror of hells half mile who decapitates tarts with sardine tins turning out to be an R.A.F. boy? My target for to night. I've been listening in to U.S.A. short waves a bellowing news item followed by "Remember pearl harbor" and the Chamber music society of Lower basin street – Dr. Hoagy wogy Pipplestein will now play "plain filth" clatter clatter bang bang bang and a new item for our South America listeners followed by *Remember* perl Harbor in swing time by the Bobcats & new yorks loveliest organist its fascinating on the short band between 19 & 20 in the afternoons. Theres a new Firth Shepheard Revue in the offing I see are you doing anything for it drop us a line how are your feet   from yours Ed.

To Gunner Chappell W.E. 979498 from Springfield, 19 November 1940

I hope you got 2 packs Craven A I sent. plenty here if you want more Drury Lane I saw was hit a picture of Sir Seymour Hicks[1] pointing to a hole I

1 *A star light comedy actor of the thirties.*

should be sorry if it was destroyed all the biscuit box horrors & Nell Gwyn apartments[1] will be left unscathed. I believe "Miss Constance Lambert & 26 danseuses"[2] are at the Opera House Manchester *Monday* yours arrived this morning. Poor Express dearie its a little hysterical & could do with a bromide. The Times is the only one that doesnt keep up a piercing shriek all the time. As far as I can see Russia U.S.A. & Japan are going to do very nicely out of gay-guere "pickings" dear on all sides "colonys" for last years model destroyers & tanks. Indo China & Baltic provinces & Comride Molytoff Ime sure has picked up a few fresh bargains. In the way of Oil & India. The suckers (us & the Germans) are going to be left stewing in our own juice. My only hope is immigration to the U.S.A. However I dont suppose Peons & untouchables such as us would be permitted to land thats reserved for the Kordas Mdme Tabouis H.G. Wells & Noel Coward who I now see has reached "Sydneay" & after returning to the U.S.A. will be at the governments service in the spring & what may have happened by then poor thing. Who can tell. Buns & strong tea are your diet I suppose do you want any chocolate I notice quite a lot here abouts wonderful shopping in Hastings everything to yourself God knows what will happen to these places I dont see whos to pay for upkeep such as it is the place is like a corpse. Refugees, dear. Ive heard no more – Here is a paradise of quiet to some places tho its supposed to be a death trap & dead mans gulch. Well I hope your not taken off by a lung complaint! yrs Ed

To Flt/Lt Gerald Corcoran from Springfield, 1940

Dear Gerald Ive been meaning to write & meaning to write. There was a bit of a *degringolade* the day before yesterday evening which made the old home shiver like an ague *Spring* dear & Etons full of spots as Byng[3] remarked My back is racked with rheumatism and I have been unable to get a shoe on the right foot as the bunion joint has been suffering from a composite mixture of old broken chilblain & *gout* poor mans gout old dear dont mistake me I had an old time chat at the firewater Inn (Bergamot[4]) with Fred Billy & Mrs Pease a witches sabbath as you might say we had lunch at a "little restaurant" called Sava not bad very cheap too & a bottle of Lachrima christi if you please lacrima perhaps more raisin than christi F of course managed to get a steak Chevaline he asked for but they swore it was purest beef sheer black market Ime sure F looks ever so well & fat so does B who is dressing Firth Shephe[a]rds new show[5] with Dorothy Dixon [Dickson] Leslie Henson etc the old stagers are beginning to show signs of wear and tear under *the strain* says B & everyone is always blind drunk. how I cant think what on? I may say we had some rum at Bergamots which was Fire pure & simple pure spirit with 1[D] worth of rum essence I

1 *In Sloane Avenue, Chelsea.*

2 *Actually announced as such in the local press.*

3 *Douglas Byng.*

4 *Berlemonts, a French Pub.*

5 *A revue called* Fine and Dandy *at the Saville Theatre (now a cinema) in Shaftesbury Avenue.*

only wish I had a private bottle but not very good for our ulcers pal. What next I wonder a fine fit of staggers with hysterics thrown in we shall be in for this summer I foresee the whole set up stinks. Fred is at Drem E. Lothian quite near Edinburgh they were busily employed blue in the face sweeping the run ways clear of snow in this hard winter and raids plenty of them he says perfect weather of course & it seems to me Ive never stopped hearing a continual engine running these last 2 days. Ive been sending a few old world mags.

from yrs Ed

To Gunner Chappell W.E. 979498 from Springfield, December 1940

Thank you for yours I had a lift to London last Wednesday I may say if they have many more such attacks there will be *trés peu* left. I went up Audley St to get to Selfridges (semi gutted) & realy every window & most of the shops blown in & as for Leicester Square! Just one mass of ruins. Lightening strikes twice alright on Burtons Piccadilly a cavity in the road an elves grotto on the sight of Burton Jermyn St in a fearful state and that arcade between Picc & Jermyn Street looked like Old San Francisco without Jeanette Mcdonald. Bunny[1] I hear is now a posh officer I can imagine the toilette jolly spruce. Wogan[2] has gone off with Hastings[3] I hear not that I didn't know so I suppose that upsets poor B[arbara] as well as everything else if you get leave let me know & we'll have a nice private little lunch & talk at somewhere unfashionable where theres no interruptions. Among other ruins I arrived at a sort of lunar landscape down Berwick St at that peculiar sort of square or open space an even wider open space now Im afraid Goodness knows what will happen They say that quite a lot of shipping has been bombed & sunk I notice very little has been said on that subject but I think of it quite a lot from yrs Ed.

To Beatrice (Bumble) Corcoran from Springfield, 1941

Dearest Bum I sent 5 onions sewn up like an operation so may busy fingers that steal them rot away. Have you gone about the Horowitz–Toscanini you might let me know & if they havent it Ill order it here and it will come in time I got a spectator & New Statesman in which poor dear Clive Bell is mystified by what "*Burra*" is? something very odd & *queer* dear Mexican Church bravely bought!?[4] remarkable but flanked by 2 insipid *guaches* – guaches my arse – strangely enough signed by the same artist *Burra* – a pseudonym for Percy Wyndham Lewis I believe he thinks it is. John Piper says worth buying for their technique alone & rich & rare imagination so I got plenty to interest me in the Nation & Spectator Let me know about the records will you? And I hope the legumes arent tampered with. theres a mysterious little exhib opening at the Leicester on the 18th I

1 Neil (Bunny) Roger.
2 Wogan Phillips.
3 Christina Hastings, ex-wife of the Earl of Huntingdon and daughter of the Marchesa Casati.
4 By the Tate Gallery.

think Paul N[ash] has been trying to make me exhibit. There were two paintings "left over" from C.E.M.A.[1] waiting to be retrieved by me so I told him to fetch them. Guaches I suppose. What is guache? He acts so terribly guache. No Savure-vivey No TON! as Mary Boland[2] would say yrs Ed.

To Beatrice (Bumble) Corcoran, 1941

Dearest B. Dont "Fret" about margerine dearie we arent badly off for fat Ive noticed from my forays *aux cuisine* the cook was away for a week-end & there seemed to me to be a good quantity. However any you *have* is always welcome. I cant imagine what is going to happen can you I go on merrily from week to week & if I think I have what I consider a nice restful week ahead with plenty of coffee & cigarettes ime quite contented we seem suspended in a sort of vacuum. yrs Ed.

To Fl/Lt Gerald Corcoran from Springfield

Dear Gerald
Thank you for your letter I soon new it was the Cafe de P[aris][3] the paper as good as said so they did all they could save uttering the hideous *mot* for a while I thought it was the Anglais. Poor Mrs Chappell (*mére*)[4] I wonder if I told you was suddenly buried in a bookcase and a mass of lath & plaster and half her daughters[5] enchanting little metroland home in Amersham taken to hospital black and blue & suffering from schock & cuts. I heard from her today her letter my dear very nearly killed me an "Emergency Hospital" its called in a ward with 40 people and a lot of children all screaming & an epileptic Jewess who shrieks "Mummie Mummie" at intervals. How I long for privacy and a bath says Mrs. C. Billy got leave to pay her a visit of course he was very upset and spent the night with little Mrs. Scott[6] who has gathered round her an unparalelled collection of monsters of Mayfayre B says really frightening. she is burning the candle at both ends with a heart thats blue & painting the town red etc such springlike weather chicks! I can see we are going to have a very jolly summer. I hope the potatoe harvest is good I wonder what that other dance hall was that got blown up it looked like Streatham or somewhere out there I gather from round about sources that they have been having quite a time in London Mrs. C's daughter & grandson fled at once to the Lake district so poor Mrs. C is alone among the epileptics & squalling children yrs Ed

To Beatrice (Bumble) Corcoran from Springfield, 1941

Dear Bum
I'm getting a little worried over the state of the vegetable basket – it seems

1 *An exhibition organised by the Council for the Encouragement of Music and the Arts.*
2 *An American stage and movie actress.*
3 *It had been bombed.*
4 *As opposed to 'fils'. A decent distinction.*
5 *Chappell's half sister Hermina Black, daughter of Mrs Chappell (*mère's*) first marriage.*
6 *Chappell's sister.*

to be getting a shade *fripé* I hope you got 2 cauliflowers looking like a *poitrine* I had to tie them round with string as the top of the *panier fleuri* was getting like a thicket or Madame Colettes wig Ime hoping there will be good fruit there seems to be a lot of apple & pear blossom & a great deal of strawberry blossom *Asperges* Im afraid are not being so good *we* get plenty but Ime sure I wont be given any to send you. Many thanks for the marge which arrived steady as a rock. Ill send Barbey D'A[urevilly] & Bob et Bobette presently.

The garden is looking *Exquis* I must say

Much love from

Ed.

To Beatrice (Bumble) Corcoran from Springfield, 21 October 1941

Ime sorry not to have written but I couldnt I felt too ill my anaemic attack transformed itself into jaundice its all to do one with the other the winter & no heating dont improve it dearie I've got a catafalque upstairs I manage to drag myself to & a fire of a few poor sticks We dont dare have central heating You know what it can be like later As far as I can gather the Ban[1] has been lifted and visitors may "enter" but not "settle" I ask you! Settle on my arse Mumsie is also having a jaundice bout in a nursing home in Birmingham you can imagine Thank God we have good fish here which I have poached & a 2 minute egg & Scotch porridge oats now & again Ive had such nausea Lord Woolpots tastey dishes have fallen very flat I prefer *dry* biscuits yrs Ed

Your letter just arrived I havent done anything about those bloody pictures they sicken me. Yes do come down I cant do anything & feel worn out & exhausted You could get me a tube of charcoal grey or pan from L[echertier] Barbe. A bomber was brought down this afternoon nr. Winchelsea I believe I heard ac ac I looked out to see if our private gun was going off but I saw a vast mushroom of smoke rising up.

To Beatrice (Bumble) Corcoran from Springfield, 1942

You might send those two tins back if you fancy some currants & raspberries Ime going to send some raspberries on Mon if they havent all gone but there looked to me to be masses Billy has a piece[2] in Penguin New Writing No. 13 April June its realy very good he's getting quite a style & not "common"[3] realy very good. Meanwhile the wheels of the OGPU[4] are grinding him to red pottage with idiot officers & 35 mile route marches etc toughening process they call it one lot got into such a state the medical officer raised a fearful stink & said if it wasnt stopped they all be ruined. The new cook is very good completely flat feet & stone deaf but not *muet* nor

1 *On visitors who were not residents.*

2 *Entitled rather pretentiously 'The Sky makes me hate it.'*

3 *Did he expect it to be? I've always wondered.*

4 *Anti-tank OCTU (Officer Cadets Training Unit) at Ilkley, Yorkshire, and not in fact the Soviet counter-espionage group.*

proud she's a great one for economies & substitutes & creamola & such like terrible common things I can see she *enjoys* cooking as long as she has anything to cook Im beginning to wonder with secret sessions & shipping etc *nous approchons les temps d'apocalyps*

yrs Ed

To Cadet Chappell W.E. 979498 from Springfield, 18 July 1942

Dearest B Let me know when you come to London I think a 5/- lunch at the Charing X station hotel would be a good place to be alone at no one

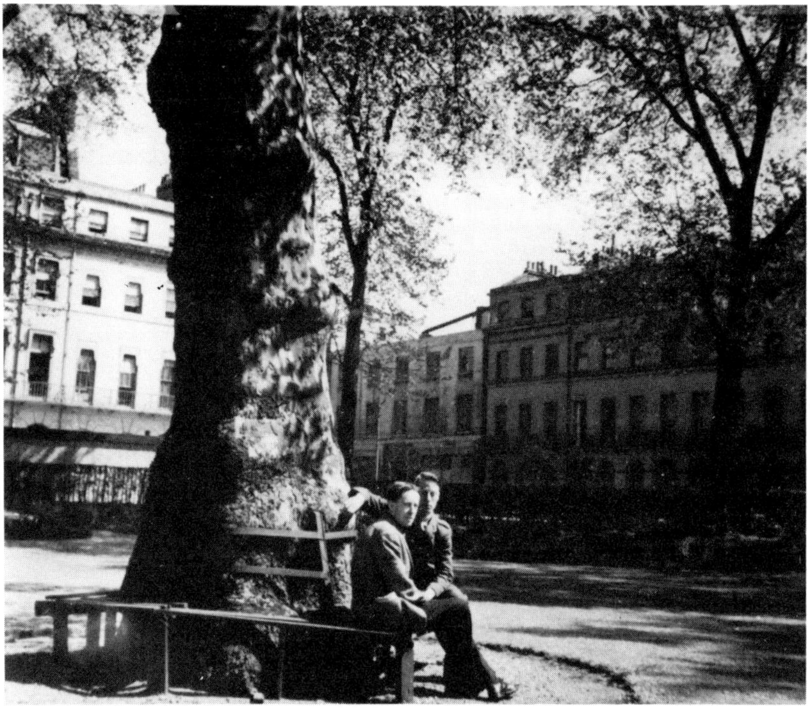

Burra and Chappell in Fitzroy Square. Photo by Ker-Seymer.

thinks of going *there*. I cant speak with more than 5 people except to bellow dreary nonsense. Small talk is getting so "teeny" I cant go on or take the trouble I used to There are rumors round here of Americans taking over evacuating Rye old people & kiddies etc etc There was one evacuation years ago[1] they all rushed off & found themselves in Dutch in Sumerset dossing down in a ploughed field There was a positive rush back to death or dishonour positively everythings been dishonerd by this time above the age of 5 before theyre rather *small* The Americans have turned out some old lady friends of Mothers they lived near Avonmouth I believe they are quite the boys for turning out the poor white trash so I hope we manage to remain hung up on our G. Strings especially with the garden produce for I feel that nice fresh dandelions & last seasons pots will be very handy as the

1 *Actually 1939–40.*

days draw in Gerald seems to be hating Harrogate I believe he was pretty well dug in at Scarborough Well dear write again I like to hear the newest horror And we all seem to be approaching a crisis if you ask old Burra Old Moore for 1943 is on sale I notice. yrs E.
The toughening process my arse. How is your mama and what is her address.

To Beatrice (Bumble) Corcoran from Springfield, 1942

Dear B Thank you for 2 pans of grey – arrived safely Mr. Minsky in the Listener is a regular sick. He tells me far more about what I've been copying than I do myself Crivelli & Ucello dearie Pierre Roy Berard I've seen about 1 Pierr Roy and another was an ad in Harpers. Ay should have thought a vague spirit of Magnasco was more to the pernt. As for the spanish civil *war*! ! ! My arse I never look *back* – Any *Riots* that may be hanging on the walls of the Redfern Gallery refer to the *future* "prophetic" dearie of the results of after war planning they even dragged Guernica in. And now children lets all sit down over a steaming cup of gall and have a lovely ideological conference over nobodys Darlan whilst the Germans settle themselves nicely in Tunis. I cant rouse myself Ide like to come up before Christmas I must say and austerity pudding you may pour a spoonful of egg powder diluted in Old Mr. Battersea Back Bedroom Bourbon over the pudding and it will burn away leaving no trace except a nasty taste. The curate on Sunday at early service Ime told took refuge in the arms of Mother church underneath the altar as the town was shot up (no bomb) I think 2 people killed and others hit and injured – I should like to see what Clive Bell tolls about the show if he tolls at all that should be very amusing. The weather is lovely and muggy & long may it remain so   yrs Ed.

To Beatrice (Bumble) Corcoran from Springfield, 1942

Dear Bum I realy am much better and am quite a normal colour. Where was I born? I was "found" in multi colored rags banging a tambourine on the steps of the Vatican my father a toreador & my mother a portuguese Duchess – My daddies a midget whats yours. I heard from Billy who said every one "took him aside" & then said "You know Ime very *fond* of —" then followed a stream of gall & wormwood Ashtonova however just burst out without the "fond" in to a stream of reproaches & abuse & then retired to Catterick where he writes insulting letters. Relations between A & Help very strained All the old theatricals going on in a terrifying way as if there was no *gué guerre fraiche et joyeuse* at all. Very quiet round here and I must get you some onions did you do anything nice with the nuts. The house has been very cold I may say but I do have a few sticks smouldering in my *Tour d'ivoire*

yrs Ed.

To Squadron/Ldr Gerald Corcoran from Springfield, 29 April 1942

Dear Gerald Biscuits and crunch fell like manna on stony ground Something very different fell on Hastings the other day I havent been to see but I was told one fell on George St where I believe one of my favourite shops full of old chairs cracked pots & Nelsons sevenpenny novels was. Id like to see if it *is*. As for Bath dear! – an old friend of ours was removed to a hospital having been buried in ruins 5 hours with broken ribs and her sister has entirely vanished away like the arabs. The Vic–W[ells] Ballet arrived just as the fun began and never got away from the station and Constant and the stage manager were made to dig about in the ruins & put out fires – no mention of Bobbie. He ought to have appeared out of a blazing pump room dressed in red spangles & a peeked devils cap. Ime waiting for dear old Oxford and ye antique spires to get it in the neck. Thank you so much for the goodies. It was very kind of you.

Yrs Ed.

To Cadet Chappell W.E. 979498 from Springfield, 1942

Dearest B. I am much better and a normal colour not that Ive been out but I may say *Automne triste et monotone* has been pouring with rain. Everyone in a teeny weeny little world is getting too much stuck together thats what it is. all those faces always watching never missing a thing in an unreal little world to[o]. Im sorry about Ashtonova but as far as I can gather he brought it on himself by enlisting so he put the noose round his neck alright and its not so easy to slip it off. Im sure its driving him crazy and that awful hanging in mid air with every leave an "Embarkation" leave. however it seems to end at Catterick O.K. I suppose the gall is all for Veuve Joyeuse Helpman for having managed to escape everything Anyway Im very glad.

Ive just received this letter – "Dear Mr. Burra Mr Lane[1] would like me to confirm to you the terms arranged with Sir Kenneth Clark (who Ive never met) for the inclusion of a book devoted to your work in our Mdrn Pntrs series for which you will receive a fee of £100 (very good I must say) I think Sir K will *have told you*!? how extremely pleased Mr. Lane is that you have agreed to *his having one of your paintings for his collection*" (Ive never agreed to anything and its the first Ive heard of it)

What do you think of that Funny H A H A or funny peculiar Theres quite a rush on yrs truly as a hedge against inflation He wants his 100£'s worth. Dont they all. I have been talked and talked into a show at the Redfern. they frame pics & if sold I pay frames & they take 25 per cent. The whole thing makes me quite ill. Gall. I may say I cant help laughing to myself. Why the discovery its rather late what do you do and where do you go when youre through with Ilkley[2] may I ask? Write again soon – maybe by Dec 2 I shall be less funny peculiar and we can meet at some *maison de tolerance*

yrs Ed

1 *Allen Lane, the head of Penguin Books.*

2 *OCTU.*

To Mrs Chappell [Mère!] from Springfield, December 1942

Dear Mrs. Chappell Thank you very much for Mrs. Henry Wood which was removed by Father at once and lent to an old gentleman before I could turn round However I hope to get it back I havent been well so I havent been able to do any shopping but will try and find something nice for you in the New Year. We have been very quiet here just lately. I believe a bomb or two has been dropped on Eastbourne which seems very popular. No cinema here now, that received a direct hit so is in no state to function. There was nobody there but the manager whose watch was still going "they" said when found. Billy is coming on leave soon I think so I hope to see him I dont know what happens after his OCTU is over & Fred seems to have got two months off[1] so I was informed I dont know how that was manoevered I seem to have had quite a successful show at the Redfern Gallerys from the reports my spies have sent in having overheard the most peculiar remarks. I wish you could find some place to settle but I always feel there might be another blitz just as you had got into a flat and then the whole thing would have to be gone through again. I wish it was all over Ime sure, to think its been going on 4 years I have lost all sense of anything at all and seem to exist in a sort of vacuum of timelessness since 1939. I must say we have been very lucky so far. Getting rather cold here Ime hoping for a green winter which fills the graveyard they say but not nearly so full as an icy one I'me having some iron injections & strychnine so I see on the box & they do me a lot of good. especially the strychnine I can take a good deal! Well all the best for 1943 I hardly dare wish it and give my love to Blair and thank you for Mrs. Wood much love from Edward.

To Beatrice (Bumble) Corcoran, 1942

Dear Bum Thank you for the fat and *Mes apprentissage*[2] which were realy very good I imagine *Le Straps* to be a notorious midget who beats old gentlemen. Willy sounds a regular old French terror anyway I suppose he made her however peculiar he may have been and very careful in his accounts there is a wonderful picture of Polaire looking like an Aubrey Beardsley in a Black costume with a huge feathered hat I keep expecting Jeannette Macdonald in unnatural colours to appear under the almond blossom at any moment as Moonyean everything is looking very pretty and full of flowers I am sending onions back in that tin I steal them at night. *Voleurs d'oignons* by Jean Lorrain I do hope Freds patriotic gala heroique[3] turns out a success & realy he has been sort of pushed out of it by all these other goings on. Bobbie is England you say? in a gold coal scuttle and a pitchfork draped in red white & Blue crepe de chine? I cant think how theyve managed to squeeze it into a Ballet. Well dearie I feel much better write again love from yrs Ed

---

1 *To do a ballet for the Vic–Wells company.*

2 *By Colette.*

3 *A new ballet,* The Quest, *with a scenario by Doris Langley Moore based on Spenser's* Faerie Queen, *and a decor by John Piper.*

To Squadron/Ldr Gerald Corcoran from Springfield, 1942

Dear Gerald
Ime sending a cutting out of the Telegraph also the Listener[1] quite a treat the Listener. Barbara overheard a conversation between Eddie Marsh & Clive Bell Clivey was stricken. such a change from the Euston Rd school B said. "This man drives me mad" said Clive "What kind of a fellow is this Burra do yo know him? they say he is very eccentric and dresses very oddly like his own drawings. He's quite young isnt he? Oh no in his middle 40's at least etc I thought it was very funny. Ime still yellow & have started my injections again but am much better. I suppose you ought to have a news cutting subscription but it would only make one sick at the ocean of balls. Anne went to the Redfern and got hold of some very good glossy print photos of some of the painting but she's keeping them to herself dear Cecil [Beaton] has been takeing Fashion photos in front of them too. Such a saucy back drop. The liquor in London seems to be getting queerer & queerer   yrs Ed.

To Squadron/Ldr Gerald Corcoran from Springfield, 1942

Dear Gerald I'm glad you enjoyed yourself & werent bored I felt terrible and was very nervous I was giving everyone flu I still have an old piece of phlegm that rattles up & down Heard from Billy who was manoevering on his motor cycle in a convoy at 8 m.p.h. in the dark & at 8 m.p.h. its almost impossible to keep the thing upright he is rather sour Ime not surprised. He told me a wonderful remark by a cockney with a squint from the Elephant who on being told to look at the sunrise by the artistic sergeant said "Gawrr I'd sooner see a grate bunch of arses belching black smowk" War is so fraytefully *coarsening* dont you find. Got a new Time (opened by the censor) which Ill send when Ive finished it   yrs Ed

To 2nd/Lt W.E. Chappell 258507 from Springfield, 15 May 1943

Good gracious what a stink do you mean to tell me you pass the door Oh realy I know Goudhurst The London bus used to pass right through it now theres no more London bus but can you get to Hawkhurst if so you can get a bus on 1 hours run or maybe we might meet there its one eyed but maybe there is an hotel we could have lunch anyway. You seem caught up in the machine. Talk about mills of God. I seem to find people are not standing up quite so bravely as they did. As soon as any body drops a bomb the whole town is to be "evacuated" it always happens to where pray that isnt stuffed up with too many people. Anyway Ill send the times of the Hawkhurst buses   yrs Ed   Ime glad you managed to have a wake of old faces. You should have had Rosin bake a cake coffinshaped to put in the middle of the table. They do say the whiskey isnt so much hooch as new & too new is raw and has these merry results Andre[2] seems to like hitting his

1 Notices for his exhibition at the Redfern Gallery.
2 André Simon Jr, son of the wine and food expert.

head on the floor Ive heard of it before especially after night clubs If you can get to Hawkhurst its O.K. we hope.

To 2nd/Lt W. E. Chappell 258507 from Springfield, 1943

Dear B
Ill come over on Saterday if yr coming in I see theres a train leaves Hastings at 10.44 & gets to T. Wells at 11.57. 12 or so if I came by that I could meet you earlier & have more time I dont know what time you arrive on the scene. The Tun W train starting from The city that God forgot is quite empty but for me a porter going home to dinner & one merchant seaman. Fred I hear has a London job so everything is fine I suppose. Yesterday was an extraordinary day so warm & summer like, everything is coming out. I went to the top of the garden & realy the view was a magic scene without a breath and wonderful pale green mist on the willow plantation & a sort of mauve shadow very "romantic" indeed it was.
Let me know about Saterday
yrs Ed.

To Lt W.E. Chappell 258507 from Springfield, 31 January 1944

How are you all. Mrs P[1] in her last work of fiction[2] said we have been looking at old photos they depressed us very much. your telling me As for old letters dearie "Aparitions" I call them I wish I had the strength to destroy them all but they might be of use "Historical" value as a guide to the horrors of the 20's & 30's Im still doing this cover for "Heart of Jade" what a name it reminds me of the Magasins Reunis tea shoppe in the Rue de Rennes 1925 le Jade period 800 or so pages of the conquest of Mexico in novel form by Salvador de Madariaga its a monument of knowledge & erudition realy & makes the Aztecs into real people no wonder the Mexicans are fierce as they were not averse to a cut off the backside as late as 1519 or so. The thing is a kind of Salambo cum Scott mixed with Chums & it remains to be seen chicks if they take anything *I* do I cant believe they will I always seem to *frighten* people I saw a photo of Madame Marx[3] in profile looking to me as though shed had the Bridge off her shnozzle[4] I always admired her nose as it is but they never can leave anything alone in the U.S.A.

Need I tell you my Jade wasnt quite "the thing" so Ime getting 3 gins I quite well knew from the first what would happen. I never can think what makes them try in the first place. I suppose they think theyre encouraging me or being progressive.
I hope its better weather now
Best wishes from
yrs Ed.

---

1 Barbara Ker-Seymer, now Mrs Humphrey Pease.
2 Her last letter.
3 Alicia Markova.
4 She had not.

To Capt. W.E. Chappell 258507 from Springfield, 28 March 1944

Dear B.
Sent you Mother finds a body Gpy Lee[1] & I hope it reaches you. Its very funny I thought there are some ghastly descriptions in it and a cabaret of unexampled squalor very well drawn from life Im certain. London is solid with U.S. MIlitary police paradeing up & down with white cast iron chamber pots rammed on their heads. I want to see Wolfits Volpone if it hasnt been incinerated before I get there London is rather like Paris 1920 style with a US influx on the exchange and all the old French people grumbling about the vulgar americans needless to say shamelessly extracting the last penny when poss everything has entwined U.S. flags & gets dubbed chicken inn etc Ime waiting for Lyons "Old Vienna' to switch to "Lindys" & Gunter suddenly come out as the Brown Derby   yrs Ed.

To Capt. W.E. Chappell 258507 from Springfield, March 1944

Dear B. I hope you get some old mags and modern Ammerican poets & another air mail letter I sent off to N.A. I hope you arent ankle deep in pumice[2] Mrs. P has taken to Warren St. Station with a small cardboard *attaché* case containing 2 pots of Elizabethan Arden 1 camera & a few diamonds & a Tin of Ideal Milk. This lovely home is tottering to its doom with no staff kept together by Mumsies grumbling she still manages to have breakfast in bed – the ghastly suffering of this war . . .

To Capt. W.E. Chappell 258507 from Springfield, 20 October 1944

Dear Pen Pal Thank you for your last letter Ive spent two days watching the Saddlers Wells infant school trying on a variety of rags Theres one terrifying aged infant gutter midget queen type suddenly appeared in a blue school cap. a very tight black & crimson lake striped football shirt & very ragged plum shorts. Everybody *roared.* he looked exactly like Caseys Court in Comic Cuts or a pink paper that had Weary Willie & tired Tim on the cover. I went to a rehersal[3] too & having wandered through the darkened auditorium & loosened the chandelier I came upon a little scene going forward on the stage in which Messia H'man was sweeping nobly about being "jostled" by members of the Caseys Court gang he was then surrounded pushed over backwards & given a good sharp kick in the balls then a knee in the stomach after that they all produced razors & slashed him in the face swept him up & over & delivered 2 sharp pokes with broken bottles in the face then followed a sort of *descent de la croix* copied from El Greco & a resurection & scotch jig when it gets realy going it should brighten up the fans. Ime told by "Barbara" my spirit voice by whom I sometimes get "in touch" with "the Messia" (Bobbie) that he has a boil on his arse & will have to have a deputy at the dress rehearsal which I very much

1 *Gypsy Rose Lee.*
2 *Chappell was in Naples when Vesuvius erupted.*
3 *Helpmann's ballet* Miracle in the Gorbals, *with decor and costumes by Edward.*

wanted to see. Sometimes I get in touch by "Ninette' [de Valois] who rattles the table a great deal & bursts into fits of laughter & "Donald" [Albery][1] hes more difficult sometimes my voices get a bit muffled. Boy[2] is now in Holland having been patched up into lovely fresh meat again & bundled off in no time at all. I hope Fred gets out. I dont know what he's doing there anyway. yrs E.

To Capt. W.E. Chappell 258507 from Springfield, November 1944

Dearest B. we had a lovely first night at the Gorbals youve no conception how I enjoyed myself Everybody was disgusted They made a very good job of it I must say Tonova[3] "disapeard" after Gorbals & wasnt seen I dont know whats become of him I saw Sophie[4] & Beryl de Zouter[5] in an astrahkan toque. she was outraged & still more so when I said I thought the razors in the slashing no ought to have been made of diamonte to *twinkle* sharper!! after 4 double gins & a few more squeezed in a basket chair in the lounge with enormous bottoms squeezed in our faces Miss Leigh[6] said she liked the set I said do you *realy* mean *that?* she said "Yes I always say what I mean". There are quite a few gas mains going off I suppose it must be the pipes wearing thin Everyones wearing thinner & thinner – either that or swollen up like a balloon – Do we look awful dearie everyone looks like kiddies to me except Bebe Daniels. I told you about Boy didnt I, being killed? Bum said she was thankful her mother had died first as she realy doesnt know what she would have done if she had been alive. Does the place look shabby you wouldnt believe yours E.

To Capt. W.E. Chappell 258507 from Springfield, 23 December 1944

Dear B. I went to the preemiair of Freds "Nocturne" Margot was beautiful, wonderfully distracted & romantic. Behind the scenes it was more distracted than romantic. I went round with Bum & we found Mrs. Siddons F[red] and Mrs. Bracegirdle B[obbie] or should it be the other way round standing "waiting" in a minute dressing room like a couple of land mines waiting to go off. Mrs. BraceG said producing 2 grey rags "please be more careful of the towels they cost coupons" Mrs. S almost in tears said "she buggered it up again" referring to poor old Alice[7] whod gone off in the hired car! They frighten me realy as I told Bar. the atmosphere is rather of the G. String school – I looked about for mothers gallstones & expected to find Ninette "slumped" in the toilet. Ime very sorry about Lupe Velez who was "found dead" from an overdose Ime always sorry when a *real* character leaves this world she was a wonderful dramatic actress as I saw a Spanish language

1 *He owned the New Theatre where the ballet performed during the war.*
2 *Beatrice Dawson's brother, already wounded and recovered.*
3 *Ashton.*
4 *Fedorovitch.*
5 *Beryl de Zoete, a ballet critic, writer and mistress of Arthur Waley.*
6 *Vivien.*
7 *Alice [Astor] von Hoffmanstal.*

version of "Resurection" and she was perfect in it. she didnt care wrapped up in a rug over her head & stains under each eye screaming about in the police court I sent you a copy of Essays by T.S. Elliott about Elizabethan playwrights & a LOOK but to your last address. I saw "Old Acquaintance" with Bette Davis & Miriam Hopkins. Hopkins didn't get good notices. I thought she was lovely as a successful lady novelist (Bette being an artistic success) they end up rather the worse for wear drinking a little left over champagne – flat – over the electric logs in B's apt to the tune of Auld Lang syne on the Wurlitzer. I enjoyed it thoroughly. Write when you can
yours Ed

To Capt. W.E. Chappell 258507 from Springfield, 22 February 1945

Dear B. I hope you have 40th Birthday Blues[1] by Palinurus[2] by now Ive been staying at Pont St. one or two days. Bum is very busy Shes been doing the Duchess of Malfi realy being done by Roger Furse who is so busy the whole thing has *realy* been drawn from Lottos works & Urbino portraits by "Beatrice". John G[ielgud] Duke Ferdinand declared he wanted to look strange & vicious? B copied out a cute costume in canary & bottle green or black for Duke F. & we thought it a bit more Dandini than Duke. I said the Duke would step forward suddenly & break into "just a fellow on a furlough out looking for a dream" whilst a large placard with the Chorus printed on it comes down in front of the arras. Just a fellow on a furlough out looking for a nightmare it ought to be from what I see around Denman St. I actually saw something I wanted to in the shape of Peer Gynt. I got a front row stall & you get your 13/6 penny worth believe me. Richardson is very good indeed & so is Dame S[ybil Thorndike]. I, Bum Larry & Vivien had lunch together dear, at the French pub!!! they were charming I thought very simple and nice & no airs or chichi of any sort whatever. V is just about to break out in "skin of your teeth" by Thornton Wilder. The ballet was an enormous success in Brussels. the dear boys particularly liked Gorbals Why of course they did so *homely* what with razors and fried fish its quite a breath of the old sod. No word of Ashton who I think only moves between the censors & the *grande monde* but if they arent going to S.A. perhaps he will do something if he escapes long enough from the maw of Hanover.L.[3] Write again soon
yrs E.

To Capt. Chappell 258507 from Springfield, 10 March 1945

Dear B. Ashtonova came to dinner and I showed him some designs I had done for Don Juan just to encourage him the Ballet has just opened in Paris. Why is La done up as a Boogie Woogie Bugle Boy?[4] Cyril Connolly

1 The Unquiet Grave, *essential reading at this period.*
2 *Cyril Connolly.*
3 *Hanover Lodge, Alice von Hoffmanstal's London home.*
4 *Bobby Helpmann, in* ENSA *uniform. Sometimes designated "La" because of his diva-like qualities.*

has been in Paris I believe as a cure for early morning tears at 40 & to find out about literary life has he been dressed up as a *chasseur maudit* I wonder – or waddling along in a civilian overcoat . . .

To Capt. Chappell 258507 from Springfield, 24 March 1945

Dear B. Colonel de Helpmans Ballet Vic de Monte Saddler has been gracing Paris all in uniform. And "One" asked oneself if one hadnt, beneath ones eyes, a curious anachronism due to the madness of a *metteur en scene distrait*. Because *avec leur joliesse fragile leur paleur pastelisée ils semblaient tous descendus de l'un de ces tableaux anglais du siecle dernier. Les filles avait des petits nez invisibles*, (like Leona's?) *des joues à peine rose; les garcons, un teint translucide, une courbe gracieuse dans le sourire, de longs cils* (Nestlés), *des regards clair et surpris*. What at dearie? There was also a cute party with Noel C. Cocteau & Berarard. no mention of Bobbie who was dipping *ces longs cils & plongeant ses regards clair et surpris* in a *gin vermut au Ritz Bar* Ive no doubt. I wish someone would take me to Paris not in a bogus uniform. I hear via friends in the censor Benjamin Britten is writing an opera & Ashton is going to make a silent appearance, *princesse du geste et reine de l'atitude*, always had a flair for operas, you remember Madame Butterfly? I hope it comes off. The News Chronicle described the Duchess of Malfi as "a new play by John Webster" he ought to write one for the Lunts Ime sure hed do quite as well as Terry Rattigan. An enormous thing fell at Marble Arch and covered the arch with the good earth bits of "gents", tree trunks, daffy bulbs, every window in the cumberland was blown in & the Odeon or whatever that cinema is was pocked about. it was at 9.30 a sunday morning so didnt do quite as much harm as it might have In an old "Shit" there were some pix of to h & h not [*To Have and Have Not*] with Bacall leaning on a specially Hollywood sanforized piano at the Club South of the border style Martiniquaise being played to by Hoagy Carmichael who actually looked quite genuine. his face looked almost dirty or maybe it was bad printing. anyway Ime told by some one who saw it on Cape Cod! that Carmichael & Bacall are wonderful. You can hardly see for the slats of the Venetian blinds trusty old blinds for atmosphere dearie. Ime told Kismet is perfectly terrifying I saw a photo of every one with terrible old satin poufs on their heads they looked like Olsen & Jolson [Johnson] in "Harem Huddles' without June Havoc. Marlene Deitrich had wrinkles at the knees in her image dance befor the prophet Ronald Colman. Ive found a little old Book with images of the dance of Death in it which I bring out whenever any one turns on the news it spoils everyones fun skeletons playing fiddles etc at the Carribean Club. Everybody is slowly crumbling away. Wonderful weather just now – write again soon from yrs E

Throughout those weeks in 1945 as the war dragged its way from the melodrama of the Berlin Bunker to the obscenity of Hiroshima, Chappell was in Naples, despatching a stream of complaints to his family and his friends in England, chafing bitterly against the delay of his demobilisation. Edward, travel starved from his years of imprisonment in beseiged Great Britain, offered him short shrift. The war had worn Edward out; and with the release from the tensions of the years he had spent lurching uncomfortably between states of tedium or terror, he felt a debilitating exhaustion. Having been ill on and off throughout the hostilities (when his physical condition was still suffering from the abominable treatment he had meted out to it during his trip to Mexico with the Aikens in 1937) it is remarkable he did not undergo a complete and utter collapse. For once he was ready to complain in detail as to how badly he felt, writing on August 1945: "Ive given up dearie & never go out . . . I realy feel like DEATH and cant go on". Not, in fact, true, for he did of course, go on; recovering his spirits and his sense of humour with what must have been a clearing of his mind in spite of regarding the peace in Europe with a faintly hostile eye, and greeting the final conclusion of the war with not much more than a cynical apathy. The lights went on again in blacked out Great Britain, yet, despite the determined efforts made to celebrate so glorious an occasion there was an atmosphere of indecision and anti-climax – provoked obviously by the meandering arrival of world peace – and suggesting nothing so much as a too long delayed and so only partially satisfactory orgasm. Only those in the services, waiting scattered across Europe and the far away places of the world, were able (after two, three, or four, years of exile) to feel something resembling euphoria. The sad and wounded hulk of Britain still appeared as a regainable Paradise, and the thought of 'going home' induced a picture of total bliss. Edward felt no bliss, only a welcome relief from tension. The pointlessness and brutality of the war had dug deeply into his guts affecting him far more profoundly than he could ever bring himself to admit. The work he had produced was quite unlike any other artist's war paintings. He saw the soldiers who had taken over the whole neighbourhood as creatures from another planet. There is something mythic and elemental about the dark brutish figures lumbering on and off lorries or crouching in gun emplacements. They are monumental, made of earth and stone; filthy, inhuman and menacing; quite unlike his mention in a letter of a 'troupe of runts'.

To Capt. Chappell 258507 from Springfield, 18 August 1945

I've given up dearie & never go out and can scarcely speak I dread going to London & put if off and cant see anyone very neurotic it seems to me but now everything is over except the ATOMS HE HE! I realy feel like *death* and I cant go on I suppose if I was to go away somewhere a long way off for a change it might do me good but you cant get away from *yourself* for long I find that spectre will always rise up at you wherever you are I had a dirge from your poor mother who said she had terrible letters from you saying everybody had stopped writing and all she longed for was a home of her own but my dear it seems absolutely impossible for people to find homes of their own or anybody elses. They are taking empty houses in Rye & poke-ing famillys into them & the mayor raised a stink by saying people should put people in their spare rooms. God knows who these people are – bombed out from big towns or something. There was a peice in the Dly Mail about Italy. they said everything was stolen, with or without violence, by organ-ised gangs. tyres simply vanished when your back was turned. someones luggage was removed from a moveing jeep. & trucks were "fired at" after dusk & were attacked by gangs in Rugby football fashion & stripped & Dumps of materials etc where broken into with Expedition & dispatch it sounded to me like a giant Cicero in the Hey dey of Al Capone only rather more so. is that so?[1] As for Hootch factorys makeing genuine cognac for you brave boys & gin on the side they are all over the place & factorys for false papers & identity cards etc in Naples – Well it seems to me this war has made people into balloons or sticks there aint no middle course of course its the heat that got off your extra fat for next winter. I just listen in to the U.S. Forces Radio all the time now so I know all about the Great Gildersleeve & Fibber McGee & Molly etc so I have a few shattering gags for you "The upper crust is just a lot of crumbs held together by its own dough" – and on looking at a lot of wanted gangsters photos in the Post office. "Gee! I aint seen so many hot mugs since the barber shop burned down". I roar with laughter The whole thing is a continuous sort of dihorea lunatic asylum drivel with I min of news on the hour every hr. I cant stop listening to it. They dont have the classy boom of the B.B.C. anyway. I see Mdme Alice & Dolin[2] are forming their own company & going on the road in the fall so I saw in P.M. Theyl end up as Alice & Pat at the Peroquet, Juarez a boarder town dear with Gypsy Lees mother hideing a corpse in the ladies toilet I dont realy feel so, as a matter of fact They have their heads on the right way. *They* wont be at the Peroquet! yours Ed.

To Capt. Chappell 258507 (still in Naples) from Springfield, 16 September 1945

Dont take on so dearie everybody is sick of waiting in queues no cigarettes nothing to drink & no clothes. Fred is thinking he's going to make his debut with Cesar Francks Variations[3] & decor by Sophie & then hopes to do Don Juan as a *grand piece du fin du monde*. Roger Furse is doing some superb piece for Helpman & the Baron[4] has been heard from going on in a whirl of intrigue & producing ballets just exactly the same but for mother who had to be kept hidden & let out once in a while for air as she was a little Jew so he told Sophie I should like Fred to do a real classical ballet for Mdm Marx I would go to Saddlers W[ells] if Mdm came back for a season. F[red] has gone at Graham Sutherlands "Wanderer"' costumes & cut off 20 ft of pipeing & what not from each & they look wonderful they all say. What kind of management is Robinson & Spiffard for Conrad Aikens story Mr. Arcularis has been made into a play & the contract has been signed production in 6 months 1st on tour & at least 3 weeks in the West End he wants to come over & see it before it folds & hopes for film rights wonderful for the old soul I think. Everybodys so glamourous except me Well youll soon be cowering over your gas ring & a pot of old tea I daresay yrs Ed.

---

1 *Yes, that was so.*

2 *Alicia Markova and Anton Dolin.*

3 *To become one of Ashton's greatest successes,* Symphonic Variations, *featuring Fonteyn and Michael Somes.*

4 *Birger Bartholin.*

To William Chappell from Springfield, Xmas 1945

Dearest B. I wasnt expecting to hear from you once the fun began and you were caught up in the mad whirl. Thank you for the BK Token and I was wondering if you would like some nice useful thing for the house as you are opening house & Ime sure you want some dish clothes and Ive got some coupons or a nice iron kettle from Harrods. Nothing but mines blowing up down here there was a terrific explosion at 2.30 this morning that sounded like an old fashioned bomb. Have you found any business premises[1] yet and if so where I went to see the sign of the cross the other day and thoroughly enjoyed it with Claudette Colbert as a vamp[2] and Charles Laughton[3] stark on a chaise longue with a dirty piece of flannel on his head hiccuping and a built on roman nose Frederick March looked very odd with a mop of curls rather like Henry Ainely gone peculiar the films have got duller & duller but for Lost week end type, when do we have bathes in asses milk now?

Take off yr clothes & come on in says the Empress to the court gossip. Ive had two or three of the Penguin they brought out about me you remember and havent dared read it as for the *paintings* dearie I should *love* to know where most of them have got to for I just have no idea. The whole thing stinks & when I look at it I feel sick. My fault of course. As for the Redfern crookery never having been there for fear of an attack of vomit I dont know anything about them. I also had a letter from somebody called John Paris or something who had written some book about English water colour paintings & was humbly apologising for not having encluded me. Realy everybody is going out of their minds I thought it was very funny. Ime reading Ulysses & havent ever read it befor its realy wonderful. I always adored puns nothing but terrible seminary jokes about Jesuits etc that and Appointment in Samarra is very good too. Well dearie theres a tearing Xmas South Wester & many happy mines bursting on the beach & I dont think we shall have a white christmas thank heaven yrs

Blessed mother Mary Anycock

To William Chappell from Springfield, 25 December 1946

Well dearie how are you with the pantomimes. And all the seasons sick and happy new vomit. I saw act I of Carmen[4] the set I mean. it couldnt have been worse painted (unless I had done it with a tooth brush to please the head mistress when she was asleep like the story in Little folks 1912 or so) but from the 10th row youd never notice any of the little nuances and from anyway further just a lovely far away dream There is a dainty tower at the back the very image of the Empire state without King Kong. and the Spanish shawls! screaming for Jose Collins[5] & a grand piano to hang them

1 *Chappell was about to start a theatrical dressmakers and designing business in Bruton Place, W.1.*

2 *Poppaea.*

3 *As Nero.*

4 *Edward had designed* Carmen *for the opera company at Covent Garden.*

5 *Jose Collins was a great pre-war musical comedy performer, star of* Maid of the Mountains *and* A Southern Maid *at Daly's Theatre.*

over so Hutch[1] can sing "a small hotel" underneath a standard lamp. I particularly liked an old scotch lodging house keeper who is a wardrobe mistress I suppose draped herself in a tremendous shawl with a design of red cabbages & 20 feet of fringe to show how it should look. Goodness only knows what it will look, too. I gather Mrs. Rhodes[2] is busy with her nose at the gas stove cooking lovely fresh food & nothing out of a can she says we shall have to have our meals separately in future but I dont know how they manage having everything "fresh" without a 2 hr wait in the Grimsby plaice queue or a dainty horse steak – I see in "Ballet"[3] "Patineurs" is considered rather frivolous in New York. I suppose they ought to have had Hugh Laing in somebodys womb to give it weight. Who is the man who does the ballet notices in The Sunday Times, hes very sour, it must be terrible for it to see all the awful things it does who ever it is.[4] We have been having a death struggle with a very doubtful turkey from heaven knows where this morning. *What* came out of *its* womb was a terrible packet of old gall stones neck & liver if it had been there one day longer Beauty Darling would have been carrying god knows what, as it was about 10 oz of little pebbles where in its gizzard or gall bladder it was very good in the end realy I must say. I never said what the gravy had been made out of. quite "fresh" of course. thank god for a thaw it has been terribly cold down here and I hope to see you before long maybe. Those tangerines in the shops are very good I keep trying to remember the tune.[5]
Yrs. E.

Edward began travelling again in 1947 when he went to Ireland to stay in Dublin and Galway City. The horrors and difficulties of the journey via Holyhead by train and sea to Dun Laoghaire might well have deterred a person of exceptional strength and vigour. It did not deter Edward. Nothing ever deterred Edward once he had made up his mind he wished to do a particular thing.

April 1948 found him back in Ireland, this time in Cork, from where he explored Bantry Bay, Limerick and Kinsale. In September of that same year he made another visit to Dublin and to Galway City. In 1949 he moved further; deep into Southern France staying in Avignon; 1950 took him to Tours and in 1951 he was in Bayonne. His sister Anne was with him on all these journeys. The letter to Chappell written on the first post-war trip to Ireland tells in detail the hazards of the journey.

To William Chappell from the Great Southern Hotel, Galway, Eire, 1947

Dearest B How are you getting on in gai Paris – I dont pretend Galways

1 *Hutch, coloured pianist and singer discovered by Cochran.*

2 *Mrs Rhodes was Barbara Ker-Seymer, who had married again.*

3 *A magazine edited by Richard Buckle;* Les Patineurs, *one of Ashton's ballets designed by Chappell, had been redesigned in New York by Cecil Beaton.*

4 *Perhaps it was terrible. Most of the* Sunday Times *ballet reviews at this time were by Frank Howles, who was really the music critic.*

5 *'Tangerine (she is all they say)', sung by Betty Hutton in* The Fleet's in.

gay but it has its moments I find & is realy very romantic – some of the caracters dearie! I dont know how they keep upright. The Galway girls by Georg Grosz not John are my favorites 2 inches high & draped in black bedspreads to the floor with a pair of mens boots or a smart pair of 3 inch heel pumps completely walked over at the heels & very stained legs not with the crushed juice of fruit & flowers this hotel looks as if it was full of commercial travellers very middle class and priests with familys. Of course if you want to drink yourself into the grave at the double & who doesnt you just must come here. its an alcoholics "*must*" for Ive never seen so much Powers & Jamiesons whiskey together in one place & you can swill non stop & I also find 2 doubles set you up quite nicely so Ime wondering if they dont add a bit of water in Old England. in this hotel it costs 2/6 a double & this considers itself the Claridge de Galway so it comes cheap. any amount of candy you want & cakes – & "Salomé where she danced" in glorious technicolor at the Town Hall! a kind of Greek tomb type in grey stone in the style Ime very fond of. I believe its imposs to take away any whiskey – they simply remove it at the customs which rather upsets me as you can get in demi Johns & the only time I saw it in nice little pocket flasks I thought no body would notice, it was dummies in the window. Theres a bus strike too so we cant go any expeditions anywhere which we were planning however I find plenty to occupy myself in monster study and staring at huge pots of jam bars of Dutch & Danish chocolate etc and realy lovely Aran tweed in large bales. theres a sort of off white type fairly smoothish that Ime sure you would be mad about. I believe you could take away a length without it being torn off you. The journey dearie is the kiss of death. I dont know how I made it as I forgot my passport & wasnt allowed on to the bloody boat after a perfect death rattle in the Irish mail in which everybody ended up upside down with their feet poked in each others eyes & grey in the face at 3.50 AM fun dearie but not good or clean. having been hummed & hawed over by the officials I finaly took refuge in the Manchester train waiting to go back to London to get my passport – all the way back to Rye & then coming back Ide missed my sailing ticket & they wouldnt sell me a return to Dublin however it was O.K. you would realy think they did everything in the world they could think of to make it hell.[1] there were queues for the boat 20 miles long with poor old creatures staggering under suitcases bursting & tied up with rope & dragging them into customs & up gangways I dont know how anybody takes any luggage they treat people like animals realy! One ought to fly obviously its the only thing. A high tearing Atlantic gale is now whistling through the seminaries, convents, retreats for the fallen, St. Mary Magdalenes laundry & Loyolas pension lunchs & dinners. I hope I ever get back but my journeys seem to get all buggered up!

Yrs ed

1 *They still do if you travel by train and boat!*

To William Chappell from Springfield, December 1947

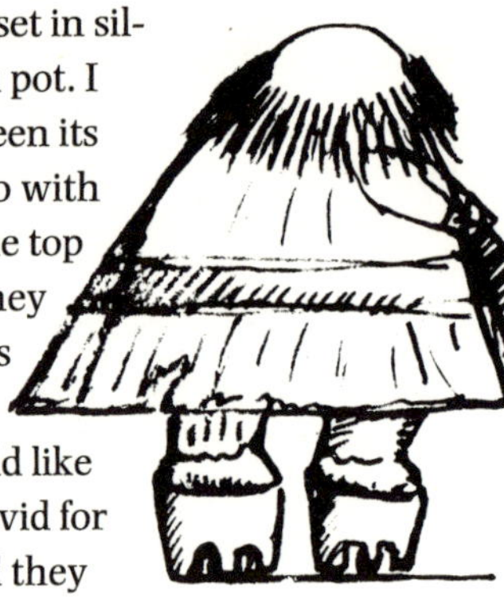

Dear B How tiresome you are giving me that beautiful book. Theres nothing here but The Tosspot letters by C.W. Lewis two ostrich eggs set in silver and several lovely tea sets all at 20£ for 4 cups a slop pail & tea pot. I shall look round. The Bosch is the most wonderful book Ive ever seen its realy a triumph I think. Especially *queux et mendiants* nothing to do with *pochettes surprises*. one very fashionable a stunted barrel bald at the top with "wedgees" specially made at the Cour des miracles Walt Disney might do the *jardin* des delices somewhat cleaned up for the kiddies Snowhite & the 7 delices[1] gluttony sodomy adultery fornication evilspeaking lying slander & malice – I was wondering if you would like a couple of shirts for a present as I saw some wonderful ones in David for about £2-15 there was one in a very small grey & black check and they had other ones. Ive got plenty of coupons so you can have them too. go and get two when you visit Miss Blairs modern style Duplex apt.[2] If you dont do that I shall be forced to by a celuloid hat box with paintings of hollyhocks up the side I must say I should like to see Anthony & Edith Evans in Anthony & Edith[3] it sounds like Lunt & Fontanne gone crazy but you get your moneys worth Im sure. I read a Raymond Chandler the other day "The high window" I think it was called. absolutely smashing, such a bunch of cheap people and variety of heels in ghastly apartments described in every detail. hes much better than an ordinary detective I cant put them down & want more now Ide like the big sleep. Blue Dahlia etc I gather the Big Sleep was very cleaned up in the movie version. We cooked 2 turkeys, Christmas morning was a perfect death struggle we even had to boil a ghastly pudding. We had masses of food all at once so every one was in a panic it would all go bad leaving us nothing, such good clean fun it all is There is another number I had en eye on about Mad Martin Blake & Fuseli by Ruthven Todd published by the Grey Walls press & illustrated. I particularly like Mad Martin who quite outdoes Gustave Doré. Theres an extraordinary one in Queens Rd Brighton the rd from the station opposite a sort of Town Hall & in a mysterious missionary religious shop of the last judgment. Ime sure its Martin. There was one in the Listener the other day too, The creation of light Ime being more & more influenced by Beatrix Potter. Well I suppose you are run off yr tiny feet as usual.

yrs Ed.

To William Chappell from Springfield, 1947

Dearest B. Come on the 27th if you want it will be O.K. wonderful weather yesterday I was taken for a ride in the afternoon and it didnt seem natural at all it was so aureate everything as dry as a bone therefore yellow & buff realy lovely I must say. I havent seen anything but Edward my son Peggy

---

1 *Edward lists eight!*

2 *Chappell's sister was living with band leader Van Phillips in Phoenix House, Charing Cross Road.*

3 Antony and Cleopatra *at Stratford and then the New Theatre (now the Albany).*

Ashcroft in a blonde wig over one eye as sireens moan staggers up saying "Bring another bottle, may husbands minister of champagne" that was the bit I preferred. Also Together Again[1] at the Victoria Palace wonderful that was I thoroughly enjoyed every moment.

Yours E

I see La Piaf has just started in a movie called "*Neuf garçons et une fille*" with *Les compagnons de la chanson*!

To William Chappell from Springfield, December 1948

Dear B. It is so dark in here in the morning I can scarcely see to write and thank you for the Goya drawings which are wonderful I think Ive done nothing at all this Chrissmus white chrissmuss why are you gray? is my new number in the Russ Morgan manner. Ive been sent "*We* called it music" by Eddie Condon & Thomas Sugrue after mother & Mrs. Rhodes have finished it you realy must read it as it is an Apotheosis of Bandboy supreme all about the Wolverines, Red Mackenzie's chicagoans & the Mound city Blue blowers etc The cracks are so deafening & come one after another nobody ever gets up till about 5 in the afternoon. Fats Waller comes out very well in all these books he must have been a realy charming sympathetic caracter – plastered all the time & I dont wonder he fell down dead in a pullman. I see another picture with Magnani[2] called "Vengeance" about a mother (M) whose son is taken away by the nazis. I hope it comes here. I suppose they have them in the U.S. because there is a huge Italian population instead of only Madame Parmigiani[3] Del Giudice[4] & Monty Banks[5] – I heard about Mr. Moreno who rang up Bar having been recommended by Len Lye. he took her out to dinner with two financiers in Percy St. & they were offerd smoked salmon roast duck a whole chicken goose turkey & Anna Neagles wig full of plovers eggs hard boiled – he also implored her to come on down to Monte Carlo for the new year. quite regardless of John[6] and baby. I should have insisted on taking baby with a trained "Nannie" in a private plane even if I was terrified into a fit. I think Mr. M must have gathered the impression B was some kind of very high class tart! The movie[7] down here is nearly ready & Im sure will be opened by Patricia Roc who will cut a ribbon and the whole thing will fold up in a heap of rubble. anyway I might catch up on my british pictures if it opens. they prefer some realy high class clean British pic like Wicked Ladye in a Buenos Aires photo section of La Nacion or some paper I saw some photos of Massine & Red slippers[8] or whatever it is no word of Helpman to read what they say

1 *With The Crazy Gang.*
2 *Anna Magnani, great Italian stage and screen actress.*
3 *Proprietress of splendid food store in Old Compton Street, Soho.*
4 *An Italian film producer working in England.*
5 *Gracie Fields' husband.*
6 *John Rhodes, Barbara Ker-Seymer's second husband.*
7 *The Rye Cinema, bombed in the war, was rebuilt (though pulled down in 1981), and is now replaced by some houses and 'daintie' shops which would have enraged Edward.*
8 The Red Shoes.

you'd think Massine had done it all I see there are a lot of English visitors in Switzerland and the treasury is at its wits end "combing hotels" to find out how they get currency its screamingly funny I think. Ive got two King Cole[1] records one "Im lost without you" I like "Babs" & Are you fer it? also a lovely song by Sarah Vaughan & Dizzie Gillespie's orch – "Lovehman wha can you be?" I also got 4 day creep I couldnt resist the name – I shall buy me a bull dog to watch ma man while he sleep. men are so doggone crookit Im afraid he'l take a 4 day creep – by Ida Cox & orch. meanwhile Im deafened by Near you which begins as boogie woogie & has a sandwich of Frank Sinatra type Kraft spread in between – it takes the place of Fersenimenalreasons. The Ri[t]chies have made a very nice little apt up here[2] with a Belling cooker behind a rare old *tapisserie* reeking of sausages & 2 bedrooms if it was in London of course everybody would be in ex-stasies. unfortunately theres no water up here but a cold tap that once its turned on you cant turn off. however theyve been here all this time – its sad about this house as it could realy be made very nice in flats. There is a daintie exhibition at the Leicester Galleries that has a grossly insensitive comic strip in it by me. That will send everybody off on a 4 day creep* my love to Mama

* especially Ramond Mortimer. I see Dali is thinking of launching a comic strip.

To William Chappell from Springfield, July 1950

Dear B. How are you getting on in your monkey act.[3] I hope at matinees you will run round the edge of the dress cercle & throw any matinee teas into the stalls and terrify any kiddies into cronic fits of epilepsy. All I can say is it was a lucky thing you got to be a monkey[4] it came in very handy. Clover is supposed to be coming on Monday for a day or two. we went to see Angus Wilson at the B[ritish] Museum to get his book. she wants to translate it. a figure emerged in a Tam with a kind of birds nest beneath, a cardigan & a bloose and a sort of navy blue nappy draped as Gandhi used to wear it! & very thin bare legs. I was transfixed by this Oh yes said Angus W. *Thats* Miss MacDonald she's translating Virgil into French she some-times gets very excited – the other day she hit another lady over the head with a museum directory. Im supposed to be going to Tours for 1 week Aug 13 by the end of the week I shall be on Vitel & a dry discuit. I shall go to all the "sights" – *Monoprix Uniprix* & the *grande Brasserie de la Touraine* etc. They say the cooking is very good in Tours – if I had strength I would stay in Paris on the way back but I cant be bothered to find a hotel or alter my ticket, its terrible but its true now I just dont care realy whether I come

1 *Nat King Cole.*

2 *In the attics at Springfield.*

3 *The 'monkey act' was in André Roussin's play* The Little Hut *(translated by Nancy Mifford), starring Robert Morley, David Tomlinson and Joan Tetzel at the Lyric Theatre, Shaftesbury Avenue. It was on a pre-London tour when this letter was written.*

4 *It was a very lucky thing and, indeed, came in very handy.*

or go. I must say I would like to see Orson Welles satire on Hollywoo' a play I gather containing an interpolated film made by O.W & le toot Paris in the *Buttes Chaumont*! in a grotto. it would be very enjoyable Im sure – there was a terrible storm I believe & Toot P got soaked to the skin – Have you read a Patrick Hamilton called Slaves of Solitude I found it at Cannon St. station for 1/- its a triumph of horror about Miss Roach in a war time boarding house at Something-on-Thames – Im so enjoying it. theres a fearful german woman in it who speaks a wonderful sort of 1925 dialect very coloquial they quarrel over a US lootenant & get taken out to Road Houses I cant put it down need I say – Dont fall off your palm tree and I hope it runs for 18 months or more.

Yours E

To William Chappell from Springfield, 24 August 1950

Dear B I saw La Hutte opened yesterday and I hope it remains open a long time.[1] I saw it was at its 1000 performance in Paris I liked Tours which has been well bombed half of old T is no more and the bridge over the Loire quite untouched & the Railway yards – need I add – however – the others[2] went to chattoos & I went & layd down after lunch. there were 2 very good little restaurants *La Rascasse* & *Le Renaissance* at Le R you got an enormous *repas* for 350 fr with a *quart de vin rouge* as for the fruit & flowers Ive never seen better & quantities of butter etc flowing about. Spent a night in Paris at the Terminus Est. rather above my station but I couldnt struggle on it was one mass of Americans & world-waize motor bus tours. setting off – very comfortable we had dinner at a beastly restaurant. however I had been well fortified by brandy so didnt care & it was opposite I dont like big restaurants I only like tiny boxes squeezed in the back room – Im longing to see Gloria S[wanson] as a half mad old star with a kept man[3] and Anna Q Nillson Buster Keaton & Henry B. Warner as bridge partners! to say nothing of Eric von Stroheim[4] I went to see *Orphée*[5] again & thoroughly enjoyed it Im looking forward to a new book by Tennessee Williams about an elderly actress who is booed whilst playing Juliet as shes considered too old. I think she returns to Italy. I saw it was on John Lehmans list well I hope you are bearing up. yours E
My love to Mama

To Clover de Pertinez from Chapel House, Rye, 31 July 1951

Dear Clo
I completely forgot all about "holydays" and all that till I was reminded by Anne asking if she could come & stay on Friday! which was a very wild stormy day rather nice I thought & today has been lovely not that I didnt see what looked like a typhoon in the direction of Cantorbury but it never

---

1 *It did.*
2 *Edward's sister Anne, and cousins Eleanor and Jill Brodrick.*
3 *In* Sunset Boulevard, *co-starring William Holden.*
4 *As Swanson's butler.*
5 *Cocteau's great film, with Maria Casares as Death.*

came here Mrs R[hodes] & Co are off tomorrow I gather to stay at Anne X Duveens & then Cagnes' S'mer. this very 6th August. John B[anting] & J[imbo] are taking off for a flat in Hastings up on the top of the Cliff just behind White Rock & the Pavilion, almost directly behind – 30£ cheaper. I thought it was very nice with a huge front room newly done up, obviously once the dining room & back bedroom & quite a good sized kitchen & bathroom 180£ P.A. including rates.

Bar said all the old ghosts Billy Fred etc on the Constant Lambert programme looked a 100! & the camera had enormous close ups of Billy, very trying. Bobbie [Helpmann] kept as far away as poss. yrs Ed.

To Clover de Pertinez from Springfield, 1951

Dear Clo. Pleased to see yer Im sure and E[1] if he so pleases. I shall come over to Brayton by the 9.37 so we might meet in the station between 11.30 & 12 I think it usualy is. Some monster of perversion a sex maniac (?) totally devoid of any sensibility bought "Judith & H's Head" for 200£! The first *prayvate* (horror of horrors) person to buy a picture from the exhib they said Mama Tilda & Anne went to Canterbury yesterday in a sort of Central American Jungle sweat bath. to see the wife of Canterbury[2] Bath & came back stricken they obviously thought it terrible. The music was very modair style I gather. David P. keeps ringing up & trying to make me go over & Im behaving very badly & saying Im out or away. Im so busy & feel so tired I cant have both and I dont care not realy – A(nne) has got some hotel in Bayonne, Capagorri 15/6 bed & breakfast so probably a good one for 9 days or so I hope it is a good one as Im tired of walk ups in all their unbridled scruffiness like the Rue Lavoisier! I dont mind St. Germain des Pres and St. Sulpice being scruffy. it must be the proximity of *St. Lazare* that adds the horror to that neighbourhood I dont realy like that part at all. The Ministere is better Im sure. A[nne] liked it very much expect she had a room on the 2nd floor overlooking the street & tumbrils bearing heaven knows what, rumbled & banged past about 4 together with a *grands concours des drags* dragging Miss Poubelle 1950 along behind them which woke her up.

There was such a crowd in Canterbury you were nearly pushed off the sidewalk. awful it sounded to me yrs E.
There was a long piece about Perse in the N. Statesman by Pritchett.[3]

To William Chappell from Springfield, 1951

Dear B.
nearly all the paintings sold were sold last year & I got the money and the mysterious man who bought Judith & Holofernes at that frightful exhib at the Funne Fayre & Dome of Discovery. Somebody was supposed to buy the

---

1 *Edward de Pertinez, Clover's son and Edward Burra's godson.*

2 *This was a ballet with decor and costumes by Edward:* Canterbury Prologue, *choreographed by David Paltenghi (a great friend of Edward) for the Ballet Rambert in 1951.*

3 *V.S. Pritchett the writer, who was a friend of Clover.*

coronation of the V(irgin) but they dont seem to have. Im usually being a recluse in the Duke of Wellington Wardour St. Done up in early Midevil Denham style nobody goes there Im so busy listening to other peoples conversations I never can leave till 2.30 when I move to "The Stooge"[1] Something very quaint happened yesterday re Recluse.[2] a young man came from the Sussex & East Something or other Express & said he was writing about Sussex artists – he began about "Recluse" dearie & said "I dont think that *at all* so, why everybody knows *you* here"! As Ide spent 3 hours in the Railway Hotel taproom on Satdy morning in a blizzard staring at him in my roll of recluse & in every other bar in town, it does surprise people – Aye have quayte a social layfe in may fashion dearie – & its got to be may fashion *or no* social *layfe* – I heard from Gerald [Corcoran] this morning He said one was going befor the Tate Selection committee & Southampton was thinking of one & thats all

love from

Tess of the Storm Country

To William Chappell from Chapel House, Rye, 15 February 1952

Dearest B How are you getting on I hear from Rhodes you are very depressed. I found a paper back of "Goodnight sweet prince"[3] which Ive not read and am glued to it. I never knew that Father went out of his mind at 56 or younger, no wonder I always thought they sometimes had a wild look. begining with Grandma Mrs. John Drew they span the 19 century!

Tender is the night,[4] has just come on & I want to see it but its one of those things that take about 4 hours and completely misses Scott Fitzgeralds style except in one moment of five minutes however Ide like to see it. its what we would have called a "society drama" in the days when Hedda Hopper[5] was allways in a garden party dress as Mrs. Van Rennslair Dupont queen of newport society. that & "A view from the bridge"[6] I want to see. not that I ever get anywhere when I go up. If I dont work I can hardly have the force to get up and stay in bed reading till 10.30 – everything seems so far from everything else – & if I lived in Islington or one of those places I know I should never leave the Angel and become a fixture in Collins pub hung with photos of Lew Lake in (the original) Splinters[7] & get even queerer than I already am – we spent quite a long time the other evening examining some old thrown out French comic books in a dustbin outside the Hamburger delicatessen in Brewer street – its a very ominous sign picking over dustbins. As for Clover – fortunately she has to work at the British council school or else she would be in all day in a crumpled

1 *A drinking club.*

2 *The Press continually spoke of Edward as a recluse.*

3 *A biography of John Barrymore and the Barrymore family.*

4 *F. Scott Fitzgerald's novel, filmed by Jack Clayton.*

5 *Hopper played elegant sophisticated women in many movies before turning columnist and becoming as unpopular (though equally successful) as Elsa Maxwell.*

6 *By Arthur Miller.*

7 *A famous First World War concert party.*

black night dress "unable to leave the house" owing to imaginary telephone calls – nearly all her mothers generation relations were quite incapable of ever going out – the only remaining aunt in Hove never step[s] outside the door! The High Salvington Aunt remained at home ordering Hats she never wore from Barkers etc & dresses – Somebody has lent or given a painting by Monsiu Desiderio to the national gallery – called "an explosion in a church" one side is perfectly alright & the other in process of coming apart in front of a Gothic altar – its all in darkness except for the plastic attack. It seems to me those planets in conjunction are having a very queer effect all round. Miss Roett is doing up the Rockingham[1] now – the people who were doing it were all told to leave by Tony Whatshisname – & Miss was ordered in & is delighted. I suppose in "Regency" – nothing contemp – *pas* the *genre de la Maison*. Suddenly got cold again here Im sorry to say owing to the planets I daresay. yrs. Ed.

To William Chappell from the Aikens' house in Brewster, Mass., 1953

Dearest B
How are you getting on. I dont seem to be getting any nearer New York where I see the Ballerinas have opened to a full house. I saw an article in the N.Y Sunday T. Mag about Margot by Sashy Sitwell with photos & a piece in time & there all booked up also I noticed the Old Vic midsummers nights dream is due next yr with Dames Moira (Shearer) & Helpman so everybodys well fixed. My favorite caracter Clare Leighton[2] came to lunch today with Mr. & Mrs. Francis Biddle[3] – "Claah", she calls it and looks exactly like Griffin of the Chelsea Polly with twists of plats – she appeared in a scotch Tartan Bonnet & got blind drunk on martinis & California Sauterne (type) with a terrific English ladies accent. shes a wonderful old 20ies piece & asked me if I remembered the "Cave of Harmony"[4] & said "Yes, Elsa was quayte a gahl in those deese! Ayme fraytefully haard at work on the mud flats studying the habits of cockles they spit at you like mean old men –" I think she does very well with her books & prints – Im getting quite worn out with all these goings on & social whirl. however I man[a]ged to paint 2 paintings & ½ way through a 3rd on my bridge table in a becoming half light I can hardly see – we went up to Vermont & New Hampshire a mere 1450 miles in all. N.H is full of Jumbo nutburgers nestling among the natch beauties & motels but Vermont realy is lovely – left to itself we went to a place called Newbury Port full of large crumbling 18th century mansions that I liked very much I wouldnt mind living there, not too far from Boston – However I cant get away from this neck of the wds They all seem tickled to death with the new house, I think its just about what they can manage & I heard from the laundry princess[5] she thought of

1 A popular homosexual bar in Soho.
2 An English artist.
3 The ex Attorney-General in Washington and his wife.
4 An 'artistical' thirties nightclub in the Seven Dials, London.
5 Barbara Ker-Seymer, now Rhodes, had set up a launderette.

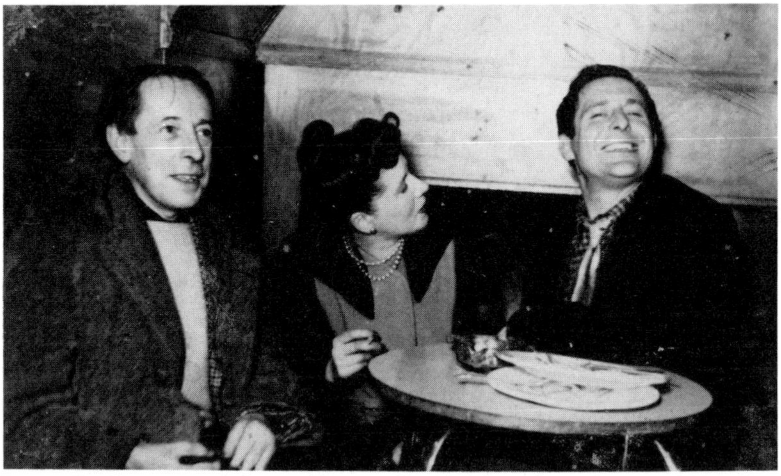

Burra, Ker-Seymer and dancer/director David Paltenghi at the Mandrake Club.

gadding off to Madrid for her hols with David Paltenghi[1] Bumble & Co who were working on some mysterious picture out there also a few handy stunt men etc. The Ritchies & milord have gone to Royan wher milord insists on going to all the restaurants mentioned in the Michelin guide, I always found the ones left out where much better. Im supposed to be sailing Oct 2 thereabouts so I do hope to be allowed to get to New York where I dont want to see a soul as if I see anymore strange people I shall scream[2] – Im beginning to be unable to keep a polite interested face. Conrad of course is ready for anybody the place has been full of visitors staying, a crazy woman called Pat Griffin an associate editor of Look appeared in full stage make up & bats wing dark glasses. She spent an hour every morning in the bathroom. C. said "She must use an enema I suppose" she was very nice as a matter of fact. hubbie arrived at the week-end with a 6 shooter attached to his belt goodness knows why & said may I mix you a gin & bitters – which I drank & felt as if Ide been hit on the head with the 6 shooter as it contained nothing but gin straight & a teaspoon of bitters in a large beer glass which I poured down all unnoticing. Well I hope to see you soon if I can make it love from yrs Ed.

To William Chappell from 41 Anderson St. Boston, Mass., 1953 only here for one week more

How are you getting along dearie? I have collapsed here for the last 5 weeks on the wrong side of the tracks so to speak – but the room is quite comfy & large – it gets more & more like Zazu Pitts in "Greed" behind a barricade of gallon jars of california claret (type) & empty instant coffee jars & old sardine tins I hope to have a little show here at the end of April. I only hope someone may buy something I went to hear Count Basie & band the

1 *David Paltenghi was an extraordinary young man who arrived in London before the war to study hotel management. He was Italian–Swiss. He decided to become a dancer, partnered Fonteyn and many other ballerinas, and ended up as a film director. He drank himself to death.*

2 *He screamed a lot – but always silently.*

other day. Im not surprised the musicians union are so careful they realy were wonderful. How did your Anouilh do[1] did it get to the West End and run They have a mysterious ruling here in Boston that you may only drink on Sundays *at Tables* do you drink less at tables or is it to do do with law of Moses being written on tables or was it tablets. I heard from David P[altenghi] who is working on Alexander the Great in Madrid he said Alexanders "Stalion" Bucephalus was played by an old grey mare (dyed) with false balls tied on I love *realism* I hope you are doing O.K love to all ED

To William Chappell from Brewster, Mass., 1953

Dear B

I just heard from the launderette girl that you have had a great success at the Hippo[2] I hope you had a joy plank with a chorus dangling electric fish that gave a schock. I havent been inside a theatre since I came here as they are rather expensive but a burlesk show at the old Howard in Boston which had Rose la Rose. I must say she really gave a wonderful performance especially her 2nd no. which she did in reverse appearing on a *chaise longue* covered in a comic strip and ended up at her dressing table in a Rose Té hostess crinoline – with a bottom that slipt off for smash exit also a member for the wedding[3] (movie) which was wonderful I thought especialy Julie Harris who gave a superb performance as F. Jasmine Higginbottom or whatever she called herself. I've been spending a week in Boston on my own[4] in a basement overlooking the N.Y. Central tracks everybody in the basement kept their doors firmly open & by the time I got in they were all drinking beer & drunk so asked me in so I never got to bed till about 3 or 4 sometimes, all Irish need I say – I spent my time visiting bars some were realy unbelievable The Novelty Bar was very good on Washington St. if you ever go to Boston its full of sailors, petty gangsters, aged whores & queens wrangling over the sailors like gulls over something thats been thrown off a boat & a Hill Billy orch magnified into an earthquake & a midget chip & cigarette seller – I also went to the Hi Hat to hear the Errol Garner Trio, very grand(?) & mostly coloured – with smart colored society ladies covered in diamonds & black cartwheels on their heads sipping pint tumblers of I dont know what quite; & Bourbons. There was also a Dixie land place that played tunes like I wish I could shimmy like my sister Kate so had to go there but that was more Harvard undergrad type with a good few dinges after which I would try to slip into my basement unseen. but you havent seen life till youve lived in a basement the landlady remarked – she was always *trés digne* untill she fell down on the floor. Im very happy here need I say Well you might drop us a line if you have time in all your successes love to FRED who has come into money I hear! ! Also Honor, your old pal E.

---

1 Time Remembered *at the Lyric, Hammersmith.*

2 *A revue,* High Spirits, *with decor and costumes by Osbert Lancaster, at the London Hippodrome.*

3 *From the novel by Carson McCullers.*

4 *Which was exactly what he liked to do.*

To William Chappell from Brewster, Mass., 1953

Dearest B – Lovely weather here & boiling hot but for a tornado in Worcester Mass, there was a terrible thunderstorm here, being drunk we thought it was all a gorgeous multiscreen 3 dimensional masterpiece by C B de Mille – Its beginning to get quite theatrical round about here with dainty little summer fire traps starring minor members of the Gabor familly [Eva] in Sailors delight & a high Brow rep at Provincetown – even Zachary Scott & Billie Burke. I imagined the coronation would be wonderful for show biz I never thought of wandering about in a drizzle looking at damp bunting. Mama said the show was wonderful on Teevey you might have been right in the abbey. we went over to Hyannis for the cinema Im so taken up I can never go to the movies, looking at the freaks – its Hastings realy. the figures dearie! I dont know how they dare parade themselves about with the most terrible gams & hanging bottoms of Babylon in very tight shorts – Brick red etc the men dont seem to go for shorts so much as in England thank god – so spend my time walking up & down drinking Beer & looking at mags in the drug store no wonder theyve got Bums after a double egg peanut mayonnaise 3 decker jumbo sandwich & a Barrel of milk. Yesterday an extraordinary lady photog arrived & took us without stopping all day Mary A[iken] was to be cook of the month for MacCalls magazine she had to cook a sea Bass for her house guests but couldnt get anything but a haddock. the "house guests" were all blind drunk by lunch time so I cant imagine what MacCalls will make of it. I hope we can have some of the photos they should be funny. Dont speak to me of living in *Rye* – I particularly dislike Rye. its everything that I most dislike – I dont want any part

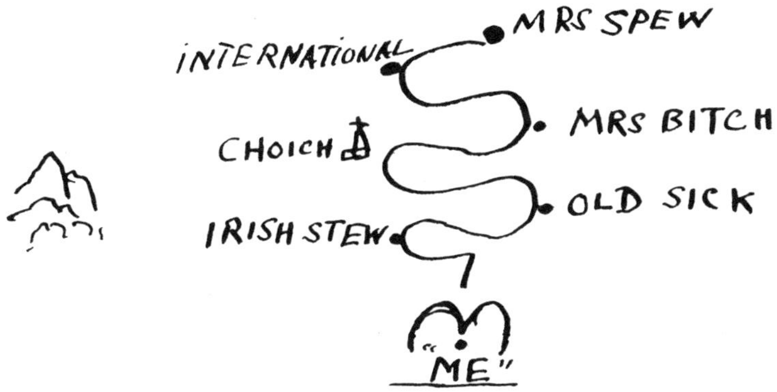

of it – Ime glad you had a lovely time at A[shton]'s shooting Box. being an heir now I consider he ought to have provided a large staff of perfectly trained Filipino boys to wait on you. Yrs Ed.

To William Chappell from Chapel House, Rye, 8 January 1958

Dear B.

Thanks for your letter The morgue has some what cleared up since the happy festival is over Mama is better but only tottering about & dear papa is struggling along Anne I hope is going to London today as she has had no holiday at all. you need have no qualms about Normans success at the Palace[1] as rocket coaches from outer Luton & Wigonovia (200000000000 layte mayles away & worked by a super turbodrop shuttle via jupiter) will be crowding the outer space port in Romilly Street Ive been reading Astounding Science Fiction.

Lynn Fontanne finaly has Alfred L[unt] murdered in that new play[2] they went to not at all a "sparkling sophisticated comedy" but a drama! that nobody was quite prepared for – german & rather symbolical – theyre too old for guardsmen. I see they are going to do some dreadful thing to the Hippodrome & turn it into a theatre restaurant show & dinner 30- & 15/- cold buffet in the circle that should be the grandest flop next to the London Casino. Thought up by Mr. Forte I believe & stuffed with gay folk from outer space. I hope you had a gay time on Hogmanay yrs Ed.

To William Chappell from Chapel House, Rye, 29 February 1958

Dearest B.
I entended to send a telegram yesterday but clean forgot to and have been very busy trying to arange one set[3] containing 2 bedrooms a Bar Lenox Avenue 2 parallel streets disapearing in a vista, a panorama(?) of Harlem a stoop, & a lobby – so I have plenty to work on, I went to an audition at the Victoria Palace, the West Indians were very insulted at being asked to speak in a 'murkan' accent! I left them to it now Mr. H[4] is in Paris looking for a girl I only hope a 'murkan.

It seems to me Charley has had wonderful notices at least The Times & the Dly Mail of course we dont know what Kenneth Tynan will say. he was terribly upset by the Potting shed[5] last Sunday anyway Im sure it will go on till Norman has a stroke. I told Mr. H to get a truck load of U.S. military personel (colored) from an Army Base to provide *color* some of those pubs near Fitzroy Square Tottenham Court Rd would provide – Well Ive no doubt I shall rush up for the day next week. I dont have time to stay just now. I wonder how much I should ask if Im not turned out befor the end! I have no idea realy what would you say Hope to see you befor long yours Ed & thank you for your letter.

To William Chappell from Chapel House, Rye, 1958

Well well we never know whats in store do we? I hope he's[6] not feeling too bad poor thing but is probably beginning to perk up about now with True Heart Susie[7] (Chappell) rushing from bed to bed playing a mandoline very

1 *Norman Wisdom was being directed by Chappell in a Frank Loesser musical,* Where's Charley!, *based on* Charlie's Aunt.

2 *Durrenmatt's* The Visit.

3 *For a play with music called* Simply Heavenly, *set in Harlem, with an all-black cast.*

4 *Mr. H was Laurence Harvey, who was presenting and directing the play.*

5 *A new play by Grahame Greene.*

6 *Thomas Elliott, a friend and colleague of Chappell, had been rushed into hospital at 2 am one morning for an emergency operation on his appendix.*

7 *True Heart Susie was a particularly sickening silent movie character.*

fast. We had a part of yr revue[1] & Dora B[ryan] on the T.V. on Tuesday I must say it made the rest of the programmes look like the Biggleswade womens Institute Christmas concert party – it had such a polish & very pretty girls. Massey junior[2] is wonderful I thought hes quite a find he was terribly good as the shepheard! also dear Dora as Cinderella. I suppose Honor makes their lives a mysery keeping up that wonderful well rehersed air! prior to that Ide been to a western with Audie Murphy the crowning of the Pope a 2nd feature etc at the Odeon Edgware Rd next the Met, the audience were purest Beckett entirely grey all over & sound asleep. Among other things on T.V we saw Joan Hammond as Mdm Butterfly or Shaun Glenville as Widow Twankey I should say It was one of the funniest things Ive ever seen rather unfair realy as at a safe distance – say in Covent Gdn she wouldnt have looked too bad but nothing is spared on T.V. I fully expected the baby to turn out to be Dora Bryan we seem to be very foggy today so I suppose a few more trains will be running into each other. let me know how you get on

yours Ed

I include a little sketch of how it looked on T.V.

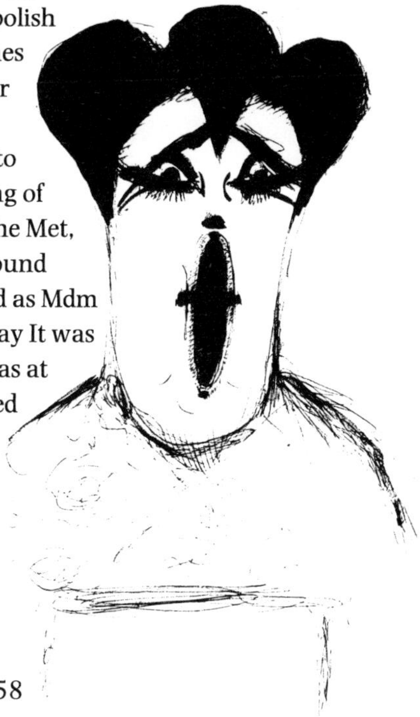

To William Chappell from Chapel House, Rye, Boxing Day 1958

Dear B

Thanks to anti biotics and moussec papa seems to be still living[3] as of writing, as the nurse gave him a terrible cold which could have finished him off. Mama is in the last stages of asiatic cholera[4] & can hardly stand up poor thing I think shes had a very high temperature The countess Ritchie has got a nose like a scarlet door knob that admits no air whatever with a sort of mixture of catarrh & synus I dont know what, so things have not been very *gai* this season. The boiler also burst & remained so for 3 weeks or so with no heat you can imagine that was wonderful here thank heaven its mended. The Lunts are opening in Brighton & I believe Lord & Lady Synus are going over to see the Sat: matinée I suppose they open today I think I should like to see Dorothy Ward & Tommy Steele at Liverpool I saw Dorothy Ward refused to have any of her long golden hair trimmed off as she said she had to compete with the longest hair in show business. Tommy S's. I saw they were planning a movie of the life of Sarah Bernhardt with Jennifer Jones! & one of Dusé with Sophia Loren. The life of Queen Victoria with Jane Mansfield. I humbly & proudly suggest getting larger & larger & shorter & shorter & blonder & blonder as the glorious years roll bye on the widest of wide screens Happy New Year & best wishes to you all yrs Ed

1 Living for Pleasure, *by Arthur Macrae and Richard Addinsell, at the Garrick Theatre.*
2 *Daniel Massey, son of Raymond.*
3 *Mr Burra was very ill.*
4 *Asian flu in fact.*

To William Chappell from Chapel House, Rye, 2 February 1959

Dearest B.

We are bathed in sun here too. I stayed the week end before last at Homer St we had drinks with Bum & she came to dinner. No sooner had she sat down than she unwound 20 foot of bandage off her leg & produced a realy lovely ulcer as big as a 5/- piece! when we went to Bums for drinks she was just having a quiet dinner party of Bunny & Compton Mackenzie! I think B[1] was rather frightened of Sir C I dont know why as hes a very urbane old thing Bunny didnt like W[est] Side Story I dont feel it would be quite him. A pot of tea & a cobra please Miss as we say at the Marrakesh Hilton Plaza. you can get chocolate covered ants Fried Bumble bees & roast caterpillars at Harrods now. also smoked sparrows on a skewer for the gourmet from the Far East. – Hong Kong to you – You can imagine all the Harrods ladies sitting in the Bank[2] chewing chocolate covered ants. We went to that little French restaurant[3] in St. Martins Lane just about opp the Shaftesbury Hotel with a Routiers sign. its very good in a plain way & no chi-chi & exactly like a French restaurant yrs Ed.

To William Chappell from Chapel House, Rye, 5 March 1959

Dearest B Am out of the clink which I was in such a state of boredom I nearly died (not of anemia) I soon picked up after the blood transfusion which took 4 hours in which your not supposed to move the food was frightful but they *tried* I'm supposed to be built-up – Heigh Ho! As for the *mumps* – everyone was furious as I felt absolutely nothing at all my face was a X between the late Sydney Greenstreet & Charles Laughton & Abbot & Costello in Meet captain Kidd I even had a swollen ball – that "they say" is too awful not for me Kidd – just a routine inflation I'm used to dropsy – but of course by that time I was in full spate with a temp of 102 an enormous spleen & a swollen liver – the Dr. from the hospital was struck dumb. however all goes well Im glad Ashton has done so well what does he want with a property abroad – hed never be there – everyon would allways want to go somewhere else. Gerald was going on about a chorus & said a revue wanted a chorus – thats as maybe but that would put [a] few hundred on the already huge weekly bill – would it not at present prices – he should stick to Nude to nite Josephine at the Grand Theatre Brighton where several nudes fell off a fan out of inanition & had to be taken to hospital you may have seen the other day – I should quite like to see Antonio.[4] Bar said he had a very good woman somebody D'Albaicin I remember a great beauty in Quadro flamenco (Diagheleff) called Maria D'Albaicin. she died of dope. I see a Member for the Wedding is on. Julie Harris was extraordinary I thought – for some reason they are showing it at the Berkley. its

1 *Was it Barbara, Bunny or Bumble? I think it would take more than Compton Mackenzie to frighten anyone of them.*

2 *The glorious Banking Hall, long since gone.*

3 *Mon Plaisir (actually Swiss).*

4 *The flamenco dancer, great at the zapateado.*

not "pop" I presume. also the Clouzot about the oil & Yves Montant etc I want to see – They have erected an enormous partition upstairs dividing off the top room. I didnt think I should be allowed to reign supreme in so much open space – however I dont care – funny I thought – I keep hearing about roads blocked etc on the radio but everything hereabouts is balmy spring otherwise duckie little TinkerBell towne is like an itsy bitsy morgue. quayte *dead* – its like Horror Comics – I am TOT – I come from the land of the living dead. you called me – Grtch Zoom – yours Ed.

To William Chappell from the Hotel Recamier, Paris, 1959

Dearest B.
We went to see Veterans of Variety a couple of days ago – that is Dame Josephine Baker & the youngest Nicholas brother[1] who sang a couple of *terribly hot* numbers in no voice but a mike. Dame Josephine who I seem to remember had a pretty but rather *small* voice is now a cross between Maria Callas & Elvis Presley thanks to a diamond encrusted mike. she has a wonderful white osprey hat & a splendid Rhinestone dress covered in embroidered flowers also a 1920ies style coat with huge great white fox? collar. but she doesnt sweep about enought for me at the end of 2 hours in the prom I felt as if Ide been hit by a 2 ton truck it was then going on another 2 I presume after the interval Mrs. Rhodes was dragged off to a hot dog at the Royale I had a nice walk up the Rue de la Gaieté & round Montparnasse! it realy hasnt changed except a huge movie next to the Rotonde its realy nicer than St. Germain des P. where the performances and *strain* are such & everybodys so busy trying to catch a big fish it worries me I cant pay attention to my Picon Citron – If Miss Roetts stomach supposed delicate stands up to the treatment its been getting it will stand up to anything – Mrs. R[hodes] is no one for weak stomachs & has taken to the Basque restaurant Clover & I go to especially *steak au poivre* which they have very good. Mrs. R has already been to the Printemps Samaritaine Louvre Trois Quartiers quartier reservée Uniprix Monoprix & Brentanos & bought a black nylon fur beehive I saw one seated in the 2 magots

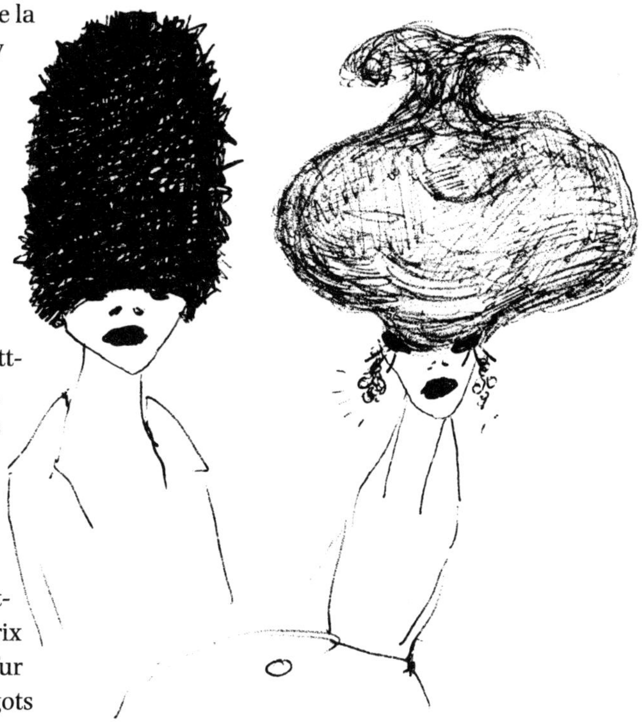

that was at least 2 feet high or more next to hair do in brightest ginger orange I went to see an exhibition *Les elumineurs Flammandes* at the

1 *Half of a famous black dancing duo, the Nicholas Brothers.*

Librairie which was illuminated books it was quite uncanny as they were 13th & 14 century & realy looked *brand* new. marvellous costumes exquisitely done in every detail & portraits of people Ime sure there was a catalogue I stupidly didnt get otherwise Ive not done a thing except be very busy running to & fro. Theres no shortage of traffic almost worse than London well Ill be seeing you I daresay   Yrs Ed

To Clover de Pertinez from Chapel House, Rye, January 1960

Dear Clo
Very sad about the accident[1] driving with Gallimards neview & wife & two children I got the obituary from the T[imes], even the Dylymyle (referd to as such by Nicholas Crabbe) had a piece about him. I couldnt have gone on with the exhibition a minute longer what with surfeit & stuffiness & all those terrible people peering at 500 ft apotheoses of Charles the 1st from a distance of 3 inches – when they should be hanging in the grand saloon about 5 feet from floor level! I must go again & see the other half. there are some wonderful things there however the contrast between the public & the paintings was too awful – even tho half the goddesses looked like very placid house maids suffering from slight nose colds & they probably were, being models – so realistic.

I think theres going to be an exhibition of paintings Spanish at the end of the month *contempry* they say they fit into the *contempry scene* & are purchased by amurkans one forgets that the 3 most celebrated modern? painters are Miro Dali & Picasso & P is having a grand retrospective at the Tate this summer with sculptures etc that ought to be good Maybe hes not contempry anymore Grande Dieu Am reading Rosmersholm. its wonderful they have that quality of a bomb ticking.

I see Mrs. Patrick Campbell as Rebecca roaming up & down wringing her hands and ticking away to herself I did see her in Hedda G[abler] well I hope you have a good journey & what about the new franc. have you found out about it?   yrs Ed.

To William Chappell from Chapel House, Rye, 30 December 1960

Dearest B –
We seem to have had about 20 Sundays. I never went out and the weather was lovely but for one awful morning. I did get driven down to the sea one day by Anne which was lovely & nobody there & we went to an obscure waste not far from Lydd full of rubble gorse gravel & ruins & people fishing in the sea with their rods on tripods what they catch I cant think. Clover is here for a week or two and wont move as she hangs on the phone waiting for Mr. P.[2] to ring up. quite like old times. I did see one movie "Shoot the pianist"[3] which is my favourite picture – so "amusing" until suddenly something *awful* happens. The pianist is [a] very cool little man Aznavour

1 The death of Albert Camus.

2 A distinguished literary man and inamorata of Clover.

3 A film of François Truffaut, starring actor/singer Charles Aznavour.

who Ive never heard of – with the bitterest dead pan Ive ever seen. it seemed to have upset the critics so unlike Les 400 coups.[1] I hope all your dinner parties past off well and nobody cried or hit each other. Mama was in bed 2 days with a liver complaint. from tiredness & 3 glasses of champagne she said but now is up again – Theres a wonderful account in the Telegraph of the policemans evidence at Raymonds Revue Bar. the most respectable place in London realy. hes being accused of running a disorderly house! Well dearie Best wishes for 1961 from your old pal E.

To Clover de Pertinez from Chapel House, Rye, 27 May 1961

Dear Clo Im glad you discovered the Raine[2] peice no wonder C[3] was so delighted with it. a Palace revolution & will it be without bloodshed? he said. Ive not heard or seen another word of anything but why would I, as Im not in the right set it will probably be hushed up & Kathleen Raine will be lured into a private lunatic asylum & given drugs & Braine washed. Ive not moved for weeks I feel very much better, I just cant be bothered to move the Academy gets very busy & tried to make me come to lunch on the 28th but I put it off till June 18th[4] I wish they would leave me alone I dont want their horrible old Academy[5] having done without it 40 odd years. Maybe Im a little tired from anaemia like pope John who seems in a very poor way. Yes do come if you want to when you come back. Frederick[6] is going for a two week holiday in July some time & then I dont suppose anyone will be permitted, but any other time is alright I'm sure – even then, if you do all the washing up & cooking. Mrs. Chappell[7] just left this morning to go & see D[ino] de Laurentis[8], it might be some little job or other its funny how B[illy] has got entangled in the movies. We were talking about restaurants & He said Smiths Tea Rooms[9] were very good indeed for lunch – entirely French & one or two Americans & none of the waitresses can speak a word of English. They have sausage[10] & mash twice a week! I must try it also a restaurant Bosc in one of those streets that run between the Rue St. Honore & the 3 Quartiers. I know quite well. also the Mediteranée[11] at the back of the Odeon very good but rather expensive – Ive often examined it & it looked rather too dear for me wonderful fish he said Bar is realy thinking of transferring her domaine from Homer St. to the Islington house. I think it would be very nice as Islington is so much more open & airy & I think a

1 *The autobiographic film that made Truffaut famous.*

2 *Kathleen Raine, the poet, had written an elaborate criticism of Aiken's work, with some things he wanted to hear and some he didn't.*

3 *Conrad Aiken.*

4 *When he put it off again.*

5 *They were trying to enrol him as R.A.*

6 *Frederick was the Burras' man-of-all-work, a person of much character. He had been with them most of his life.*

7 *(Fils)*

8 *Dino de Laurentis was an Italian movie mogul.*

9 *In Paris over W.H. Smith's bookshop in the Rue de Rivoli.*

10 *Walls, flown over from England.*

11 *All this when Chappell was working in Paris with Orson Welles on* The Trial.

Back garden & larger rooms & near Bar Roetts mama & near you. E said you were being bribed back for a visit in January to go to Malaga – which would be nice, where has the money come from, winnings at Poker? we did go a little drive with Anne yesterday through the mists up to the Fire hills at Fairli' near where you had that house – Its really very attractive up there. we came up from the Winchelsea Beach direction, its a strange labyrythine region covered in verdant richness covering up Ferdinand Céline-shacks[1] & bungalows. nobody in sight dead as a door nail not even *la chére grosse mignonne* lurking in the scrub   yrs Ed.

To Clover de Pertinez from Chapel House, Rye, June 1961

Dear Clo
Yes do come from Dover the trains are still running one every hour I think I imagine they will run through the summer. Ive not heard any more about Kathleen Raine. perhaps shes been walled up. Im better but my blood count hasnt gone up as it ought so the Dr. has produced some kind of Swedish iron injections guaranteed non carcinoginous in rats. I had one yesterday & felt Ide been kicked in the arse by a mule! I actually went into Hastings as I wanted to see a film & when I came back I was so tired I had to go to bed at 9.30 & Im supposed to go to the Academy & have lunch & sign a book & recieve a diploma or something I should be dead after that so I shall put them off. If these mule kicks dont raise me up I dont know what theyl do. anyway left to myself Im perfectly happy & alright so long as I dont do to much ie "rushing about" Yes dear you may cook & wash up & make a steak & kidney pudding & shop. What a squawk dearie because Mr. Profumo has been to bed with the same tart as an attache at the Russian Embassy! I dont know about Doc Boyd I feel he's been running the poshest call girl racket with abortion on the side Im sorry for La Belle Keeler who seems to be chased from pillar to post never a moments peace poor thing West Indians shooting through the door Mr. Profumo Dr. Boyd and all it should make good reading in France Dimanche. Let me know about July 1st but its not for a week or two I expect E[dward] will enjoy the Boda
yrs Ed

To Clover de Pertinez from Chapel House, Rye, 12 August 1961

Dear Clo. Thank you for yours.
I went to Hastings & you could hardly stand. however it made no difference at all to the merry throngs of French teenagers & juvenile delinquents and other human wreckage, milling about. I had all my hair cut off. I hope you got my card from Boolong on the continong. I realy enjoyed my trip on the Isle of Thanet. I seem to remember that from long ago – double gin & tonic for 3/6 & very large mesures too – everybody was stuffing sandwichs tea biscuits & chocolate from a slot machine – there are wonderful shops in

1 *Louis-Ferdinand Céline was a French novelist of the realist school.* Voyage au Bout de la Nuit *was probably his most famous book.*

Boulogne – huge sort of galleries full of everything you can think of & marvellous mens shops full of beautiful things & very expensive – it didnt seem to me any of the inhabitants ever entered them – they all[1] looked the purest Ferdinand Celine. we had lunch in a trippers restaurant. quite a good sole meuniere I had however & a bottle of blanc. The patty maison had been frozen to such a state it was impossible to unfreeze it. we had a lancashire lass at our table who embarked on a mountain of mussels. They looked very good but from the smell I notice rising from the port I thought sole was safer. there are 2 quite good libraries. I got a Butor about Baudelaire! which looks very interesting. there was a small chapter about *Le vin de l'assasin* so apt for a day trip. *Je serai ce soir ivre mort: alors, sans peur et sans remord*

Je me coucherai sur la terre, very bad taste and we wont include it in our selection. Bumble rang up this morning and asked me to stay a few days & she had tickets for Luther & I couldnt face it, I shall only start drinking again if I go to London, out of desperation & here Im not tempted to except on a day trip to Boolong & the next day I didnt feel very good – I wish the telephone was torn out by the roots. I had a pc from Bar who says all the other guests are like Dame Sybil Thornbyke & Mary Merrill & the book shelves are full of Nelsons sevenpenny novels encluding Berta Ruck. Also heard from Billy who seems to be very grand in Ischia in T. Rattigans schloss. expecting Graham Green to lunch. B said he was rather nervous as he didnt know what to say to high style authors & GG always looked so sour yrs Ed.

To William Chappell from Chapel House, Rye, 29 August 1961

Dearest B

And what fashionable watering place have you moved on to now? Baden or Homburg? There is a saucepan lid placed over the country of grey cloud. it rains in other places but here its just plain aluminium colour & bone dry – I hear poor Miss Roett has developed an acute case of chicken pox at the Ca Frollo. she hides in Maxs pyjamas wrapped up in a sheet & her face covered in lumps its worse than Death in Venice. She went to see some cousins just befor she left & they all had chicken pox, such a wise thing to do especially if youve not had it. its very infectious & I hope dear little Max has had it and Mrs. R[hodes] – Im expecting Clover & Edward next weekend & Miss Dawson announces (unless she can find something more suitable) shes coming too which means some one will have to sleep on a sofa & Clover is absolutely terrified of being driven – so we shall see what turns up (later) They turned up in full about an hour late for lunch having been held up for hours in a block – Bumble & Clover had been to Luther[2] & both said they thought it was awful! poor Finney had to pull constipated faces as Luther was constipated Miss D. said she didnt think he was quite

---

1 *The inhabitants, not the shops.*
2 *John Osborne's play.*

up to grand parts yet. he hasnt played very many however – Miss D is going to Italy this week I think to somewhere not very far from Venice to take the waters & bathes. She was terribly stiff & kept falling asleep at the wheel. I suspect her of taking millions of pills & anadin etc to assuage the aches – she has to be prodded by a companion. The Ritchies have been a few days in Edinburgh & are now on the way to Oban & thick drizzle & Le Toot Glasgow in dripping cowboy hats with dripping fringe round the edge – the last 2 days have been marvellous here – & Im glad to say we had a splendid week end – I went again to Boolong with my cousins – very happy time. no nasty sea air as I firmly took up my position seated in the Bar surrounded by everyone stuffing pork pies & tea so as they wouldnt be poisoned by anything dreadful in Boolong. we had quite a good lunch at the restaurant du Theatre exactly behind Le Theatre it *was* called Le Coq Hardi The Theatre has a terrible grey ciment sort of 1920 contempry modern front but the back is pure 1825 or 30 & the back streets also *very* quiet & no traffic at all. delightful I thought quite madly unfashionable positively nobody would be seen there dead – Gerald & Co. didnt enjoy Capree a bit according to Bum & spent over £1000 on it I cant think why they do it as Im sure they are much happier at home but I suppose they must "go away" Ide rather like to read Mrs. Moores book about Byron[1]

yrs Ed.

To William Chappell from Chapel House, Rye, 28 January 1962

Dearest B.

I was meaning to write to you at the Villa Rose & then I got your letter. I was sorry about the week-end but I didnt really feel very well on Saterday and by the evening I developed a swollen face. it looked like the worst mumps – an abcess but I brought it down with penicillin. Clover didnt come Bar said as she was living in her (what realy is a) daydream wicked old P sent roses & a book & fobbed off Mdm with tales of wifies bronchitis & then he had flu poor little man all he wants is peace I feel. I heard once or twice how well the roses were lasting Theres a terrible Vadim film called Blood & roses in natural Blood & rose tints which I suspect has been distantly based on that Sheridan Lefanu story about vampires. it hasnt had very good notices but I think I shall go & see it I saw "Splendor in the Arse" the new one by Elia Kazan that I enjoyed with the new young man brother of Shirley Maclaine[2] – *I* thought it was well acted. Mom frightened the daughter into a fit with stories of the awful things men do and we girls dont enjoy it but to get darling kiddies after which I went to Bardot in "La Verité" & la verite *is* that Brigitte *enjoys* what men do. all men. even if they dont do anything much & ended by cutting her wrists & killing herself – So its a mugs game dearie. There was a trailer of the Roman Spring of Mrs. Leigh which I must say I enjoyed very much – also with Shirley's brother as the gigolo he was excellent in the part. Dame Blanche[3] looked very styl-

1 The Late Lord Byron.
2 *Warren Beatty in* Splendour in the Grass.
3 *Vivien Leigh.*

ish also a shot of Lotte Lenya – as the Marquesa Terribili Birnbaum de Battifolia or some name like that – a *maquerelle* who obtained S. McL's brother for Dame B. who is going to play in the Trial? I expect O[rson] has people in mind it sounds very promising & interesting to me and will make quite a change from Shaftesbury Ave! Not that you want a change but who knows to what it may lead.[1] I was so put off by the season of uncomfort & joy I didnt know what to do. you know what this[2] is like in an easterly *gale* no less – Christmas eve when I did a little Christmas shopping was so seasonable it actually managed to half empty Tinker Belle Towne with all its twinkling lights twinkling for only me who was buying a bottle of Kirsh in the wine merchant. I gave it to Anne who never stopped drinking thimblefulls of it. I realy meant it for fruit salad – however eternal thimbles wear away a bottle. A couple here – Scotch I may add, went up to the N.W. of Scotland at Christmas & it was marvellous. very bright with black distant mountains & a sea of indigo & bright orange hills – the dead bracken goes a bright orange & the sun stays down low – they said it was very beautiful. On the train back when they arrived in Edinburgh they stepped into a sleeper & soon found nothing came out of any tap & there was a peice of ice in the water bottle – so thoughtful for martinis – when the heating came on every single pipe burst & they travelled back with a soaking floor. British Reelways lead the world – Theyd just been dumped on a siding & nobody had bothered to empty off the water – too much trouble.

I saw a lot of set reproductions of drawings and photos of "L'A[nnée] derniere à Marienbad & they looked lovely. the only Robbe-Grillé[3] I read was called La Jalousie. & started off from the floor up minutely describing every nail & completely leaving out the caracters. there all like that now – one I read called L'observatoire de Cannes by Jean Ricardou literally about nothing but? they went up in a horrible railway on a string & everything was minutely described, no names & no plot – and another one. not *realy* in the groove tho, called "La distribution" which consisted of an interesting *drame du Boulevard*. taking place in a posh Riviera hotel & with absolutely no dialogue – no one uttered a word & the whole thing was stage directions, minute ones I must admit and nobody ever had a name. it realy was rather good by a man called Marc Supportas very old French familly it sounds. Theres a very good exhibition at the Academy of from Giotto to Picasso I went with Bar – I shouldnt mind going again & theres Spanish abstract paintings at the Tate I must try & go. Clover translated the catalogue which she said was purest jargon balls & crap.

Mama is pretty well – so long as she doesnt go for a long walk & has made you a shawl! It will do nicely to appear at the off licence of the Sherry Bar on Sunday mornings in a petticoat mens boots untied & entirely wrapped up & vanished into the shawl but for one eye & a claw holding a milk jug for the guinness[4] Let me know how your getting on   yrs Ed.

---

1 *It led to very little, in fact.*   2 *Rye.*

3 *Alain Robbe-Grillet had written the script and dialogue for Alain Resnais's film.*

4 Galway Girl *by George Crosz (not John): a very nice costume for Sunday morning but the shawl was for reading in bed as since the war Chappell had always slept naked; it is still in use.*

no longer the Abbé Dawson[1] but the vicar of Bray where they make that film.

To William Chappell from Chapel House, Rye, 9 March 1962

Dearest B. The weather has been freezing here for the last 10 days and it was icy in London last W.E. which I spent at Geralds where they now have a terrible old Spanish cook. shes not bad realy but they have rather a high standard & were completely ruined by a Portuguese lady they had who was a *superb* cook Ive never had such food quite unobtainable in a restaurant – anywhere in London anyway. It was very warm[2] & a lot of gin, I was taken out to dinner with some gentleman & his new wife who had a picture of mine. I havent been to the Albany since Hodge! that dinner didnt quite come up to our standard. I thought it was pidgeon but it was realy a very old frozen pheasant (3) There was a terrifying middle aged lady with a bust & good legs & a face like a grey Du Buffet who roared anecdotes in a sort of stagey bellow in Geralds ear & was blind drunk and a Mr. & Mrs Gutteridge friends of John Devonport[3] I found I went to see Lannée derniere a M[arienbad] & I was glued to it and not bored at all I hadnt the least idea which *année* it was or whether the heroine had been shot or the Hero suddenly fallen over a balcony & that hotel[4] is realy wonderful.

Ive not seen the Bars for about 2 weeks or so. having blotted my copy book by going out to lunch & getting blind drunk & not arriving at the cinema Bar was furious. I ended up in the Capacannina Club? with the manager of Wheelers who kept saying I realy *must* get back to Bayswater & not going need I add.

Desmond[5] appeared in a very sharp suit for work at the galleries! digne de Bunny.[6] with a very long double waistcoat with buttons in a V & very high at the neck. it was beautifully made but he must have drugged the Tailor to have induced him to produce anything so oo tray it looked very nice. his supposed chief girl friend Jocelyn turned up – shes very pretty but a genuine bitch G. says. I can see Phyl cant bear her D[esmond] told her they didnt *like* her I must say in those circumstances Ide never enter the house. You cant accuse me of doing anything[7] as I purposely hide & dont see a soul for weeks. I find its the only way I can work so see much fewer people than you see at Fregene[8]

– Yrs. Ed.

Did you see that Arthur Macrae died[9] the other day in Brighton? an X-Italia Conti pupil he was no age.

---

1 *Another of Bumble's titles.*

2 *In the Corcorans' house obviously.*

3 *John Davenport, a journalist, parodist and musician.*

4 *It was filmed in a great palace near Munich, the Schloss Nymphenburg.*

5 *Desmond Corcoran.*

6 *Bunny Roger.*

7 *Like finding himself blind drunk in the Capacannina Club with the manager of Wheeler's?*

8 *Where Chappell was staying with Orson & Paola Welles in their house near Rome.*

9 *Of cancer. He wrote four of the revues Chappell directed, and many successful comedies.*

To William Chappell from Chapel House, Rye, 30 March 1962

Dearest B

I would have written befor only was at Homer St & didnt get your card till I got back. It all sounds lovely to me I always like to be in Paris. Bum came to dinner & she is realy rigid poor thing Ive never seen her quite so stiff – she seems very busy however doing a film & a play I think – I also saw Lord Churchill[1] who was babbling gaily on in the Rockingham which little Bar has been painting up. We had an *exquis petit repas* at Chez Solange which Ive always looked upon with great suspicion & its very good we thought. presided over by a band of French women. they know their stuff the decor is a shade on the wild side with double damask wall paper & assorted christal chandeliers & I rather liked it, not contempry anyway. I saw Never on Sunday. Melinda Mercouri was splendid with the biggest mouth in Pireus – and all the tarts were perfectly *sweet* and nobody has ever heard of a Mickey Finn or anything nasty. she seems like a sort of comedy Blonde Magnani I should like to see her in a tragic part as her face is a tragic face realy. In the local paper I saw they had been doing Scenes from the Long distance runner at Camber among the sand hills & they should have been very realistic in the East wind. Mercifully warmer now. I think your hotel[2] was the one Arthur[3] took his overdose in have you been seeing ghosts of an elderly marquise doing embroidery on a frame seated by the fireplace – I always like Van Cleef & Arpels[4] window & a ruby & sapphire scottie emerging from an emerald dog kennel etc I wouldnt mind a nice ring. All George Orwells books have been coming out in Penguin & I got Wigan Pier & Keep the Aspidistra flying. he has an eye for monsters like no one. Ide forgotten how good he was. I wish they would bring out Down & out in L[ondon] & P[aris] again. I believe Zagreb is a wonderful place[5] with the Palace of somebody or other Domitien? & other remains or am I thinking of something else. Ragusa.[6] thats it. I seem to remember Clover stayed there with Mum & Dad years ago. You do seem to be moving in quite high cercles with Anthony P[erkins] & [Jeanne] Moreau Anthony is the darling of (teen age) Paris I thought & is going to do a film entirely in French – so I saw in the Times which also said Orson W was finishing Don Quixote & begining a version of The Trial. Are Perkins & Moreau and all going to Zagreb too? There seems to be an epidemic of terrible "Japanese" films in which huge american ladies disguise themselves as *mousmées* & do the most awful things. Rosalind Russell on all fours teasing Alec Guiness by creeping round him to say nothing of Shirley Maclaine in the Geisha as a gheisha I dont know whats the cause of all this. I wonder what the Japanese think. if Jerry Lewis was a gheisha Ide go & see it. Mrs. Helpman

---

1 *Peter Spencer Churchill.*

2 *France et Choiseul, in the Rue St Honoré.*

3 *Arthur Jeffress.*

4 *The great jeweller in the Place Vendôme.*

5 *It wasn't really as it turned out: extraordinary yes, but run down.*

6 *Now Dubrovnik.*

has been playing a dear old gentleman (a cross between Mephisto & Bransby[1]) in a wheelchair & crutches opposite Beatrice[2] Lehman as an old lady disguised as Boris Karloff who speaks like a parrot in a Strindberg play on T.V. I'm very sorry to have missed it Anne & Colin are going to Germany! BONN I dont know whats BONN there HA HA they dont like beer but there are walks. A hasnt been well. she gets colds & promptly runs a fever. I shall not go any place till Autumn when I get no further than Réaumur–Sepastopol where there are lovely walks & beer & Picon Grenadine an old country remedy Well let us know how your getting on in the Rue St. Hon.

Yrs Ed

To William Chappell from Chapel House, Rye, 12 May 1962

Dearest B. I think Zagreb sounds rather nice. Have you been anywhere else? I had a weekend at Homer St. Miss R[oett]s uncle arrived from Brooklyn (N.Y.C.) to stay with Mum & came to dinner just a little familly affair as Miss R was rather afraid for unkle who is a positive Damon Runyon thin little short man & a heavy drinker Im afraid. hed been all over too from the Ritz Bar to Collins Islington via the Tower of London – anyway who should walk in on the little familly party but Mickey[3] – Charles Boxer,[4] & a courtly old world american gentleman who looked exactly like President Isenhower – Uncle never stopped talking & drinking for a single second he realy fascinated me as for Mickey – I did notice signs of wear towards the end of the soirée – Geoffrey[5] was also there as a familly member – he had been asked. I went to Liason Dangereuses & realy after all that to do they didnt seem very "dangereuses" to me. The only caracter who seemed to have any style at all was Gerard Phillipe as Valmont the others looked like very common rich French people & there were a terrible couple of sub Bardots. it bored me rather We also went to see "Sweet Bird of Youth". The Paige as the declining star was absolutely *superb*! She was rather in the manner of Brenda Dean Paul. P[aige] has a very grand manner & says to Newman – Er – bring me my spectacles – I like to see what Ive been to bed with – yes – hum Ive done better but I *have* done worse – at the Coliseum which is full of *ghosts*!

You have a few little treats of a sort awaiting you in Gai-Paris consisting of Dame Deitrich at Olympia & a marvellous Mexican exhibition of everything you can think of sugar skeletons. sculpture – & heads shedding real tears with real eyelashes & all. Ide very much like to see it – at the Petit Palais I might struggle to that I went to see A walk on the wild side which isnt a very good film but I enjoyed it. Capucine is lovely to look at like a very grand lady in her own well chosen environment but what gentleman

---

1 *Bransby Williams, the music-hall performer who did characters from Dickens.*

2 *Beatrix, the actress sister of John and Rosamond Lehmann. The play was* Spook Sonata.

3 *Mickey is Emily Hahn, an American writer who worked a lot for the* New Yorker.

4 *Charles Boxer is married to Mickey.*

5 *Geoffrey is Dr Dove, the only doctor Edward showed faith in, and a great friend of his.*

would dare presume in a New Orleans brothel I ask you & old Barbara Stanwyck as the Madame was acting away – I didnt think old [Laurence] Harvey was so bad as *that* – I would never be surprised if he didnt end up a "*Star*" I mean a real one for they dont act realy. I rather enjoyed Christopher Issyvoos[1] Down there on a visit its very realistic Theres a splendid Brian Howard type on a greek island & a well known Amurkan [male] whore at the end who was very well done I thought – who on being recruited for the Forestry fire fighting corps or something in the war said. "Since your Aunties taking the veil, she might as well go the whole hog & have *all* her hair cut off! & murmured "Aunties last Pick up" when getting into the pick up truck that was to take her to the camp! he seems terribly frivolous for a high class auther dont he? Another remark of La Paige was Give me a cigarette. One of the ones that gives you cancer (theyd been getting high on tea). Miss Beatrice D[awson] is doing the costumes for Uncle Vanya at Chichester S Lorances production

yours Ed.

To William Chappell from Chapel House, Rye, 26 July 1962

Dearest B

And where is my wandering boy to-night? you havent been to Madrid by any chance – Clover has returned & stayed here a day or two on the way – I went to see Harold Lloyds world of comedy a string of old comedies strung together heaven I thought. especially the supporting caracters all of whom I know intimately by sight and masses of terrible tram cars whirling into tunnels & rushing backwards in the old Hollywood hills. The Maison Dawson (absolutely rigid when last seen & unable to bend) is doing a few dresses for Miss Judy [Garland] in the Lonely Stage – Miss Judy had a lot of lovely dresses made specially in Amurka but wore them about town so she naturaly got rather 'tached – one moment you can do anything with her & the next she becomes terribly grand! However she seems to [be] very nice. they seem to get on well. I spent last week end in Homer St. & they are shortly off to Ischia which I hope wont be like Blackpool Beach in wakes week – Not very good here realy as far as supposed summer weather goes – the caravans are empty they say and milord the laird o'Rye Harbour is nearly driven cracked by the vast camp around the house with distant music all day which stops for an occasional voice saying "Will Mrs. Bunthorpe please go to Caravan 102 at once". They've taken another lovely spot in Iden & Im wondering what Fate has in store there – some nice council houses & a Battery of Battery Hens perhaps working night and day with "distant music" to encourage laying – Very sad about poor Harold[2] dropping down dead outside the dressing room door after taking a class – I suppose his heart must have been strained & I see in the Times obituary Raquel Mellor has died in Barcelona where she started her

1 *Isherwood.*
2 *Harold Turner of the Royal Ballet.*

professional career at 19 – aged 74 – she appeared in London in the 20ies in Albert de Courvilles Joy Bells – I wish theyd show her old picture of "Carmen" – she looked so winderful in it – but I suppose its not "artistic" or all the copies have been lost – & Violettes Imperiales! Well let me know how you are getting on if this ever reaches you!

Yours Ed

To William Chappell from Chapel House, Rye, 14 December 1962

Dearest B.

Im very worried about poor Mama as I think she feels permanently sick (except in bed) which is the last place she wants to be, cant eat anything & is very feeble & an awful cough. a stomach cough she says. I wish they could stop it or it will stop her. However she couldnt be more comfortable than she is here – waited on all the time & comparatvely warm at huge expense. The dear little streets have all been dug up & new sewers put in so you can imagine what it was like – vastly improved I thought with a gang of Irish laborers in western hats from Woolworths & about 50 pneumatic drills, scoops & dirt removers all full on – we had an old lady friend to lunch who said "Theyre so *good looking* arent they? so YOUNG! and never a bad word or tipsy (?) There are some nice photos in Wardour Street of Baby Jane[1] presenting a roasted rat on a plate on a well appointed tray to a shrunken ruin in bed (Joan) and one of Baby Jane giving Joan a hard kick on the floor Sir Lawrence will want to be in the next one they make as Baby Janes illegitimate son who has been chained to a tin bed in the attic for 40 years and forgotten human speech – I've been reading "*Occupe Toi D'Amelie*"[2] it never stops for a minute! Like Dr. NO – Its very funny too because the characters are all so matter of fact & real – but I dont know what it could have been like in English, as Im sure theyd tone it down & get terribly coy. I can see Vivien Leigh being very good as Amelie. Theres La Dame de Chez Maxim in the same book which Im looking forward to I didnt know he wrote it. I saw in Time Romi Shneider was here in a film "The Victors" with Mercouri & Moreau as well – I shall look forward to see her as "the nymphomaniac Leni" in O.W.'s the Trial if it ever gets printed or whatever they were trying to do. What about money I wonder?[3] I enjoyed "Le Beau Serge"[4] a lovely village I thought, Bar thought it gloomy but such places dont depress me. Oxford strasse & all the Bright (dead) lights in the West End *depress me*! to such a state that I must be drunk then I feel quite cheerful – For a *time* – They dont have half enough electric bulbs – I noticed Harrods was covered in bulbs in a very old world style. Everybody was blind drunk in the Village drinking from the bottle when

1 *Bette Davis in* Whatever happened to Baby Jane? *with Joan Crawford.*

2 *By Jacques Feydeau; it was put into English by Noël Coward as* Look after Lulu *and the characters were not matter-of-fact or particularly real.*

3 *Practical Edward – a good question. Chappell was kept hanging about in Paris for two months before he was paid and then only received half.*

4 *A film with Simone Signoret.*

not giving birth to mongol kiddies in a thick snowstorm or being seduced in the cemetery – not the least bit depressing in my point of view – I suppose it was by way of a homilly against alcohol. Well you must come down when theyve[1] gone back to the village school House if we're still alive!

Yrs Ed

To Clover de Pertinez from Chapel House, Rye, 26 December 1962

Dear Clo

Thank you for El Bosco. I had a very good book on him but it vanished. I think I gave it away. It has been bitterly cold quite bright and everything a dry grey colour as hard as stone. The whole house is full of monstrous christmas cards of an unparalleled size and vulgarity – a great many weeny feetus'es dressed as choir boys with huge heads & also "Red candles on the festive Board" consisting of 3 oranges & a prickly pear against a red church window etc all from loving pupils of the Ritchies. Ive been getting through Christmas with "The Naked lunch"[2] which is wonderful starts off realistic & ends up outdoing Maldoror.[3] They make wonderful remarks I must say. The Lesbian, concealed in a papier maché Arc de Triomphe, fills her great lungs & looses a *tremendous* bellow – "Oh Say do that Star Spangled Banner yet wave?" by the time it gets to "Hassans Rumpus Room" (smart club?) it turns into a X between Maldoror, Justine, & W.W. Jacobs. and I also have a tiny paper back Mary [Aiken] sent of only 650 pages (& abridged) about slave breeding on the old plantation where everyone had a marvellous time but the white ladies as young mastuh suh was always in the slave quarters trying to get Pearl in the family way & give birth to a high yaller girl they could get a huge price for in New Orleans! M said you wont be able to put it down if you can stand the style – I dont see how they can make that one into a movie![4] its called "Mandingo" we seem to have got over the wreck pretty well and mama seems better. company cheered her up & is even eating more not that thats very much – but better. It snowed 20 hours in Marseilles & in Barcelona France has been freezing. I listen to Radio Lille which is very loud here Ive very much enjoyed both Occupe toi d'Amelie & La Dame de Chez Maxim and am enjoying Messieurs les ronds des cuirs about the ministére des Dous & legs – its brilliant and in a wonderful style this time, dedicated to Catulle Mendes & with a foreword by Marcel Schwob I got them at Harrods.

Fancy!

hope you Keeping warm in I

yours E

---

1 *Anne and Colin Ritchie.*

2 *William Burroughs' novel.*

3 Les Chants de Maldoror.

4 *But they did!*

To William Chappell from Chapel House, Rye, 11 April 1963

Dearest B.

It was just as well I didnt come to the party[1] as 10.30 Wednesday I ejected everything on sight till about 2.30 when I fell asleep there being nothing more left but a raging thirst. I got terribly anemic according to the Dr. who took a blood test. I must say Ive been feeling terrible, tired I suppose more than terrible realy – and am eating protein (?) & pills & was told to walk up hills & stairs as little as possible! what is may *layfe?* but walking up hills & stairs? anyway I havent been out. Hes coming next Wed to take another test & it should have gone up. He also said I mustnt go to London for fear of catching something else which would be very bad. The party went off O.K. I expect – everyone loves it. The Times critic was a shade sour but its only the 2nd time theyve ever even noticed me at all as they dont much care for me realy & [I] will never be seen at the Venice Biennale. they reproduced a picture however I cant think why – its very strange all these little Fart politics & things that go on. perhaps there will be more on Easter Day if theyve got any space left over from ads for Holidays – they go on so I dont feel I ever want to go away again except to Pittsburgh PA I send you this card with the Mortal Man[2] on it and I found it in the automobile book too. I thought it lovely and a splendid view down the valley. A[nne] & C[olin] are going to Devonshire next wed for a holiday in which they dont have to do anything at all. I wouldnt mind going down there. Max is become a poet & turned over a new leaf I hear altho the house reeks of tobacco smoke. whats to become of that 35£ unplayable steel gittar? could you pawn it? Well I suppose we shall see some Bizarreries down here over Easter yrs Ed

To William Chappell from Chapel House, Rye, 19 April 1963

Dearest B

The Dr came and said my blood count hadnt gone up but was stationary so I am still on protein & mustnt do anything at all. I dont care about not doing anything *realy* but I do feel much better. I did dare walk to the post office yes do come down if you want but not from Tuesday to Fri next week as Tilde – Mrs. Loeb – old friend of mamas comes & never stops murmuring compulsively about thousands of caracters perfectly charming men & people etc whose names Im sort of begining to know when they turn up in the flood rather like the last act of the Mill on the Floss! & how mein Vater was very fond of the old Emperor & drank mustard & water to ruin his voice as he didnt want to be in the choir of the old vienna something or other. she drives poor mother out of her mind! I also managed to get Scott Wodehouse who came down for the day in his Volkswagon (by courtesy of the film co) to drive me over to the A.B.C. in Astings where they were having a try out of Baby Jane very appropriate for Hastings my dear where I feel any amount of Baby J's are lurking in bed sitting rooms. she[3] was

---

1 Private view for his exhibition at the Lefevre.

2 An hotel in the Lake District.

3 Bette Davis.

wonderful I thought & gave a splendid Bravura performance – not realy a good film as it seemed old fashioned in treatment & could have been more "frightening" but Bette was marvellous – I see she has made a personal appearance at Warners with her daughter aged 16 who sang "Ive written a letter to Daddie" (his address is in heaven above) The Beatles might beat it up into a pop no.

If Mrs. R[hodes] thinks she going to stop Max from smoking & drinking shes got another thought coming to her "Mothers are the last to know" my new number for Baby Jane Im longing to see 2 for the see saw on in H next week I suppose I shouldnt drag there? I also want to see Summer lady or whatever its called here, in the USA "The Stripper" about a middle aged lady who falls for a boy of 18 so far fetched dont you think? anyway Im afraid it didnt last long at the Carlton & "To kill a mocking bird" which I thought was a very good book sort of Faulkner for the little ones! a little diluted and middlebrow it was realy very charming & Im scarcely ever charmed but I quite was by "To K a Mbird" I heard a long extract of Michael Machelmore?[1] in his Irish literary numero on the Foreign service of the BBC I was glued to it and I dont care for "talking" but he was very amusing & has such variety – quoting a Druids prayer he says The gift of the gab by God – since before Chroist! If you come down & have finished it will you bring down Under the Volcano[2] as I like dipping in it now & again *dipping* I had a first edition that I leant Clover & that was the last of that. and I must have a copy

yours Ed

I keep getting letters from the R.A. about terrible dinners that I always forget – the whitebate dinner was the last. I believe the speeches at the Academy Banquet where of an unbridled boredom according to Lord Ritchie – what all this has to do with "Fart" I cant think I even heard from Henry![3] I should answer that.

To William Chappell from Chapel House, Rye, 4 June 1963

Dearest B

I have noticed that East Anglia had an East wind & fog off the North Sea all the time I thought of you at the Festival[4] It looks a dear little place *un si joli petit plage* – I realy ought to have gone and visited at Mrs. R[hodes] last week end but I couldnt move & finaly ended up in Hastings where I bought a pair of black shoes like the ones you gave me only much commoner & very comfortable too, I finaly was fortified to go and try them after 3 beers – I thought I could refuse them if they didnt fit but theyre marvellous and made in Yugo Slavia! which seems odd – and I got a pair of black jeans

---

1 *Macliammoir, the splendid Irish actor.*

2 *By Malcolm Lowry.*

3 *Henry Rushbury, who with his wife Florence (Birdie) Rushbury took Edward and Chappell to Paris for the first time in 1925.*

4 *Aldeburgh, where Chappell was directing. It is* far *from being 'un si joli petit plage'.*

much to the sellers disaproval who tried to make me buy a nice pair (with turn ups) and suitable to Mr. Kruschev. theyre very good for work as they are made of cast iron! the zip will draw the lightening and the iron monger in that part had wonderful brass lamps gold style exactly like we used to have in the nursery about 1911 not for electric light but parafin! 59/6 beautiful round opaque glass globes. I should rather have liked to have seen Dead Souls given by that Russian Co even if I dont understand a word I dont feel it would matter Im longing to read it again now and there *was* a copy but not now natch. Ive Been deep in my favourite style book called a "long and happy life" by Reynolds Price – southern ton up heartless boy with fiancey – called Rosacoke also one I read "Catch 22" about a U.S. air force outfit in the war! I hate war books but not this one which is frightfully funny in a nasty way & will not feature Richard Attenborough. I saw Irma la Douce as I wanted some place to lay by in – the *Set* is terribly good & must have been copied stone by stone but the tarts! are just as *Francéy* as Pig feet black eyed peas & 7 up! make dear Gloria Swanson as Sadie Thompson look like our dear Queen as she looked this very week at Epsom. any respectable french whore would sooner drop dead than look like *those* tarts! let alone be arrested on the spot – Its quite amusing tho – see you soon I hope   yours Ed.

To William Chappell from Chapel House, Rye, 12 June 1963

Dearest B

Thank you for your letter.

It seems to me as if Mrs. Rhodes might realy move to Islington. The Doctor isnt satisfied with my progress so has produced some Iron injections, swedish he says and have not produced cancerous tumours in rats (so far). I must have spoiled my progress by going to see "Hud" at the ABC in Hastings. I enjoyed it thoroughly. Paul Newman crashes about in a pink caddy poor Mr. Profumo has nothing on him as he only has married wimmin. Brandon D Wilde is becoming better looking & for a moment I thought was going to be seduced by the cook, a change for her, as she was usually being attacked by P.N. when drunk. I should love to see Freaks at the Paris Pullman & Edgar Rice Burroughs describing his own film with a dead pan face Dead Pan is the word for any photo Ive seen of Mr. Burroughs. I have a passion for the midget in Freaks Harry Earls who was a baby in a film I once saw with Lon Chaney as a dear old Grannie pushing prammy, Baby would seize in its tiny fist any pearl necklaces kind ladies wore & break them into the pram then be wheeled home & given a cigar. from the sweetest "Baby" face it would put on a face of unbelievable venom. Perhaps you would care for a card for the Academy Soirée? (evening dress Tux & decorations) I have one or two and even a ticket to park the cah. & I think Im supposed to go to lunch on Tuesday any way I cant now unless somebody drove me there *& back* in a cah. H A H A the whole thing seems so quaint Yes do come down anytime over a week after you left 2 lbs of the sausages were unearthed in the Fridge! even I, didnt dare eat them I wish

Ide known – they must have thought I was saving them for my little gathering of Dark Things on the Gibbet marsh   yrs Ed

To William Chappell from Chapel House, Rye, 23 December 1963

Dearest B   Thank you so much for the lovely shirt Ive been wearing it ever since. its such nice stuff and I must wash it soon. I like the colour I have a tendancy to DARK creatures of the DARK and crocodile people buried for countless eons of unrecorded time and mysteriously appearing in a small colony in the Bronx – I hear from Miss Well informed you are off to Paris staying with Terry going to all the places or what remains of same that havent been torn down & made into discotheques or Drugstore. Im deep in "The Day of temptation" William le Q[ueux][1] I cant put it down about an Italian adventuress madly in love with a nice young Englishman they spend the summer in glamerous Leghorn she dressed in black lace & jet with a smart little toque or a dove grey suit & large black picture hat. it must be period 1902. Shes always cycling – its quite the thing and in the bois as the pretty countess cycles by with her hands off the handle bars & fixing her chic little toque with a hat pin. the smart young men are heard to whisper Stories!? all that, & "diplomatists" & the good old piss of Europe is hanging in the balance as usual. hes realy a terribly bad writer! but you cannot put them down – or I cant this would make a wonderful movie with the late Monro[e] as the countess who had a face of singular "*innocenza*" & was a dazzling blond[e]

Desmond & Judith are back from USA they do seem to have had quite a time & a luncheon with George Cukor with all sorts of people (& Terry) suddenly the Toulouse Lautrecs & Gauguins etc flew up to the ceiling & a vast wide screen came down from heaven with a new picture with James (is it James?) Garner & everyone said doesnt he look *turrible* or isnt he ugly. They loved San Francisco. I feel very HUM DRUM after all there glamerous carryings on. but I know I would be only permanently feeling sick from a hangover –

Well – happy new year (*again?*) etc we are expecting the usual tomorrow at lunch My Lord. Colin & Anne. Mama isnt realy too bad considering

Love to all from yours Ed.

To Clover de Pertinez from Chapel House, Rye, 26 February 1964

Dear Clo

Have been at Islington this week-end which is very nice indeed not nearly so claustrophic as Homer St. Very quiet but for the children in the playground. we went to Whitechapel yesterday to see Rauschenburg?[2] I think – who is very good he uses old pants & signs and various different ways & techniques with a wonderful result and there is a lovely series of Drawings supposed to be Dantes Inferno which are rubbings & pencil scribblings

1 *Edward was reading this novelist with equal fascination at his preparatory school.*

2 *The American painter, then exhibiting at the Whitechapel Gallery.*

with faces appearing they are a beautiful greyish colour – american he is of course. the academy struggles on sending invitations to assorted nightmares & obituary notice[s] of completely unknown people. & Ive never been to Goya! I realy cannot face the horrible people every fartstudent en beatnik & leather filthy hair & Beatle wigs even at Whitechapel of course I quite like that – There were also one or two very neatly dressed Daddies. I saw John Banting a few days ago & he said of course Jimbo isnt a heavy drinker realy he just likes to get drunk 3 times a week. J[ohn] likes to be a teeny weeny bit high all the time I suspect – he said he had asked John Devonport to stay! that should be curtains for quite a long period[1] – The crayme of Padre Amaro Ive been reading translated (quite well) by somebody called Nan Flanagan I also read Miss Lonelyhearts & the day of the Locusts & End as a man by Calder Willingham I just read them over again. we didnt have many friandises when E[dward de Pertinez] was here only scrambled egg.

Yrs Ed

I should love the sequence [sequel?] to Guignols . . .! I reread it & Vauboode la nuee[2] & macredit! There is also a new Nathalie Sarraute entirely about literary criticism "quotations etc from, which has caused quite a flutter in a weeny *cercle* I expect it is on her theme of snobbery & *lieu communs* Jargon! Im sure its very funny if you think that funny

To William Chappell from Chapel House, Rye, 1 May 1964

Dearest B. I dont know, but it was only a Pc I sent from Rotter.d[am] – which I adored. the entire place was knocked down but for a few old streets period 1870–1900! So it now is a sort of demented Madison Avenue rearing up from a pile of rubble & old tramways whirling backwards & forwards like a Mack Sennett comedy – it was naturaly freezing cold & a frightful wind but everything was boiling central heating like 'Murka so very cosy. I found some Bars in a little old dockside corner near the home for dipsomaniac sailors & U S Lines very small & all called the Pub – MAEWEST LANDSEND accent on end but you may stay so long as you dont *fall asleep on the Bar!!!!* for if you do you are turned out *at once.*

The Golden Gate had a Bar lady whose mouth was a golden Gate who said "a Beer dear?" then I went to another one I dont know the name which had the drunkest people in it Ive seen since I left Avenue B. & a screaming queen who flew in a towering rage with his Boy friend. a very neat young man in a smart overcoat & a hairdo, & suddenly bellowed in English Get OUT! and denounce me if you DARE!! No one took any notice at all & Madame then made the Barmaid – in a neat afternoon dress with a satinette ocelot front change him a cheque in the middle of which he suddenly remarked in English & FUCK the working classes – by that time everyone was being treated to Beers by a blue grey figure who had obviously been on the bar for days as he had quite a patina! I couldnt think

1 *John Davenport was a very heavy drinker.*
2 Voyage au bout de la nuit.

why I was surrounded by glasses. I then retired in fairly good order as I felt another quarter hour & I should have never gone till the following day or 2 or 3! & Amsterd[am] which we visited in a torrent looked marvellous I thought I must go *there* – the museums are superb & we also visited the Hague which I very much liked & it has some eccentrics I noted of the first water – they are getting rather *rare*. there was a lovely Gibson girl 75 & not a day younger with a mop or rather romp I should say & a huge orange flat wool Tam with a pompom in the middle – she must have had it made her friend looked like a X between Sybil Thorndyke & Edith Sitwell & was having a nip of old geneva with her coffee – I didnt care for Brussels nearly as much I realy prefer the Golden gate & MAE WEST. Some very good shops in the H[ague] & Rotters – both high class & Monoprix types – I never saw a soul on stilts & in a Dutch cap & wearing clogs – and I arrived home a wreck! whenever I come back Im a wreck – Friday I went out with Banting and Jim we ended up at the Pipemakers Arms which had an extension till midnight for a Farts match accent on Farts. they have a huge public and a Juke Box! the public look like a cross between Bodger[1] and screaming Lord Su[t]ch with streaming screaming golden hair and Navvys from all the surrounding Pylons, atoms & constructions & a few *Debs*(?) more like the Elephant & Castle than tinker Belle Towne. the next day I was a wreck as usual & that evening John rang up and said do come round and have a few Bloody Marys I was so horrified at the idea I screamed NO NO I realy cannot spend my life feeling ghastly all the time & I suspect J gets "bored" & just wants company, he can talk to me and no holds barred! We went to see at the Nat Film theatre an antient 1930 musical called Drei men und Lilian [Harvey] with Willi Fritsch Kurt Gerron Olga Tchekowa & Lilian who swept about in a sports car with a musical horn in picture hats & chifon she realy was a freak but somehow managed to create an illusion. huge legs & feet & no body & a huge head. no eyes & a pretty mouth! She was so espiegle & delerious with gaminerie & mous & blinking & finger sucking you could hardly see her – die dry men all wore skin tight jackets and enormous flapping pants! it had tremendous pace & go there was a cabaret of 4 Tiller girls in satin trousers & jackets dancing on 4 pianos Tap & Buck & wing & bent down & kissed the pianists on the bald spot. causing applause & ending with splits you would have just *loved* it!

Yrs Ed.

To Clover de Pertinez from Chapel House, Rye, 18 August 1964

Dear Clo

Had a p.c from Corfu of a pillared arcade a cafe evidently – very Italian & rather olde worlde as Bar said – I dont mind that kind of olde worlde (about 1860 I should say) I believe Billys show is off now & dear little Mrs. Thea[2] is living or rather laying in "the downstairs room" at Thurloe Sq! always

1 *A character from the Flook comic strip.*

2 *Chappell's elder sister.*

such a little lady Thea was & to end up with cirrhosis[1] of the liver poor thing – however it stops her – her gentleman friend drinking all Billys drink.

I dont think people are (realy) shocked at anything – murders etc. why should they be, hell fire was the only deterrent, so you may "do anything" (if you can get away with it) The Marquis de Sade has come into his own dear old man, scribbling away in the Bastille! Im in the middle of Portrait of a Lady, very good & very long – I notice that Luis Bunuel has made a movie of Journal d'un femme de chambre with Jeanne Moreau as the femme! (Ive not read it yet!) but I re-read Nadja they spend their whole time wandering in the streets & visiting a Bar at the corner of the Rue Lafayette & the Fbrg Poissoniere & visiting L'Etreinte de la Pieuvre the last episode at a cinema in the Blvd Bonne Nouvelle in which a chinaman invaded New York by duplicating himself 25,000000 times over, "President Wilson ota son bin ocle!" Im not surprised. Give my love to Antonio. hell be having cirhossis too if he isnt careful. if they got him in the hospital they probably would operate for cancer & peptic ulcer & pills at *once*! hed never get away
yrs Ed When you come will you bring The Groves of Academe as *I* would like to read it oddly enough.

To Clover de Pertinez from Chapel House, Rye, 15 September 1964

Dear Clo
Mama is very much better & the Doctor said she realy collapsed from inanition as she never eat anything & hadnt for years – so if she wants to be able to get up & cease being bed ridden she had better pull herself together & eat something also of course she had been constipated for years & the Dr gave her pills which have moved mountains as you might say. Scott & Monica Wodehouse[2] came down Saterday, no, Thursday & we finaly arrived in Hastings old town end & had tea in a dainty shop with home made keykes (made in Hong Kong) about 5 or so. it was lovely but a tearing gale & brilliant sun. Monica made us go to a tea shop She gets more & more ladylike. (sort of) Bumble came to lunch on Saterday she was staying with 2 gentlemen wig makers[3] somewhere at Beckley or Northiam & looked very well – we went to that antique shop. & examined a very pretty little garnet necklace (40£) & a couple of shells on stands which were about 8 pounds each or something enormous. & she bought a nice painting of cats done in 1875 I think. Madame the proprietress was very interested in Bumbles rings & Mine! she would have bought them Im sure. I heard from Billy who said hed already spent 200£ on Theas illness & that she looked like Belsen but was very bright & wouldnt admit how ill she was poor thing I wonder if shell live. and no Ischia of course. Le Reve should be called Le

1 *It killed her.*
2 *Scott and Monica Wodehouse were lovers; she had simply adopted Scott's surname. She became a good friend of Edward.*
3 *They ran a firm called 'Wig Creations' and made the wigs for practically every West End production.*

mievre realy – its so exquise about l'awfeleen who was found in the snow by 2 *chasubliers* who live in the cathedral shadow in an *ambiance moyen-ageux* & the awfeleen becomes a marvellous embroiderer & dreams of St. Agnes & the *Legende D'orée* & of course meets a *jeune ouvrier* – I suspect Monsignors nephew in disguise. & realy dear. It badly needs Huysmans "*mais le mal hereditaire (des (Rougon Maquart) couve*" it unfortunately does no more than *couve*. I think she dies in an odour of sanctity at the end. There was a terrible thing in F[igaro] Literaire by Jean Cau about St. Exupery whose style was very suitable for young people, it wont do much good or much harm.

Mi Tintin, mi Dostoievski!
middle brow. yours E

To Clover de Pertinez from Chapel House, Rye, 3.30 am Wednesday Thursday. F. *8 October 1964*

Dear Clo
I am sending back Brouillon which is a masterpiece I think and I should like to read the other 2 – Miro comes off on Saterday I see. it was a lovely exhibition I thought. There was a downpore yesterday Mama is better but very feeble & one nurse however she seems able to do without a night nurse I hope Frederick doesnt have a nervous breakdown is all – Im sick of hearing about peoples insides I hear from Gerald who has arranged to have a large joint show with Fisher or is it Fischer? the year after next & *next* a show at the Lefevre in May – if we live till the year after next we shall see, of course theres no artist like a dead one is there I expect you could come on the 5th November there aren't many people here now but of course a huge crowd comes for Bonfire night yrs E
Et ces deux grands debris se consalient entre eux – (Chamfort)

To William Chappell from Chapel House, Rye, 25 December 1964

Dearest B.
the marsh looked lovely this afternoon having been snowed on & Ive discovered where Newchurch[1] is – several miles from anywhere it seemed to me especially busses – it must be about 3 miles from Dymchurch & a bit more from Ham St – but it may be nearer some other point – we cooked a nice lunch of Turkey & brussel sprouts & roast pots & Colin Anne & Ken were here K or whispering[2] Ritchie whispered away, I cant hear him very well as Ime deaf & used to howling all the time but I should soon get used to it anyway I think its marvelous & he looks much better & Im sorry to have to say, younger & *slimmer*, having been removed from the late Lady J's cuisine, entirely of double cream & butter – I see theres a nice panto at

1 *Chappell had just been given a cottage at a peppercorn rent in Newchurch bang in the middle of Romney Marsh by Erica Marx, the poet and wonderful encourager of young poets, whom she published through her Hand & Flower Press.*

2 *Kenneth Ritchie [Lord Ritchie] had just undergone an operation on his throat and had to learn to talk all over again. He made a remarkable recovery.*

the Palladium with Cliff Richards as principle Boy – he hasnt the presence or figure for it has he? not like Dorothy Ward. Just befor I left Islington Max arrived & I heard what I imagined was Blind Boy Williamson mixed with little Richard, or rhythm & Blues going on in the kitchen – definately I thought from Birming*ham*[1] – it was his group, they realy were very good. It would be rather funny if he had a career rushing from Odeon to Odeon in a mini bus – followed by a howling mob[2] they had cut a disc. nobody ever makes a record, not now. I hope you noticed Orson is backed by the Spanish government & evidently was supported by Margaret Rutherford as M. Quickly I suspect "If nothing succeeds like excess" it should be a smash[3] – also John Gielgud was mentioned – I can imagine the team of Welles & Rutherford. Its been quite peaceful here over this happy season as everybody thinks they will tire mummie & havent dragged along all their terrible children & so on to see Aunt Trudy who just *loves* to see them. Well dearie I hope we shall have a happy 1965? There will probably be terrible riots in Camden market owing to the soaring price of Junk & maids furniture with the varnish removed. If I was very rich I should have my house done up entirely Louis quinzey (Genuine peices & china to match)

Love to all yours Ed

Monica Wodehouse was a fan who – through sheer boldness – became a friend. Had she known the extent to which Edward usually resented an invasion of his privacy by a total stranger she might well have listened to her friend (and lover) Scott Wodehouse whose name she had taken and who – lurking behind the garden wall – had thought it to be in no way a good idea to ring the bell at Chapel House. Something in Monica's approach pleased Edward. Unpredictable as ever he not only invited them in but later went out in their company for a drink. The discovery that Monica's mother had been a dancer in Paris and had understudied Mistinguette in a revue at the Casino music hall was enough to intrigue Edward, 'Mis' being one of his favourite performers. Proof was produced later in the form of a splendid photograph of Monica's mama wearing the famous 'Rose' costume. All this combined with the fact that Scott worked in the movies sparked off a friendship; and the letter he wrote to Monica the following day was the first in a correspondence (begun in the summer of 1960) which continued throughout the rest of his life.

To Monica Wodehouse from Chapel House, Rye, 8 June 1965

Dear Monica
Thank you for the P.C. The exhibition[4] has been going on in a cloud of puke from the Times and a very flattering peice by the critics[5] or George Melly I realy think – 9 pictures have been sold so far. The notice in the T was very

1 *Alabama!*
2 *Edward would have enjoyed such a situation a great deal.*
3 *His suspicion is absolutely correct: she was wonderful in Orson Welles' splendid film* Chimes at Midnight. *Welles was a marvellous Falstaff and Keith Baxter was a remarkable Prince Hal.*
4 *At the Lefevre Gallery.*
5 *On BBC radio.*

funny realy it infuriated Barbara Rhodes Billy Chappell & Mrs. Pertinez to such a pitch they wrote an abusive letter to the Editor! John Banting wrote another to Nigel Gosling as he thought his notice was corny, he was only living up to Observer, which is so terribly *avec* it must give the staffs sleepless nights keeping *avec*. I also had a fan letter from a Bus driver post marked Stoke Newington but unfortunately not signed & no address There was a large troupe of morris dancers suddenly appeared on Sunday & danced outside our door on the green sward & dog shit I was laying in a trance feeling sick in my bedroom & I heard a sort of bawling & clicking of sticks being knocked together & there they were trolloping round with straw boaters trimmed with daisies & all and a strange transvestite looking exactly like George Orwell in a tweed shirt & carrying a parasol was threatening people & terrifying them into giving money! it was winsome. Monday I went out with Banting & "Jim" & got quietly pissed & no morris dancers I thought I should feel iller than I *did*! Ive just read a clock without Hands for the 1st time & Reflections in a Golden Eye 2nd time by Carson McCullers & a new James Purdy about a successful rapist, they all love him, it was very funny I thought I hope you are getting on nicely with the dear children & they arent seeing ghosts or murdering somebody in childish fun or anything that children do nowadays. We went to a Chinese restaurant in W. India Dock Rd the other day called "old friends" it was the best Chinese food Ive had the whole house is dining rooms from top to bottom – & I particularly liked the decor which consisted of a Dado of paper tiles on the top was a pretty wallpaper of roses & hung with large coloured photos of Hong Kong & framed pictures of cocks & chrysanthemums embroidered in silk – then to one of those pubs which have a roaring lady singer. with the aid of a microphone she managed to be heard quite clearly. It was a nice pub old style & no chandeliers or Frying Pans & nothing contempry it hadnt altered since about 1901 I should think – with a very long Bar made of wood not melted down false teeth dyed blue write again if you have time   yours Ed

To Clover de Pertinez from Chapel House, Rye, 14 September 1965

Dear Clo.

Thank you for your letter I walked all over Florence[1] & went to all the things – If you look at the wrong pictures you wont find a crowd of Fart Haters being bawled out by a lady guide as they rush back to Les cars du midi or some old Danish char a banc – all the shops were having "sales" so werent at their best but there are some very good ones I can see nobody wears high heels or winkle pickers. They all were tied with huge Bows – & rather low cuban – & nearly always black – most of the grand people are away or hidden from view – The weather was never too hot & lovely but for the last 3 days when there was a thunder storm – none of that terrible Roman visitation. Italy cut in two we saw in the papers – The Travel

1 *Where he had stayed with American friends, Jennings Rice and his wife.*

agencys were cut in two I may add – Marie is a very good cook Italian style – so we had Tripe osso buco Lassagna Baked Fried Fish & paella its very difficult to get Safran – & some very good roast beef cooked in a saucepan 20 mins to the pound it came out red & beautiful and of course plenty of pasta & green figs. I was even dragged to the convent on the top of Fiesole. Florence or what I consider Florence hasnt changed *at all* since 1927, its only grown down the Arno Valley. I got back despite "Italy cut in two" very nicely in an empty *rapido* to Milan – The Milan Calais train was a battlefield. full of families all returning to Basel Metz Strasbourg etc where they were working & even to England – there was a very cheerful caracter (Italian) in the carriage & absolutely *blind drunk* waving Beer Bottles & roaring out of the window for more. He fell out at Como! in a deluge of empty bottles – not what *I* connect with Cow Mow.

Yours Ed.

To Monica Wodehouse from Chapel House, Rye, 19 November 1965

Dear Monica

Thanks for your last about grannies so different from Giles cartoon or are they. Theres quite a little colony in Islington of very special Grannies who I should not like to Cross. They must have plenty back biteing to do – and the REX cinema has Greek pictures Sundays Ive always wondered if they are Greek pictures in Greek or The Nutty professor dubbed in Greek. It realy sounds very like a friend[1] of mines experiences who lived with "Grannie" in Granada during the war. She crept out to buy 2 oranges at the local store – Grannie was *dans toots ces états* when she came back, and said she had lowered the family as people would think they couldnt afford servants. She ruled the roost with a rod of iron – sweet old thing They finally managed to escape to Madrid where Grannies cant make themselves heard over the traffic. Its a pity theres not a tidal wave as Grannies gather in sea. Im reading a paper back as usual "The World of Violence" by Colin Wilson complete with cover of men being shot etc. Not a word of Vaylance that aye can see – but a fascinating autobiography of his early days and 2 uncles one of whom left him 20,000£! ! who were excentric to say the least verging in fact on madness, one was taken away and the other ended up in a windowless room of his own contriving & would allow no one but his wife in to clean up once a week. even Aunt Dinah was odd and deeply innarested in spiritualism. she had Colin to the house & she drank a jar of rum & lemon juice – & C eat cake – So far no ones been tampered with exept his duckie little sister went into a spinney with a nice man, in fact *the* nicest man (she said) who told her she must take off her dress as the sweeties he was going to give her were made of treacle At that moment Colin caught up – Also reading La Bâtarde leant me by someone who got stuck in it. I havent got stuck, but she never tries to *please* – the reader or herself – quite the opposite of Colette & she obviously hates her appearance

1 *Clover de Pertinez.*

& her large nose – but she seems to get off with quite a few people enclud-ing Maurice Sachs. I have seen "Darling" which I thought was very good & a very nice exhibition of Corot at the National Gallery some of them were lovely and even the nymphs (some of them) one or two were a shade brown soupy. I go and stay the week end at Islington & spend a happy Sunday morning in Chapel Market & surrounding Bars full of crones & Irish men – and various members of the "oldest North London criminal families" conspiring in corners – sometimes they even dance – & some pubs are more disreputable than others I wouldnt care to X any of them crones – Ive no doubt with winter coming on, gas & electricity cuts, a Bread strike with Q's of 2000 in Birmingham waiting for a sunblessed loaf & soon the points will all be frozen so there wont be any trains – you are happier among the back biteing in Pireus. I hope this reaches you safely and isnt steamed open
yours Ed.
A bit of violence has appeared in Colins Book by P. 124.

To William Chappell from Chapel House, Rye, 15 April 1966

Dearest B.
I am very sorry to hear about Thea[1] and all the awful sequel – I suppose she must have been worse than she seemed poor thing. I dont know if she was older than I am I think younger.

I hope you will come to the cottage when you come back from Norway, goodness knows what thats like! ! under snow & ice I should think – Norway I mean – We've been living in a semi melting grey sorbet here which has now vanished in a flood (more or less) there were 2 large snow-balls still in the church yard left by the vampires

Hope to come up to Charlton not this W.E. but the next. Im feeling very much better and cough gone but I still get tired especially going up very steep hills and its anaemia – its a sign. I noticed it a bit on visiting Banting as Hastings is always up a precipice or down one except on the front – our little visit to East Anglia quite stopped the cough & cherry syrup which is nothing but a sleeping draught –

Dear Noels play sounds wonderful I think – I like him as an actor and it sounds *very well acted* from the notices Ive read –

Hope to see you soon and I daresay struggling in Norway will take your mind off all this for a time anyway –
love from Ed.

To Clover de Pertinez from Chapel House, Rye, 21 June 1966

Dear Clo
I went over to Newchurch & saw Billy – & Bars who were there. John [Banting] was staying the night at Charlton P[lace] after the Wing Ding & Fish Fry! He arrived to day over here at 2.30 and stayed till after 5 &

1 *Chappell's sister had died from a cirrhosis of the liver.*

enjoyed it all very much the Fish Fry I thought hed wangle it one way or another & even had words with Marcel Duchamp The public was mostly young & non lion hunting realy. they began to take sly looks at Peter Pan when they say him hob nobbing with M.D.! John didnt know anybody but Alan Reynolds he got the ticket through Julian Trevelyan I think who didnt go as he cant speak, but with difficulty and the frustration of not being able to would have killed him. J said the 7/6 Chianti was very good & the supper wasnt bad. He also went to several exhibitions & was careful not to take too many pills which go to the legs if mixed with drink! Bar went to the P[rivate] view I think. I found the Pview card on getting back.   Yrs Ed

To William Chappell from Chapel House, Rye, 11 September 1966

Dearest B.
I was wondering what had become of you – The gate theatre will make a nice change I declare if I wasnt going to stay again with those people in Florence I would have payd you a visit but Im off to F for a fortnight & I hope by this time there wont be quite so many cars or people milling about looking at Fart that bores them all to death & preventing me from looking at it I found a lovely William Le Queux the other day (a Newnes 7d) called "in white Rayment" I remember reading it at school. all the caracters turn blue & gasp "The phial! in the left hand drawer of the Bureau in the study" & have mysterious tattoos under their seed pearl dog collars Mama couldnt put it down. Did Miss K[er] S[eymer] tell you that whilst visiting Sammy in Paddington Hospital, (S. had a broken ankle) she saw a corpse figure – lieing motionless with hair all over its face & never uttering & it was Jeanne de Casalis? I realy think its too awful poor thing nobody seemed to come near her, & about 3 weeks ago I saw a long obituary in the Times. she seemed to be quite unconscious however. Another thing was the other day "a voice" rang up that turned out to be Tom Driberg who asked me out for a drink at the George with "them" all, & them consisted of an attractive driver (French) & one other gentleman & Miss Joan Littlewood! I was very surprised when I saw Miss L seated in there. I thought she was rather nice – I had only just come down from Towne & wasnt feeling quite as *well* as usual! & I dreaded they would want to go to every bar in Town but they were only on the way through. Mr. Banting was very pleased with the manuscript book about Brian Howard, many contributors. among them Bar & himself I think & 2 Books about Nancy Cunard are in the offing! so the 20ies are getting the treatment. Well drop us a line scented with Tullamore Dew

love from yrs Ed.

To Clover de Pertinez from Chapel House, Rye, 27 November 1966

Dear Clo we quite by chance happened to see Douglas Cooper explaining the wimmin in Picasso's life at the Grand Palais. at the end a pneumatic man controlled from eons away in an outer galazy. said Les Dames D'avig-

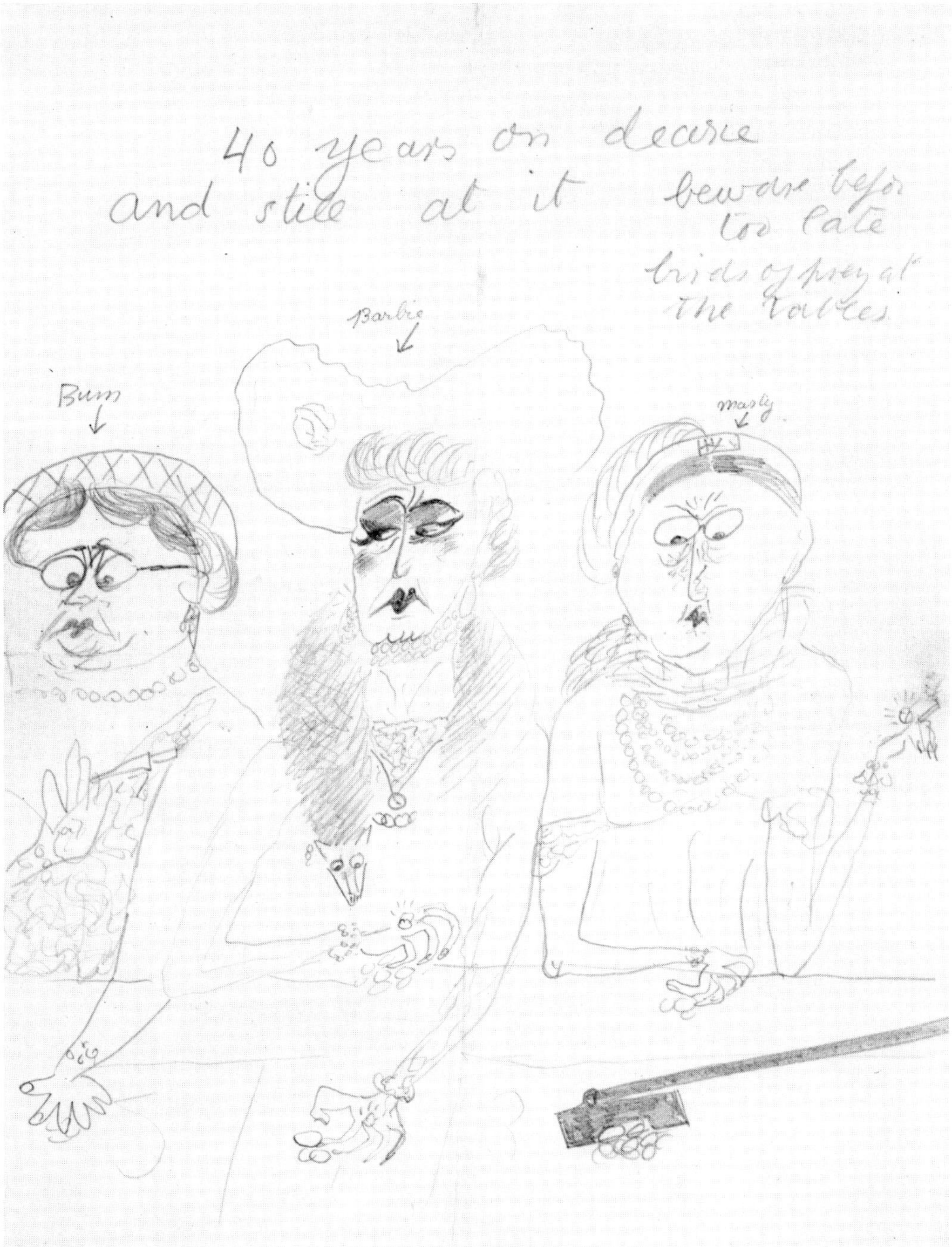
40 years on dearie
and stile at it
beware befor
too late
birds of prey at
the tables
Barbie
Bum
masly

non was a vastly overated painting & Kandinsky Mondrian & Malevitch were the most significant painters of the 20th cent. I was fully expecting Douglas to draw a pistol & shoot him – now I notice a large Kandinsky exhibition is opening or open at the Marlborough gallery – Piccy is far too *representational* my dear – when I left Max was refusing to get up & laying in bed waiting for the Ting a ling a ling from his agent who was supposed to be getting "them" a job. they seem to me to live in a sort of myth world. I never could, I never ever believed anybody. Bar tells me he has £6 a week so that is something! I actually received a letter from the poet[1] who has realy been in a terrible state with his skin complaint. they were at last in Brewster & going to Savannah Dec 1st I think he was realy very ill & of course poor M was nurse, having just recoverd from her op. I was pleased to hear as I began to think it was the end. Gerald has finaly found out from the Tate that they are not considering a retrospective exhibition of Burra so they can continue with their plots at the Marlborough Gallery that should cause a scandal   yrs Ed.

To Clover de Pertinez from Chapel House, Rye, 5 February 1967

Dear Clo

Ive been meaning to write for sometime. Did you see a long piece about Malcolm Lowry in the T. litry sup – last week I think. Gerald mentioned it and sent me a copy M has been having quite a doing over with the "Letters" I noticed in the windows of Guldens the paper & stationers in the Hy St: the 3 vols of Childermass! that face – "the nastiest face I ever saw" (Hemingway) was stareing down – I just finished the last volume, where Pullman is assumed into Heaven! at the end was a very interesting little unpublished article by somebody who of course I forget who said the whole thing was realy part of a huge work containing "T[ime] & Western man" the Apes of god & large peices of unpublished manuscript Im sorry Ive finished it. Bar Roett is busy making over a huge great place belonging to Gladys Calthrop so she has her work cut out we went to the Chelsea Potter in the Swinging K[ings] Rd at lunch all Booteeks & Beatneeks layabouts etc & mini skirts, but not the *thigh* dearie *that* very often is anything but mini especially in white stockings its quite fascinating almost like Montparnasse in the 20ies! you can see all these from the windows of the Chelsea P. just a little lower down on the other side from Chelseas House of enchantment! I went to the young contemprys at the Tate with Bar we enjoyed it very much – I like to see a lot of Bright colour. All done with the most perfect meticulous technique – no botching about. Im not so sure whether I cared so much for the sculpture(?) I must go & see Millais John Banting says one of his aunts or great aunts was the little girl seated in a church pew! He is suffering from aches & pains & a stiff hip. Bar Roett has been attacking Mrs. R[hodes] about Max & making him "do something" but what? if she says "leave my house lazy layabout" he will go off & not get a job & realy lay

---

1 Conrad Aiken.

about & "loose all his standards" Mrs. R says! he usually manages to have a pound or two in his pocket. She thinks if he was to leave home he would become filthy dirty & live in squalor. I think she thinks he will end up a successful business man[1] like Papa – you never know, if he marries & finds he wants money. difficult isnt it, all these people with realy *no* vocation to do anything at all – But lay about? yours Ed.

To Clover de Pertinez from Chapel House, Rye, 8 April 1967

Dear Clo I was away a couple of nights in E. Anglia with A[nne] and we finaly got into Peterborough which fascinated me or at least a Tea shop we went to did. one of those they dont have in the South of England. There was an enormous woman & her obese daughter in trowsers & aged about 15 who sat down to a slimming diet of an enormous plate of thick bread & butter salad & cold meat & vast mountains of fish fried in batter and an avalanche of chips there were also a couple of commercial gentlemen in a corner tucking into toasted scones & cream buns. and an entire familly straight out of T.V. in the hotel Bar were celebrating "Grannies" 80th birthday. one of grans relations was a wonderful old queen who came rushing in screaming "Ive got me present" & produced a bottle of Cointreau. they all had an enormous familly dinner in the restaurant. there was also a large dinner party of very glum young men & one blonde with a bouffant hair do. goodness knows how it didnt catch fire as the head waiter kept turning up a terrible sort of methelated spirit Mount etna & flambant everything in sight. strictly □ the fashions in P. I note but there were some very kinky figurines in Norwich! not in the Castle Hotel which was strictly businessmen starting up a thrombosis. what I like are the Pork butchers & "real" butter you can buy in the market.

I went over to H[astings] to see John yesterday and returned sound asleep and didnt wake up till Ashford. thank god the train went back again – Im always doing that and going to A by mistake. I did it the other day in the early morning too & dead sober going to see Billy & had to take a smart Mercedes Benz taxi to Newchurch. We went to a realy wonderful church or rather huge monastic remnant called Wymondham Abbey. Magnificent it was with a huge ruined tower with a black gaping archway – in fact there are 2 towers & surrounded by twisted fir trees. I bought 2 or 3 postcards – Bury St. Edmonds is a nice little town with 2 market days which I love. I hope you all are alright. Jolly Roger[2] had a stroke the other day but has made a good recovery & is home again Im supposed to be going to stay the week end with Bumble next W.E. having always got out of it sort of up to now yours Ed.

To Clover de Pertinez from Chapel House, Rye, 1967

Dear Clo
When I got back I found a letter from Gerald enclosing a copy of a cable

1 *She was not far wrong.*
2 *Roger Senhouse, who lived in Rye.*

saying Ide won the Mazarotti Prize of 3 million lire £1,750 & a post card from Bar saying I must leave the money in Italy – well dearie I *was* surprised as I never thought they gave prizes to anything that wasnt "abstract" & the size of the Front of Warner bros – disgusting isnt it? what will they say? The Telegraph gossip column said E Burra (age 62) was recieving the prize in Valdagno(?) Italy today Sat! If so Italy is realy very like Tinker Belle Towne all cobbles & English Tourists and Bogus Beems! It was for a painting called "the Fates" what ever that was and done about 30 years ago I should think. I heard from Billy at Chichester who is fed up with actors & is living in a large flat with 3 chattering girls a barking dog, a cat & the Rices little boy who never stops talking. he hopes to come to Pump Cottage soon which has been turning to jungle, no one having been near it for months. You dont make very much producing at "Festivals" – Well maybe I shall see you at August Bank holiday if it isnt named something else more refined & all goes well – love to all – yrs Ed.

To Clover de Pertinez from Chapel House, Rye, 11 January 1968

Dear Clo
I went to the Academy Show[1] and we very much enjoyed it especially husbands & wives series.[2] sitting at dinner tables of huge size & looking mooney & one of Mdms back in a bustle leaving the drawing room & hubbie – in full evening dress of course placed in front of the fireplace looking very snuffy called "The first shadow"

"A visit to the Borgias" & some wonderful Alma (marble) Tadema & groups of very indecent nudes with all their hair shaved off being interviewed by Aristophanes – also a series of nude ladies with red hair sticking out of a lilly pond being interviewed by a phone (fawne?) or maybe a? goatherd[3] – There was a very good Sargeant of the Sitwells also "darnation silly, silly pose" & a very good Whistler of the Thames & Fantin Latour some lovely Richard Wilsons & a fine Etty nude being given a very close once over by two very unvictorian satyrs – & Stubbs in fact you get your moneys worth. we also went to BOOM which I very much enjoyed dear Noel gives one of his better sketches as "the Witch of Capri" & is invited to dinner by Elizabeth Taylor (Elizabeth in a Kabuki? costume) he says "Theyre saying very strange things about *you* in Capri my dear! they say your *dead*!" Max is doing very well selling *vices* at the Home Boat exhibition at Olympia leaving wads of 10£ notes about the place. Bar says hes very careful of his money – when I said she might pinch one or two she said he knew just what was there & he never gave her any money & asked her to buy him tooth paste & razor blades! I went over to see John yesterday and was driven over to Pump Cottage today. John & Jimbo came over on Boxing day here & we had lunch & spent the morning in the Railway Hotel

1 *Victorian painters.*
2 *By Orchardson. These were like exquisitely painted versions of stills from some wonderfully stylish period film.*
3 Hylas and the Water Nymphs, *by Waterhouse.*

& the afternoon boozing here. The cottage is getting on. all the floors the underneath of which were found to be wringing wet, have been taken up & have to be cement. we havent had any snow here or so little it vanished at once Hope you are all well & not having Kabuki Flu

Yours Ed

To Clover de Pertinez from Chapel House, Rye, 15 January 1968

Dear Clo Thank you for yours arrived today I was going to London last week-end but at the sight of snow on Sat I was certain British Railways would stop for 4 hours at Orpington whilst the guard boiled a kettle on his spirit stove to pour on the points then it got quite warm raind and the whole thing melted. Had 2 cards of splendid Baroque churches from E It sounds very attractive Peru not that I shall ever get there.

We are staggering on here at the rate of heaven knows what a week about 50£ or more – on night nurses & day nurses – A is almost at her wits end. Frederick is busy biteing everybodys head off – as he's never not answering mumsies bell & emptying the commode & we live on Junkie time too as the pills are like clockwork no need of a sun dial. John has a copy of Brians Bible,[1] 600 pages long so no wonder its 70/- did you hear that broadcast? it was realy very good. Harold Acton was very funny – as Mrs. Howard told Mrs. A[cton] (who came from Chicago) that Chicago wasnt the least *chic*, not like Mrs. H who was a Southern Belle from W. Virginny. He didnt know if she was quite sure he was a suitable friend for B – who was only to mix in the most aristocratic circles at Eton etc. She sounds like Lady Cunard & Nancy I feel the kiddies were rather a disapointment after all!

Aubrey B[eardsley] looks much better in the original as they had at the V & A exhibition. They are so *strong* & unfussy realy positively monumental! copyers took the chi chi & left the framework I got a copy of Under the Hill, finished by an unknown personnage of Maurice Girodias Olympia P[ress] stable! Aubrey could get away with murder, and it all seemed the lightest and gayest thing, but the finish didnt quite keep it *up*. not for the want of trying & it had some drawings too all for 12/6 paper back in the well known O[lympia] P[ress] green covers. I think the O.P has finaly collapsed now, theres so much competition. I suppose you cant get any servants in Gabia now all having removed themselves to Belgravia & the Grand Hotel Scarborough. perhaps theyl be *squeezed* back again!

love to all yours Ed

To Clover de Pertinez from Chapel House, Rye, 8 February 1968

Dear Clo
Can you order this order at the Toffee works? ? These are the ones she wants, written down – I must go to the Academy & Gwen John not very

1 *A book about Brian Howard by all his friends.*

much approved of by John Banting – but some of Gwens portraits looked wonderful to me – there was one in the Times of a "lady in white" 1909 who looked as if she was nearly mad with acid stomach. it looked very good but not J's style exactly[1] but then I enjoy everything having no teest my dear – & you mustnt enjoy the actual peenting of the peenting one *bit* none of that morbid delectation in pigment – I saw a copy of the last London magazine on the cover of which there was an envenomed looking ruin who caught my *eye* none other than *l'affreux* in person or Ferdinand,[2] with quite a long article inside & it mentioned the forbidden Books! I always did say he was the greatest 20th century french novelist & had an enormous *affreux* underground influence Ive kept seeing pricking its ears in the underbrush ever since Voyage au booo de la nuit.

I had a pc from Mexico of the university building entirely covered with a vast fresco from top to toe by O'Gorman! no one would have the courage to do anything so huge & whole hearted here – imagine the screams & hysteria of hatred & protest Yrs Ed

To Clover de Pertinez from Chapel House, Rye, 14 February 1968

Dear Clo
I enclose cheque for £1-7-6 thank you for ordering same. And for LSD acid as we call it such a pity its not legal as it would do far less harm than alcohol – That story about students staring at the sun whilst under the influence of LSD was a fabrication it seems – I daresay the London magazine is in the public library – it ought to be. I went to see "The anniversary" with Bette Davis – she was wonderful as a high class Hollywood vixen with a very curious T.V playstyle English familly with a cockney accent. well worth seeing & Belle du Jour – Belle herself is rather like Princess Grace attending a Fate de Bienfaisance![3] but the rest of the cast are *splendid*! also the Pre Raphaelite film in Technicolor in huge close ups. talk about LSD – maybe it was laudanum! In those awful staid old Victorian days, so puritanical people were able to *enjoy* themselves almost how they wanted to. They have to do whats good for them (& the govt) now dont they? Saving their lives up for the BOMB HA HA It always kills me when Mdme Barbara Castle "saves lives" on the Rd – keeping them for a cancer I daresay. But we must definitely be creeadive *not* Destructive! He doesnt seem to have "*seen*" anything The Watts[4] until he took acid *natural* objects trees & trunks etc People dont see a thing I believe, they never look at anything realy, People in the train never look they give me the creeps. Antonio being so very old cant be expected to wash anything up remember yrs E.
Juan O'Gorman apparently designed the mosaique on the MEX[ican] Nat Library 2 sides & literaly about twice as high as Harrods & quite half as wide – it looks very remarkable – sheer size & mosaic.

---

1 *John Banting was a punk long before the punks and a natural surrealist.*
2 *Louis-Ferdinand Céline.*
3 *Bunuel's film* Belle de jour *starred Catherine Deneuve.*
4 *A well-known pop musician.*

To Conrad Aiken from Chapel House, Rye, 13 May 1968

Dear Conrad

Thank you for yours. we have plenty of underground & underground papers.[1] The International Times ? OZ among them all good old fashioned Anarchist I shall send you some to read. yes dear I have got letters, there must be quite a lot as I never throw them away but they are in a confusion everywhere in a book or in a box & I expect some interesting documents got lost when we left Springfield some of the things might cause a slight outbreak of acid stomach & the horrible aphtosa if they were printed. Im afraid poor Mama is about on her last legs – in fact the afternoon nurse said she didnt think shed last the night. I felt it terribly about 2 years ago when she first had an illness & I thought she was dieing, but its been going on so long & shes so worn down to a shadow Im used to it all now poor thing. I dont know what Im going to do as I hate houses & dont care about them at all or furniture or dinky all atomic kitchens or anything like that *at all.* nor do I care for this horrid little Beautee spot now becoming a kind of overblown gifte shoppe with pottery plaques with the name of the house on every sweet little place all the old inhabitants have moved or moved themselves to council estates on the outskirts so the centre is completely given over to gyfterie, & other forms of perversion lansakes! I suppose it is a way of preserving it. I had a p.c. from Florence where Jennings & M[2] have installed themselves in an apt as per usual – so I must write a letter & soon or J will be in a huff again It seems to suit them & they *know* it which is better – the traffic & the noise is something terrible I think let alone crowds of milling visitors. The place to go in the summer is obviously Valenciennes or Bradford – Leeds might do. It now is freezing & 3 weeks ago it was quite hot youd think it was November but of course its colder in than out owing to damp – God knows whats happening we are all disintegrating it seems to me! & fast

love to all yours Ed

To William Chappell from Chapel House, Rye, 15 May 1968

Dearest B. I expect you know all the horrors by now. Poor Mama died about 3.15 yesterday morning or was it the day before?

I was in a terrible way when she was first very ill 3 years ago? & I got Anne back from Scotland as I thought she was dieing, and its been hanging like a bomb ever since. she realy was in such a state of misery & discomfort & half doped. Im glad shes dead & its all over, she has been in a coma realy this past week. I was going to stay with Bar this week-end but put it off till the one after as the funeral is on Monday. so ring up if you are at Pump & available & Ill come over. I went to that Marzotto show Ive not seen any notices so I suppose so many beastly *Figurative* painters & foreigners too are being ignored. What grandeur![3] compared to the

1 *Mostly on the floor of his studio work room.*

2 *Jennings Rice and his wife, with whom Edward often stayed.*

3 *In the new Royal College of Art building.*

crumby old joint when we used to go to the common room in Queens Gate, my gracious! Did you enjoy "Reflections"?[1] I thought they were all very good encluding Brando – you didnt realy have to hear him as he gave the impression as in those terrible lectures he kept giving. I plan to retire to a modern Bungalow with a picture window with nylon lace curtains criss cross across it like the above.[2] not in Tinker Belle Towne. I always thought those windows would be good for a studio.
Hope to see you yrs Ed

To Clover de Pertinez from Chapel House, Rye, 1 November 1968

Dear Clo Ive been meaning to write for ages, but all I do is sit by the fire & read papers – just come down on Tuesday from Geralds with a hangover that I hoped was wearing off on Wednesday but today my god is Dehydration Day Yes brothers & sisters I feel as if I was permanently in a subway with head noises – we actualy went to "Hair" I realy rather enjoyed it very jolly & very moralistic I thought about as indecent[3] as the MacFisheries & they show nude Fish. somebody said Fuck but as everyone is always saying Fuck its lost its cherry as you might say I liked the band then off to the Savoy Hotel! realy my dear tayme had stood still, all the diners looked as if theyd come direct from Leeds & Bradford & every minute there were Happy Birthdays. There was a terrible chorus it opened with one of those Bamba Bamba numbers – about as much Bamba as running for the 8.15 from Acton Town! theres a violent thunderstorm going on just now. Its been so wonderfully warm long may it go on is all well
love to you all Ed

To William Chappell from Chapel House, Rye, 3 November 1968

Dearest B.
I realy quite enjoyed Fun in a Bake house,[4] all it wanted was G.S. Melvin to come on & sing Im happy when Im Hippy in long hair & pince nez wearing a beaded 1920's dress with fringe over puce pants & it would have brought the house down. It was quite a change of pacc the Savoy Restaurant! I thought I was switched back to 1930 they would have had a twinkletoes competition for 2 bits & every 2 seconds it was Happy (not Hippy) birthday to you & very plain & dowdy. isnt it odd how plain the rich are? Phyl said! it was a good dinner however.

Mireille[5] supported why God knows by 3 zombie women in powder blue night dresses – an acordeon Im glad to say pianist etc & one million mikes for every instrument so it sounded far too loud, but she has "the voice" and when shes been robbed & beaten black & blue by some no good snake hips

1 *The film of* Reflections in a Golden Eye, *the novel by Carson McCullers.*

2 *He had drawn his ideal bungalow.*

3 Hair *was the musical where full-frontal male nudity was seen for the first time (for 50 seconds in the finale of the first half) and gave rise to a (possibly apocryphal) remark from one critic to another in the interval: 'There wasnt time to notice who was circumcised.'*

4 *Edward's title for* Hair.

5 *Mireille Mathieu, the French singer supposed to be the natural successor to Edith Piaf.*

man she may have the temperament. but shes no Piaf, Yvonne George or Damia yet & I wish she wouldn't sing English no's or "Ma pomm-eux" in a funny costume. she looked a bit like a smart English golfing lady who had been given a Hashish cigarette by a caddy! I saw "Faces"[1] which realy is wonderful – all done with a swinging hand camera and the acting is so good its like looking through a keyhole. there was a terrible seen when a sort of lay about brought some girls back from the Bar they all hang out at waiting to hook somebody & one was a very elderly battered old tart who fell heavily for the young man as he did a dance with her & asked him to kiss her which he did – & went off with somebody else – she said I shall drop down in the street! I shall fall down dead like an animal in the street & no one will know or care, Im old etc – by that time I was sobbing into a handkerchief. Balthus I managed to get to and I wonder what they think of *him?* I feel, with nearly all of them, that *something* has happened or will do, as soon as nobodys looking – & that "something" will be *very* reprehensible & odd indeed. I should like to have a few carefully chosen, one would always have something to think about. yrs Ed Hope to come up the 17th Nov? I hope –

To Clover de Pertinez from Chapel House, Rye, 1 February 1969

Dear Clo
Ive been staying with Gerald and rather broke out on Sunday as I went to see Drag Queen with Judith Desmond & Sarah Ponsonby who paints horses from photos in the Pink ['un] (not exactly) more like the U.S. Racing journal – she told me "I flog them to my friends in the Shires" G says she does very well anyway she asked us back to tea. Then I went back to Judith & D's grand establishment full of horrid pictures of huge legs in High heels & nasty old phantasys by Edward Burra of nudes emerging from smoking guns & Mae West even that old painting of La Nina de los Peines[2] at the Circo Price! I had 2 large gins & Sarah P then arrived & said Im stoned with her hat over one eye I said *I* feel nothing and we passed round an asthma cigarette I then burst into fits of laughter at the sight of Sarah & continued going off into gales every time I caught S's eye I said we are getting to be like an old laughing record (circa 1909) a little friend of mine once had. We then left for Bumbles birthday party I think it went with a swing Bumble said *some* definitely did – a lot of film people – they must have been. Sandy tipsy & Bunny looking wonderful in black. suddenly I noticed a tiny person in white with a huge bright red vagabond hat. Judy Garland who was murmuring on a sofa She soon manoevered herself into our little circle, she was fascinated by Ponsonby. On Monday got taken to unfunny girl rather a bore I thought but for American Brides in the Zeigfield Follies with every one hung in pearls walking down a staircase pausing on each step.

Barbara Streisand is very good wonderful to look at and moves

1 *A film by John Cassavetes.*
2 *A great old flamenco singer.*

beautifully but is a tragedy queen realy. she ought to be doing Magda & Hedda Gabler! & is very like Fanny Brice not quite so grotesque of course. The Tate is having a large exhibition of René Magritte. I shall enjoy that. Another thing that amuses me "they" seem to be discovering Blaise Cendrars & his Black humor in Moravagine etc the mills of god do grind slowly. I havent heard from Bar & if she still has Pat Highsmith lurking about. Billy is in Nottingham producing "The Entertainer" at the Playhouse. I dont know what they think theyre doing in Spain Im sure they seem to do nothing but arrest lawyers!

love to you all Yrs Ed

To Clover de Pertinez from Chapel House, Rye, 1969

Dear Clo

I went to stay with Bar last W.E. & thought she looked rather odd about the eyes & shed been having migraine – Billy came to dinner & B Roett went out to some discotheque or something & we all had to see Auntie Crawfy[1] in the Queen Bee – in which she wears a different dress by Adrian in every shot & drives the familly to drive *her* over a precipice The Irish were celebrating St Patricks by roaring in Wards Irish house draped in bunches of dead shamrocks & an enormous Free state Flag draped across the end of the room I could see Roett was rather worried. the last time befor that I stayd with Mrs Indefatigable[2] who spent the whole of Sat preparing steak carbonade for Judy [Garland], Johnny Ray and his "manager" I dont know if I told you about this visit or not – anyway I was quietly drinking gin all oblivious & Bum came in & said would you like *a Biscuit?* it gave me quite a turn! – & said they are one & a half hours late for dinner! why, I said thats *nothing* – They had surpassed Madame who is late sometimes but not that much Judy was in a mini skirt skating outfit in black – Johnny Ray is very nice I thought – Sunday we went to Geralds for lunch & as Phyl was tired from her op we went to the Academy me for the second time Bum carefully looked at everything I realy thought Ide fall dead. then we went to what I thought was a trade show of *La Folle du Chaillot* at Warners own private theatre & found some people there – Dame Evans & Gielgud & his friend who came to dinner after etc as we were sitting there having been given a drink who should materialize but a phosphorescent very buttoned up little person who looked lit up from inside accompanied by a young man in a duffle coat Margaret & Tony! Bumble did a backward curtsy into my gin & then after a bit of standing up the picture began – befor that I said how do you do to a surly pudding face that I suddenly realized was Mr. Heath! goodness knows why I should say how do you do to him – the film is one huge long crashing whimsy bore. Katharine Hepburn is no more mad than Mrs. Golda Meyer & all far too clean the only other mad woman who could have been mad was Margaret Leighton looking like a tipsy old gaiety Girl!

1 *Joan Crawford.*
2 *Bumble Dawson.*

The cottage looks wonderful I must say & is as good as ready. Various odd persons have been giving this wreck[1] the once over no one has bought it yet & it wants a good bit *done* to it!

Am reading the Life of Huysmans by James Laver. I think I have read it before but Im enjoying it very much & a life of W.C. Fields – they have points in common – ! I hear you are too fat, last Autumn I seem to remember you were quite thin – I'm glad I dont have to be on the go! I can only think if [I] stand still & stare four hours in the kitchen or sit in a gloomy undone up pub *if* I can find one not a stockbrokers Boudoir

Love to all yrs Ed

To William Chappell from Chapel House, Rye, 3 June 1969

Dearest B.

Dont worry about proper food as I have it quite good. meat and Fish I had a marvellous peice of Skate I fried, dredged in flour with some of that mysterious herb of Annas[2] & peices of Beef I get – Annas Spinnach was lovely & the sorrel I made into soup with the remains of that curry & carrot soup we had Thank her & say how much I enjoyed them all & the Herbs next time you see her! You must come again on return from Bermuda the land of make believe. Gerald & Phyl are off to "dear old Capri" where they sit in the cheif café & sun bathe etc & case the Bootiques and appreciate *grande comfort* in the hotel I dont know what Norman Douglas would say – plenty for his pen – well realy I must come up & stay at Charlton P[lace] its too awful – anyway Ive no doubt they will be down here befor long.

The BBC wanted me to appear Gerald said & discuss FART. I cant do that as horror of horrors I have absolutely *nothing to say at all* on the subject! see you later on I hope   yrs Ed.

To William Chappell from Chapel House, Rye, 30 September 1969

Dearest B. Thanks for yours and on Wednesday I went to London for the day and had lunch at George Mellys house with J. Banting there – we wanted to go and see the ICA of old bits & DADA realy is what I liked a tape worm made of very battered little boxes as for John he walked round writing Marcel Du Champ & M. Du Champ on all the exhibits I got quite nervous but nothing *happend, it* was a happening or an agro-so that is why you got no reply but what happened on Thursday I dont know, I must have been out somewhere anyway let me know next time.

Ide rather like to meet Hockney his paintings at that huge POPFART show were very good and one wonderful portrait – not very POP it seemed to me. Im glad you got to Chichester & Dame Leighton as Egypt[3] – all Ive been to is "The Italian affair" Noel had one of his little *vignettes* as a very very shady prison master at a wonderful looking prison Ime sure was a

---

1 Chapel House, Rye.
2 Anna Pollak, the opera singer.
3 Margaret Leighton as Cleopatra.

real one – it wasnt bad & now they have Ow what a luvly war & I realy dont want to see it having seen the trailer and everybody being madly brilliant & witty and semi musical comedy. I dont care for any war straight or twisted. I realy want to see Midnite cowboy & Easy Rider. I know the London Opla Centre[1] which Im sure was once a movie[2] & I saw Sophie Tucker & Shapiro do their act there – it must have been in 1936 or 7 or thereabouts! not inconvenient for Islington as I believe theres an Angel bus passes the door. I hope to see you   yours Ed.
lovely day today it realy was.

To Clover de Pertinez from Chapel House, Rye, 1969

Dear Clo
I feel so tired I cant do anything more or care less Ive never seen such piles of dirt. have managed a good many books that I never want to see again & God knows what else junk – but the trying thing is feeling so exhausted. In having a telephone as Anne said she would never have a moments peace & be dead with worry if I didnt £20 instalment fee. It doesnt worry me not having a phone. somebody in Hastings is doing some curtains Im nearly crazy & have lost the bill I cant remember anything. I hope there wont be too much furniture as I hate it.[3] Gerald sent me a copy of the Spectator & in it was a peice by Bryan Robertson, I didnt think he cared much for Burra but I was wrong it seems. Yes I should like to come up at Whit if Ime not in an asylum by then. Poor old John [Banting] was moaning this morning about swollen ankles & knees! I said my ankles were *huge* by the time I sat down to read the Dly Mirror at 8 at night having walked to & fro through piles of rubble all day "doing up" beastly things. The move is a Thursday Ive not seen John Russell but there was a very good one in the Dly Telegraph love to all   yours Ed
I havent heard from Bar, shes probably annoyed with me!?

To Clover de Pertinez from 2 Springfield Cottages, late 1969

Dear Clo Ive at last got moved in and am feeling much better but havent done any work as Im always doing something or dragging about assorted rubbish and am "unsettled" as they say – I found one suitcase full of letters from Madrid pre war & letters from Gledstanes Rd & Balham! I havent dared to read them – even some from the Hôtel Gellert! Jane Hodge[4] and some gentleman[5] want to see any letters I had from Aiken – & Ive dug up quite a few – Ide kept a good many evidently & keep finding them in books. I feel that some people wont be too pleased at what they faynd tucked away there, but Ive not read them. I heard from Bar who said she hoped I was feeling less hostile! I couldnt well have been more but I was so

1 *A school run by Covent Garden Opera House to train young singers and musicians: Chappell was going to teach there once a week.*
2 *It was a very splendid huge art deco cinema originally, and offered a stage show as well as movies.*
3 *He none the less took some nice pieces with him from Chapel House to Springfield Cottages.*
4 *Conrad Aiken's daughter.*
5 *Joseph Killorin.*

exhausted I didnt want to do anything but lay down. Any way Im supposed to be going to stay with Gerald for the week end Sat next. I dont realy want to move anywhere. This is very comfortable with plenty of hot water & warm & easy to turn on some heat for a while, and its a relief to be out of dear little Rye which is already crowded with people gapeing & crazed with boredom? Ive been re-reading "the mysterious Mr. Bull" by P[ercy] W[yndham] L[ewis] its very funny Ive found several *lesser known* works! Im looking forward to look at "The old gang & the new" "The diabolical principle" etc & "Hitler" & "the Apes of God Blasting & Bombardiering" – all *madly* hostile my dear – one or two novels – They might bring out "the Roaring Quean" now. or is it in such fraytefull bad teyste? but in a very different way to Last Exit to Brooklyn etc – Last exit to Wyndham Lewis – They realy should

Yours Ed

To William Chappell from 2 Springfield Cottages, 20 December 1969

Dearest B
I[m] sending you a little tip of 5£ just to buy ribbonds & thimbles & other Gew-gaws at Owles & Beaumont! when ever I go to shops, Im dragging about an enormous canvas bag full of toilet paper vinegar carnation milk amonia Scrag end of neck etc & can hardly drag it along. They are still moaning on about *la neige* on the Radio. all it seems to me to be is cold but not *nearly* so cold as it will be if there is a week long electricity strike on Jan 6th to welcome in the happy new year. I am fortified with a new Beatrice stove with no Pink Petrol & no jerry can and no coal as far as I can see – only unlightable coke – Its no good bothering my dear. I notice Duckie little Rye twinkling its Red eyes in the High St covered in electric bulbs is getting rather full of very *douteux* Hippie types! definately not here to sing carols. I dont think there are many empty houses to stage a squat in. Well hope to see you after all this drag & so on is over – wishing you a happy
C & New Year
O God yrs Ed

To William Chappell from 2 Springfield Cottages, 1970

Dear B
I hear you are back again[1] private or public this time? I hear from Bar you are having another one I hope they know what they are at is all – we suppose so. I havent been "Put off" yet by Gerald so I hope to see you on Sunday or Saterday & Monday. *they* are very lazy & dont whirl madly about all over London never drawing breath! like some people we know of. I hear Sir [F. Ashton] is off to the mugging – a curious old puritan fertility festival brought over on the Mayflower – Poor Honor must be in a flap & already out in a rash B[arbara] said, its a pity she cant have some "Jasmine tea" & be off in fits of giggles [or] sound asleep! Jim[2] has been layd off from

1 *After an operation on his leg for a blocked artery.*
2 *Banting's lover.*

the Atomic plant at Lydd we are all sorry to say as he had a steady job for it must have been 5 years! & now is "resting" with a whiskey bottle Poor old Roger Senhouse is very tottery We went over to Tenterden last Saterday to do some shopping & Anne said, Ive never seen so many rich common people I suppose they all live in the loveliest made over Sussex farmhouses & workmens cotts with carriage lamps – they rivet me in a dreadful way. I hope to see you improved when I see you.

yours Ed

To Clover de Pertinez from 2 Springfield Cottages, Spring 1970

Dear Clo Thank you for yours I love Penzance,[1] quite unspoilt & full of lovely little terraces without carriage lamps & pottery Plates[2] with St. Anthonys Piss House written on them – and the people in the pubs all talk loudly to each other & dont look pinched (only purple) we went to a garden near P all going along a long drive & they had yellow Rhodedendrons which are lovely very pale lemon yellow ices with brown spots in the flowers. Magnoleas, & large camelias brown round the edges from the wind. even tho' they were very shelterd all planted in small divided walled gardens. The Queens hotel was very comfortable & realy very good food. Far Far better Anne said than the grandiose *manoir* with a golf course they went to after to meet Ken. I went back on the train from P on Sunday & thats when I went to see Billy[3] & the next day now hes at 34 Charlton P. He went for a week-end to the Rices.

I remember Gladys Rees[4] she realy was rather nice, & that great Scotch mist with huge feet & a maxi overall was "Graham" and was a friend of Juliets.[5] talking of *costumes*, do you remember Juliets sister, not at the P, but she came to dances & things & was permanently disguised as an Augustus John Gypsy with Sombrero & her hair in tiny plats – large gold drop earings shawl & all! Talk about Fancy dress my dear! I notice that Gypsys are *in* again! more like Pola Negri than Augustus this go round tho – Borer wasnt quayte out of the top drawer & was very jolly & covered in acne. I cant find any Jean Rhys in Penguin & I know the one about Montparnasse I particularly want when she lives in an hotel & has a littery lover who throws the price of a dinner on the bed. *not* a bag of boiled sweets – it seemed *familiar*[6] to me! I started one about 2 girls on a theatrical tour when I was having lunch with Bum. Judith Corcoran was there to lunch in a maxi & a maxi coat somehow she looked *quite* in a maxi, & not at all like a manic religeuse who has just been raped by Monk Lewis, & is just going to be walled up!

---

1 *He had been on a visit with Anne.*

2 *These were popular in Rye and Playden.*

3 *After the second of two operations on his leg.*

4 *The people mentioned here were students at the Chelsea Polytechnic in the Art School when Edward, Chappell, Ker-Seymer and Pritchard were there.*

5 *Juliet Wigan, later married to the architect Brian O'Rourke.*

6 *It paralleled Clover's situation in Paris with Jules Romain.*

garden & banks are covered in primroses & daffodils & look very pretty but I wish the weather would improve.

yrs Ed

To Clover de Pertinez from 2 Springfield Cottages, June 1970

Dear Clo Ive been meaning to write for ages. I went over to Pump Cottage Bar came & fetched me Billy & her came down for 2 nights, & I dont think he could stay there alone as he gets tired. The Dr I may say said he would take 6 months to recover which is what I said. Jim is still out of a job but all goes gaily on amidst flowing cut price Haig from Wayne Wayze & cut price cigarettes from Tesco, We went to the Lord Nelson in the old town to study (bogus) life all with one gold earing & fancy dress – all in a day dream and I wonder what they do in the week. If it gets any drier & no rain there will be no vegetables or anything else & Im pouring detergent & washing up water on the plants they seem to like it.

I took an extra hour getting down from London in the train as they were relaying the track after a derailment & we went a delightful tour round Kent – rather nice realy & boiling hot. Billy went to have a drink with Honor & Van Phillips & Sir F. was there who said he had been made a companion of honour. Van P said *he* had been a companion of Honor for years! Ha Ha – very witty I thought. I read in the Daily Sketch that Sir F keeps all his orders in the waters[1] hanging by the wall Mrs. Rhodes got one of those Marx & Spencer chickens that look like a hand grenade & are boned. Ive often wondered about them – she roasted it & cut it in peices in a dish, it was excellent, & actually tasted of chicken! Imagine that – they also have some quite good tinned mince which is generally uneatable but theirs makes a very good shepheards pie. I have a lot of Spanish books & Ill send some if I can muster up time & force to tie them up & get them to the P.O – yours Ed.

To William Chappell from 2 Springfield Cottages, 9 October 1970

Dear B

Ive not seen the exhibition but I hope to stay with Gerald Oct 17 week end & go then Im glad our letters did get there and were delivered I allways did feel something vaguely institutional about Saddlers W & the Old Vic! It was a sort of Tea feeling cum Salvation Army with a touch of Borstal and everything elevating. John & Barbara Bagnal went to Rogers wake at a church in Covent Garden. many were there, then they retired to the Tate for lunch or so B Bagnal suggested and was steared into some dreadful dram shop. yesterday John recived a letter at the pub which he said was saffron. it was a (supposed) piece of hash like a small bit of dried shit – which we later smoked & drank & did everything possible with absolutely *no* result *whatsoever*, so I presume J was diddled by some "man" in Eastbourne somebody put him on to! It was exactly like a very nice cigarette for

1 *The lavatory.*

asthma & the bronchial tubes an old lady used to give me in Rye when I went to tea! however the whiskey made up – & beer earlier! ! Hay Ho – well the weather apart from sudden deluges, isnt at all bad realy, and looks wonderful very melodramatic over the sea with sun one side and an inky shower with a livid light the other. Ive been making chutney with apples & quite nice too but I dont suppose it would keep are you going back to Thurloe? or dont you dare! I hope your not knee deep in sewage & head over heels in crap. The only things in my dustbin are empty ½ Haig bottles & tins of evaporated milk – otherwise I burn, & the rats bats starlings and other waylde creatures not dead from chemicals finish off the rest. I suppose I shall have to bring in the geraniums? yours Ed.

To William Chappell from 2 Springfield Cottages, 23 June 1971

Dearest B.
On Monday Dr. Rothenstein the nutty professor Barrie S. Penrose & a young lady came down and we went out to lunch (eon) at some terrible restaurant Dr. R is writing something in the Observer about Il comendatori Burra. he wanted to buy a painting of Ebbw Vale Ide just painted & I realy dont want to sell it so I asked 500£ for it & he said he wd have to think about it. The house is pretty well scourd *out* & there is nothing, literaly *nothing* left. I put them all on to J. Banting who I hope may get an exhibition & loves having people Barrie P & Mr. Postan from the Hamet Gallery & the Boss of the H. Gallery too & is having a wonderful time with it all hes very social of course – they all begin to drive me into a state of Paranoia & advanced persecution mania. mercy how they all agitate. white folks fussin. Im ungrateful. I hope the command performance[1] wont be too trying and none of the old drops[2] dont drop on the head of an old Liverpool personality playing tea for two on the musical glasses. Did you see Ellaline Terriss[3] has died aged 90 or was it 100? I heard her talking & singing "the honeysuckle & the Bee" from her daughters garden in Wimbledon last year! Strong voice & very cheerful. We just went to Spalding & drove about and ended in Cambridge on the way back very restful I find all I do is [be] driven about & get DR–K in the evening & no trouble no fussin or hysteria Hope to see you Sunday yours Ed

To William Chappell from 2 Springfield Cottages Playden, 18 August 1971

Dear B.
Thank you for your letter and do come down for a week-end if you fancy. Realy a heated swimming pool?[4] What would Beatrix Potter think. Youl be asked down to cook for the Queen Mother next. like Rosa Lewis for Edouard 7. Mr. Penrose came down with some money & gave me 2 sets of wood cuts. very posh they look. I also had a very funny letter from Nan

1 *In Liverpool before the Queen, who was opening the new Mersey Tunnel.*
2 *Backcloths.*
3 *The Edwardian actress, married to Seymour Hicks.*
4 *At Frederick Ashton's country home.*

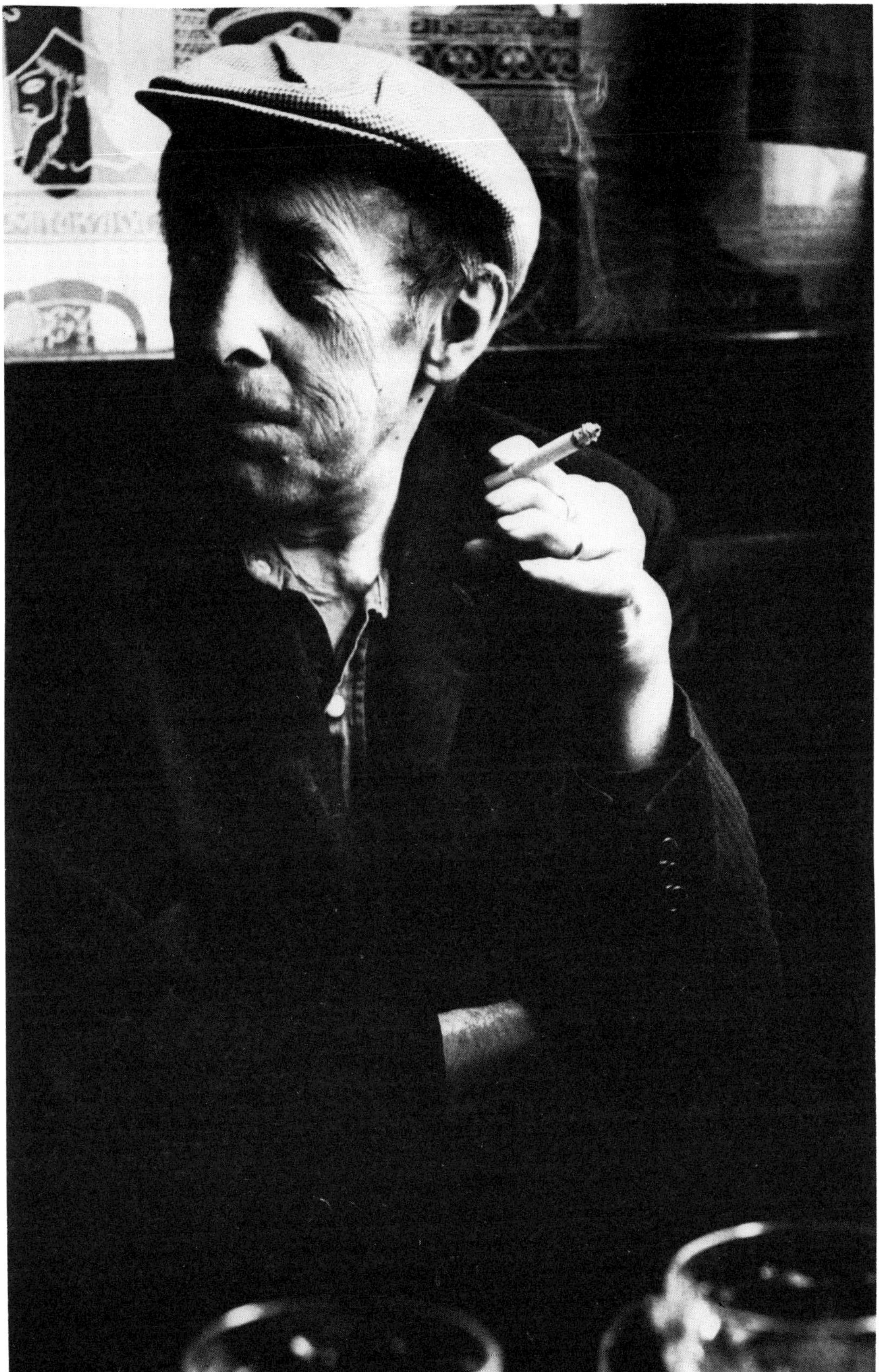

Redfern–Kivel, who said *he* had a *set?* from about 40 years ago at least & they were obviously printed (badly) by me. I dont believe he has them all & how may I ask did that little man get hold of them & kept them mum, until all this who HA? and asked me & *Johnny* Banting to stay at El something, is it in Tangier? very cheap markets – artists love it(?) I showd it to "Johnny" who was livid with fury at being referd to as "Johnny" so belittleing he said – How the vultures gather at the smell of carrion! also saw Desmond Ryan who turned up to lunch at J's bringing a bottle of what he called Green Peril. I must say after gin and peril I was quite sober but couldnt walk straight. dont mention it to the watch committee. Anne & Colin are off tomorrow. And fill every glass for gin inspires us & fires us with courage love & joy![1] I got a hand of pork & trotter the other day for 40p very good too. I suppose you would call it rather a rough joint as you cant cut dainty beautiful slices off it but its a good buy Am just ending a vast shoulder 70p – we were forced down to Rye on Tuesday & it was absolutely stuffed in every sense – a huge bus 20 feet wide swept through that arch[2] & up into the High where it encountered a Pontins[3] HA HA van parked & there it all remained. The *rest* of the Hay was divine & became a pedestrian precinct no traffic of course could get by. I shall have a bus to do just that every time I want to go to Rye – Yours Ed

To Clover de Pertinez from Cottages, no date, autumn 1971

Dear Clover Thanks for yours. Yesterday I went to a cabaret at a caravan sight at Bo Peep Hastings to hear George Melly with John & Jim and various members of the Melly familly. it was quite a rivetting performance in a huge sort of cabaret 2 Bars & an amusement arcade full of blind drunk peices of rock in Boofong hair does & sort of sub George Bests. not the best bests but not bad, there was also a mountainous woman in blue sequins with a sort of diamond strip down the front who roared into a mickrophone & ended up with Pack up your struggles in your old Shit bag & Puke Puke Puke (my version) also Auf Weldersehn Maytcar! all the kiddies were up & in the amusement arcade till a good ½ past midnight dressed in skin tight pink knickers with a coat made of rags & stockings with rings round them. I never got back till about 1.30 & then I was in such a state I boild a peice of bacon & never went to bed till between 2.30 & 3! We had a very nice time in Wales & one absolutely perfect day "Snowdonia" is beautiful – of course the day we just passed through you couldnt see Snowdon at all – it was shrouded.

Mr. Alexander Postan left us some copper plates for etchings & says hes going to print them so we're doing a few prints! I dont particularly want to realy. Im going to Charlton P on Wednesday so I hope I dont vanish & return blind drunk & unable to walk & blot my copybook it can stay blotted!

---

1 *Edward's version of the song from* The Beggar's Opera.

2 *The landgate.*

3 *A holiday camp at Camber Sands.*

Mrs. Chappell[1] is now landed with Cathleen Nesbit (aged 90?) who can never remember what theatre they are rehearsing at let alone her lines so Im sure he's going to return blind drunk! shes taking Dame Gladwys place in the Chalk Garden. Dame G was indisposed. I may inform you before I forget John (at the Cabaré) was dragged on to the floor by man mountain Dean in a very smart business diplomatic suit & a pair of blue sand shoes with toes painted by himself on the outside! He was a great success. Gerald [Corcoran] was made to go to a nursing home – as the doctor said he wouldnt be "responsible" – & proceeded to make all the nurses drunk on Champers, so Desmond told me. I think he's out now again so they are expecting some pepper at the Galleries. I hope you got 2 cards from Harlech! 1 of the horse & lion by Stubbs & the cute little "Stone breaker" by I forget who now. quite small its a lovely little painting.

Nobody ever looked at those early drawings of mine exept to say nasty things if possible so I gave up doing them its realy very funny except all I feel is a strong urge to vomit & I dont want to see any of the fucking crap whynt they stuff themselves with them?

Theres no Fartist like a dead one dearie – Im dead I suppose if theres a horrible exhibition at the Tate. they will have a horrible dinner (by candle light!) I realy shall have to be away or sick or dead I can imagine what that will be like. Yrs Ed

To William Chappell from "Sprcotts' Pleedun Raye Wednesday Soir
postmark 20 Jan 1972

Dearest B.

Thanks for yours. I went to see John this afternoon at St. Helens Hospital where he was being ministered to by belle negresses and is having an operation on Tuesday next for the rehabilitation of his arse which will be combined with his cock and he says its distinctly Picasso cum Heath Robinson. it frightens me alright. but he looks very well & the ward is very nice sunny & beds not too close together plenty of space between & you can be curtained off. he's been having trouble at that end for 18 months or more past & I *hope* when this is all over with will be better! if it doesnt finish him off but I dont think it will. Everybody seems to be in the last stages dont they? Gerald looked blooming in among the hyacinths. I hope to see them all as I hope we shall go there to lunch on Sunday next. I dont know why Bar thought I was not too good Im sure. a touch of hangover from ruminating for hours in Wards Irish House drinking double bells with an occasional pint of guiness! what I realy enjoy doing & then going to the cinema & having egg & chips after. I wonder how Doris [Langley Moore] is? we shall have to run down to the Pump Room & stay at the Francis Hotel & hope to see Mrs. Moore with a face twisted into a sort of crucifixion, sailing down the dining room carrying books papers Dly papers etc – complaining bitterly about the city council who are obviously a bunch of crooks if thats anything to be surprised at & busy ruining the goose that lays the golden eggs

1 *Fils.*

– if they but knew – by destroying irreplacable 18th century buildings. Im glad T. Rattigans benefit[1] went off well with poor old Sir Noel a long days journey alright! Yrs Ed.

To William Chappell from 2 Springfield Cottages, Sunday postmark 31 Jan 1972

Dearest B.
I enjoyed our little party. I love Miss P[onsonby] she realy is a natural. I wish you could have seen Sir John [Gielgud] in very tight sort of jersey jacket. he has quite a "good figure" I must say *à son age*! I went over to see John yesterday who is in bed with a pipe up his nose stuck on with sticky paper one arm done up in gauze and a peice of plastic with a pipe in it connected with a sort of fancy art style gin bottle on a stand & pipes leading down to a plastic sack under the bed. talking between gasps but talking – I must say considering his state, hes not doing at all badly, but I should think hed be in there for *weeks*. and doesnt want to go to a rehabilitation centre afterwards. Jim can do the shopping etc hes sure not to be working (unfortunately) or maybe fortunately in this case – I hope to come up on Wednesday week. I wanted to come up at the week end but Mr. Smith is coming down on Sunday to discuss god knows what my past life. and wants to see Anne too. it bores me to death as I never can rem[em]ber my past or what date it was when or why – some of those old letters would give them all a turn never a mention of Art more like Fart with a capital F. This weather is getting a little trying just in time for power cut tayme. Blackouts tomorrow honey I hear by courtesy of the Daily mirror on Radio Luxembourg. I want to see the French Connection. I realy want to see a pop sort of vaudeville bill with a lot of stars among whom Ike & Tina Turner who I want to see particularly & sort of musical cowboy film called "Zachariah" at the New Victoria. I havent dared mention such a thing! well I hope to see you soon – Yrs Ed.
Monday The power is off so the place is freezing but I *have* got a fire.

To William Chappell from 2 Springfield Cottages, April 1972

Dear B.
Well, if you *want* to know dearie I thought the whole thing[2] was deadly. I particularly dislike talking about "Art" or "myself" & being questioned. Nobody ever gets very Far. they should have learned that by this time youd think? Having been photographed cooking 4 sausages from the butchers for myself & Bars lunch I was asked to sit down & eat them being photographed of course so I firmly refused to & they had to be satisfied with 2 bites. why we shouldnt have lunch in peace I dont know. They[3] question & "me" talking was at the end & I very nearly blew up. I have been brow beaten into coming up on Monday to go to some Fucking pub in the Harrow Rd George Melly to be there etc & I said I must return here the next

1 *A matinée at the Haymarket.*
2 *The making of a filmed television interview for the Tate restrospective.*
3 *Peter and Carol Smith, who were making the film.*

day. Mrs. S[mith] swore shed drive me back or get a car! They are coming down on Monday for what I cant think. If Ide known all this would go on I wouldnt have had anything to do with it at all. as I dont realy care a Fart! Mind you I like Mr. & Mrs. Carter de Haven-Smith very much indeed – Im very fond of them, and theyve been very good realy! We shot a pretty little scene in the Village grocers – it might have been out of "Grumpy" stoll version

Yours Ed

The camera crew are very nice.

Come & see "The Little Lost Charwoman" featuring Marguerite Fuck at the Electric Palace!

To William Chappell from 2 Springfield Cottages, 28 April 1972

Dearest B.

Thank you for yours –

having just completed Super Market Susie retitled Mrs. Wiggs of the cabbage patch, for Vitagraph I dont want to go anywhere and would like to do some *painting*! Its all over now I hope. Carole & Peter S. were very nice & the camera crew – of 4 no less, one other one they payed not to come! it made quite a crowd – Youl *thrill* to Susie trapped in a flood of flaming Mazola and a human vampire in the cellars of blazing Tescos – Sob at Mrs. Wiggs watering 3 dead geraniums, shudder at the flames of hate! created by a lot of greasy paper & old Daily Mirrors & a Fire lighter be horrified at Susie Wiggs dragged through scenes of unspeakable vayce & degradation in the lowest dens of harrow Rd by the notorious George Melly & be hartwarmed at the human interest of Mrs W leaving Rye Station for the last time from the wrong platform. & they say there are "pictures" too! whatever they are – I enjoyed the Drag Pub.

Miss Phyllis Monkman in a pink negligée & a huge blond wig looking like Louie the Ritz with delirium Tremens & a giantess sang Burlington Bertie very good I thought. What was that mysterious rout they gave at the Lefevre? I was so drunk all the time of Mrs. Wiggs that I never took anything in at all? *My* idea was to get off on my own down the village buying packers chocolates All seemed *luxe ordre beauté volputé* etc at 35 Charlton P. with Miss R[oett] back on her step ladder – I should like that wall left without being paperd – its wonderful. Miss R thinks so too. far too bare for Miss K[er] S[eymer]! I shall see you befor long I daresay Yrs Ed

To William Chappell from 2 Springfield Cottages, 4 August 1972

Dearest B. Thanks for your letter. I reaaly cannot go away with *luggage*, and once I get my clothes on I cant change them or dance reels (I may reel but thats a different thing) or keep "bright" for very long. I was reeling somewhat on Monday having fortified myself with one or 2 wee double drappies befor lunch – a lot of white wayne and a double scotch & 2 vintage ports offered us by dear Francis[1] who is a dear man and one at Miss

1 *Francis Bacon, the painter.*

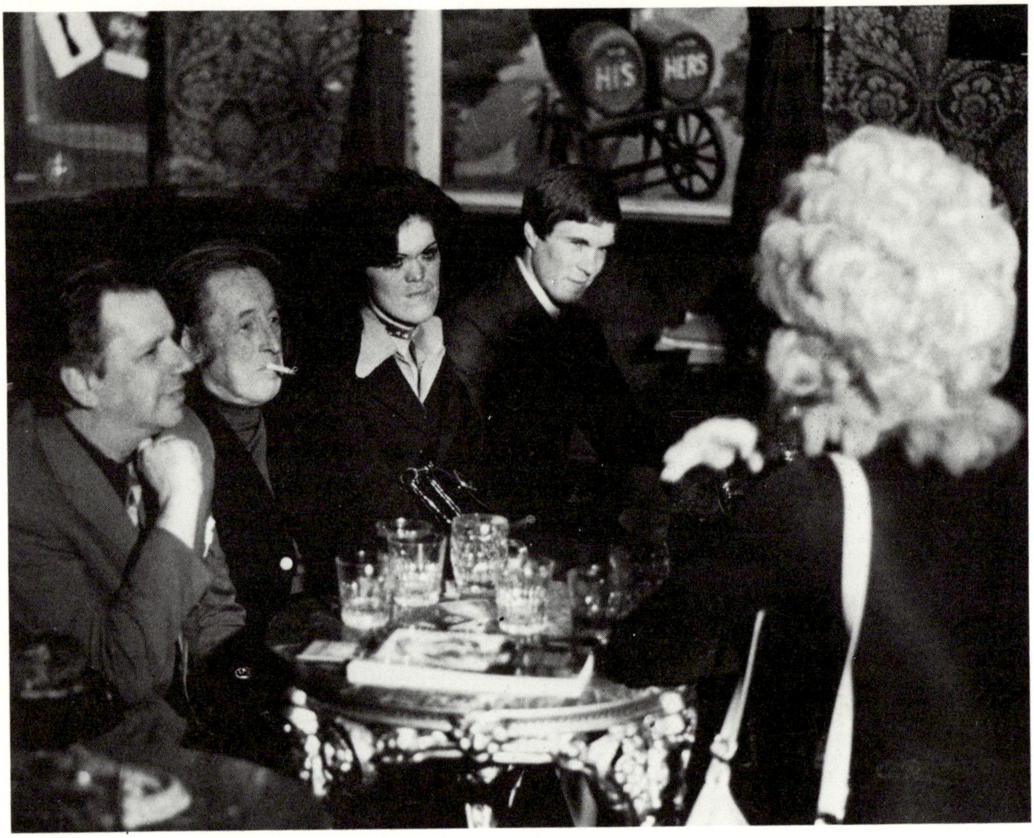

Mews.[1] I actualy managed to get to Dirty Harry so I must have been high as a kyte when it suddenly dawned on me time was marching on. Too many people is a mistake realy as you cant concentrate or I cant. Ive been living for the last 3 days on Irish stew! having bought 2 lbs of Best end of neck, very good it is & I also had 2 cutlets off it for lunch one day – The weather is very queer indeed with a grey lid on it & a high gale I may see you after you get back
yrs Ed.

To William Chappell from 2 Springfield Cottages, 16 August 1972

Dearest B.
Ive not been to Caledonia stern & wild[2] since the war Anne & Colin go every year. I used to go all the time. Mama was born in George Street Edinburgh! Its marvellous I must say I always have disliked the South of England (I dont count Cornwall) now its rapidly turning into a sub-Croydon with gaps. Much nicer to drive realy Ide think – I dont say if its pouring rain & a thick fog but the weather is very good harvesting going on in full fling. Well I suppose Terry [Rattigan] being *a professional* – thats a

1 *Miss Muriel, high priestess of a famous drinking club in Soho, the Colony, much patronised by painters.*
2 *Chappell was staying in Bunny Roger's house in the Scottish Highlands.*

pejorative word now did you know? is interested in the theatre so likes to go & see plays *en province* – Im sorry about Bar[1] I hope the megrims are recovered it must have been the shock at finding it wasnt drizzling. Such a heresy. I prefer salmon to trout that seems to me to be rather tasteless & muddy I never dare say so only to you between ourselves. Happy Sandy to be stoned. I love to be stoned. it quite prevents one from doing any work so I can rarely be really stoned except when the film was being made what else was there to do. Poor Carol has lost her job. I hear owing to some Hanky Panky however she threw a tape recorder at someone Im glad to say thereby showing her breeding The film is finished & there it will remain I expect. I saw [that] at the first night of J.C. super star Danny La Rue said he should be up with them playing Mary Magdalen. I had been casting it (prayvitly) myself & I had cast him for Herodiade Mdm Alice Delysia as Magdalen, Stowitts[2] as J.C.S.S. W.H. Berry as Pontius Pilate & the Dolly sisters as Martha & Mary & the Jackson Boys as the 12 apostles. Postan came down today & I gave him 2 engravings (itchings dear) he plots to publish in a portfolio of 3 & sell them separately we hope to make some money meanwhile Ive been "going on with my paintings" all very dull nothing but landscapes. Yes my dear do come down when you want. very *humble* Im afraid after all those lobsters & salmon & Barons of Beef! however theres whiskey the more important bit to me (& Sandy so it seems) love to all
yours Ed

To Clover de Pertinez from 2 Springfield Cottages, 30 August 1972

Dear Clo
I expect there were peices in the Times about Jules "Remains".[3] & this one Bumble sent me I think its from the Paris ed. of the N.Y. Tribune a SKINFLINT I notice among other things I wonder who wrote this one. I was up at Charlton P[lace] & they seemed to have enjoyed Dundonnell Miss R[oett] got so bitten with midges she positively developed an alergy – They vanished to Geffreys surgery at 9 yesterday as G said allergys sometimes swell up the tongue & choked you – you may imagine what opportunities for *Drââmes effroyables*; & in the middle of this Bar brought up some brekker for Miss, & when she picked up the handle of the tea pot it came off & in trying to catch it gave her hand a terrible gash – Billy is doing a play an old one by Preistley & was going to see the old thing yesterday. he wasnt alltogether looking forward to it Im sure P has his own ideas on what *he* wants

Anne & Colin are in the Isle of Mull & then Rothsay Perthshire she says Mull is beautiful but you can never see it on a fine day a haze – & bad weather a mist   yrs Ed

---

1 *Who took to her bed at Bunny Roger's.*
2 *Hubert Jay Stowitts was an American dancer who had partnered Anna Pavlova toward the end of her life.*
3 *Jules Romains, Clover's former lover, had just died.*

To William Chappell from 2 Springfield Cottages, 23 September 1972

Dearest B.
I hope you are all right and not feeling too badly.[1] I hardly dare write but Ive no doubt Preistleys play has helped to remove brooding too much on the subject. Just befor I received your letter I met Alice Binnie in the grocer at Peasemarsh & she said she had just come back from Greece. I said you dont look tanned & she said as the temperature was 96 all she was looking for was a bit of shade – I thought later it couldnt have been any help that heat. You mustnt let it worry you. We are going away on Sat 30 for (about) a week to the north Cumberland or Northumberland Im not expecting a temp of 96! but thats not my object as you might say That white lily with three heads has come out finaly! very late Its been lovely down here lately yrs Ed

To Conrad Aiken from 2 Springfield Cottages, 6 December 1972

Dear Conrad Ive been meaning to write but didnt want to bother you with all your troubles & activity. They have suddenly put my apothosis at the Tate next year instead of 2 yrs on so I get consultations which mean nothing to me as I dont know where any of the pictures are & dont care anyway. it might have been FUNNE 20 years ago – but now, No. not much. Mrs. Rhodes tells me that some people would be in bliss – The last one was how they should be hung. and I said you hang them anyway you like honey –! Johns[2] house is very nice indeed I thought. I shouldnt mind it at all but this ever increasing muddle suits me well enough & I can go & spend a weekend in London where I get blind drunk (in the morning when Ime doing the shopping) so I end up buying 20 paper backs books none of which I remember buying. I read SCIFI & magic & witchcraft sword & sorcery some are realy crazy – its like a vice realy it gets you I cannot pull myself together or move I can manage three days in London & keeping up on doubles (whiskey) it makes it feel not quite so awful! when not being refused a drink in pubs! they dont quite *approve* of me – I always ask why? & they get very up tight. quite sober too but difficult to *place* & all the pubs in the West End are getting paranoid over hippies & drug takers "drugtakers" HA HA I know quite a few only its not called that as it comes from the Dr. on prescription. Pills with everything & everybody cross eyed at the drop of a hat. They are thinking of changing the licencing Laws & I might go to the movies more as I never can go to an early performance as its good drinking time, its a perfect farce the whole thing. They might just as well keep open some pubs as everybody drinks themselves silly at home anyway – like little Miss Griffin who started at 5 or 6 she says (see extract in the Dly Mail) I hope you all are keeping going – just – Christmas horrors will soon be here

Yours Ed

---

1 Chappell's favourite sister had just died in Greece from a brain haemorrhage.
2 John Aiken, Conrad's son.

To William Chappell from 2 Springfield Cottages, 12 December 1972

Dearest B

I can see Chez Victor will be quite impossible now Princess Anne goes there for dinner, having gone to Private Lives, very sensible of her. Next time you come down well have a pot roast for a change. Yes lets have lunch Monday I should think? or Sat if it comes to that? Ive begun to notice a horrible feeling of rush & gathering of rubbish going on Rye was very crowded & no where to paranoia park Wayne Wayze was frantic & I could hardly fight my way to the whiskey shelf it makes no difference to me my dear wether its Holloeen or the day Billy crossed the Boyne. I must get some Mack.[1] I suppose mothers [Barbara's] Megrims are "a protest" against everyones horrible behavior! I swear whiskey would do her good. She says she cant get drunk but she hasnt *realy tried* "keep pegging away" as they used to say in my school report. everything would seem much smoother – For a time –

Poor old Amy Shuard was BOOED at La Scala Milan when she was opening in Turandot & there was a riot! because she was a Foreigner she says – well – F[2] was BOOED in Munich!

Let us know about luncheon

Yrs Ed

To William Chappell from 2 Springfield Cottages, 20 March 1973

Dearest B

Yes I do hope to come up on Sat? if they dont all go back on a disruption course in a huff. It was thingummy Sands[3] where we were to meet you. round about 2.30 or something it leaves London about 11.30 I believe so realy it doesnt take all that time.

When they started talking of this film, *I* thought it would be just the paintings & perhaps a photo or two of me. little did I know it was to be a quaynte personality sketch in the manner of Bransby Williams![4] I love the Savoy Grill. proper style that is and very good cooking never messed up and exactly what it should be. Ive got a pound & a half of shin stewed with carrots onions turnip Bisto & an oxo cube & some Knorr powder very non U Im sure. Its now turned into a solid galantine you could eat it in slices it might be rather good. Theres another nightmare in store for May 19 when they put a plaque on Paul Nashs house "the friends of Paul Nash" they are to be allowed into the house by "Miss Warren & then forgather at a Hostellerie for lunch" so I shall be forced to go away I cant bear those kind of things & everyone in Rye Ive been avoiding for years will be there Im certain. They depress me these things – plaques etc

yours Ed

---

1 Macgregors, a less known brand but more reasonably priced.

2 Ashton.

*3 Grange-over-Sands (which Edward later calls Grange*mouth *Sands).*

4 The music-hall actor who did impressions and characters from Dickens etc.

To Clover de Pertinez from 2 Springfield Cottages, Friday the 13th *April 1973*

Dear Clo

The lakes looked wonderful as the tops had snow, & there was a marvellous sunny day we seemed to see too much and it all has run together – befor the snow it was very dry & all the water falls dry as a bone but when the sun came out everything was pouring & running. we picked Billy up at Grangemouth Sands.[1] I rather fancy Grangemouth S which has miraculously remaind fixed between 1880–1900! "The Sands" & views of Pennines beyond are lovely – also went to Furness Abbey realy magnificent. it must be one of the finest wrecks in England. red with viridian & pale whitey green moss & in a beautiful situation – not many people go the man said "the surroundings" are not very lakey & Touristy Im happy to say. I never expected for one moment you would come to this frightful exhibition.[2] I could have told you so 6 months ago – I dont answer anyones letters & am thinking of going away if I could pull myself together – I dont care if I see it or not. I might if I was left entirely alone & not pesterd to go to a party or any deadly affair of that sort. Fearful scandal my dear! we forgot to go & see Beatrix Potters House etc close to Newby Bridge where we stayd I went on about it & then we clean forgot – we stopped at Cambridge & I got "Une page d'amour" & another one. The heroines darter goes rigid *comme son aieule* you may remember *La Fortune des Rougon*. Granma was rigid for days – Blood will out Ant[3] seems to be being particularly *Rougon Maquart* brandishing knives but from boredom not *l'heredité* I swear he was less bored in Harrogate

yours Ed

To William Chappell from 2 Springfield Cottages, April 1973

Dearest B

I hope you were none the worse for whirling round *petit suisse*[4] in 57 varieties of different weather and never allowed to stop but for 2 whiskey macs under pressure I cant imagine how we ever stopped in Peterborough! Yesterday they gadded off again to Aberdovey. Colin *may* actually stop on the way. they are spending a night at Cheltenham. Ken likes his drink which goes on as late as possible (like Fred) & then play bridge after dinner which A[nne] doesnt very much like realy. I thought of coming up this W.e maybe but I just collapse. and I dread all the terrible horrors being brewd up over this Tate affair – surely they have *everything* they want by now but me and they can leave me alone. its like a night mare to me – very wrong Im sure but there it is. Poor old Picasso seems like the passing of a world but he was a good age 91. now we can imagine what a cage of apes it will be over the 20000000000£ or whatever "The fortune" is supposed to be – we shall hear more no doubt. Ive got your horse radish, I took a bit. and

1 *Grange-over-Sands in fact.*

2 *His retrospective exhibition at the Tate.*

3 *Clover's husband. Antonio de Pertinez.*

4 *The Lake and Peak Districts.*

have put it in the ice box. We whirled at such a rate round the Lake district It all seems mixed up & run into each other. I thought Derbyshire was lovely & that place with Damsons. I think Mr. A. Postan is coming down tomorrow. yrs Ed.

To William Chappell from 2 Springfield Cottages, June 1973

Dear B.
We realy had very good weather over the moors & dales & they looked marvelous its wonderful to go quite a *long way* & never meet a soul. & ended up in Cambridge at that terrible Blue Boar Trust House, quite a change, everything suddenly burst out Bogus. & the town was full of "Beggars" gypsys & strange begight in Bawdkins and kirtle withawl. I just got your letter and I am coming up Sat or I hope to so you can let me have the books[1] then I looked at one in "The Series" called "Lud in the Mist" or something like that by somebody Mirlees and I thought it a shade *whimsical* William M[orris] & George M[acdonald] are both entirely without a grain of whamsy dead straight – Im sure that brains & singing dont go but if they do happen to be a grain of brain you get a great singer. tho I dont know if Melba or Caruso were great brains?! shrewd I dare say Sir Thomas Beecham considered *all* singers fools! if only it would get a shade warmer. Hope to see you then yours Ed
I have been having a large coal fire.

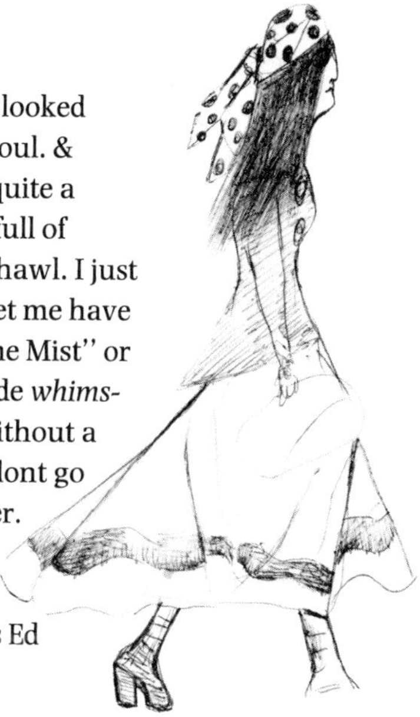

To William Chappell from 2 Springfield Cottages, 11 June 1973

Dearest B
It wasnt shocking at all & I love curried eggs but I never can realy eat a great deal if Ive been drinking by Tuesday evening I was not my best. I went to the White Swan at the end of new Row there looks a nice butcher there. The Tate sent me 7 catalogues one with binding what in Gods name Im supposed to do with them I dont know one is enough youd think. there was a very good notice in the Financial Times Anne gave me. Its the most inconveniently situated place in London the Tate as you well know – miles from anything any one ever *wants* spiritualism/whiskey I wish you were here enjoying this weather. I heard from Clover raving on at everything & *she* wasnt included & nobody took *her* picture. & I daresay Smith might have paid her fair from Harrogate – but Granada is a bit too much on a narrow budget. I cant understand any one careing.[2]

I had a very sweet letter from Mrs. E. Toft 20 Victoria Rd Haworth Keighley Yorks. saying I watched your exhib on Thurs night I realy enjoyed the paintings my daughter who is 8 years old thought you very nice it is the first time I have ever wrote to anyone in my life like this But I just have to say to you thank you for ½ an hr of yr wonderful work yrs faithfully Mrs. Toft. She must have meant it yrs E

1 *Fantasy fiction, no doubt,* Conan the Barbarian *very probably among them.*
2 *And yet he didn't like it when people did not care.*

There is something touching about Edward's P.S., 'She must have meant it'; almost incredulous, as thought he found it difficult to believe so spontaneous an expression of pleasure in his work, directly and clearly stated and far removed from any hint of the 'Fart' talk he detested. It is clear Mrs Tofts meant every word; and so did the bus driver from Stoke Newington who reacted with the same unaffected sense of discovery; and the lady who came upon Edward's work almost by mistake and fell into helpless and delighted laughter at his painting of topless waitresses. All three of them saw immediately what Edward wanted to be seen: the strength, the reality, and the humour of his work. Very different to the thin wail of Raymond Mortimer's tortured sensibility, 'They're so LOUD', when confronted for the first time by Edward's paintings at the Redfern Gallery during the war. A quite gloriously gutless reaction. Equally so an 'Art Critic' of the Morning Post *for 30 May 1932 who, after several paragraphs of positively orgasmic waffling over some fearfully dainty silk* collages, *dismisses Edward in a sentence: 'One is safest in silence in the next room where Mr Edward J. Burra's imagery might lead one to violent language.'*

There is no record of Edward's reaction. Had he shown one his language would not have been violent; only down to earth: 'Oh lor! What a proper pisspot!'

To William Chappell from 2 Springfield Cottages, 26 July 1973

Dearest B
We started in Boston Lincs then went from there to Grassington where we stayed 3 days going round. I must say its less tireing than one night stands! on way back we stopped at Cam[bridge] rather stormy but the deluge took place on the Sunday night we were at 'Bernis'' 6 Bars & 2 Jumbo Fish fried in turkey carpet and double double steak & luscious Smedleys processed natural peas etc. Grassington is a very cosy hotel with central heating (if you care to turn it on) Mrs R is very keen on that hotel & very nice food – beautiful surroundings – we went over to Richmond from Grassington I love R – I visited one very quiet pub & then I went to one called the Bishop Blaise crowded with the dear boys from Catterick Camp & a coach load of Harpies of a certain age who steadily yelled at the top of their lungs & treated our dear boys to beer they accepted & took no notice at all. we were very fortunate about food which was good even at Fortes Trust House at Matlock where we stopped a night on the way down. let us know how you are getting on facing the public. I might come up not *this* week-end but the following?   yrs Ed

To William Chappell from 2 Springfield Cottages, 3 August 1973

Dearest B.
Monica, who you've no doubt heard mention of, & has been recuperating from nembies in an asylum at Haywards Heath came over from Brighton By Bus – shes *quite* undaunted & since being off the nembies, has developed a driving energy that exhausts me to a rag – & brought photos of Mum in some of Mistinguets costumes, She was underst[ud]y – One of those of rose petals I know well with a hat 20 feet high, & she left a photo of an un-

known 1913 belle who we cant think *who*? Gaby Deslys or Lilian Braithwaite when young I thought or Lily Elsie[1] as she was in the widow at Dalys. She told me she had written a letter of 15 pages to Mrs. Rhodes "explaining everything"! Mrs. R. does not approve of M realy. Mrs. R is becoming terribly Boorgwah in her old age. its those relations in Summerset or wherever Flower shows & wimmins institutes & that – Blood will out Monica had a little boy now a rather *big* boy who shes not seen since I dont know when & shows no interest in & Mrs. R thinks that so terrible and is economising for the future she told me well well dear I should have thought the future was NOW. I feel everything is so fluid Ime very doubtful about "the future". Clover swears shes coming over in Sept & Edward wants her to spend the winter in Brum with the central heating. in Graná shes boiling with a temp of 85 inside the apt & then proceeds to freeze in the winter. Monica has a play Pictorial of the Bing Boys – Mum was in that. & there is a picture of Vi Lorraine in an oriental? costume. I cant describe it but you can imagine it. her "ordinary" clothes were very elegant & Lorna & Toots P[ounds][2] were very *chic* indeed & looked quite modern & very stylish! I was very impressed by them at the age of 9, when I was taken to a *matinée* I remember Toots was very pretty in a Dolly Varden Hat. Mum has a signed photo of George [Robey], with "I love your face" George written on it! Do come down when you are able & if you are too. Yours
Ed

To William Chappell from 2 Springfield Cottages, 4 December 1973

Dearest B
I'm sorry the trains were Sunday but you were enriched by human contacts in the Rly Tavern? I always like an oportunity for a surprise drink. I suppose that diary[3] was never meant for other eyes but why did he put it on paper? only later. I presume – I think its a nice trait to employ yr old friends[4] but I suppose it was left to Cocky to give them the bums rush when they were found to be totally inadequate – I never much cared for Gladys C[5] – I had a p.c. from Lincoln & one from Kelso about which I know nothing & yesterday went out to lunch with John Aiken & Paddy with an old mutual friend at her house – very careful of the Bawbees – only 2 glasses of wayne & a glass of sherry. however I managed 2 scotchs befor I left the cott. knowing what dear Margaret McKechnie was capable of in the way of lunchtime O'Booze – NO word of Mdm Rhodes – they havent had time I suppose & are getting over the cholera – Thanks for yr call dearie! you neednt worry on my account – Im only too pleased to be left in peace and I dont want to go to London at all. I hate to answer the telephone for fear its something I cant think up an excuse fast enough to get out of. I dont want

1 *It was Lily Elsie.*
2 *Famous music hall and revue 'sister' act.*
3 *C.B. Cochran's personal diary.*
4 *Noël Coward was notable in keeping an eye on his friends' well-being.*
5 *Calthrop.*

to move – Arrive in Rye at 9.15 & find all the shops empty & theres a bus at 10.30 so its quite easy, I dont mind walking down at all. I dont *want* to walk *up* dragging a heavy bag, but dont need to, if I time it well – not much traffic today. I suppose they saved it all up for Bank H yrs Ed

To William Chappell from 2 Springfield Cottages, 6 December 1973

Dearest B this weather is perfectly divine down here & I havent had any heating on the last 2 days but for a nice fire yesterday (when it stopped smoking & was burning well) Well I have a little drama of my own Mrs. Ritchie thought I should buy a stove so I got an Aladdin & 2 Jerry cans of Blue Paraffin. the next morning I thought Ide light the fucking thing. I thought the wick was burning a bit yellow & a little uneven but I hoped it would get OK & retired to the bathroom & was putting on my pants when I heard a sort of *roaring* & thought OH God what now? & went in the kitchen – there was the stove *blazeing*. so I realy was terrified – & I thought the Tanks will blow up & another minute the cottage on fire & picked it up! I burned my thumb & burnt off a lot of *hair* & burned my forehead but got it on to the doorstep! & slammed the door & thought well – ! theres 17£ written off – Mrs. R arrived later & was very surprised to see the stove on the doorstep. there wasnt a thing the matter with it but a bit blackened – Mrs. Smith lit it perfectly – Im terrified of it & dont dare touch it – another result of the Drame was my face suddenly swelled up on the side but is sinking now I looked a proper mess like the rest of the country my dere – I also suspect there may be "trouble" on the railways from next Tues – midnite – I hear Lady Diana M[1] is arranging – from her bed in Maida Vale to save fuel – a gala opening for Cockie! Well dear I *hope* to see you. I shall buy a bottle yours Ed

To William Chappell from 2 Springfield Cottages, 23 December 1973

Dearest B
I felt the show, now all is known that it isnt a million pound spectacle with staircases & show girls draped in electrically lit tangerines but is a nice little Review! would do well– but what with variegated strikes especially the suburban Southern region being to all intents & purposes non existant & petrol it has a few handicaps Im afraid. You can get petrol here quite easily & *no queues* – dear little Yuletyde Tinker Belle Towne is stuffed with cars & Mrs. R quite paranoid about parking. Alls well here & Aladdin is working beautifully – & is very useful & burning Blue one seems to be able to get Blue Paraffin. its supposed to be for old age pensioners & elderly people. I dont know if meths drinkers are counted in? probably not. I had a glowing account from Mother Ker Seymer of the opening night & Itty Jessie[2] in Rose & Mrs. Glenville[3] with orange miracle whip on her head (hair) & diamonds

---

1 Lady Diana (Manners) Cooper.

2 Jessie Matthews.

3 Dorothy Ward.

twinkling I wonder what Jessie thought? also Dorothy Dickson it must have been quite a gathering. Well a happy Christmas & no trains or coal & "very few petrol stations look like being open" throughout the Glad new year!

Yours Ed.

To William Chappell from 2 Springfield Cottages, New years Day *1974*

Dearest B
I wrote to you just before you left. In wondering about trains on the Southern region. long distance may be OK but commuters seem to be non existant & I dont know about the Hastings Ashford line – if that deigns to run Anyway everything is quite cosy & the man came to service the boiler and said he thought there would be FU-EL like those jolly Xmas stamps – so Apt – Apter than they ever dreamed at the time of designing Im sure – *If* you could afford to pay for it. La demoiselle Roett developed "a germ" one of those germs theyre always developing in the stews round the Angel & vanished on Xmas day leaving Bar to cook everything on the N.S. gas which either left everything raw or burnd it to a cinder – she says it wont simmer – there was no lack of work & washing up of 999 plates etc. – I dont think she enjoyed it – All was *luxe ordre beauté* & *volupté* at Fayre Meadow with Colin Anne & Milord – after 6 double scotches in the kitchen & a glass of champagne I fell into a deep sleep in the afternoon after getting back here & finished up with some porridge! When you told me you were going "North" it sounded so grand I felt certain it was to Bunnys – having quite forgotten Oh Kay[1] – later it *did* occur to me something wasnt quite right & you werent deer stalking and making Cabinet pudding. Comets are supposed to foretell disaster arent they so this one is right on time, a pictorial list of comets in the daily Mail after every comet since 563 B.C. or so theres either "the beginning of the 100 yrs war" or 110000 Incas stewed in onion juice or an eruption or a prolonged famine Well I daresay I may see you

Yrs Ed

To William Chappell from 2 Springfield Cottages, 15 February 1974

Dearest B I enclose a letter from Mrs. Ritchie about our little promenade, she told me all, & I said I should completely muddle everything up – so she wrote it down. I had a little note from Beatrice Dawson. I dread it. asking me if I could be induced to *stay* & I dont want to I realy *dread* coming to London the only place I can bear at all is Charlton P. maybe in the good old summer tyme I shall feel more like it – I dont like staying with people realy I prefer the Grand Hotel Harrogate listening to monsters & mooning over double scotch that or assorted derelicts in Liverpool St. Buffet. I realy dont know about having another show as Ive got plenty of money (worthless paper) to go on for some time & anything more if there would be anything

1 The George Gershwin musical, a production of Chappell's.

more will be removed by the Inland Rev & V A T and a wealth tax Im sure & *I* might keep some paintings, I would like to talk seriously (if possible) with Gerald over this! anyway – I suppose it doesnt matter what one does Im begining to think creepy gnomes have delivered *oil* to my tank I believe without me seeing. it will be *a bill* to send to my accountant. running great "buisness" I run "Novelties" & "Gyftes" – plastic cunts made into salt pepper & mustard in different shades. a very good line, & thats not the ½. If I hear any more about Solzynitzn I shall have one of my awful screaming fits. I think they are playing him up as an antidote to "Heath & Wilson". Cross talk artistes supreme – this week the Scunthorpe hippodrome next wk Biggleswade La La! off they go on Solzynitzn again I must turn off

Yours Ed

To Monica Wodehouse from 2 Springfield Cottages, 11 March 1974

Dear Monica
Ive meant to write but what with one thing & another havent brought myself into a fit state to do so I had an attack of gout in the left toe & my ankles swelld up xtra however its better now well I wrote a letter to Scott to his little grey home in East Camberwell and promptly lost the letter so it was delayd somewhat. I think O Kay may do quite well. Amanda Barrie the leading girl is very good. Shes a good dancer can sing & is also a comedienne a funny one too there arent many such

That photo you gave me is Lilly Elsie there was a peice about Lilly in the Dly Telegraph picture supplement with other photos & shed been around from the age of 6 before she got to the Merry W. "Little Elsie" at the age of 10 was on the halls imitating Hetty King & Harry Lauder & then was "on tour" in Chin Chin, TINTIN, CHEE CHEE, TEE HEE etc all the musical shows seemed to have names like that. there was one photo, it looked like by "Lenare" but might have been Cecil Beaton taken in the 1930ies & she looked wonderful then I havent been up to "towne" much, once for the week-end & for the day & had lunch at the gallery yrs Ed
Thanks for the p.c. it must have been nice in those days.

To William Chappell from 2 Springfield Cottages, 3 April 1974

Dearest B. Thanks for yours. I might see you this week end as I have enquired if I might come up You do seem very busy running from Place to Place aided & abetted by whiskey I hope. when you can pause long enough. I dont know why I dont look at Book Boxes more – many a treasure yet if you can face going through it all. I got a paper back by James Hogg. known as "the Ettrick Shepheard", a Scotch worthy who wrote a book called Memoirs of a self confessed? Sinner about a monstrous religious maniac. realy dear if you liked that Lefanu you might like the memoirs or confessions! It was published in 1924 & later in 1947 by the old Cresset P[ress] it realy is a sort of masterpiece in its fashion[1] Anne

1 It was a masterpiece with no qualifications. Hogg worked for years for Walter Scott.

found an 1895 copy (illustrated by an illustrator I well know) of Dr. Nikola. my dear I cant put it down! Dr. N is a sort of FUMANCHU cum Dracula caracter. the book belonged to a circulating library with a stamp on every illustration & somewhat dogeared but none the worse. The luncheon[1] went off very well Bunny Bumble Judith Phyl & Michaels lady friend & Gerald of course. the cook rushed in & said the *croute* round the *fillet de Boeuf* had stuck to the pan & she couldnt unstick it! it was none the worse I may add. Phyl arrived with 2 Fur Coats and an obstetric instrument of solid silver – it turned out to be a shoe horn. for Desmonds birthday – Judith at once said he wanted shirts! Phyl said she was beating the Budget a *Silver Fox & a mink*. the silver F was lovely. it was a boiling hot sunny day so Bunny said "You can wear them both cant you dear!" every one tried them on the mink cost a £1000 & History doesnt relate what the Fox cost. Goodness knows what they thought of "carnation creams & methylated spirits" Gerald said it would do beautifully but I dont think anyone took it in realy
yours Ed

To William Chappell from 2 Springfield Cottages, 9 May 1974

Dearest B.
You may bring out your candles and yew, luckily for you, have *gas* as I hear the Power Stations may be affected by Mr. Bumwhole Scanlons engineers strike! I hear you cant get your new shoes on nor can I but I have hopes however Ive got a nice pair of imitation (Malaysian) Dunlop non slip yachting shoes & they do very well & cost £1.50 in Rye
yrs Ed

To William Chappell from 2 Springfield Cottages, Thursday L'heure exquise *28 June 1974*

Dearest B
Thanks for yrs. I heard from the chatelaine of Charlton who said all was well so I shall struggle up Sat on the train arriving 20 to twelve about – we all hope. Its been raining with remarkable results to the mange too – beans and the pot plants I hope you have a lovely time in Brum looking at the property developments – The Chatelaine said that one little "sketch club"[2] brought £2000! at Sothebys – Methylated Mavis the meths Queen had flogged it for 15£ Ive no doubt ready cash – Clover said it was hanging in the passage at Springfield. Well well. splendid isnt it? "Somebody" I wonder who? sent me a cutting from an Australian paper saying Mr. E. Burra had been given a prize of 5000$ (Aussie) for his 30 min film! ! could it have been Bobbie?[3] yours Ed

1 *One of many at the Lefevre Gallery.*

2 *The sketch club was an exercise each month with a set subject at the School of Art in the Chelsea Polytechnic. Edward used this subject always to his own advantage.*

3 *Robert Helpmann.*

To Clover de Pertinez from 2 Springfield Cottages, 3 or 4 August 1974

Dear Clo
How busy the bombs have been in Brum! and so many things worthy of blowing up (according to Billy) Prayvit Aye has been having some very odd things about Brum! talk about Dan Smith & Lady Forkbender! a picture of whom was in the Sun front page, buck teeth and a sort of Portia costume for the Lords. "Mrs Terrible in the role of Porsher" I encourage deadly nightshade – I have a large vine climbing up one of the apple trees. No doubt there are rats. I saw one yesterday eating crumbs they come from an old man opposite who keeps chicken on [a] sort of midden behind his cottage – its an outrage to metroland – not that mine isnt one too with a front garden full of old dock leaves & brambles let ramp instead of a lamp post old style several wagon wheels & some hideous roses looking like plastic & synthetic dye

Ive seen quite a lot about cholera in the Algarve where the tourists go. Tourists are a *hardy breed* nowadays & they just have an injection & go.

Dont speak to me of Chypre.[1] Im pro Turk & I prefer the Arabs – being a heartless totally unfeeling brute the palestine refugees are the wrong sort no one bothers about. not a bit like the PAN-OFFS Id like to have been a fly on the wall at that reception for them in St. Johns Wood. They are pestering me to do Flowers[2] – and I thought of a nice bunch of plastic like they have in pubs

yrs Ed.

To Monica Wodehouse from 2 Springfield Cottages, 3 September 1974

Dear Monica
So youve been on the cruise again? looking for rough trade I presume? What more do you want than Mr. Scanlon (living on the unions expense account) at the T.U.C. Congress? where he has somewhat upset Harolds apple cart – & also Mr. Liberal in person, without his hovercraft –

Im told Josephine Baker at the Palladium (for a week) was marvellous & brought the house down – if I had been in London I would have gone but Im so passay I cant summon up force to do anything unless Im pushed 68 she admits too but I suspect her of being 70. Anyway she rushes around & does everything & had wonderful costumes. There was a terrible storm this morning and a gale blowing – I heard on the BiBiCee every life boat between Ramsgate & Southend had been out gathering up people from plastic rowing boats plastic Cabin cruisers mattresses plastic yachts rafts etc that ye mariners from the Marina were trolloping around in, in fancy marine dress. They seem to think the sea is a sort of round pond! Its always put the fear of God in me I must say

Yours Ed

1 *Cyprus.*
2 *A subject which had proved a best-seller.*

To Clover de Pertinez from 2 Springfield Cottages, 19 September 1974

Dear Clo

Our letters must have crossed. 11,000 tons of apples & half of 2 trees[1] descended burying the oil Tank finaly & completely but mercifully J. Cox, came and removed them – at once & not in 6 weeks, which generaly happens anyway Im not surprised as there seems to have been a hurricane for days I notice the car ferries have been rock & rolling outside of Dover unable to force an entry well I suppose this boreing farce[2] will begin soon J. Cox – my favorite caracter – remarked on some mistletoe in the apple trees & said "A *Parasite* – like members of parliament" HA HA! What a pity about the yacht "morning coffee"[3] Mr. Heaths very own dream boat! and he wasnt on it. Mrs. Chappell at the Express dairy super markitette was suddenly handed a bag by the lady assistant who he hobnobs with who said this is yours I think – 1 lb of *sugar!*[4] Mrs. C drew back as if offered the Baptists head on a salver – but took it with many thanks – he doesnt take sugar but it was very kind of her & useful for guests –

Well I do hope a hoarding advertising Win with Labour hasnt fallen on you

Yours Ed

Channel moderate I see this morning

To William Chappell from 2 Springfield Cottages, September 1974

Dearest B.

Well dear there were no raving old folk tearing each other to the bone over a crust at Jempsons which has bread & we never got there till well after 12. Yes Bar could *not*, simply could *naat* bring herself to ackcherly say what she got – she said she got what she asked for from the HAMAMMET de Claridge gallery[5] but not *what* she asked – It amuses me very much – She says the bottom has faln out the Fart market – it wouldnt surprise me considering the exorbitant prices asked. And what other treasures have you been offered this week in the way of meat whiskey etc etc? anything useful? Perhaps I shall see you Saterday if all goes well. Bar said Miss Roett had gone off to stay in a damp cottage in Zummerzett or wherever to satisfy her masochism! I like the country & I dont realy mind the weather! Imagine that. I *dont* like wet weather in Oxford St. talking of masochism.

Yrs Ed

To Monica Wodehouse from No 2 Gasoline Alley *22 October 1974*

Dear Monica

Having come to being gently layd out in an ambulance I went to the Westminster Osp- Casualty ward where I was set on by about 7 internes & a

1 *Enormous – very prolific & very old.*

2 *Christmas.*

3 Morning Cloud, *which had foundered.*

4 *It was two pounds in fact. There had been a shortage and it was under the counter.*

5 *The Hamet Gallery.*

doctor who gave them a lecture on the *enlarged spleen*. Mine is huge & happily hadnt been ruptured – & the doctor gathering up my hands & saying note the typical manifestation I was Xrayed & by that time felt all I wished to be was left alone – so was left on an ambulance[1] in the casualty ward by that time Dr. Geoffrey Dove Billy & Bar had arrived so we was then bundled off to the Lambeth osp where I spent the night & thank god Dr. D got me out the next day & was 2 days at Charlton P. in bed my ribs & shoulder were terrible & as I also had a frightful cough every time I coughed it was like being stabbed – however all is very much better now and I feel almost normal but a shade groggy. I suppose I have been lucky it wasnt much worse, & it could easily have been – Goodness alone knows what hit me![2] & nor does anybody else it seems to me. I realy feel like doing nothing! but read. I said to Billy, to think it was only last week I was knocked[3] down it seems like a year & he said it was *3 weeks ago – dear*! I have been enclined to be vague as you see from that. Hope to see you later on in a week or 10 daze or so   yrs Ed

To Clover de Pertinez from 2 Springfield Cottages, 11 March 1975

Dear Clo
That old crone I was talking of – & you were wondering who – lives opposite Mrs. Rhodes ever since she came with only one Toilet in the back garden & *owns* the house with a suppurating leg & cant move & was looked after by a sacrificing darter who was recently squashed flat by a trailer truck that slewed sidewase! no one to empty the commode – Im not at all sure about Portugal some very queer things seem to be a-foot – a Mr. Michael Foot in mouth. I think Portugal will end up with a dictatorship (as usual) till next time round – Its rather funny as the Comunist Paty are becoming quite *Boorgwah*! and respectable almost *establishment* – compared to the Trotskists Red Moles Marxist Leninist workers pot Venessa Redgrave and old uncle Tom Cobley & all the others & MAO. There has been a mysterious disapearance of Chinese white water colour! *Why* I wonder. there was none at Windsor & Newton *or* at another placc. Mrs. R found some in BOOTS! where "artists" dont often go to buy coulors I imagine.   yours Ed.

To William Chappell from 2 Springfield Cottages, 5 May 1975

Dearest B.
Thank you for yrs. Yes I would like to come on the 10th if all goes well Bar asked if Ide like to she wrote from Cornwall so just had room between the clotted cheese creams served with jumbo Saffron Buns & boiling crabs etc etc etc & had been to a lovely pub in Falmouth full of Porto Ricans – I wish

---

1 *A tilted stretcher.*

2 *As he was (he does not mention it in this letter) dead drunk, it could have been the kerb, the pavement, or a building which he crashed down on. For a detailed account see* Edward Burra: a painter remembered by his friends.

3 *He had a lump the size of an egg on his forehead.*

I had – ! and not gone out every day – but I dont want to *miss* anything in such a short time you realy want a week or 10 days. very suitable for me Dublin would be – good for tottering (or rushing along in rags shouting!) I find my legs are better since Ive given up making white sauce. Fatal to me, not Fatal to *eat* but standing stareing & stirring it! if I keep my legs up all the time they are much less swollen (& I daresay those pills), I couldnt think *what* was wrong with me this afternoon & discovered I was frozen so put the pipes on & Fuck May I feel rather better now. what price conserving energy & save Fule? I got a response from the minister of Piss & Social Security – of a kind a reciept for the payment of my last card & 65£ in back pension cheque crossed & thats all! I was surprised as I was begining to think some people were much older & dearer & sweeter & better than some other olde folke! I suppose if I hadnt written that letter I should have been quietly ignored? They dont like paying out but they *love* clawing it *in*.

I expect to come on the 11.30 so perhaps we can have a gloomy nip in some run down old joint? full of everybody in the last stages.

Yours Ed

Wherever has Greta Keller[1] been all these yrs? In the U.S. I suppose – such a plump pretty little blonde hiding her chins! singing away in cocktail Bars.

To William Chappell from 2 Springfield Cottages, 16 June 1975

Dearest B.

I hope nothing terrible has been happening and your not throwing flowers about in Hollyhead docks. rosemary for remembrance, Heres Henbane! & vipers bew gloss but I expect things are thickening at the Gate and nothing is arriving on time. A is off today for the west country so I hope for some cider & Somerset cheese.

end of next week for the Railway strike dont forget Annie [Duveen] has arrived to go to the dentist I was wondering about her summer season so I havent seen Bar but Ive "heard" quite a lot as we write I think shes terrified to have me to stay without Nurse Chappell. Its simply wonderful here but today Im afraid its passing. That painting of mine I was doing is just finished – very distasteful peice of work Ime sure. I cant always be pretty realy – being terribly *hostile* – as you know – A voice calld up, one of those flat rather mournful muttery type that I can never hear "a student" Im sure, & asked to come & visit. just a social call. Im afraid I said for gods sake leave me alone – ! also somebody from a mag called SUSSEX wanted to *interview* me which is my idea of utter nightmare of horror & boredom I never answered the letter I think 3 paintings were sold in the show[2] – quite good I should think, considering the state were in, busy going over the chutes towards a general strike & railway strike etc over a thousand pounds went to VAT. so after 33½ per cent & those frames I make a fortune & far exceed the Soshulcontrack dont I? Grey again today so I suppose its

1 *Greta Keller was a popular central-European cabaret singer in the twenties and thirties.*
2 *At the Lefevre Gallery.*

going to be pudding lid type of weather. The Sprew is keeping up very well, Fri at *9.30* in the morning we went down to Rye, & the shop I go to get it was so full of solid protean & great bottoms of the world I simply left it – but luckily the shop opposite the butcher was OK but imagine if its like that at 9.30 by they time "they" begin arriving in force its hell – Oh for Scunthorpe & the wide open spaces of yer High Street & yer Marks & Spencer

Yours Ed.

To Clover de Pertinez from 2 Springfield Cottages, 26 July 1975

Dear Clo. Thank you for yours I realy dont know what the Duke of Barcelonas? papa is it? is doing upsetting an already tottering apple cart, imagining he's something out of Valle Inclan? I dont know what we're out of here, the frying pan would it be? & into the grill – Billy says its so nice to be somewhere where everybody is what they are[1] meaning all the servants in the hotel. Barmen porters, waiters people shop assistants Barbers actors & everyone, is *IRISH*! Imagine! No west Indians pakistanis cypriots chinese, Spanish waiters & maids! there are Jews, but they turn into "*Mr. Bloom*" – He suffers from ghastly cosmopolitanism at Souse Kensington – you can scarcely get into the tube theres such a Babel & fuddle – Artists (bona fide) can live in Ireland Tax Free he says. I should love it but I fear, am too old & decrepit now to manage to do it—All together for the floral dance my dear now Italys gone "communist" or whatever their version may be & the portuguese version? Our version would contain a strong MORL tone! as soon as I he[a]r MORLS mentioned I begin to shudder – everything to do with the present govt is strongly MORL even Lady Forkbender is MORL not like Christine Keeler. Im glad Mr. Profumo has been honoured. I believe Len Lye & wife are expected to dropover from Annecy where Len has been judging cartoon films they asked Bar to go to Annecy expenses paid but she found it took 14 hours & you arrived at 1.30 in the morning I said if it had been 30 yrs ago I should have gone at once 30 years ago I probably would have thought it boreing and *not* gone! I hear on the Radio The Observer is in trouble & if its to go on there must be redundancies. I never can read anything but the commonest papers – the others all seem to be never ending print & come to the same thing in the end as the SUN!! yrs Ed

I never seem to have a chicken I cant get anything out of the oven without dropping it I might boil one

To William Chappell from 2 Caseys Court *August 1975*

Dearest B

You will be pleased to hear that Ken, on being asked what he would do with Thurloe – said he had several "irons in the fire"? & wasnt giving it up as he felt he might get bored being at Bosney all the time! Now he's in St. Helens Hospital Ore having had a hemorage from the arse. said to be from the liver – "*They*" dont say anything – nor do "they" know anything –

1 *Dublin.*

more than "*Les medecins de Moliere*" if you ask me. I realy think Ken shows spirit. I wrote to Bar and I cant move this week end or pull myself together at all I just layd in some frozen cod – & shall live on fish pie – & got some marvellous beans from Rye which was full of giant drifting flowered beds all sucking sucking ice cream cones from that shop where they sell bars of rock & "sea side pebbles" They must be *dragées* – & it was packed with Eyetalian Teen agers & they were sucking sucking Iced Lollies.

One day when you come down I shall go back with you I might face it with company. Did you notice the pictures of Elvis in the Dly Mirror who has *given in* to cheeseburgers & ice cream? When I think of Jail House Rock & Blue Suede Shoes etc its sad realy – I always did think he looked like Decaydent Rome or Antioch & in that mysterious gladiators toilette he had on & his size – he lookd even more so now

yours Ed

To William Chappell from 2 Springfield Cottages, 22 September 1975

Dearest B

I see you have been suffering from the Dawson syndrome a state of *extreme agitation*! & eternal running to & fro I expect she feels shed better keep well in with old John G[ielgud] who might be influential in giving her a peice to do. I cant face being dragged round like a Brown paper parcel. We went over to Tenterden so I snatched some frozen cod VODKA & WHISKEY as we rushed on. Poor old Lord[1] has been driven up to towne by Cyril today Sunday & (I think) is going to Edward 7th Hospital? and of course has his own Doc in London, so he can stay & he can have something done or not but anyway looked after for a time poor thing – Nothing has risen up & New Life from outer space materialized in the plum chut[ney][2] – it looks perfect in every way! Monica came over a for a good *release* & now is rereading Lilith & has developed a mania for George MacD[onald] When I was in Tenterden I picked up a copy of "Flames" (Robert Hitchens) & am glued to it now & I cant put it down Its a poor mans Dorian Grey with Valentine & Joolian – Valentine lives in an exquisite Flat in Victoria St! I hope not Artillery Mansions – date 1897 very much influenced by Oscar need I say Valentine a Christ like figure who has *never* wished to sin begins to think hes missed something – & wishes to change souls with Joolian [who] is a naughty girl & always trying – someone NEW – until he meets Valentine – *a tout petit petons* – who improvises on the piano his saintly face fixed on an exquisite painting of Christ kissing a wounded knight – Heigh Ho – anyway Im like Mon[ica] & "Lilith" with it. I do remember reading it at the age of 11 or thereabouts Im so glad theyve fallen on this apartment in Tropea I envy them I feel I shall never go abroad again. A refuses to drive on the continong – so I shall never get I had a p.c of Tropea it looked perfect – tottering on the top of the cliff where its been tottering for a long time. I feel. Yes do come down – any time you fancy. yours Ed

1 Kenneth, Lord Ritchie (Anne's brother-in-law and Chappell's landlord), who had become very ill.
2 A large amount of very good chutney made by Edward and Chappell.

To William Chappell from 2 Springfield Cottages, 1 December 1975

Dearest B.

I entend to come up next W.E and Ive no doubt Mary A[1] will be furious but I cant help it. & dont entend coming up on Sat *13th* I should be run over, fall down in a bus, fall down in a pub and fall down in the train or at Ashford–Well, they went moaning off to the event[2] at St. Martins and the Stock exchange male voice choir – followed by a Buffett wake at "the office" & Margaret wont leave A says so I shall leave her to go back in the train It suddenly developed such a thick fog this afternoon it got pitch dark at 3 – I hope it didnt catch them on the way up. Ive just finished that Jewish book "The Manor" by Isaac Bashevits Singer & I cant wait to get "the Estate" Vol 2 now I shall start off on F. Hugh Benson! very different Im sure. Isaac B is very good on Poles. Some of them are real terrors & stop at nothing. Ken Russell is doing a life of Rudolph Valentino with Nureyev as Valentino! can you imagine what theyl get up to. he should do W.C. Fields with Fred as Carlotta Monterey – Sir Ralph Richardson might do W.C.F. with (not very) much alteration. Well I hope to see & hear from you how your getting on & on

Yrs Ed

The Benson is another perfect period peice. he has a sharp eye!

To Monica Wodehouse from 2 Springfield Cottages, Friday – now NEXT FRIDAY *postmarked 12 December 1975*

Dear Monica You can see how I somehow got innarupted by going to spend a week end in London and [by] Mrs. Mary Augusta Aiken a very old friend of mine who has taken a cardboard plastic olde worlde Fyre Trappe upper very slippery wooden ladder in Ye Mynt Rye! and being American promptly turned every electrical appliance full on in every room in the house! talk of conserving *energy* dearie and I dont dare dream of the electricity Bill. Poor Billy Chappell is working from 10 o'c to 10 o'c producing an unheard of Opera by Gluck[3] with a cast of millions (of pupils) in the Opera Centre – Commercial Rd – (The X.Odeon) & 400£ to make the dresses out of plastic tissues from cheeses & three old ostrich feathers from Covent Garden (lent) so he feels a little tired just now. When in Towne I saw a terrible film of Blood & Sand with Tyrone Power Rita Hayworth & Linda Darnell! Nazimova was Tyrones mother she was very good – it was frightful & of course I remained glued to it till the bitter end. Ritas pad was realy the Alhambra Hilton Hotel (enlarged) another one who was good was Anthony Quinn (looking about 19) who should have been playing the bullfighter Tyrone Power is a great Irish Beauty – but no actor I fear. I havent seen any Christmas shoppers etc but in the Victoria Wine Co in Tenterden – but theres always a crowd of old soaks in there cum rain or cum shine & Christmas my foot The only other sign was the girl in the cash desk

1 *Mary Aiken, widow of Conrad.*

2 *Memorial Service for Lord Ritchie.*

3 Alceste.

in Liptons super mkt gave me a paper with a Number on it, & said it was "for the stuffed lion" – not a new line of cannd monosodium glutamate & soya meat protein but a *huge* orange stuffed lion, That you would have to take away in a wheel barrow – absolutely useless & hideous & no child could move it I should think. If it had been a ½ bottle of VODKA it would have been quite different. I dont ever go out further than Chapel Market & the Duke of Pisspot when Im in Islington & never get up till 11! it is a rest from washing cooking shopping painting – even *that*! I get stuffed in a cab & go & see Gerald at the Gallery & then I go back to the bottle & read Sci-Fi. There realy are quite a few things Ide like to see but its all Too much.

Yours Ed

To William Chappell from 2 Springfield Cottages, 14 March 1976

Dearest B.

On Monday Sheila Hutchins Dly Exp cookery book will be in the bookshops price 95p (Collins) so get a copy at once! get one for me – what a treat. I went down to Rye (at 9.30) & got some croissants at that Swiss patisserie – they were the best croissants I have had in England light and made of the best materials & simply lovely. I wish I could get there *more*, & very convenient to Salmons[1] too. Bar says she wants to buy that painting of Falmouth for 500£, the day before. Gerald rang up and enquired about getting the pictures framed – I am trying to collect enough paintings and I dont want to sell it & would like to *exhibit* it – it being one of the Best ones – & its a terrible struggle getting enough – otherwise I would be pleased to sell it to her. Its realy very difficult – Anne couldnt get 3 singles in Tenby but has in the other place I forget the name! on a "cut price week-end"? whatever that is – do they have a cabaret & paper hats? and we are starting here so come down the night befor on a Thursday – April? all fools day? Im between paintings so am wretched and cant start – my 255 gallons of oil cost £74.54 I suppose thats a lot of money but its quite a lot of oil.

yrs Ed.

To Monica Wodehouse from 5 Fair Meadow, Rye, 25 June 1976

Dear Monica

about 6 weeks or so ago I fell off a step on to the pavement & broke a leg & cracked a hip & they operated & I went to the E. Sussex Jumbo Hackerey in Hastings a huge hospital – They were very good I must say I was in agonies if I was turned round for bed sores – then after a week I was 3 weeks in St. Augustines a nursing home in Hastings – very kind they were & am walking with a Zimmer[2] or getting about – I hope to walk without it in the end & then came here to my sister. I realy felt if I didnt get out of that home I should kill myself being deadly depressed from about 20000 anti Biotics didnt help at all – however things are better now & they couldnt

---

1 *The fishmonger in Cinque Ports Street.*

2 *A walking frame.*

have been kinder than they were. So thats why I havent been heard from. I spent some time in St. A reading "one flew over the cuckoos nest" Bar lent me I hated Big Nannie to such a degree I could hardly bring myself to read about her the bk is very good. I can imagine Jack N – Bar said Nannie was very good in the film. Did you enjoy Nureyev at the Colliseum? there was a nice picture of Mdm Fontaine being visited by Liz Taylor & Jackie Onnasis von Kennedy at the Met doing the Merry widow Mims[1] monumental benefit & general Fish Fry seems to have had more publicity than anything. it was all far too long & went on & on & on it wanted a firm director to cut it. I must write to Scott now I see Amurkan money is coming back in quantities into the business & there hasnt been so much doing for yrs – lets hope the unions dont bugger it up   yours Ed

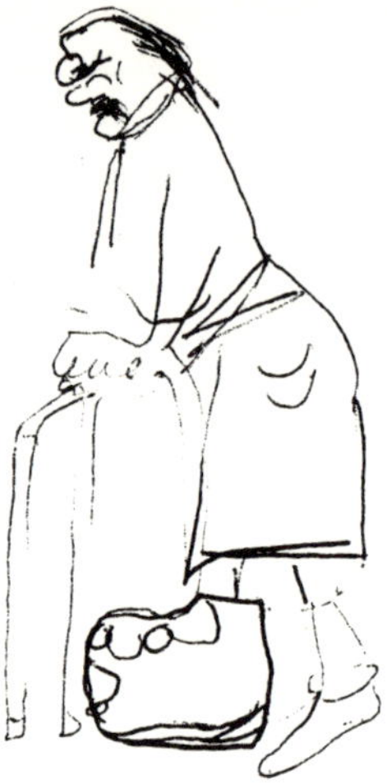

To Barbara Ker-Seymer from Feeve Fayre Meadows Ree Sx, *1 July 1976*

Dear Bar I seem to be getting on nicely on Scotts porridge oats. Ambrosia Rice etc. & a few small soles which seem to be very good just now. seedy raspberries & everything dried up to a bone in a howling Sirocco with skies of azure I dont think it will ever rain again & every one will wither off with starvation & thirst! Wambledon we have which I dont mind. I also saw the outbreak of the 1st war in Upside Downside[2] which depressed me to death & the Pallisers rather good I thought I have been trying to walk alone & *almost* can. leaning on the furniture. I hope it will get better after a while. Billy has taken rooms in Alexander Grants basement[3] I hear, much cheaper than 40 T[hurloe] Sq but not "cheap"[4] he can keep some furniture there, for I think there are still some bits & peices lurking round here kept by neighbours to be gathered up. I hope Annie [Duveen] is enjoying her visit to tropical London – nudes in Brighton laying about & a huge mass of bloated sucking flesh in Rye looking realy lovely no wonder the BOTTOMS Fallen out of the Meat mkt "Daddies" are speshly Fat & they all stop dead in the High Street & block the pavement – Love to all from Ed

To Monica Wodehouse from 2 Springfield Cottages, 11 August 1976

Dear Monica
Wednesday the 18th would be fine if it suits you. Who do you think turned up 2 or 3 days ago but Scott who seems continualy busy & done a lot to the house & garden – Wendie is getting married again so I said he wouldnt have to pay *her* alimony – he still pays for the children. Wendie asked for £7000 & him to buy *her* a house! I am getting a bit more spry – but still need the ZIMMER sometimes however I walked round Hales Stores in Peasemarsh this morning I must say I like to buy my own things & Im thankful to be back here & doing a bit of painting too I dont believe its ever

1 *Marie Rambert.*
2 Upstairs, Downstairs.
3 *Actually a ground floor flat with garden.*
4 *It was cheap.*

going to rain again – & the country is Bright yellow! like gamboge & chrome! very beautiful in a way. Yes Scott was going on about the Turks & the Greeks – who wont be permitted to blink – I suspect Mummie Russia & Daddie U.S will see they toe the line (I hope) and all will be sweetness & OUZO on Lesbos where burning Sapho loved & sung – hope to see you

Yrs Ed.

To Monica Wodehouse from The Shambles [*2 Springfield Cottages*], Thursday Friday, *August 1976*

Dear Monica

Ive been meaning to write but have been swamped in riseing tides of rubbish and old bottles & dirty clothes. I think Billy is coming down tomorrow & he wont stand for it, nurse Chappell will soon have it ship shape (I only hope) I had a P.C from Samos did I say? of *L'Eglise de la metamorphose* – & Mrs. Rhodes from Calabria where everything is a fairyland of fried fish – pasta & motor bicycles – I must say it sounds lovely jokeing apart – the journey is not quite so lovely & the return wont be a bit lovely if they arrive at a ferry & the ferrymen are on strike rocking the economy & killing the cow that lays the golden eggs – (later) Things look quite green now & Ive even noticed grass but they are Qing up (in pouring rain) in Devon at taps in the street with beer bottles & plastic buckets – in that case I wouldnt have any water as I couldnt hobble with it. Nurse Chappell did a bit of cleaning but once again the tide is rising. Nurse comes down again on Monday bringing an oxtail & a chicken – the ones at Peasemarsh are now uneatable from Farmers Horror Farm they have a very old faded taste of dead fat thats died of some horrible disease & exude a horrible yellow grease. & theres no escape from them in our little rural super Ms. Marx & Spencers are very good indeed but I cant *get there* as you know –

Im sending a picture of Nureyev in B & S[1] and I must say Ide like to see it – The young man who was going to play the gypsy (who was a lead in the Festival B & very good looking) dropped dead!

Not so Henry [Miller], going strong at 84.

Yrs Ed

To Barbara Ker-Seymer from Shambles once more, *3 September 1976*

Dear B

Nurse [Chappell] left on Friday having made apple tarts and cleared up (its back to normal now of course) and is going to Eire next week to give the Rivals a once over & *tighten them* up for some special perfs for the Festival.

Rope W[alk] seems to me to be ready & Billy has found rather a pretty paper very cheap for the bathroom.

Whilst her ladyship & his lordship[2] were away on the grouse moors the house has been broken into & all the silver pinched & a few brooches of senimenal but no value & all the whiskey drunk and poured over the fur-

1 *Blood and Sand, an excerpt in the film* Valentino.
2 *Anne and Colin Ritchie.*

niture Too bad isn't it. you realy cant go away unless someone remains behind in the house Scott [Wodehouse] has come back from Samos he enjoyed it very much – very few tourists at all there & nothing – as its not a fashionable island I hope they dont build a Pontins at Tropea! with Italian contadinis as waitresses & a pasteurised swimming pool. I was terrified there was going to be a seamans strike – which would have been lovely for you when you arrived at Calais
Yrs Ed.

The above letter written to Barbara in Calabria was to be the last she received from Edward. A few weeks later he was dead.

'Nurse' Chappell, on returning from Dublin at the beginning of October, went almost immediately to Playden for the weekend. Early on the Sunday evening Edward became suddenly and dreadfully ill. On the following day he was taken to hospital where he died on 24 October. For seventy-one years he had fought a valiant and impossible battle with his always-ailing body. Now the fight was finished; and the fruits of the struggle were to be seen in those brilliantly alive and highly personal paintings scattered through galleries, private collections, and the homes of his friends and his family. From infancy he missed no speck of his surroundings, whether interiors or exteriors: every inch, every yard, every mile of cities and countryside; each face, each body (with very carefully observed feet), and skies, and the way light fell through cloud; the most truthful and delicate images equally with the most violent and alarming. He painted as though possessed by a huge physical energy. He had, in fact, none. But his blazing will-power, harnessed to an imagination wild, fertile and surprising, acted as a powerfully energising stimulant into his frail person and his arthritic bones. It was little wonder that the fight finally wore him out. The paintings are a testament to his belief in life as an actual substance. Something as strong as iron, soft as silk, smooth as gold, cool and glittering as rough water, and wild as wind; a substance to be walked on, wrapped in, slept with, floated in and flown through. Everything he saw he absorbed into his inexhaustible memory through his faintly mocking, infinitely wise, and very wary eyes.

For centuries British painters have excelled in the use of watercolour. Over the years Edward explored its possibilities more fully than any painter before or since. There is genius in his absolute control and understanding of his chosen medium. The wide, luminous landscapes he worked on during the last two years of his life show few signs of human habitation. Serenely brooding, they might be waiting for something strange to arrive. In two of his last pictures that 'something' is seen: beings of a vaguely human shape, but of a substance belonging only to the earth. They are formed from shifting, fluttering masses of leaves, grasses, and feathers; from the stalks, roots and petals of flowers: everything in a constant rustling state of growth, fadeing and renewal. They vanish into their surroundings; the fields, woods and hedgerows, and re-emerge: beautiful, remote and alarming.

Edward Burra is better known as a painter in his own country; and best known there among other painters, collectors and students of paintings; he is not yet world famous. He will be.

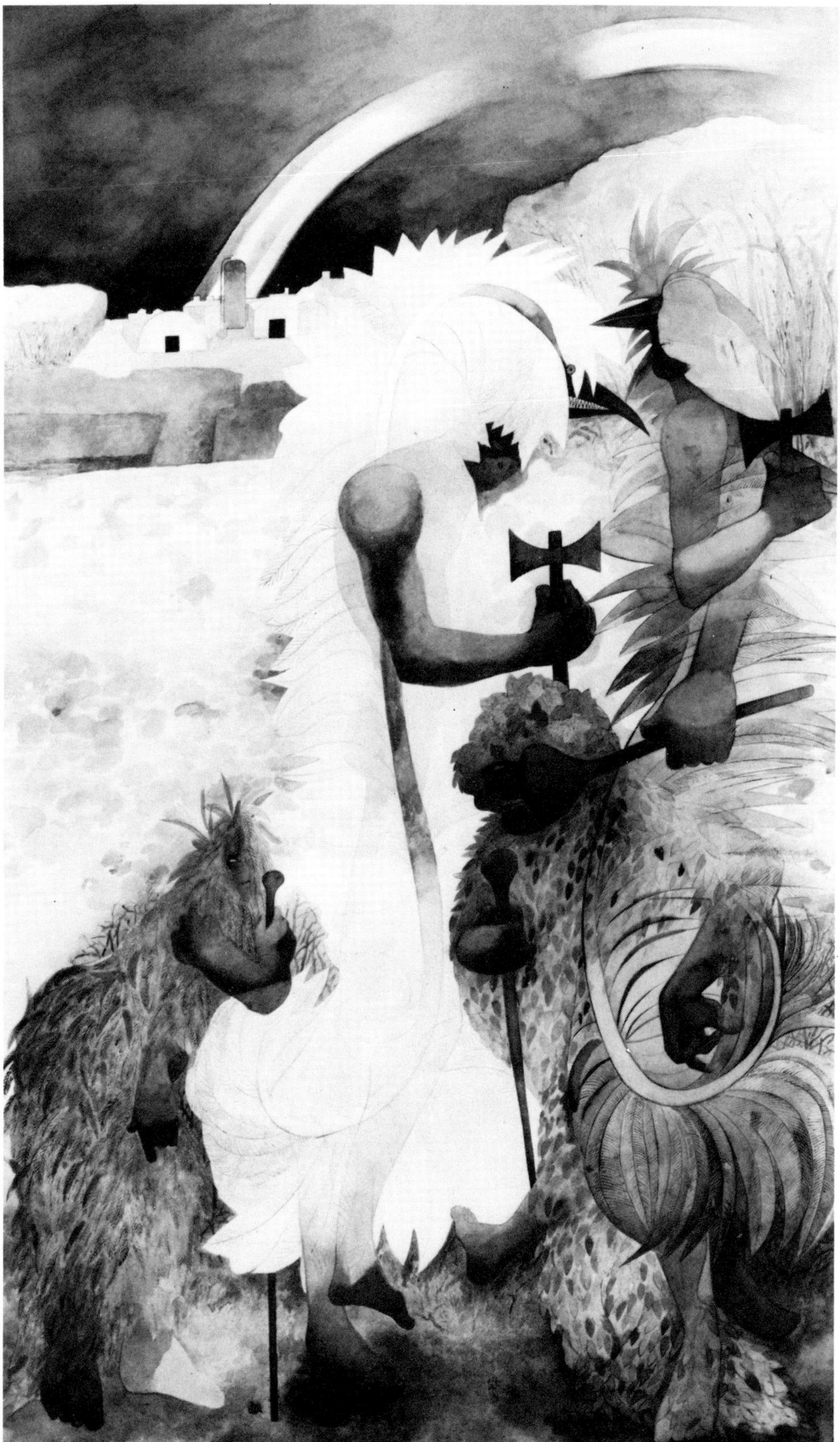

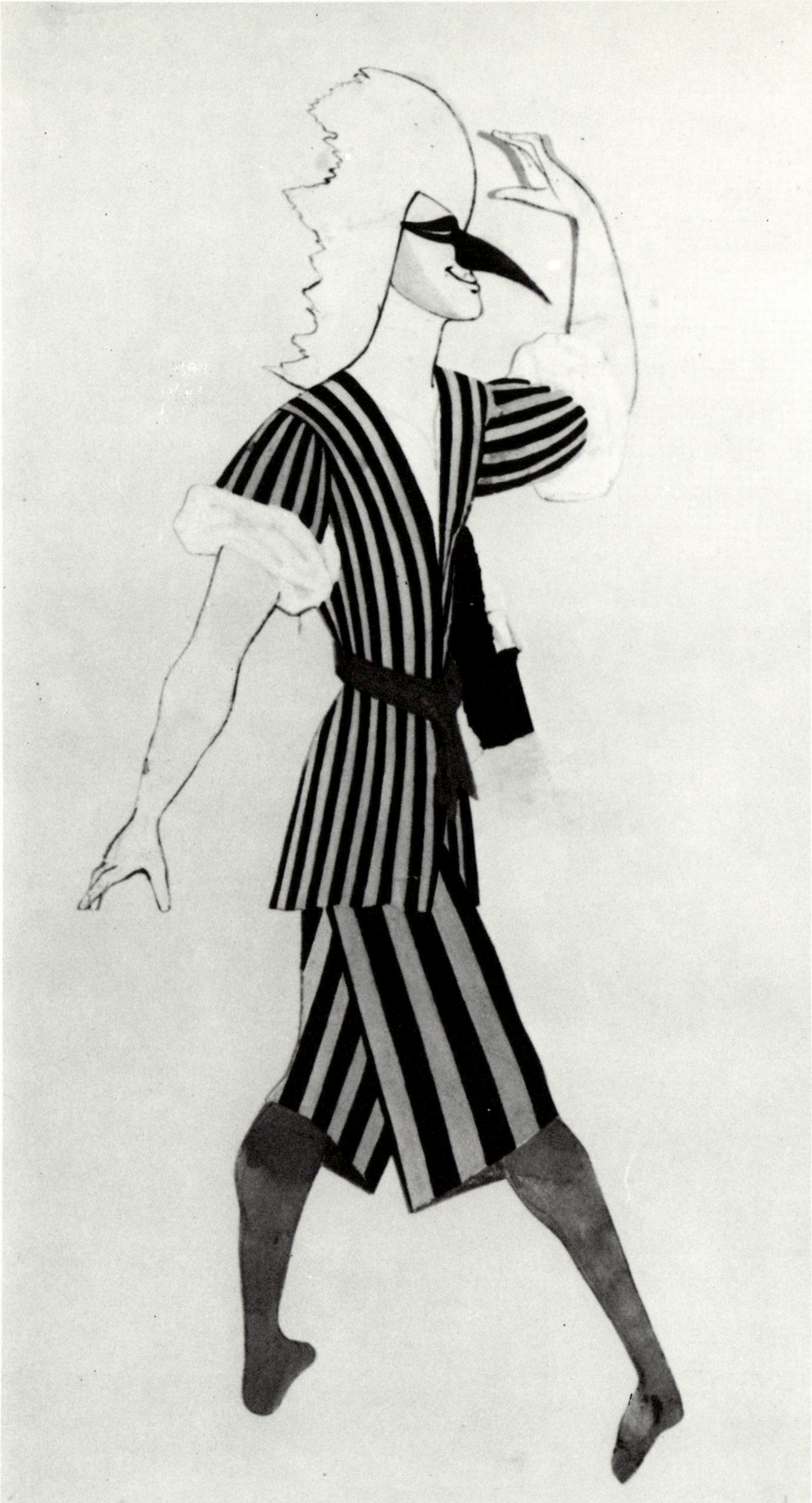

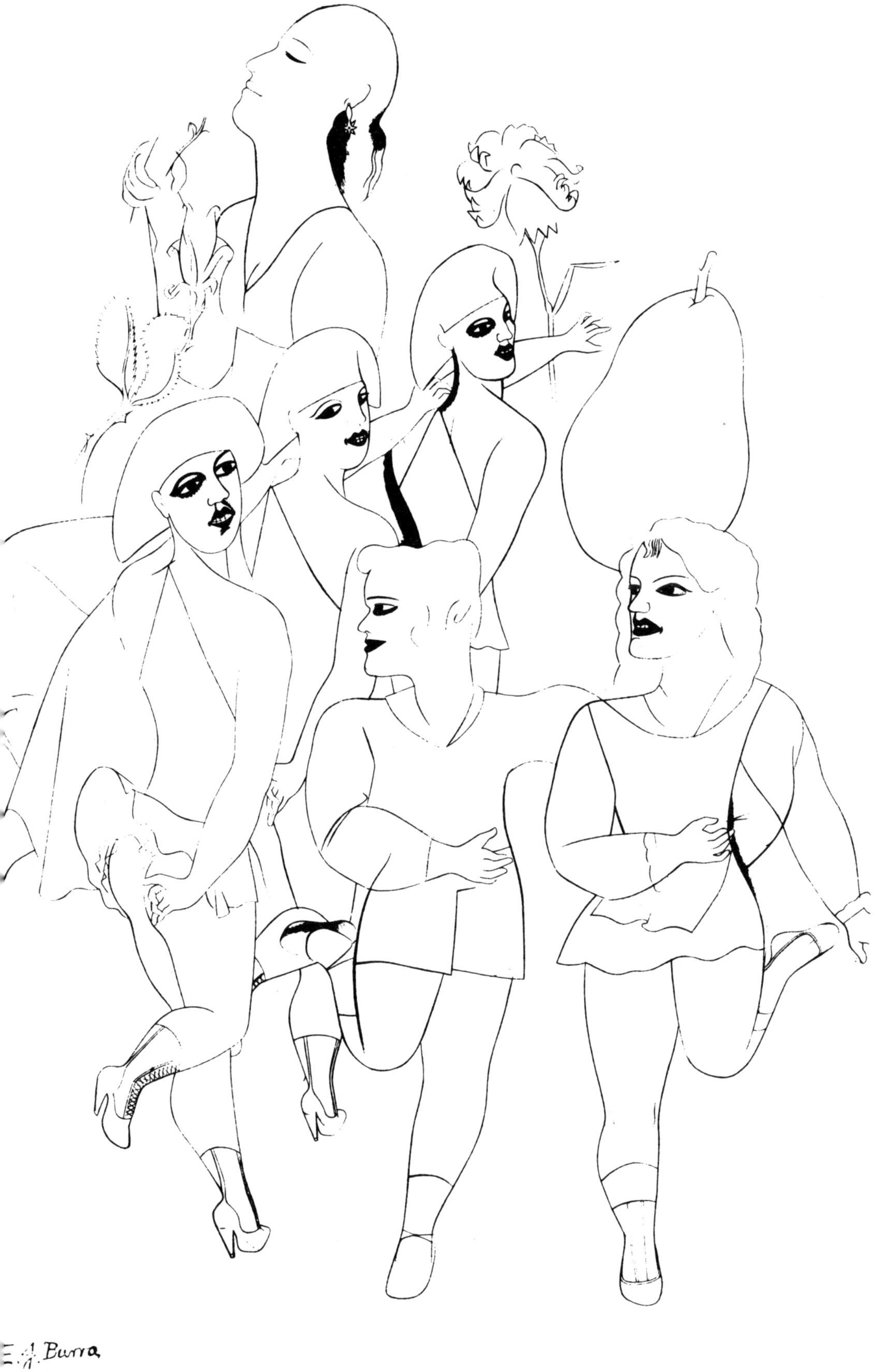
E. J. Burra

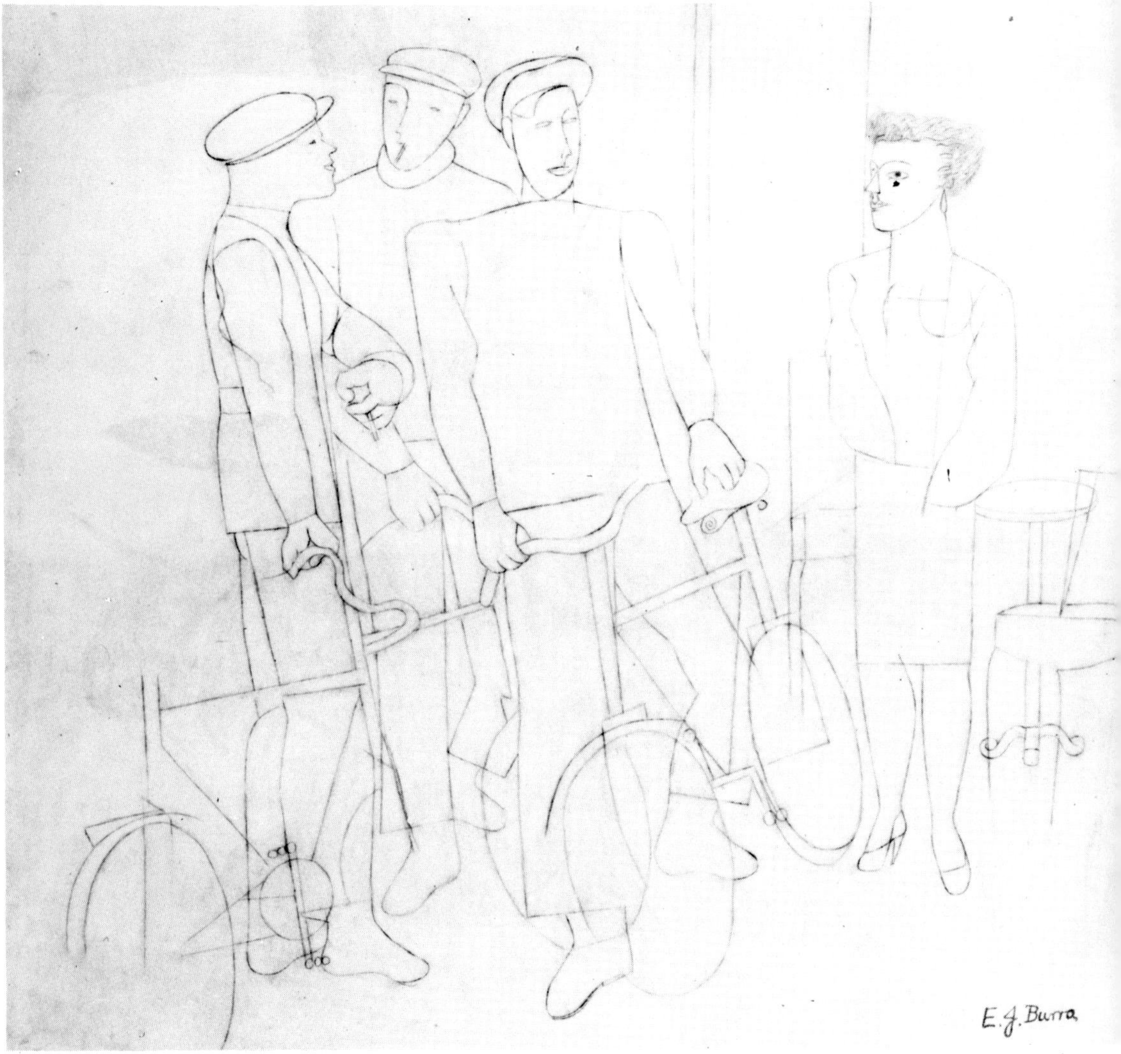
E.J. Burra

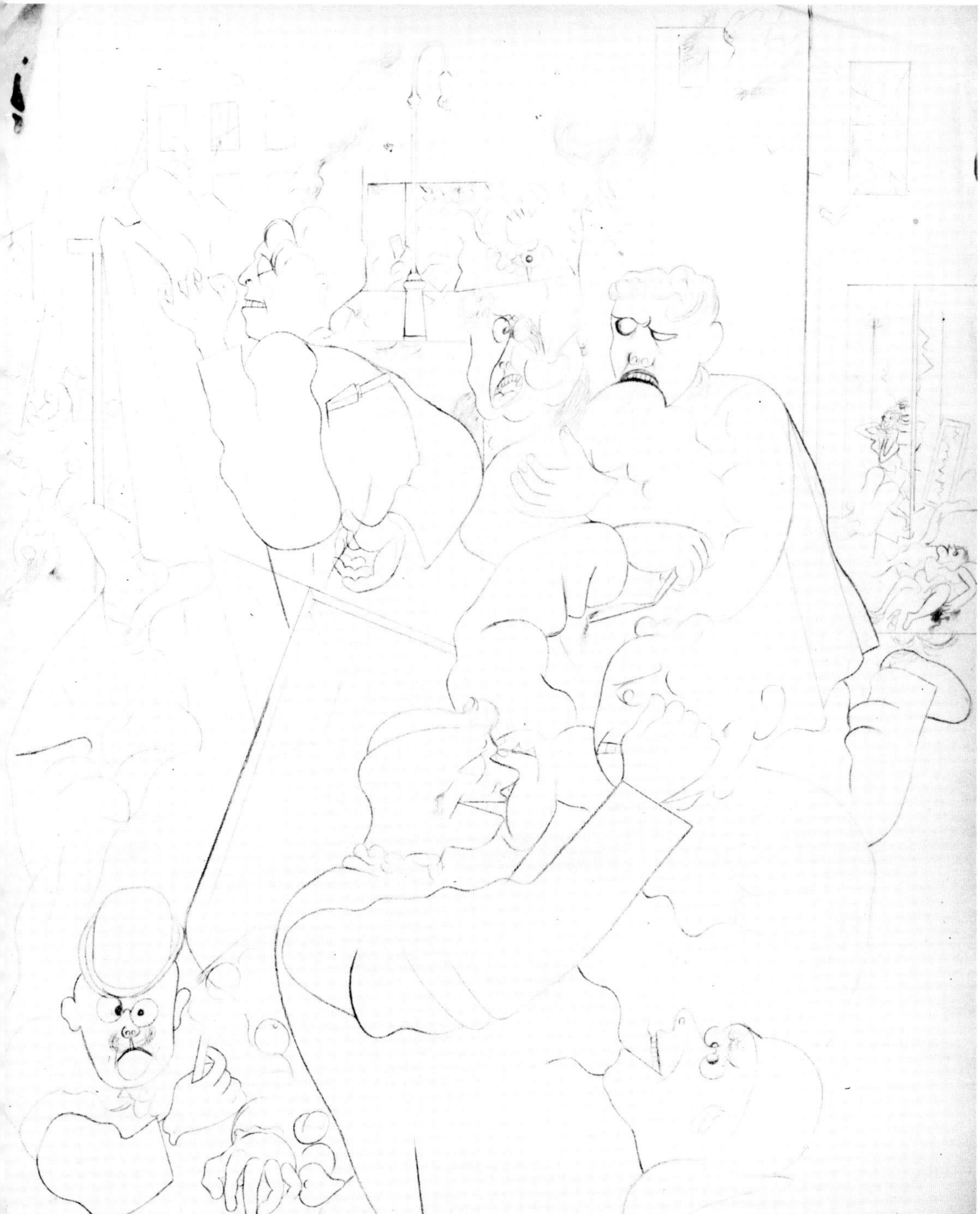

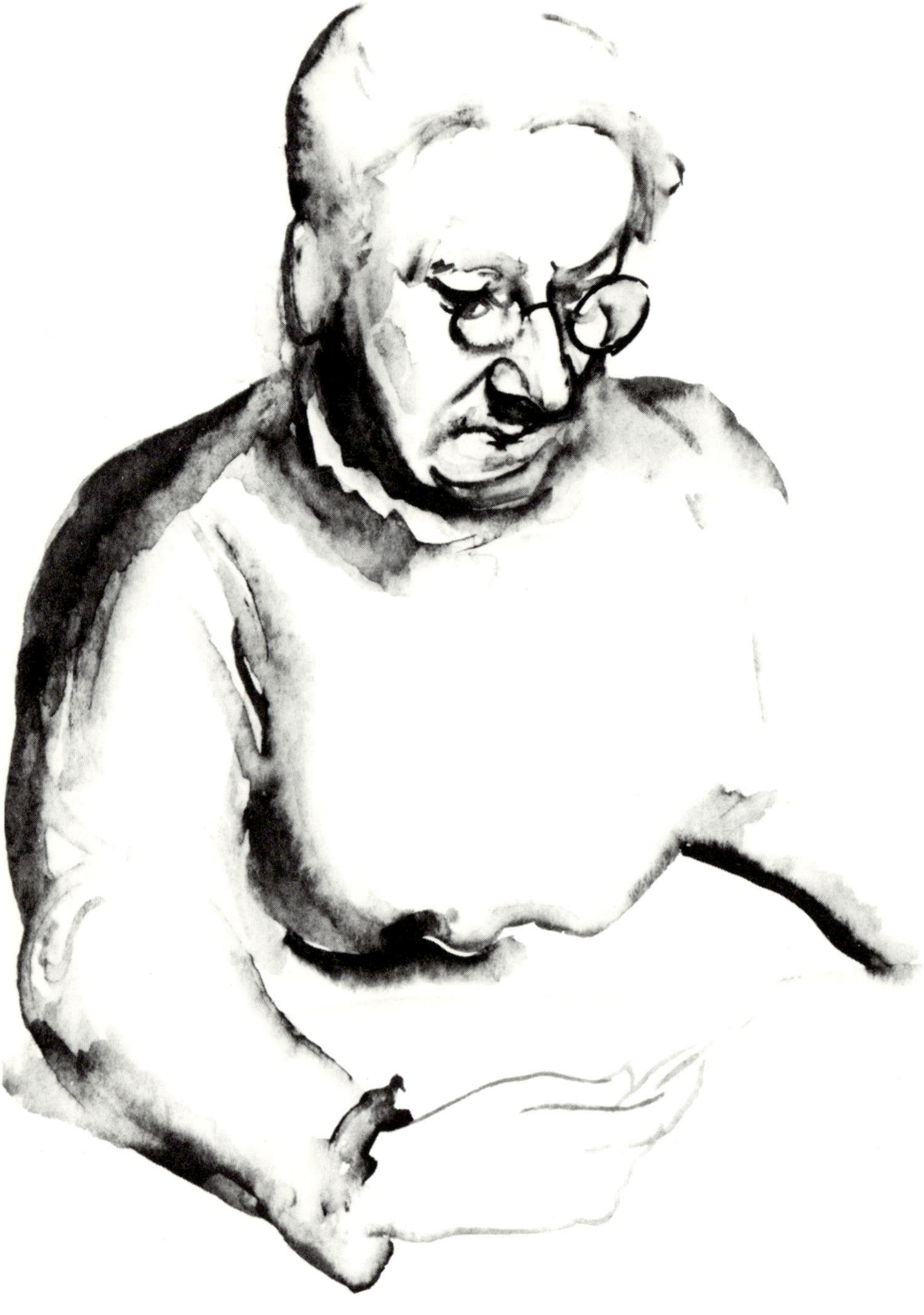

INDEX